FOLLOW ME!
Disciples in Markan Rhetoric

SOCIETY
OF BIBLICAL
LITERATURE

DISSERTATION SERIES
Michael V. Fox, Old Testament Editor
Pheme Perkins, New Testament Editor

Number 145

FOLLOW ME!
Disciples in Markan Rhetoric
by
Whitney Taylor Shiner

Whitney Taylor Shiner

FOLLOW ME!
Disciples in Markan Rhetoric

Scholars Press
Atlanta, Georgia

100784

FOLLOW ME!
Disciples in Markan Rhetoric

Whitney Taylor Shiner

Ph.D., 1992
Yale University

Advisor:
Wayne Meeks

© 1995
The Society of Biblical Literature

Library of Congress Cataloging in Publication Data
Shiner, Whitney Taylor.
    Follow me! : Disciples in Markan Rhetoric / Whitney Taylor Shiner.
      p. cm.—(Dissertation series / Society of Biblical Literature ; no. 145)
    Thesis (Ph. D.)—Yale University, 1992.
    Includes bibliographical references.
    ISBN 1-55540-940-7 (alk. paper). —ISBN 1-55540-941-5 (pbk.)
    1. Bible. N.T. Mark—Criticism, interpretation, etc.
    2. Apostles—Biography—History and criticism. 3. Biography—To
    500—History and criticism. 4. Bible. O. T. Apocrypha.
    Ecclesiasticus—Criticism, interpretation, etc. I. Title.
    II. Series: Dissertation series (Society of Biblical Literature) ; no. 145.
BS2585.2.S48 1995
226.3'066—dc20

                                             9345598
                                             CIP

Printed in the United States of America
on acid-free paper

To Jane B. and John H. Shiner

TABLE OF CONTENTS

LIST OF FIGURES

Preface

This book is an unrevised version of my dissertation submitted to the Yale University department of Religious Studies in 1992. As such it reflects many ideas developed in courses, seminars, and discussions with friends and mentors. Its strengths result from the value of those relationships. Its weaknesses result often from unheeded advice.

In trying to place the Gospel of Mark in its first century literary and rhetorical context, this work investigates in some detail a number of other ancient works that make rhetorical use of a student-teacher relationship. While that part of the study forms the basis for the interpretation of Mark and should be of great interest to readers concerned with narrative and rhetorical interpretation or the historical milieu of the Gospel, I have tried to keep the Markan portion of the work in Part II as self-contained as possible for the benefit of readers who are primarily interested in understanding the Gospel itself.

I would like to thank everyone who has provided guidance, support, and friendship during the production of this dissertation. Wayne Meeks, my dissertation adviser, has been instrumental in helping find ways of grounding my interest in narrative interpretation within the historical context of the first century world. His criticism, advice, and encouragement have been invaluable at all stages of the work. Richard Hays provided many seeds for this present work in a seminar he taught on the Gospel of Mark. My fascination with Mark and with Mark's view of the world owes much to him. Abraham

Malherbe provided many insights into the ways that Greco-Roman literature can illuminate the texts of the New Testament and gave many helpful suggestions for this project. Hans Dieter Betz first showed me the importance of rhetorical analysis of New Testament texts in his seminars at the University of Chicago.

   Some of the ideas in this study were presented in papers at the Society of Biblical Literature meetings, where I received many helpful comments. Joanna Dewey and David Aune graciously provided copies of unpublished papers relating to this work. I would particularly like to thank Elizabeth Malbon for her encouragement and advice. Robert Berger provided an excellent index. Most importantly, my wife and children have been unstinting in their loving patience and support. Without their help this project could never have been completed.

ABBREVIATIONS

AAAH	Acta Academie Aboensis, Humaniora
AB	Anchor Bible
ABSA	*Annual of the British School at Athens*
ACNT	Augsburg Commentary on the New Testament
AIARS	Acta Instituti Atheniensis Regni Sueciae
AJA	*American Journal of Archaeology*
AJP	*American Journal of Philology*
AJT	*American Journal of Theology*
ALUN	Annales littéraires de l'Université de Nantes
AnBib	Analecta biblica
ANET	J. B. Pritchard (ed.), *Ancient Near Eastern Texts*
ANRW	*Aufstieg und Niedergang der römischen Welt*
APAPM	American Philological Association Philological Monographs
AS	*Ancient Society*
ATDan	Acta theologica Danica
AUG	Acta Universitatis Gothoburgensis
BBB	Bonner Biblische Beiträge
BETL	Bibliotheca ephemeridum theologicarum lovaniensium
Bib	*Biblica*
BLS	Bible and Literature Series
BR	*Biblical Research*
BRel	Beiträge zur Religionswissenschaft
BTB	*Biblical Theology Bulletin*
CalC	Calvin's Commentaries
CBQ	*Catholic Biblical Quarterly*
CBQMS	Catholic Biblical Quarterly—Monograph Series
CCM	Connecticut College Monographs
CGTC	Cambridge Greek Testament Commentaries
ClassQ	*Classical Quarterly*
CLL	Classical Lives and Letters
CP	*Classical Philology*
CSCP	Cornell Studies in Classical Philology
CUAPS	The Catholic University of America Patristic Studies
DJD	Discoveries in the Judaean Desert

NTS	*New Testament Studies*
OBO	Orbis biblicus et orientalis
PA	Philosophia Antiqua
PC	Proclamation Commentaries
PCAS	*Proceedings of the Classical Association of Scotland*
PG	J. Migne, *Patrologia graeca*
PGC	Pelican Gospel Commentaries
PMLT	Père Marquette Lecture in Theology
PP	*Past and Present*
PPFPM	Philadelphia Patristic Foundation Patristic Monograph
PSS	Pubblicazioni del Seminario di Semitistica
PSV	Phoenix Supplementary Volumes
PW	Pauly-Wissowa, *Realencyclopädie der classischen Altertums-wissenschaft*
QIFGUP	Quaderni dell' Instituto de Filologia Greca della Universita de Palermo
RB	*Revue biblique*
REG	*Revue des études grecques*
RheinMus	*Rheinisches Museum für Philologie*
RIL	*Rendiconti dell' Instituto Lombardo*
RSR	*Recherches de science religieuse*
RSV	Revised Standard Version
SBLDS	Society of Biblical Literature Dissertation Series
SBLMS	Society of Biblical Literature Monograph Series
SBLSP	Society of Biblical Literature Seminar Papers
SBLTT	Society of Biblical Literature Texts and Translations
SBLSBS	Society of Biblical Literature Sources for Biblical Study
SBLSCS	Society of Biblical Literature Septuagint and Cognate Studies
SBM	Stuttgarter biblische Monographien
SBT	Studies in Biblical Theology
SC	Sources chretiennes
SCHNT	Studia ad corpus hellenisticum novi testamenti
SCL	Studies in Classical Literature
SecCent	*Second Century*
SLA	Studies in Late Antiquity
SNTSMS	Society for New Testament Studies Monograph Series
SO	Symbolae osloenses
Str-B	[H. Strack and] P. Billerbeck, *Kommentar zum Neuen Testament*
StutB	Stuttgarter Bibelstudien
TAPA	*Transactions of the American Philological Association*
TBA	Tübinger Beiträge zur Altertumswissenschaft

TCGNT	B. M. Metzger, *A Textual Commentary on the Greek New Testament*
TCH	The Transformation of the Classical Heritage
TDNT	G. Kittel and G. Friedrich (eds.), *Theological Dictionary of the New Testament*
TRev	*Theologisches Revue*
TSJTSA	Texts and Studies of the Jewish Theological Seminary of America
TST	Toronto Studies in Theology
TTH	Translated Texts for Historians
UCSCP	*University of Chicago Studies in Classical Philology*
VC	*Vigiliae christianae*
WS	*Wiener Studien*
YCS	*Yale Classical Studies*
ZAW	*Zeitschrift für die alttestamentliche Wissenschaft*
ZNW	*Zeitschrift für die neutestamentliche Wissenschaft*
ZTK	*Zeitschrift für Theologie und Kirche*

1 _____

INTRODUCTION

_____

This century has seen numerous methodological developments in the study of the Gospel of Mark.[1] In the nineteenth century, the Gospels were often understood as historical records from which the life and teaching of Jesus could be reconstructed directly. In this century, however, the historical reliability of the Gospels became suspect. In large part this was due to William Wrede's analysis of Mark, *The Messianic Secret*, which argued that Mark's own theological interests played a great role in the structure and content of his Gospel.[2] Mark's editorial work was also stressed by Karl Ludwig Schmidt in *Der Rahmen der Geschichte Jesu*, which argued that Mark worked with independent units of tradition and that the chronological and spatial framework of the Gospel was the creation of Mark himself.[3]

The methodology of form criticism developed directly out of the observation of the apparent independence of individual episodes in the Synoptic Gospels. For the form critics, the Gospels served largely as mines for units of tradition that were studied as independent entities. In the fifties, however, scholarly attention began to turn back to the

[1] An excellent summary of Markan scholarship is found in Sean P. Kealy, *Mark's Gospel: A History of Its Interpretation* (New York and Ramsey, NJ: Paulist Press, 1982).

[2] William Wrede, *The Messianic Secret* (Cambridge: James Clarke & Co., 1971). German edition published in 1901.

[3] Karl Ludwig Schmidt, *Der Rahmen der Geschichte Jesu: Literarkritische Untersuchungen zur älteste Jesusüberlieferung* (Berlin: Trowitzsch, 1919).

1

Gospels themselves and the contributions of the individual evangelists in creating them.[4] The redaction critics retained the construct of independently circulating units from the work of the form critics but concentrated on the way in which the units were transformed by the Gospel writers. The work of the evangelists was understood primarily in its relationship to the pre-existing tradition.[5]

Narrative criticism, which has developed over the past two decades, is in part a reaction against the tendency of form and redaction critics to treat the Gospels in terms of individual units and conjectured reconstructions of the units' prehistories. Narrative critics, while not abandoning entirely the historical reconstructions of the form and redaction critics, have insisted on interpreting the Gospels as integral texts. The meaning of the Gospels, they have argued, is to be found in the text rather than in the prehistory of the material found there. To assist in the interpretation of the Gospel texts, the narrative critics have borrowed from various schools of contemporary literary criticism, applying the methods of literary criticism to the Gospel narratives. The use of literary critical models has allowed the narrative critics to sidestep the issue of historical veracity, which consumed the nineteenth century critics, to concentrate on explication of the world created by the text itself.[6]

The methodology of narrative criticism, however, has not been without its own critics. Mark Allan Powell has conveniently summarized those criticisms into five points:

1. Narrative criticism treats the Gospels as coherent narratives when they are actually collections of disparate material.

---

[4] The first major redaction-critical study of Mark was Willi Marxsen, *Mark the Evangelist* (Nashville: Abingdon, 1969). German edition published in 1956.

[5] The major works of form criticism relating to the Gospel of Mark are discussed by Kealy, *Mark's Gospel*, 115-158. The period of redaction criticism is discussed on pp. 159-197. For an important recent critique of Markan redaction criticism, see C. Clifton Black, II, *The Disciples according to Mark: Marcan Redaction in Current Debate*, JSNTSup 27 (Sheffield: Sheffield Academic Press, 1989).

[6] A very useful introduction to narrative criticism is provided by Mark Allan Powell, *What is Narrative Criticism?* GBS (Minneapolis: Fortress Press, 1990). The relationship between narrative criticism and earlier methods of interpretation are discussed on pp. 2-10.

2. Narrative criticism imposes on ancient literature concepts drawn from the study of modern literature.

3. Narrative criticism seeks to interpret the Gospels through methods that were devised for the study of fiction.

4. Narrative criticism allows subjective interpretation by its acceptance of the possibility of multiple meanings.

5. Narrative criticism rejects or ignores the historical witness of the Gospels.[7]

Those criticisms all reflect different aspects of a single complaint: narrative criticism has misperceived the nature of the Gospel narratives. The Gospels build their plots out of relatively independent episodes rather than a continuous narrative line as in most modern fiction. The nature of Gospel characters is extremely different from the nature of characters of modern fiction, biography, or historical narrative. The purpose of the Gospels is different from the purpose of modern fiction. As works that may be described as ideological, propagandistic, or didactic, the Gospels were intended to persuade their hearers to accept or reaffirm a particular point of view. In particular, the Gospels were intended to persuade their hearers to accept a particular point of view concerning a set of historical facts.

These criticisms, then, are not criticisms of the enterprise of narrative study of the Gospels so much as criticisms of the literary models that scholars using the narrative approach have adopted in their interpretations of the Gospel. The Gospels do present a narrative of the life, death, and resurrection of Jesus. There can be no complaint, on principle, of the attempt to interpret those narratives as narratives. It is a matter of some note that the Gospel writers chose a narrative format for their presentation of Jesus. A number of other formats for the presentation of a great teacher, leader, or religious figure were available in the cultural milieu, including collections of sayings, dialogues, and the topically arranged biographical form. If the Gospel writers chose a narrative format for their presentations of Jesus, the

---

[7] Powell, *What is Narrative Criticism?* 91-98. For the literature from which these criticisms are drawn, see the notes provided by Powell. The points are quoted from Powell, except for number 4, which I have restated for the sake of clarity.

narratives must reflect the writers' purposes for the composition of their works.

What is needed, then, is not the abandonment of narrative criticism but the development of a style of criticism that adequately reflects the nature of the Gospel narratives. Although it is possible for narrative criticism to be applied in an ahistorical manner, narrative critics generally have used our knowledge of the historical situation of the early church to illuminate the text and have sought in turn to use their narrative interpretations to illuminate the nature of early Christianity. If the goal of narrative criticism is to understand the meaning of the Gospel texts within their historical situations, often referred to as the intended or original meaning, then narrative criticism must be understood as an historical enterprise. While it is certainly not desirable to ignore the insights that modern literary criticism might provide into the Gospel narratives, if they are to avoid anachronistic readings, narrative critics must be cognizant of the differences between the Gospel narratives and the narratives found in modern fiction and must adapt their method accordingly.

The Nature of the Markan Narrative

A non-anachronistic reading of the Gospel narratives must take account of a number of points.[8]

The Gospels were intended to be read aloud. The narrative must be understood as it was heard rather than as it appeared on the written page.[9] Silent reading was relatively rare in the first century, although

---

[8] An excellent discussion of the way the Gospels would be experienced by their original readers or hearers can be found in Mary Ann Beavis, *Mark's Audience: The Literary and Social Setting of Mark 4.11-12*, JSNTSup 33 (Sheffield: JSOT Press, 1989) 13-44.

[9] This point has been made most forcefully by Thomas Eugene Boomershine, "Mark, the Storyteller: A Rhetorical-Critical Investigation of Mark's Passion and Resurrection Narrative," Dissertation, Union Theological Seminary, New York, 1974; *idem*, "Peter's Denial as Polemic or Confession: The Implications of Media Criticism for Biblical Hermeneutics," *Semeia* 39 (1987) 47-68; Joanna Dewey, "Oral Methods of Structuring Narrative in Mark," *Int* 43 (1989) 32-44; *idem*, "Mark as Interwoven Tapestry: Forecasts and Echoes for a Listening Audience," *CBQ* 53 (1991) 221-36; H. Van Dyke Parunak, "Oral Typesetting: Some Uses of Biblical Structure," *Bib* 62 (1981) 153-68; *idem*, "Transitional Techniques in the

there is evidence that non-literary documents such as private letters and inscriptions were read silently.[10] Literary documents, even when read privately, were vocalized.

It is unlikely that many Christians would have had an opportunity to read a work such as Mark in private. Books took considerable time to copy and were very expensive. A copy of the Gospel of Mark might cost the modern equivalent of six-hundred dollars.[11] Many Christians would have been illiterate and would have been unable to read the Gospels themselves even if they had access to a copy. The Gospel may have been written for presentation at a particular time to a particular community rather than written to be put into general circulation, but even if it were intended originally for publication, it is unlikely that more than a single copy of the Gospel would have been available for a church or group of churches. Thus it is most likely that the Gospels were intended to be heard by groups of Christians. The presentation of the Gospel may have taken place in a catechetical setting or in an assembly of the church.

The Gospels would have been read expressively. First century students were taught to read expressively. Rhetoric was one of the principal subjects of higher education, and people thought of words in terms of their expressive power. Students were taught to familiarize themselves thoroughly with a text so they could deliver it expressively.[12] As a result, the dramatic power of the Gospels, and especially of Mark, in which action predominates over teaching, would have been fully evident.

Bible," *JBL* 102 (1983) 525-48.

[10] B. M. W. Knox, "Silent Reading in Antiquity," *GRBS* 9 (1968) 421-35; cited by Beavis, *Mark's Audience*, 187, n. 43.

[11] At the time of Diocletian, a scribe received 20 to 25 denarii for copying 100 stichoi of text, and thus it would cost 320 to 400 denarii to have the 1,600 stichoi of the Gospel of Mark copied by a professional scribe. At the same time, a laborer received 25 denarii a day and a skilled craftsman 50 denarii. A copy of the Gospel of Mark would cost thirteen to sixteen times a laborer's daily wage, not including the cost of the papyrus or parchment. That would be the modern equivalent of about six-hundred dollars (Kealy, *Mark's Gospel*, 10-11).

[12] Beavis, *Mark's Audience*, 23; citing H. I. Marrou, *A History of Education in Antiquity* (New York: Sheed and Ward, 1956), 161-66.

The Gospel of Mark would have been heard as an authoritative pronouncement. It is likely that the author of Mark was a figure of some importance in his community. His writing would embody his authority in much the same way that the letters of Paul embody the authority of the apostle. It is Mark's authority that inclines the audience to accept Mark's account as a true account of Jesus. One of the significant aspects of oral delivery is the authority that the speaker's presence lends to the spoken word. It is likely that the Gospel of Mark would have been presented to its original audience by a speaker with considerable status in the community, whether that original speaker was the author himself or some other community leader. If the Gospel was read in a catechistic setting, it is most likely that the reader was the catechist.[13]

The Gospel of Mark is primarily an ideological or didactic work. Luke tells Theophilus in the preface to his Gospel that he has written the account so Theophilus "may recognize the truth of the matters about which [he was] taught" (Lk 1.4). John is equally clear in his intention: "These things were written so you may believe that Jesus is the Messiah, the Son of God, and that by believing you may have life in his name" (Jn 20.31). Mark does not tell us the reason for the composition of his Gospel, but there is little doubt that, among other things, he intended to reinforce his audience's conviction that Jesus is the Messiah, the Son of God, and to teach them their own responsibilities as his followers.[14]

Most narrative is ideological to some extent, since it presents or reinforces a particular view of the world. There is, nevertheless, a great difference between works that are intended as entertainment and

---

[13] Robert M. Fowler takes an opposite position, that the Gospel's reception is not based on the personal authority of its author (*Let the Reader Understand: Reader-Response Criticism and the Gospel of Mark* [Minneapolis: Fortress Press, 1991] 62-64). While it is true that the text of the Gospel itself makes no claim about the author's authority, it is entirely another question whether it was heard in terms of the author's authority.

[14] Scholars are generally agreed that Mark wrote for a Christian audience. For a recent argument that Mark had a non-Christian audience in mind, see Beavis, *Mark's Audience*. Beavis sees the Gospel as a work intended to convince its audience of the Christian understanding of Jesus. Whether the intention is to convince or confirm, the ideological aspect of the Gospel is just as important.

are only incidentally ideological and works that aim at persuasion rather than entertainment. In the interpretation of such explicitly ideological works, the persuasive intent can never be lost from sight, and the interpretation must pay particular attention to the rhetoric of the work.

The narrative of the Gospel is considerably more episodic than most modern literature. The Gospel of Mark is constructed from individual episodes that can, for the most part, stand independently. Although Mark has structured these episodes into a chronologically ordered narrative, the episodes retain a greater independence than do episodes in most modern novels or short stories.

There are many examples of works in antiquity in which individual chreiae or biographic episodes are strung together according to theme (as in Iamblichus' *Pythagorean Life* 31-33 or Xenophon's *Memorabilia*) or with no discernible order at all (as in portions of many of the lives of Diogenes Laertius, e.g., the life of Socrates 2.30-37). Narrative continuity did not play the same role in the expectations of ancient audiences as it does in those of modern readers. Narrative continuity is in part an illusion that the audience itself participates in creating, and an audience without an expectation of continuity will tend not to fill in the narrative gaps to create continuity where the narrative itself does not provide it.[15]

The narrative independence of the episodes is reinforced by the rhetorical structure of the Gospel. Since the rhetorical discourse is primary, sequences of episodes often are structured by the rhetorical progression rather than the demands of narrative continuity. As will be shown in more detail below, for example, the first call stories follow almost immediately on the proclamation of Jesus as the Son of God in the prologue in order to create a coherent rhetorical unit. Similarly, Mark creates a coherent rhetorical sequence by having a crowd of people appear out of nowhere in 8.34 to receive teaching that

---

[15] Wolfgang Iser has stressed the importance of the reader's filling in the gaps in the text (*The Act of Reading: A Theory of Aesthetic Response* [Baltimore and London: John Hopkins University Press, 1978]). Iser's work has been extremely influential in narrative criticism of the Gospels.

they cannot understand without the knowledge of the passion that they do not possess.[16]

Mark's audience was probably familiar with much of the material in the Gospel, and that familiarity would also reinforce the discontinuity of the narrative as perceived by the audience. The extent of such familiarity would depend on whether Mark wrote for his own community or for another. Mark's own community probably would have been familiar with most of the pre-existing material used by Mark. Other communities might not have been familiar with as much of the material, but it is likely that any community to which Mark would send his Gospel would be one in communication with his own and that such communication would create a shared pool of Jesus material. At the very least, the community would have been familiar with similar types of material. While Mark's placement of this material into a narrative framework alters to some extent his audience's perception of the episodes, it is not sufficient to free the material from the familiar meanings already associated with it in his listeners' minds. To the extent that these pre-existing meanings are assigned to individual episodes in the narrative, the meanings tend to isolate the episodes in the listeners' minds and to prevent the incidental information from one episode from spilling over into another.

The resulting narrative is considerably more continuous than the chreia collections of Diogenes Laertius but considerably less continuous than most modern fiction. While the form critics certainly erred in overemphasizing the independence of the episodes within the Gospels, narrative critics tend to overlook the lapses in continuity because the narrative theories from which they borrow generally assume that continuity exists in the narrative or is created in the mind of the reader.

Characters in Mark's Gospel serve primarily to further the portrayal of Jesus. In all narrative, there are characters that fulfill roles of varying importance. Most important are the central characters

---

[16] See below, Chapter 6, pp. 184-86, and Chapter 8, pp. 266-67. For other examples of narrative discontinuity, see Fowler, *Let the Reader Understand*, 134-40. For Fowler, the existence of gaps "offers the reader many empty spots to fill in" (*Let the Reader Understand*, 134). I am suggesting that ancient listeners were much less prone to fill in gaps than are modern readers.

or protagonists. In the formulation of W. J. Harvey, the novel "exists to reveal them."[17] Then come secondary characters, who are subordinated to the main characters but are still of interest as characters. Finally, there are the ficelles, who exist as personified plot functions.[18] Allan Culpepper's observation about the Gospel of John is equally applicable to the Gospel of Mark: "Jesus is the protagonist and most of the other characters are ficelles."[19] The Gospel exists to portray Jesus as the Messiah, the Son of God. The other characters serve as plot functions (the opponents oppose and cause the crucifixion) or help reveal who Jesus is.

The Nature of Markan Characters

The difference between characters in novels and real people, according to E. M. Forster, is the accessibility of their inner lives. He explains the difference in this way:

> In daily life we never understand each other, neither complete clairvoyance nor complete confessional exists. We know each other approximately, by external signs, and these serve well enough as a basis for society and even for intimacy. But people in a novel can be understood completely by the reader, if the novelist wishes; their inner as well as their outer life can be exposed. And this is why they often seem more definite than characters in history, or even our own friends; we have been told all about them that can be told; even if they are imperfect or unreal they do not contain any secrets, whereas our friends do and must, mutual secrecy being one of the conditions of life upon this globe.[20]

[17] W. J. Harvey, *Character and the Novel* (London: Chatto & Windus, 1965) 56; quoted by R. Allan Culpepper, *Anatomy of the Fourth Gospel: A Study in Literary Design*, FFNT (Philadelphia: Fortress Press, 1983) 104.

[18] Harvey, *Character and Novel*, 58, 67; Robert Scholes and Robert Kellogg, *The Nature of Narrative* (New York and London: Oxford University Press, 1966) 204; Wayne C. Booth, *The Rhetoric of Fiction* (Chicago: University of Chicago Press, 1961) 102.

[19] Culpepper, *Anatomy of the Fourth Gospel*, 104.

[20] E. M. Forster, *Aspects of the Novel* (San Diego, New York, and London: Harcourt Brace Jovanovich, 1985) 47.

A novelist is successful in his portrayal of a character when he creates an impression that the character is explicable and is understood by the novelist. It is this impression that makes characters in novels seem more real than people in daily life.[21] Even flat characters, those that can be summed up neatly in a single sentence, exhibit an inner life. The portrayal of their inner life is limited to a single characteristic, but it is a single internal characteristic.[22]

This revelation of an inner life is conspicuous by its absence in the Gospel of Mark. The characters in Mark fulfill roles, but their inner life, even when recorded in a perfunctory manner, is largely irrelevant to the story.[23] The lack of characterization is underscored by the fact that most of the characters in the Gospel of Mark, other than those who make cameo appearances, are groups rather than individuals. David Rhoads and Donald Michie, for example, divide their chapter on Markan characters into Jesus, the authorities, the disciples, and the little people.[24] These groups are not characters in the modern, novelistic sense, since their common inner life is restricted to the particular point that unites them, their support of or opposition to Jesus.

The opponents of Jesus, for example, fulfill the role of opposition, but the reasons for their opposition remain sketchy at best.[25] It

[21] Forster, *Aspects of the Novel*, 63.

[22] Flat and round characters are discussed in Forster, *Aspects of the Novel*, 67-78.

[23] The contrast between the Markan use of characters and the modern, novelistic character is clear in modern retellings of the Gospel stories. For two very different retellings, each of which fills in the missing psychology of the Gospel characters, see Arthur S. Maxwell, *The Bible Story*, 10 vols. (Washington, DC: Review and Herald Publishing Association, 1957), a children's story Bible; and Alain Absire, *Lazarus* (San Diego, New York, and London: Harcourt Brace Jovanovich, 1988).

[24] David Rhoads and Donald Michie, *Mark as Story: An Introduction to the Narrative of a Gospel* (Philadelphia: Fortress Press, 1982) 101-36. Theodore J. Weeden, Sr., lists as the major Markan characters "the religious 'Establishment,' the ubiquitous crowds, the disciples, and Jesus" (*Mark—Traditions in Conflict* [Philadelphia: Fortress Press, 1971] 20). Powell notes, "Scholars are widely agreed that the religious leaders constitute a character group in Matthew, in Mark, and in Luke, and so can be treated as a single character in each of these stories" (*What is Narrative Criticism?* 58).

[25] For literary studies of the opponents in Mark, see Stephen H. Smith, "The Role of Jesus' Opponents in the Markan Drama," *NTS* 35 (1989) 161-82; Rhoads

is only at 15.10 that the listener is told that Pilate perceived that the chief priests were envious of Jesus. The characterization of the opponents serves primarily to disqualify them as representatives of God.[26] The listener is told in 1.22 that the scribes do not teach with authority and in 3.5 that the opponents (probably the Pharisees) are hardhearted. The Pharisees and "some of the scribes" from Jerusalem are condemned as hypocrites in 7.6-8 for observing their own traditions rather than the commandments of God. The scribes are condemned in 12.38-40 for their love of honor, their greed, and their hypocrisy. This disqualification of the opponents is vital if they are to fulfill their role as opponents. Their outward position as religious authorities gives them the potential for acting from God's point of view, so their legitimacy must be denied if they are to oppose Jesus.

The much-remarked insights into the mind of the Markan characters generally serve to develop the plot or to define a narrative or rhetorical role rather than to develop the characters as characters.[27] Mark provides his listeners with an inner view of the opponents at their first appearance in the healing of the paralytic. The scribes, we are told, "were questioning in their hearts, 'Why does this man speak in this way? He is blaspheming! Who is able to forgive sins except the one God?'" (2.6-7). Even though this is an inner view, it serves as part of the action of the plot, since Jesus answers their unspoken criticism. The scribes' mistaken identification of Jesus' words as blasphemy reveals their opposition and foreshadows the opponents'

---

and Michie, *Mark as Story*, 117-22. For a study of Jewish authorities, including those who are not opponents, see Elizabeth Struthers Malbon, "The Jewish Leaders in the Gospel of Mark: A Literary Study of Marcan Characterization," *JBL* 108 (1989) 259-81.

[26] On the characterization of the religious authorities from the perspective of the rhetoric of ancient polemics, see Luke T. Johnson, "The New Testament's Anti-Jewish Slander and the Conventions of Ancient Polemic," *JBL* 108 (1989) 419-41.

[27] On the inside views of characters that Mark provides, see Norman R. Petersen, "'Point of View' in Mark's Narrative," *Semeia* 12 (1978) 116-18; and Rhoads and Michie, *Mark as Story*, 37-38. Culpepper's observation about the Gospel of John is fitting for Mark as well: "These inside views tend to be limited rather than detailed and shallow rather than profound. The evangelist shows no interest in exploring the more complex psychological motivations of his characters" (*Anatomy of the Fourth Gospel*, 26).

later charge against Jesus at the trial, but Mark does not help the listener to understand the motivation for their opposition.

The inner life of the scribes that Mark portrays reveals their role rather than their character in the modern, novelistic sense. We know nothing of why they mistake Jesus for a blasphemer or why they oppose him. Are they devoutly religious men who truly love God and believe that any deviation from their received faith is an attack on God? Are they men mechanically acting out religious formalities with no belief in God's ability to act in the present? Are they hypocrites using the words of religion to mask their own ambitions? Are they apprehensive conformists fearful of anything new that might undermine their identity? These are questions that might interest a modern novelist, but for Mark, they are not important. It is only important that the scribes oppose Jesus.

Some narrative critics have labeled the Markan disciples as round characters.[28] While they are certainly round characters when compared with the single-scene ficelles (such as the poor widow of Mark 12.41-44), they are not round characters in the same way that the characters of a modern novel, or a Platonic dialogue, are round. In most episodes, the character of the disciples is as flat, or nearly so, as that of the poor widow. In each episode, the disciples fulfill a single rhetorical role. Unlike the opponents of Jesus, however, whose rhetorical role is fixed throughout the Gospel, or the poor widow, who makes only a single appearance, the disciples' rhetorical role varies from place to place within the Gospel, often very quickly from one episode to another (as in the sequence of 8.27 to 9.13, where the disciples represent in succession inability to comprehend the meaning of miracles, confession of Jesus as the Messiah, concern for Jesus' life, witnesses of Jesus' transcendent glory, and recipients of explanatory teaching). When the flat disciples of the individual episodes are strung together "as pearls on a string," they can be seen as multisided, but it may only be our modern penchant for complexity of characterization that we have discovered. The narrative role of the disciples is broad

---

[28] Rhoads and Michie, *Mark as Story*, 123; Elizabeth Struthers Malbon, "The Poor Widow in Mark and Her Poor Rich Readers," *CBQ* 53 (1991) 601.

enough to encompass a number of rhetorical roles, but still the disciples are not characters in the modern, novelistic sense.

There are times when Markan characters do exhibit at least a rudimentary novelistic inner life, but those points are relatively few, and the characterization is confined to an episode and does not become a permanent feature of the characters. There are two particularly prominent moments in the narrative, the beheading of John (6.17-29) and Peter's denial of Jesus (14.66-72), when the audience's attention is sufficiently diverted from Jesus for other characters to rise to a level of independent interest. In both these cases, the protagonists of the episode, Peter and Herod, are quite effectively characterized as men caught between competing pressures and giving in to their less worthy impulses.[29] The spite of Herodias and the bond between her and her daughter are also quite vivid. It would appear, then, that the general flatness of characterization is not due to the author's inability to create vivid characterization so much as to a lack of interest in doing so. His focus on Jesus is nearly complete, and his characters exist in order to assist in his portrayal of Jesus.

Attempts at Historically Accurate Readings of the Disciples

The difference between ancient understandings of literary characterization and modern views has been recognized before. Three notable attempts to understand the Gospel of Mark from the point of view of ancient understandings of characterization are Theodore J. Weeden, Sr.'s *Traditions in Conflict*, Mary Ann Tolbert's *Sowing the Gospel*,[30] and Vernon K. Robbins' *Jesus the Teacher*.[31]

---

[29] These characterizations also serve a clear rhetorical intent. Each of Mark's three principal discourses—4.2-34, 8.34-9.1, 13.3-37—address the problem of persecution and the other cares that might lead Christians to give up their faith in Jesus. Peter and Herod serve as negative examples of those who gave in to similar pressures. The classic discussion of Peter's denial from a literary-historical viewpoint is that of Erich Auerbach (*Mimesis: The Representation of Reality in Western Literature* [Princeton: Princeton University Press, 1953] 40-49).

[30] Mary Ann Tolbert, *Sowing the Gospel: Mark's World in Literary-historical Perspective* (Minneapolis: Fortress Press, 1989).

[31] Vernon K. Robbins, *Jesus the Teacher: A Socio-rhetorical Interpretation of Mark* (Philadelphia: Fortress Press, 1984).

Theodore J. Weeden, Sr.

Weeden's book, published in 1971, preceded the recent interest in literary approaches to the Gospels, and although it is written from a redaction-critical perspective, in many ways it anticipates the later interests of the literary critics. Weeden stresses the importance of characterization, concentrating particularly on the character of the disciples, and seeks to demonstrate a development of the characterization of the disciples that is roughly equivalent to the literary-critical interest in plot. By and large he interprets the Gospel as a unified whole, but unlike more recent narrative critics, he is still willing to dispose of ill-fitting passages by attributing them to a pre-Markan stratum.[32]   After twenty years, the book still stands as the most thorough presentation of the thesis that Mark wrote his Gospel as a polemic against a faction of the church that he attacked through his representation of the disciples.

The general principle enunciated by Weeden is precisely that which is argued here: "The only way to interpret the Gospel as the author intended it is to read his work with the analytical eyes of a first century reader. That means in some way assuming the conceptual and analytical stance of a reader in the first century."[33]

Weeden attempts to recreate the first century stance through an analysis of the educational techniques of the time.[34]   Drawing on H. I. Marrou's work, *A History of Education in Antiquity*,[35] Weeden notes that the study of the classics involved "a meticulous investigation of characters and events." "Interest in characters was particularly pronounced." Much of the initial investigation of characters concerned facts that seem trivial to modern readers, but Weeden's interpretation is based on the final step of the analysis, the understanding of characters as examples of moral principles: "The final step in a Greek student's investigation of a literary work was 'judgment.' This

[32] E.g., Weeden, *Traditions in Conflict*, 139-49, where he consigns 4.10-12 and 4.34 to the dustbin of heresy.

[33] Weeden, *Traditions in Conflict*, 11.

[34] Weeden, *Traditions in Conflict*, 12-19.   Quotations in the following discussion are taken from pp. 13, 14, 15.

[35] Marrou, *History of Education*, 160-70, 277-81.

involved extrapolating some moral principle from the thoughts and behavior of the characters."

It was not only teachers who were interested in the use of characters as moral examples. Weeden argues that from the fourth century BCE Greek historians "wrote history not so much in the interest of accurate information as in the interest of guiding the reader to a moralistic interpretation of the world." It was primarily through characterization that such moral judgments were elicited. Livy is cited as an example of such a moralizing historian, and Weeden notes that rather than providing explicit commentary, Livy interprets history through the way that he depicts his characters, leaving judgment to his readers. Weeden argues that the Gospel of Mark was based on the model of moralizing history and that through his use of characterization, Mark intended to lead his readers to make moral judgments concerning the characters. In particular, he intended his readers to make a negative judgment of the disciples.

Moralistic characterization is certainly apparent in the literature roughly contemporary with the Gospels, but as our investigation in this study will show, there was a much greater variety in the approach to literary characterization than Weeden allows. It is particularly problematic to assume that Mark would have adopted such a moralistic stance, since his presentation of Jesus as one who is tolerant of sinners and includes them among his followers undermines the conventional moralistic stance. The other major characters in the Gospel do not wholly fit the moralistic pattern. The opponents are villains rather than negative examples. Jesus does serve as a positive example, but Mark is more interested in his divine identity. Weeden's contention that Mark would have followed whatever literary conventions were available overlooks the fact that authors generally write in accordance with their purposes.[36] While Livy was interested in history as a museum of moral examples, Mark was interested in the portentous divine meaning that lay masked behind a seemingly insignificant historical event. The two writers have very different purposes in writing, and it is reasonable to presume that they might adopt different approaches to the use of character.

---

[36] Weeden, *Traditions in Conflict*, 17.

The most problematic part of Weeden's approach, however, is his concentration on the disciples as the key to the meaning of Mark. Although Weeden lists four major characters or groups of characters— the religious establishment, the crowds, the disciples, and Jesus—he disposes of the religious leaders and the crowds in a page and a half each while he devotes twenty-nine pages to the disciples.[37] The character of Jesus does not merit a separate discussion. His character is discussed only in terms of christological conflict. Certainly, not all characters are created equal, but Mark is not writing a history of the disciples. He is writing the good news of Jesus the Messiah the Son of God (1.1).

The examination of the philosophical biographies in this dissertation indicates that supporting characters, even if they rise to the position of independent moral examples, as they often do, tend to be subordinated to the characterization of the protagonist.[38] Followers seem to fall especially into the position of subordinated characters. While the various rulers and philosophical brotherhoods that populate Philostratus' *Life of Apollonius of Tyana* are clearly presented as contrasting models of proper and improper behavior,[39] the followers generally are used to characterize Apollonius. This may take the form of contrasting behavior (1.18; 1.23; 2.7; 4.11; 4.37; 7.11-13) or similar behavior (1.40), but in both cases their behavior is used to emphasize the conduct of Apollonius. Thus, before we speak about the character of the disciples, we must first examine how the disciples are used in each individual episode in the portrayal of Jesus. The extent to which the disciples possess an independent character portrait can only be determined subsequently.

The subordination of the character of the disciples to that of Jesus is even more pronounced in the Gospel of Mark because of the episodic nature of his narrative. For the most part, Mark constructs his narrative from freestanding narrative episodes that create their

---

[37] Weeden, *Traditions in Conflict*, 20-51.

[38] An exception to this is found in the portions of Iamblichus' *Pythagorean Life* in which Pythagoras and his followers are blended together to produce an image of the ideal philosophical character (especially chapters 30-33). That, however, is hardly the model followed by Mark.

[39] See below, Chapter 4, p. 134.

collective meaning by the juxtaposition and accumulation of their individual meanings. Since the focus of each episode is Jesus or his teaching, it is not clear that we can legitimately speak of a character of the disciples at all. The disciples present us with a collection of supporting roles that Mark may or may not have unified into a single characterization.

Mary Ann Tolbert

The most ambitious attempt to interpret the Gospel of Mark from the perspective of ancient literary conventions is Tolbert's *Sowing the Gospel*. Tolbert presents a thorough and consistent interpretation of Mark based on her understanding of the parable of the sower and its interpretation (4.2-20) and the parable of the tenants (12.1-11) as summaries of the Markan plot. Unlike Weeden, who drew parallels between the Gospel and ancient historical writing, Tolbert uses the ancient romance as her model for interpretation.[40] While Weeden's parallel between the Gospel and history is based on subject matter— both are narratives of historical events—Tolbert's parallel is based on style. Both Gospel and romance may be grouped stylistically as popular literature.[41]

Tolbert defines the nature of ancient literary characters as follows:

> In ancient literature, characters were more illustrative than represen-
> tational.... The illustrative characters of ancient literature are static,
> monolithic figures who do not grow or develop psychologically.

---

[40] Tolbert, *Sowing the Gospel*, 55-79 and *passim*.

[41] Tolbert, *Sowing the Gospel*, 59-78. Tolbert's use of the term "genre" with respect to popular literature is unfortunate, since "popular literature" is a much broader category than genre. Both popular literature and elite literature can be divided into a number of genres, and some romances may be properly classified among the elite category. According to the Suda, Achilles Tatius, the author of *Clitophon and Leucippe* wrote as well "a treatise on the sphere, and works on etymology"; Photius praises his literary style, and Thomas Magister refers to him as a rhetor (E. H. Warmington, "Introduction," in *Achilles Tatius*, LCL [Cambridge, MA: Harvard University Press; and London: William Heinemann, 1969] ix-xi). Tolbert's classification of the Gospel and the romance as a single genre leads her to a somewhat uncritical use of the romance model that overlooks the significant differences between Gospel and romance that she herself notes in her discussion.

They have fundamentally the same characteristics at the end as at the beginning. They may, of course, change state, from good fortune to bad, from unknown to known, or from insider to outsider, for example, but such shifts are always implicit in the actions or principles the characters are illustrating.[42]

Tolbert understands the characters, or character-groups, in the Gospel as illustrative of four types of responses to Jesus presented parabolically in the parable of the sower (4.2-20), which she identifies as a major plot summary. The opponents are the ground along the way, who reject the word from the beginning. The disciples are the rocky ground, who receive the word with joy but quickly wither. Tolbert has more trouble finding a group that represents the thorny ground, the ones who receive the word but fall away due to the cares of the world, but identifies two examples, Herod in 6.14-29 and the rich young man in 10.17-22. The good earth, those who bear fruit, are identified with the ones who are healed or saved by their faith.[43]

While Tolbert's awareness of the gulf between modern and ancient notions of character is quite promising, her specific application of that insight is problematic. Her identification of the parable of the sower as a plot summary is unconvincing. Those passages conventionally identified as plot summaries, such as 1.14-15 and 3.7-12, appear to be much better candidates. In fact, Mark closes the parable discourse with a summary passage that indicates that the parables are to be taken as illustrative of a general principle, that Jesus taught in parables and explained their inner meaning to his disciples (4.33-34). Tolbert draws a parallel between the oracles at the beginning and ending of Xenophon's *An Ephesian Tale* and the parables of the sower and the tenants,[44] but the passion predictions offer a much better parallel with the oracle-as-summary. Nor does she show a parallel from the romances for a plot constructed out of contrasting character

---

[42] Tolbert, *Sowing the Gospel*, 76-77. For her understanding of ancient characterization, Tolbert draws on Scholes and Kellogg (*Nature of Narrative*, 88) and Tzvetan Todorov ("Narrative-Men," in *The Poetics of Prose* [Oxford: Basil Blackwell, 1977] 66-67).

[43] Tolbert, *Sowing the Gospel*, 148-75.

[44] Tolbert, *Sowing the Gospel*, 104-05, 125.

types. Philostratus does, in fact, construct the plot of his *Life of Apollonius of Tyana* in large part according to such a principle, but the romances are much more action-oriented, and their plot summaries are summaries of action rather than character type. Like Weeden, Tolbert sees the Gospel as primarily about the secondary characters rather than about Jesus himself. Her plot summary is a summary of responses to Jesus rather than a summary of the activity or identity of Jesus.

Her analysis also breaks down with her inability to identify adequately groups that represent two of the four types of ground. Two unrelated examples are hardly sufficient to represent the thorny ground, and neither of her candidates matches the description. The focus of the Herod story is the death of John as a foreshadowing of the passions of Jesus and his followers, not the character of Herod. Herod's attraction to John, like Pilate's perception of Jesus' innocence and the envy of the chief priests (15.10, 14), is a conventional detail used to underline the injustice of John's death. The parable, in its progression from immediate rejection of the seed to the seed's bearing fruit, suggests that those represented by the thorny ground should receive the word for a while and later lose their faith. Neither Herod nor the rich man ever really accepts the word.

The identification of those healed through faith as the good earth is also unconvincing. Is Mark presenting the self-interested seeking of favors as the true response of faith? The discourse in 8.34-9.1 shows that following Jesus places great demands on the follower. Who among those healed venture to lose their lives? Where do we ever see their commitment tested as Peter was tested in the courtyard of the high priest? Their faith may be paradigmatic for the hearers of the Gospel in some ways, but it is only a partial, self-serving, and untested faith. If the disciples are to be faulted for their slowness in perceiving Jesus' identity or their resistance to the passion, how can those healed, who are not even conscious of the question of Jesus' identity or the troubling fact of his impending passion, be raised up as examples of true faith? As in the story of Herod, Tolbert avoids the central point of the healing stories, which is not the faith of the healed but the power of Jesus.

Tolbert provides a much more nuanced view of the role of the disciples in her discussion of Mark's narrative strategies. In this discussion, she identifies two ways in which Mark makes use of the disciples in the construction of his narrative. She notes that the disciples provide an opportunity for Jesus to teach and serve as foils to Jesus, emphasizing through their contrary actions the exemplary behavior of Jesus.[45] Unfortunately, she isolates this analysis from her dominant typological paradigm and does not consider how the episode-by-episode use of the disciples in the portrayal of Jesus affects the listeners' perception of them as characters.

Vernon K. Robbins

Unlike both Weeden and Tolbert, Robbins understands the disciples not as independent characters but as one term of the complementary social roles of teacher and disciple. He analyzes the Gospel of Mark as an intermingling of conventional patterns from Hellenistic and Jewish literature to portray a three-stage "teacher/disciple cycle."

Robbins offers a third possibility for understanding the genre of the Gospel of Mark, suggesting that the ἀπομνημονεύματα is the closest analogy to the Gospel form.[46] This suggestion has the advantage of being supported by the usage of several church fathers. Papias uses the term ἀπομνημονεύειν to describe Mark's writing of his Gospel, and Justin, Eusebius, and perhaps Tatian refer to the Gospels as ἀπομνημονεύματα,[47] though it must be born in mind that the use of the term, associated as it seems to be with writings about philosophers, may have been influenced by an apologetic intent to make Christianity appear as a legitimate philosophical school. Unfortunately, the only extant example of the form is Xenophon's *Memorabilia* ('Απομνημονεύματα in Greek). This is also the earliest known example of the form, and it is difficult to tell from the scattered references and citations of other ἀπομνημονεύματα how representa-

---

[45] Tolbert, *Sowing the Gospel*, 221-223. Tolbert exaggerates the extent to which the disciple as foil runs contrary to the conventional expectations concerning disciples or followers. Philostratus is able to use both Damis and Demetrius as foils to Apollonius even at the end of *The Life of Apollonius* (Damis and Demetrius, 7.12-14; Damis, 7.31, 38; Demetrius, 8.13-15). The biblical example of the Israelites as unfaithful followers of Moses would certainly be known by Mark's audience.

[46] Robbins, *Jesus the Teacher*, 60-68.

[47] For citations, see the discussion by Robbins.

tive it is. Quotations from ἀπομνημονεύματα, according to Robbins, tend to be aphoristic, but aphoristic material tends to be more quotable, so the proportion of aphoristic material that the works contained is unclear. Some ἀπομνημονεύματα were collections of material about various philosophers. Favorinus' Ἀπομνημονεύματα contained material related to at least eleven different philosophers, while that of Dioscurides contained material relating to at least two. Thus, while the term ἀπομνημονεύματα may, in fact, be an accurate genre classification for the Gospels, the uncertainty that surrounds the meaning that the ancients attached to the term minimizes its analytical value.[48]

---

[48] Robbins reconstructs the genre as an account of a person of wisdom that exemplifies the wise person's system of thought and action through the wise person's interaction with rival persons of wisdom, disciple-companions, and others. The account contains scenes from the adult life of the person and may contain scenes from the death of the person but show little or no interest in the wise person's birth or childhood (*Jesus the Teacher*, 62-63).

Even this vague definition, however, is disputable. The only extant writings that the ancients referred to as ἀπομνημονεύματα are Xenophon's *Memorabilia* and the Christian Gospels. Two of the Gospels do contain birth accounts, although the absence of birth and childhood material is one of the major ways that Robbins distinguishes ἀπομνημονεύματα from the genre of βίος. There also is no common denominator in the structuring principle of the *Memorabilia* and the Gospels. The Gospels are at least ostensibly arranged according to chronology, while the *Memorabilia* has an overall apologetic framework, with individual dialogues loosely organized according to topic. It seems more likely that the distinguishing feature of the genre is not structure or subject matter as much as the relationship between the accounts and their subjects, that is, that the accounts are, as the name implies, "things remembered." Xenophon claims that his *Memorabilia* is an eyewitness account, for the most part, and the material concerning Socrates' death, which occurred while Xenophon was abroad, is given through the report of another eyewitness. The Gospels were thought to be either eyewitness accounts or reports of eyewitness accounts, and it is reasonable to suppose that the church fathers used the term with reference to the Gospels in order to underscore the eyewitness nature of the material. Zeno wrote an ἀπομνημονεύματα of his teacher, Crates, and while there are no extant fragments of the work, we may assume it contained personal reminiscences. The ἀπομνημονεύματα of Dioscurides (first century BCE), Diodorus (first century BCE), and Favorinus (second century CE) were clearly not firsthand accounts, but they may have been collections of material thought to derive from eyewitnesses. Since at least two of these works dealt with more than one personage, it may be that the term ἀπομνημονεύματα referred to two distinct genres, one being a personal reminiscence and the other being a loosely organized collection of chreiae and aphorisms thought to derive from eyewitnesses. The biography of Apollonius of Tyana by Moeragenes was

There are a number of advantages to the approach adopted by Robbins. He focuses on Jesus as the main character in the Gospel and treats the disciples not as independent characters but as part of a student-teacher relationship. He includes a significant number of substantive comparisons in his discussion. His analysis recognizes that the Gospel of Mark is a rhetorical work in the sense that it seeks to create or reinforce certain ideas and attitudes in the audience. He is aware of the way in which social expectations can influence the understanding of a work such as the Gospel of Mark.

Robbins' study is extremely valuable in demonstrating how the Markan portrait of Jesus in his role as a teacher is related to Hellenistic teaching models found in the Greek philosophical literature as well as Jewish models of prophets and teachers. There was considerable Greek influence on Palestinian culture by the first century CE,[49] and the portrayal of Jesus in a Greek language work like the Gospel of Mark is likely to show further traces of Greek influence. Robbins effectively demonstrates the necessity of recognizing the Hellenistic aspect of Mark's cultural milieu and of interpreting the portrait of Jesus in relation to both its Greek and its Jewish cultural influences.[50]

Unfortunately, Robbins' discussion of Jesus and the disciples in Mark is marred by his choice of analytical tools. His analysis of the Gospel is based on the discussion of form in Kenneth Burke's *Counter-Statement*, and his interpretation of Jesus and the disciples is framed as a discussion of "conventional form."[51]   Burke defines form as

---

also called an ἀπομνημονεύματα, according to Origen, see below, Chapter 4, nn. 42-43.

[49] Many of these influences are detailed in Martin Hengel, *Judaism and Hellenism: Studies in their Encounter in Palestine during the Early Hellenistic Period*, 2 vols. (Philadelphia: Fortress Press, 1974).

[50] A precursor to Robbins' monograph, *Jesus the Teacher*, was an article that focuses primarily on the fusion of Jewish and Hellenistic culture in Mark's portrait of Jesus and the disciples, "Mark I.14-20: An Interpretation at the Intersection of Jewish and Graeco-Roman Traditions," *NTS* 28 (1982) 220-36. In *Jesus the Teacher*, this interest remains, but Robbins' focus shifts more toward his analysis of Mark in terms of form.

[51] For Robbins' theoretical discussion of conventional form, see *Jesus the Teacher*, 10, 53. He identifies pp. 53-196 as analysis in terms of conventional form. For Kenneth Burke's discussion of form, see *Counter-Statement* (Berkeley, Los Angeles, and London: University of California Press, 1931) 124-38.

follows: "*Form* in literature is an arousing and fulfillment of desires. A work has form in so far as one part of it leads a reader to anticipate another part, to be gratified by the sequence."[52] A conventional form is defined as form that appeals as form. The examples that Burke offers of conventional forms include the Greek tragedy, the sonnet, the invocation to the Muses, the theophany in a play of Euripides, the processional and recessional of the Episcopalian choir, the exordium in Greco-Roman oratory, the Sapphic ode, the Jew-and-the-Irishman of the Broadway stage, and certain expectations about how works should begin or end. A conventional form is a fixed expectation that the reader brings to the work, formal expectations in the mind of the reader to which the work must acquiesce.[53]

Robbins applies the concept of conventional form to the characters of Jesus and the disciples in the Gospel of Mark. Mark's audience, according to Robbins, would have had certain expectations concerning teachers and their followers and the way that they are portrayed in literary works, and the meaning of the Gospel is in part determined by the way in which the portrayal of Jesus and the disciples meets or fails to meet those expectations. These expectations Robbins identifies as a conventional form, and he identifies that form as a "teacher/disciple cycle."[54]

There is a great difference, however, between the forms that Burke identifies as conventional forms and the much broader expectations of readers or listeners concerning student-teacher relations, which would include the whole array of possibilities that are part of the cultural repertoire. Simply put, there was no one fixed form for student-teacher relationships. Instead, there were several sets of conventional expectations concerning different kinds of teachers as well as various possibilities for each kind of teacher. Robbins acknow-

---

Conventional form is discussed on pp. 126-7 and 204-12.

[52] Burke, *Counter-Statement*, 124.

[53] The concept of conventional form can be applied to the discussion of episodic and continuous narrative earlier in this chapter. For modern readers, narrative continuity is a conventional form. They expect, even demand, to find it. For the ancients, narrative continuity does not appear to be a conventional form. Episodic structures are also acceptable.

[54] Robbins, *Jesus the Teacher*, 82.

ledges this in his discussion, although he tends to oversimplify the range of possibilities by organizing them into two sets, Greco-Roman patterns and Jewish patterns. Nevertheless, he remains convinced that there is a single conventional form, the "teacher/disciple cycle," that the Gospel of Mark shares with the accounts of the Greek philosophers.

That cycle contains three primary phases: "a phase which initiates discipleship (1:14-3:6); a teaching/learning phase (3:7-12:44); and a phase of farewell and separation from the teacher (14:1-15:47)." In the initial phase "the teacher and the disciple-companions accept the complementary roles of communicator and students." The second phase "features a programmatic introduction of the teacher's system of thought and action to the disciple-companions." The final phase "features the separation of the teacher from his disciple-companions when the teacher accepts a death penalty that the disciple-companions consider to be unjust and unnecessary to accept."[55]

There are two primary difficulties with Robbins' analysis. First, the teacher/disciple cycle that he identifies as the controlling rhetorical form of the Gospel is constructed by Robbins from various sources and does not match the form of any one source. Philosopher-teachers, whom Robbins sees as the pattern for Mark's presentation of Jesus, were presented in a variety of ways, including lists of sayings (as in *Secundus the Silent Philosopher*), dialogues (as in Plato's Socratic dialogues), pseudonymous letters (as in the Cynic epistles), compendiums of biographical information and teaching material (as in many of the lives in Diogenes Laertius), as well as chronologically arranged narratives such as Mark.

An examination of the specific sources cited by Robbins as philosophical parallels to the Markan cycle shows that none of them are organized according to the teacher/disciple cycle that he has identified. Robbins notes that he first identified the teacher/disciple cycle in Xenophon's *Memorabilia*,[56] presumably in book four, which he repeatedly cites. He suggests, following E. C. Marchant, that the fourth book may have been an independent work at some time,[57] but

---

[55] Robbins, *Jesus the Teacher*, 82-83.

[56] Robbins, *Jesus the Teacher*, xiv.

[57] Robbins, *Jesus the Teacher*, 120, n. 27; citing E. C. Marchant's "Introduction," in *Xenophon IV: Memorabilia and Oeconomicus, Symposium and Apology,*

the independence of the fourth book is highly unlikely, since it is well integrated into the work as a whole.[58] The *Memorabilia* of Xenophon is organized as a refutation of the charges against Socrates; it shows the philosopher in dialogue with a variety of different people, some, but not all, of whom might be described as students, and it is only in book four that Socrates is shown as initiating a relationship that lasts longer than one or two conversations. Even book four does not contain a true example of Robbins' teacher/disciple cycle since the Euthydemus cycle (4.2-6), which contains the first two parts of the alleged teacher/disciple cycle, breaks off before the reports concerning the death of Socrates in 4.8. The report about the death of Socrates is intended to show (1) that Socrates was not foolish in accepting death (4.8.1) and (2) that Socrates' death was a most noble one (4.8.2-3). The discussion between Socrates and Hermogenes (4.8.4-10), who has not previously appeared as a dialogue partner, illustrates those two points. The issue is the character of Socrates rather than his relationship with his followers, as Robbins' placing the scene in a teacher/disciple cycle implies.

Robbins' other examples deviate even further from the alleged pattern. The Platonic dialogues can be placed into various places in the assumed cycle, but no one of them shows the cycle as a whole. Philostratus' *Life of Apollonius of Tyana* shows Apollonius interacting with a variety of philosophers and rulers, and it is the progression through these dialogue partners that provides the basic organization for the work. Students attach themselves to Apollonius at various times throughout the narrative and disappear without farewells. Damis, the alleged source of Philostratus' information, necessarily attaches himself to Apollonius near the beginning of the narrative (1.19), but he receives only a one-line benediction from Apollonius at the end of the work as he is sent on an errand unaware of the philosopher's impending death (8.28). It is, moreover, stretching credibility to maintain that everything in between is "a programmatic introduction to the teacher's system of thought and action to the disciple-companions" as Robbins

---

LCL (Cambridge, MA: Harvard University Press; and London: William Heinemann, 1968) xvii-xxiii.

[58] See the discussion below in Chapter 2, pp. 38-42, 54-55.

claims.[59] At times Apollonius does instruct Damis, but much of the time Damis simply records the activity of Apollonius. Of course, anything that Apollonius does might be very broadly interpreted as a lesson to Damis in how to live like Apollonius, but that ignores the apparent intention of the work, to record the character and the activity of Apollonius rather than his instruction to a particular follower.

The final phase of the alleged cycle, featuring the unjust death of the philosopher, is confined primarily to the Socratic material.[60] Robbins mistakenly claims that Apollonius was killed by the emperor Domitian and thus fits the model,[61] but Apollonius faces down an unjust charge brought by Domitian (8.4-9), is reunited with his companion after the trial (8.10-14), and lives into the reign of Nerva (8.27-28) before either dying or being assumed into heaven (8.30).[62]

One can in a much broader way discuss the range of expectations about teachers and their followers, especially in specific situations, and the place of Mark's portrayal of Jesus and the disciples in that range. That is the approach taken in this dissertation. To attempt

---

[59] Robbins, *Jesus the Teacher*, 147-55. See the discussion below on Apollonius' lack of structured instruction, Chapter 4, pp. 122-24.

[60] David E. Aune notes an interest in martyrdom and violent death in biographies of the late Hellenistic and early Roman periods. This interest was not confined to the portrayal of teaching figures, but can also be found in the lives of poets, political figures, and prophets. Aune cites only the late lives of Diogenes Laertius as examples of the interest in philosophical biography ("Greco-Roman Biography," in *Greco-Roman Literature and the New Testament*, ed. by David E. Aune, SBLSBS 21 [Atlanta: Scholars Press, 1988] 122-23).

[61] Robbins, *Jesus the Teacher*, 154-55.

[62] It is certainly appropriate to speak of a *topos* of confrontation with political authorities in the depiction of the lives of philosophers. The confrontation of Apollonius with Domitian fits that category, as does the confrontation between Pythagoras and Phalaris mentioned in Iamblichus' *Pythagorean Life* (32.215-16), the interchange between Secundus and Hadrian in *Secundus the Silent Philosopher*, and stories told of many other philosophers. Philostratus lists a number of these confrontations in *Life of Apollonius* 7.2-3 in an effort to show that Apollonius showed greater courage than any of the other philosophers. The death of Jesus in Mark, however, does not have the same purpose as the accounts of confrontations between philosophers and despots. In the philosophical literature, the emphasis is on the character of the philosopher, the strength of his convictions, and his courage in the face of tyranny. In Mark, it is the death and rejection of Jesus rather than his courage that is important. A scene such as the prayer of Jesus at Gethsemane (14.32-42) is hard to reconcile with the philosophical examples of courage.

to construct a single expectation, however, is counterproductive because it shifts attention away from specific rhetorical and narrative presentations to a level of abstraction that provides little assistance in interpretation. It is ironic that Robbins' construct of a shared conventional form, the teacher/disciple cycle, which is intended as a tool of rhetorical analysis, keeps him from analyzing in any detail the specific rhetorical aims of the various works that form his comparative base.[63]

Secondly, the choice of the alleged teacher/disciple cycle as the overarching form of the Gospel leads Robbins to overemphasize Jesus' role as a teacher. Clearly, Mark's audience would recognize Jesus as a teacher. Jesus is addressed as διδάσκαλε ten times and once refers to himself as ὁ διδάσκαλος, "the teacher" (14.14). His activity is described repeatedly as teaching (διδάσκειν), and his followers customarily are referred to as μαθηταί or students. Nevertheless, that is not the primary focus of the Gospel.[64]

Jesus' primary identity in the Gospel of Mark is determined by the christological titles Son of God, Messiah, and Son of Man. Robbins acknowledges that Son of God and Son of Man "give special identity to Jesus," but his analysis of the Gospel on the basis of repetitive form leads him to understand Jesus' primary identity to be that of a "disciple-gathering teacher." This judgment is based on the observation that references to Jesus' teaching activity are more

---

[63] The term rhetoric has two distinct meanings, one being an analysis of the ways in which persuasive speech or writing accomplishes its persuasive function, the other being an analysis of literary composition. Burke's rhetorical analysis of forms, on which Robbins bases his own analysis, is rhetorical in this second sense. Robbins' analysis of the dominant conventional form that structures the Gospel of Mark, the alleged "teacher/disciple cycle," is a discussion of narrative form, and as such, it should be understood as a type of narrative criticism.

[64] It is a well-known fact that the Gospel contains relatively little teaching. Robbins seeks to avoid this problem by claiming that "both exorcisms and healings are part of Jesus' role as a teacher" (*Jesus the Teacher*, 114), a dubious claim based on the circular argument that "the important consideration was not whether a person performed healings but the social identity in which he performed them," that is to say that once Jesus is identified as a teacher, his healing and exorcism can be seen as part of his activity as a teacher. For Mark, however, the healings and exorcisms are signs of Jesus' authority (to forgive sins, 2.10; to plunder the possessions of Satan, 3.27).

numerous than references to the christological titles.[65] Once again,
Robbins' theoretical construct, in this case Burke's concept of repetitive form, confuses his analysis.[66] Sheer repetition, by itself, is not
enough to determine the audience's understanding. The christological
titles occur at central points in the narrative. Son of God appears in
the superscription (1.1), and twice the voice from heaven refers to
Jesus as "my Son" (1.11; 9.7). Jesus acknowledges himself to be the
Messiah, the Son of the Blessed (14.61-62), and is executed as the
King of the Jews (15.26). There are two discussions of Jesus' identity
that hinge on his capacity as a representative of God (6.14-16;
8.27-30), and the answer that Peter gives to the question, "Who do you
say that I am?" is that Jesus is the Messiah (8.29). The narrative force
given to the christological titles thus far outweighs the sheer repetition
of references to Jesus' teaching capacity. In addition, a significant part
of the Gospel is devoted to the question of Jesus' divine identity and
the difficulty people have in understanding it. Much of Jesus' teaching
refers to the consequences of his divine identity.

Mark's audience naturally would compare Jesus' teaching
activity with other reports of teachers with which they were familiar.
Robbins' teacher/disciple cycle, however, distorts our understanding of
those comparisons by assuming greater uniformity in the presentation
of teachers and students than actually existed and by directing the
comparisons away from the concrete episodes where the comparisons
can yield fruitful results.

Methodology of the Present Study

This study was conceived originally as a literary analysis of the
Gospel of Mark. Instead of proceeding through the application of
modern theories of narrative created in large part through the study of
the modern novel, I determined to study the character of the disciples
through an analysis of analogous characters found in literature from
approximately the same period as the Gospels.

---

[65] Robbins, *Jesus the Teacher*, 198-99.

[66] Robbins discusses repetitive form in Mark in *Jesus the Teacher*, 19-73,
198-99. Burke defines repetitive form in *Counter-Statement*, 125.

My own study of the literary presentation of students in ancient portraits of sages is similar in some ways to that of Robbins, but the theoretical framework is very different. Robbins has structured his study on the basis of the categories of form found in Burke's *Counter-Statement*, and Burke's theoretical construct dominates the discussion. What I have attempted in the present study is more empirical. I have examined four didactic and propagandistic works describing teachers and students that come from approximately the same period as the Gospel and have allowed those works to suggest ways in which the portrayal of the disciples may function rhetorically within the Gospel. Although I expected to find considerable similarity between the approaches of the various works, the particularities of the works far outweigh the similarities. As a result, the studies of contemporaneous works provide a typology of possible approaches that suggest possible ways in which the disciples might function within the Gospel of Mark. In my analysis of Mark, I sometimes found similar strategies at work, but I found more differences than similarities in the overall portrait of the teacher and his followers.

I have also concentrated much more than Robbins on particular episodes or themes within Mark and the similarities and differences between them and comparable episodes or themes in the other literature. This is, I believe, the only way in which the analysis lets Mark's own structuring of his Gospel speak for itself. It is particularly appropriate given the episodic nature of the Markan narrative. In pursuing this study, I have come to the conclusion that the disciples do not maintain a single, stable rhetorical function throughout the Gospel. Instead, the rhetorical role of the disciples varies as the rhetorical argument or plot of the Gospel advances. The Gospel is the Gospel of Jesus, the Messiah, the Son of God, not a Gospel of Jesus and the disciples. Throughout the Gospel, the depiction of the disciples is subordinated thoroughly to what Mark wishes to say about Jesus at that particular point in his presentation.

I originally approached the subject in terms of narrative rather than rhetoric. I was interested in the way Mark's original audience would understand the character groups in his Gospel in the light of their cultural expectations. I chose the disciples as the group on which to concentrate because of the controversy concerning Mark's view of the disciples.[67]   If an examination of cultural expectations could adjudicate between the various claims concerning Mark's view of the disciples, then the value of the approach would be demonstrated. While the discussion of Mark's purpose in portraying the disciples as he does concerns rhetorical aims, the discussion often has been pursued through a narrative methodology. The nature of the Markan portrait of the disciples as a whole was determined first, and then a judgment was made concerning the rhetorical aim of that presentation.

In the course of this study, however, it has become clear to me that Mark's rhetorical aims affect his presentation of the disciples not only on the macro-level of the Gospel as a whole but also on the micro-level of the individual episode or group of episodes. In fact, I have come to believe that Mark's presentation of Jesus so dominates his Gospel that it is questionable whether he intended any coherent characterization of the disciples. Rather, it seems that the characteriza-tion of the disciples in each episode or section of the Gospel is for the most part determined by the rhetorical point that is being made about Jesus in that particular part of the Gospel. The resulting portrait of the disciples is coherent only to the extent that it fits within a range of characterizations that Mark understood to be appropriate for the disciples of Jesus.   For example, the rhetorical purpose for the disciples' lack of understanding appears to be the portrayal of Jesus as hard to understand rather than the portrayal of the disciples as slow of understanding; nevertheless, Mark understood a portrayal of the disciples as lacking in understanding to be within the range of appropriate characterizations.

The method followed in the comparative studies is to ascertain as clearly as possible the social setting and rhetorical purpose of each of the works. Then the treatment of the sage's followers is analyzed

---

[67] Mark's portrayal of the disciples has been the subject of great controversy among Markan scholars. Much of the debate has centered on the question of whether Mark intended his Gospel to be a polemic against the disciples or a group of the church represented by the disciples. A cogent summary of the major positions is available in Frank J. Matera, *What Are They Saying About Mark?* (New York and Mahwah, NJ: Paulist Press, 1987), 38-55. A more exhaustive listing of various positions may be found in Bertram L. Melbourne, *Slow to Understand: The Disciples in Synoptic Perspective* (Lanham, MD; New York; and London: University Press of America, 1988), 1-23.

in terms of its description of the social relations that define discipleship, the literary role of disciples within the work, and the rhetorical functions of the depiction of the disciples. The particulars of the analysis in each case are determined largely by the nature of the work under study.

In the Markan section of the study, I have attempted to apply as directly as possible the results of the four comparative studies. Rather than analyze the Gospel as a whole, I have chosen certain passages and sections of the Gospel that are of central importance for the understanding of the disciples. Two of these passages, the calling of the disciples (1.16-20; 2.14) and Peter's objection to the passion (8.31-9.1), have rather direct parallels in the comparative literature. In these cases, I have created a typology of rhetorical and narrative functions fulfilled by the parallel passages and then analyzed the Markan passages in order to determine similarities and differences. In addition, I have analyzed the theme of the disciples' misunderstanding in Mark 4.1-8.21. Because of the coherence of the theme throughout this section and the interrelationships among the passages contributing to the theme, it was not possible to focus on a single passage. Instead, I have shown how themes develop throughout the section and have compared Mark's use of the themes with the use of similar themes in the comparative literature. The passages that are analyzed are far from exhaustive, but they cover much of the significant material about the disciples in the first eleven chapters of the Gospel.

It should be stressed that this study is not an historical investigation of the actual relationships between any of the sages and followers discussed here. It is only concerned with the literary depiction of those relationships. Some of the works treated here present social descriptions of the relationships between a sage and a follower, but those social descriptions directly serve the rhetorical purposes of the authors.[68]

---

[68] Xenophon wants to prove Socrates is not a "teacher" and to minimize any facet of the relations between the philosopher and his followers that might give credence to the charge that Socrates was forming a dangerous political faction. Iamblichus is concerned to present Pythagoras and his followers in continuity with the school setting in which his biography would be read and thus to emphasize the links between the foundation of the Pythagorean/Platonic tradition and the present.

Selection of Material for Comparative Study

In selecting material to be used as a basis for the analysis, primary consideration was given to works with extended portrayals of relationships between teachers and students. I chose four works, three that might be classified broadly as philosophical biographies— Xenophon's *Memorabilia*, Philostratus' *Life of Apollonius of Tyana*, and Iamblichus' *Pythagorean Life*—and one example of Jewish wisdom teaching, the Wisdom of Ben Sira. Since it is not structured as narrative, the Wisdom of Ben Sira provides fewer direct parallels with the Markan material, but I felt it was important to examine at least one representative of a Palestinian type.

The rabbinic material has not been used in this study because of the relative lack of biographical material in the rabbinic collections and the difficulty in determining the rhetorical purpose of such material within the overall structure of those works. To quote Jacob Neusner on the rabbinic material:

> No story about a sage serves a biographical purpose. None carries out a purpose defined by the requirements of the sustained narrative of an individual life or a major episode in a biography.... I cannot point in either the Bavli or the Yerushalmi to a biographical narrative of the length even of an ordinary chapter of the New Testament Gospels.[69]

Like the Gospel, the works of philosophy and wisdom examined here are primarily didactic and propagandistic. They seek to teach and to persuade. With the exception of the *Life of Apollonius*, the entertainment value of the works is strongly subordinated to the authors' ideological purposes.

The use of Greek philosophical biographies as a base for comparison does not necessarily mean that the Gospel of Mark should

---

See the discussions below, Chapter 2, pp. 46-49, 50-51; and Chapter 3, pp. 75-76.

[69] Jacob Neusner, "Death-Scenes and Farewell Stories: An Aspect of the Master-Disciple Relationship in Mark and in Some Talmudic Tales," in *Christians Among Jews and Gentiles*, ed. by George W. E. Nickelsburg with George W. MacRae (Philadelphia: Fortress Press, 1986) 188-89.

be understood as a biography of Jesus. The biographies simply provide the best material for an analysis of the rhetorical role of students in the portrayal of sages. Other comparative bases might be more appropriate for an analysis of other aspects of the Gospel. Nevertheless, it is worth noting that the distinction between the Gospels and the philosophical biographies often has been exaggerated. Much of the discussion about whether or not the Gospels fall within the genre of biography has minimized the differences that exist in the social settings, form, and rhetorical intent of ancient biographies.[70] As a result, the uniqueness of the Gospels has been exaggerated. While the Gospels certainly are unique in many respects, each of the three philosophical biographies treated in this dissertation is unique in respect to form, purpose, and social setting when compared with any of the others.[71]

The four works that have been selected for comparison span an extremely long time period, dating from the fourth century BCE to the fourth century CE. The danger of using material from such an extensive period is clear and can be justified only by the lack of adequate material from the first century. With the earliest and the latest of the four works, however, there are factors that reduce the risk of anachronism. Socrates played a major role in the cultural understanding of many people in the first century Greco-Roman world and was a model for a number of philosopher-teachers. Xenophon's *Memorabilia* continued to play a role in the culture even though it was written much earlier. Iamblichus' *Pythagorean Life*, on the other hand, while it was written in the fourth century CE, contains considerable amounts of verbatim quotation from earlier works.[72] While the overall structure of the work is late, many of the parts are much more contemporaneous with Mark.

---

[70] See the discussion in Charles H. Talbert, *What Is a Gospel? The Genre of the Canonical Gospels* (Philadelphia: Fortress Press, 1974) 1-23, and the literature cited there. For a recent summary of the debate about biography and the Gospel genre, see Adela Yarbro Collins, *Is Mark's Gospel a Life of Jesus? The Question of Genre*, PMLT 21 (Milwaukee, WI: Marquette University Press, 1990) 1-37.

[71] The complexity of the biographical genre has been recognized by David E. Aune, *The New Testament in Its Literary Environment*, LEC 8 (Philadelphia: Westminster Press, 1987) 27-36.

[72] See the discussion below, Chapter 3, pp. 70-72.

Two of the works I have selected for study concern major figures in the construction of the so-called θεῖος ἀνήρ type, Pythagoras and Apollonius of Tyana.[73]   In these cases, one can study the reactions of followers to the divine aspect of the sage as well as their actions in the student-teacher relationship, but these similarities should not be exaggerated.   Both Pythagoras and Apollonius are primarily philosophers.   They are teachers and embodiments of the philosophical life.   Their divine identity is incidental to their literary depiction.   They are philosophers first, and their divinity, however it is conceived, is expressed in their roles as teachers and embodiments of philosophy. Whatever additional divine attributes are reported of them, those attributes serve to validate the essential attribute of divinity found in their philosophical roles.

Jesus, on the other hand, is the Son of God first and foremost and a teacher only incidentally.   He teaches about himself, his own significance, and the significance of the time that derives from his presence.   He teaches his disciples what it means to follow him.   What he offers is not a system of thought and action.   What he offers is entrance into an elect community, a new Israel.

Following Jesus, as described by Mark, cannot really be compared to following any philosopher or teacher of wisdom, no matter how radically he might demand the reformation of one's life, since the purpose for following and the rewards of following are so fundamentally different.   Nevertheless, the outward form of the relationship is close enough that an examination of these works can provide a valuable matrix for understanding, first, the kinds of expectations that Mark's audience may have held concerning the disciples in their role as followers and, second, the functions that the disciples might be expected to play within the rhetorical strategy of the Gospel.

---

[73] The index of Ludwig Bieler's seminal work, ΘΕΙΟΣ ΑΝΗΡ: *Das Bild des "göttlichen Menschen" in Spätantike und Frühchristentum* (2 vols. in 1 [Darmstadt: Wissenschaftliche Buchgesellschaft, 1967], includes more citations for Pythagoras and Apollonios of Tyana than for any other figure.

PART I

PHILOSOPHICAL AND WISDOM WRITINGS

2 _____

XENOPHON'S *MEMORABILIA*

_____

Xenophon occupies a prominent place in the development of Greek biographical writing. While there was a significant development of biographical interest in Greece during the fifth century BCE, no specifically biographical works from before the fourth century have survived to our day.[1] In the fourth century, however, several true biographical works were produced. The Socratics played a particularly important role in this development. Xenophon himself wrote several works that were important in the formation of the biographical tradition: the *Agesilaus*, the biography of the Spartan king; the *Cyropaedia*, a largely fictional account of the early years of Cyrus; and the *Memorabilia*, in which Socrates is presented as a moral and intellectual guide.[2]

The *Memorabilia* deals almost exclusively with Socrates as a moral guide. It includes none of the details of his life, such as his birth, family heritage, and education, which frequently are found in an encomium, nor does Xenophon present the periods of boyhood, youth,

[1] Arnaldo Dante Momigliano, *The Development of Greek Biography* (Cambridge, MA: Harvard University Press, 1971) 8. Some fragments of works exhibiting biographical interests have survived.

[2] Momigliano, *Greek Biography*, 46-57. For bibliography on the *Memorabilia*, see Donald R. Morrison, *Bibliography of Editions, Translations, and Commentary on Xenophon's Socratic Writings, 1600-Present* (Pittsburgh: Mathesis Publications, 1988), 38-58 for texts and translations, 58-67 for commentary.

All translations of the *Memorabilia* are taken from, or are based on, the translation of E. C. Marchant in the LCL edition.

and manhood as he does in his portrait of Cyrus in the *Anabasis* (1.9). Although five chapters of the work are devoted to matters of military leadership, there is no mention of Socrates' military exploits that won him a name for bravery.   Socrates' personal life goes practically unnoticed. His wife is mentioned only incidentally in a discussion with his son about honoring parents, and there is no discussion of his children other than his eldest son, Lamprocles. A few anecdotes are presented that show Socrates outside his role as a moral and intellectual guide, such as his confrontation with Critias and Charicles when they sought to prevent his conversing with the young men of Athens (1.2.31-38 and 4.4.3), his refusal to illegally condemn Thrasyllus and Erasinides (1.1.18 and 4.4.2), and his refusal to make an illegal arrest of Leon when commanded to do so by the Thirty Tyrants (4.4.3). These examples, however, occur in the rebuttal of specific charges brought against him or serve to show that his life was congruent with his teaching. There is no explanation of the events leading up to his arrest and conviction, no explanation of the hostility that his enemies felt toward him, and no depiction of his trial and death.

Xenophon's work came early in the development of biographical writing, and, as far as we know, he had no ready-made models on which to base his work. He knew Plato's dialogues as well as those of Antisthenes, but unlike the Platonic dialogues, the *Memorabilia* presents within a single work a wide range of situations and discourses that illustrate the whole range of Socrates' work as a moral and intellectual guide.   Individual questions are not elaborated in depth within a single dialogue as they are in Plato. Instead, Xenophon uses a variety of characters and situations to elaborate a theme.

Unity, Date, and Purpose

For many years, modern scholars, following Theodor Birt,[3] believed that the *Memorabilia* was not a unified composition but consisted of a defense of Socrates, occupying 1.1.1-1.2.64, originally

---

[3] Theodor Birt, *De Xenophontis Commentariorum Socraticorum Compositione* (Marburg: Impensis Elwerti Bibliopolae Academici, 1893). Cf. *idem*, "Zu Antisthenes und Xenophon," *RheinMus* 51 (1896) 153-54.

published as an independent work, and a series of later dialogues that had no integral connection with the earlier composition.[4] In 1961, however, Hartmut Erbse demonstrated that the work exhibits a unified structure, based on the model of political defense speeches such as those presented by Lysias,[5] and the consensus since then has been that the *Memorabilia* is a single unified composition.[6] While there is no unequivocal indication of the date of the work, the dialogue with the younger Pericles (3.5) suggests the period of Theban supremacy that followed the battle of Leuctra in 371 BCE,[7] and thus the work might best be dated in that period, approximately thirty years after the death of Socrates in 399 BCE.

Although the *Memorabilia* follows the form of an apologetic speech, it would be a mistake to understand its sole purpose as apologetic.[8] The purpose of the work is not simply to refute the charges against Socrates but to show that Socrates actually deserved "high honor from the state" (1.2.64), that he was "all that a truly good and happy man must be" (4.8.11). Apologetic and encomium are intertwined closely in the work since the sections that praise Socrates serve as well to refute the accusations brought against him. Since the greatest part of the work defends Socrates by praising him, however, it may be argued that the apologetic form serves largely as a vehicle for encomium. Socrates remained controversial enough that any work praising him would have to deal with the criticisms of the philosopher as well.[9]

---

[4] Anton-Hermann Chroust, *Socrates, Man and Myth: The Two Socratic Apologies of Xenophon* (London: Routledge & Kegan Paul, 1957) 44. Marchant found four independent works in the *Memorabilia* ("Introduction," ix-xviii).

[5] Hartmut Erbse, "Die Architektonik im Aufbau von Xenophons Memorabilien," *Hermes* 89 (1961) 257-87.

[6] William Edward Higgins, *Xenophon the Athenian* (Albany: State University of New York Press, 1977) 39, n. 86; Leo Strauss, *Xenophon's Socrates* (Ithaca, NY: Cornell University Press, 1972); Momigliano, *Greek Biography*, 52.

[7] Marchant, "Introduction," xv; Erbse, "Architektonik," 257; Chroust, *Socrates*, 45.

[8] Momigliano notes that Xenophon has adapted the apologetic form for a biographical function (*Greek Biography*, 53).

[9] Ca. 343 BCE Aeschines expressed approval of the Athenian condemnation of "the sophist" Socrates in the speech he made to substantiate the accusations he had brought against a rival (*Against Timarchus* 173).

The work is not intended to defend the ongoing communities of Socratics who lived in Athens at the time of its composition. Xenophon had been banished from Athens shortly after the turn of the century and thus had been absent from the city from the time of his departure to fight with Cyrus in 401 until his return in 366/5. There is no indication that Xenophon considered himself part of any of the Socratic communities. Of the most prominent Socratics, Plato is mentioned only in passing,[10] Aristippus is taken to task for the hedonistic doctrine that he later espoused (2.1; cf. 3.8, where he also appears in an unfavorable light), and Antisthenes is given a few lines in one of the shortest of the dialogues (2.5).[11] There is nothing in the work that suggests an ongoing community of Socratics. On the contrary, Xenophon avoids portraying a clearly defined Socratic community even during the life of the philosopher.

Both apologetic and encomium are served by Xenophon's portrayal of the thought of Socrates, which is presented in a relatively systematic manner. Undoubtedly, Xenophon and his readers had an interest in the thought of Socrates. In addition, Xenophon had an interest in educational theory and the approach to education taken by Socrates. In the *Cyropaedia*, Xenophon described in an idealized manner the education of Cyrus, and he wrote several instruction manuals on various topics.[12] In addition to several passages on Socrates' approach to education (4.1.2-5, 4.3.1-2, 4.5.1, 4.6.1, 4.6.15, 4.7.1-10), the bulk of the work consists of concrete instances of Socratic education in action.

Structure

The approach to the portrayal of the followers of Socrates varies among the different sections of the *Memorabilia*. The first two chapters of book one are written in a mode distinctly unlike the rest of the work. This section, about half of the first book, is a logically

[10] He is mentioned at 3.6.1 as a relative of Glaucon. It is clear from the passage that Socrates was favorably disposed toward him.

[11] In addition, he is mentioned as a constant companion of Socrates in 3.11.17. The depiction of the Socratics will be discussed in more detail below.

[12] *Manual for a Cavalry Commander*, *Horsemanship*, and *Hunting with Hounds*.

argued refutation of the charges brought against Socrates at his trial, that he brought in new gods and corrupted the youth. Xenophon devotes the bulk of his argument to the second accusation. In his treatment of this charge, he seeks to refute a number of specific arguments that had been made against Socrates in Polycrates' speech, *Accusation of Socrates*, published about 393 BCE.[13]

For the most part, Socrates' companions appear in this section as an abstract group. For example, Xenophon states, "Many of his companions were counselled by him to do this or not to do that in accordance with the warning of his δαιμόνιον" (1.1.4). The exception to this treatment of the companions is the extended discussion of Critias and Alcibiades, two of Socrates' former companions infamous for their later political adventures. Polycrates had introduced their association with Socrates as proof of the charge that the philosopher's teaching was detrimental to the state.[14] Xenophon devotes over half of his refutation of the second charge to a discussion of these two associates. This discussion includes logical arguments that show Socrates cannot be held responsible for their later activity and introduces dialogues that illustrate in specific instances some aspect of

---

[13] For the arguments that indicate Xenophon is answering the charges made by Polycrates rather than those advanced at the trial, see Chroust, *Socrates*, 71-72; Erbse, "Architektonik," 261-63; and the references given by Erbse, 261, n. 1. For a reconstruction of the content of Polycrates' *Accusation* based on the *Memorabilia* and a rejoinder to the *Accusation* written by Libanius ca. 350 CE, see Chroust, *Socrates*, 72-100, and the references on p. 72, n. 396. The argument that Xenophon was answering the charges of Polycrates was first advanced by Carel Gabriel Cobet (*Novae Lectiones Quibus Continentur Observationes Criticae in Scriptores Graecos* [Leiden: E. J. Brill, 1858] 662-63).

The major arguments include the following points: (1) Isocrates notes that one of the points raised by Polycrates was Socrates' teaching of Alcibiades (*Busiris* 4-5), a point that Xenophon attributes to his accuser; (2) it is highly unlikely that Anytus would have advanced the argument concerning Critias in the trial because it violates the terms of the amnesty that he supported after the overthrow of the Thirty; (3) there is a close correlation between the arguments of Xenophon's "accuser" and those in Libanius' rejoinder to Polycrates.

Apparently, Xenophon's lack of specific arguments supporting the first charge arises from Polycrates' exclusive concentration on the charge of corrupting the youth (Erbse, "Architektonik," 261).

[14] Chroust, *Socrates*, 95-96.

the relationship between each of the infamous companions and his former mentor.

The second section of the *Memorabilia*, from the point of view of the treatment of the companions, occupies the remainder of book one and all of books two and three. In this part of the work, Xenophon deals in an orderly way with different aspects of Socrates' teaching. The subjects that he covers are piety and self-control (1.3-2.1), human relationships (gratitude toward parents, 2.2; relationship between brothers, 2.3; friendship, 2.4-10), and service to the state (military leadership, 3.1-5; political leadership, 3.6-7). The section ends with a discussion of miscellaneous unrelated subjects (the good and the beautiful, 3.8; various virtues, 3.9; art, 3.10; erotic love, 3.11; physical hardiness, 3.12-13; table manners, 3.14). This section consists mostly of individual dialogues with companions or opponents that show Socrates' advice or argument in a specific situation.

The third section (4.1-7) deals with Socrates' approach to education. While Xenophon makes several general observations about this subject, the bulk of the section illustrates Socratic education through the specific example of his conversion and training of a single follower, Euthydemus. A typical course of Socratic education is illustrated, with discussions of piety, justice, self-control, dialectic, and the use of definitions. One anomaly in this section is the discussion of justice, which is illustrated by a dialogue between Socrates and the sophist Hippias and does not involve Euthydemus.

The final section (4.8) treats the trial and death of Socrates. In this section, the philosopher's noble attitude toward death is illustrated by a dialogue with his companion Hermogenes.

The Infamous Associates of Socrates

Xenophon deals in some detail with two former associates of Socrates who fell into disrepute, Critias, the leader of the oligarchic revolution of the Thirty Tyrants, and Alcibiades, known both for his dissolute behavior and his demagogic manipulation of the populace. It was not uncommon in antiquity to praise or blame a teacher based

on the quality of his students,[15] and Xenophon selects Polycrates'
attack on Socrates through these followers as one of the major points
for rebuttal.[16]

In part, Xenophon answers the accusation by logical argument.
Critias and Alcibiades followed Socrates out of ambition, to learn
proficiency in speech and action, rather than to emulate the philosopher's life and thus never intended to acquire the moral character that
Socrates understood as the central point of education (1.2.14-16).
Socrates' example inspired the two to prudent conduct as long as they
consorted with him (1.2.17-18). Socrates cannot be blamed for the
conduct of former companions after they have ceased associating with
him (1.2.19-28). In addition to these arguments, however, Xenophon
seeks to separate Socrates from his former companions by citing
specific incidents that distance them from the philosopher.

---

[15] In 307/6 BCE Sophocles of Sunium sponsored a law in Athens outlawing the
philosophical schools. In defending the propriety of the law, he argued that the
number of pupils of the Academy who had become tyrants was sufficient reason
for the suppression of the schools (Athenaeus, *Deipnosophistae* 11.508f-509a).
Athenaeus cites this incident in a speech attacking the philosophers in the
Deipnosophistae (ca. 230 CE), illustrating the persistence of the attitude. In 343
BCE, Aeschines cites with favor the condemnation of Socrates as the teacher of
Critias (*Against Timarchus* 173). The moral rectitude of a teacher's student also
may be used to exonerate him. According to Hermippus (fl. 210 BCE), when the
sophist Anaxagoras had been condemned to death by the Athenians, "Pericles came
forward and asked the people whether they had any fault to find with him in his
own public career." When they replied that they did not, he stated, "I am a pupil
of Anaxagoras; do not then be carried away by slanders and put him to death." As
a result of this intervention, Anaxagoras was released (Diogenes Laertius 2.13,
LCL tr.). For a discussion of Jesus' responsibility for his disciples' actions in the
Gospels, see David Daube, "Responsibilities of Master and Disciples in the
Gospels," *NTS* 19 (1972-73) 1-15.

[16] Xenophon devotes thirty-seven of the sixty-four sections of his chapter
refuting the charge that Socrates corrupted the youth to a discussion of Alcibiades
and Critias. Undoubtedly this reflects in part Xenophon's preference for dealing
with specific cases rather than general ideas. For Xenophon's choice among the
arguments of Polycrates, see Erbse, "Architektonik," 263.

The opinion of Alcibiades held by Xenophon and Polycrates was not held by
all Athenians. Isocrates criticizes Polycrates for advancing the argument of the
connection between Alcibiades and Socrates since, in his opinion, Alcibiades
should be honored by the Athenians for his service to the state (*Busiris* 4-5).

Critias

In the case of Critias, the incidents related are quite effective in creating the distance.[17] Xenophon relates how Socrates had criticized Critias for attempting to seduce Euthydemus (1.2.29-30). As a result, Critias held a grudge against him, and after seizing power, he passed a law forbidding Socrates to teach (1.2.31). Socrates had criticized the governance of Critias and the rest of the Thirty Tyrants (1.2.32), and when Critias summoned him to prevent his teaching, Socrates forced Critias to admit that the prohibition was intended to silence criticism of the Thirty (1.2.33-38). In the face of this conflict between Socrates and his former associate, it is hardly reasonable to hold the philosopher accountable for the very activity that he opposed.

Alcibiades

Alcibiades provides the second example of the false follower of Socrates. Xenophon defends Socrates' connection with the demagogic politician by indicating that Alcibiades was out of sympathy with Socrates and was seeking only political advancement (1.2.39). As evidence, he repeats a conversation between Alcibiades and his guardian, Pericles, concerning the nature of law (1.2.41-46).

This dialogue is the only dialogue in the *Memorabilia* in which Socrates does not take part. Since Alcibiades is presented as a false follower of the philosopher, the dialogue must be understood as a false form of Socratic dialogue.[18] In the dialogue, Alcibiades is able to demonstrate that Pericles cannot define the meaning of law.

On the surface, the dialogue seems to show Alcibiades' superior reasoning ability, but for Xenophon, it illustrates a rhetor's trick. Alcibiades has learned to discuss according to the external form of a Socratic dialogue. He has learned how to cross-examine his partner to

[17] This is not necessarily intended to imply the truthfulness of these accounts, which has been called into question (Chroust, *Socrates*, 61-62; Arthur Kenyon Rogers, *The Socratic Problem* [New Haven: Yale University Press, 1933] 173-74).

[18] Strauss says of the dialogue, "Not only is the refutation or the answer Socratic; the very question is Socratic." This judgment, however, is based on the Platonic image of Socrates. The only purpose for introducing the dialogue in this context is to demonstrate that Alcibiades was not truly Socratic. If Xenophon's audience could not recognize this interchange as a perversion of a true Socratic dialogue, the effect would be to establish Alcibiades as a true Socratic.

reveal the shortcomings of the partner's understanding, but he does not share Socrates' purpose in undertaking such discussions. Socrates' purpose is to improve the moral condition of his companions and to enable them to better carry out their duties within the community. Alcibiades and Critias, however, are concerned simply with using their skill in argument to prove their superiority. "So soon, then," Xenophon tells his reader, "as they presumed themselves to be the superiors of the politicians, they no longer came near Socrates" (1.2.47, LCL tr.). They were not interested in their own moral improvement and resented their mentor's efforts to reform them. Pericles' retort to Alcibiades, "At your age, I may tell you, we, too, were very clever at this sort of thing" (1.2.46, LCL tr.), reflects Xenophon's judgment on the emptiness of dialectic skill in itself.[19] The actual art of statecraft is very different. Pericles' comment, however, is not a condemnation of Socrates, because for Xenophon's Socrates, the dialectic process is aimed at molding the character and practical skills that allow someone like Pericles to lead the state.

The same type of argumentation used by Alcibiades is found in the dialogue in which Socrates converts Euthydemus to the pursuit of philosophy (4.2). Socrates convinces Euthydemus that in spite of his pretensions to learning, he does not understand the meaning of justice (4.2.11-23). After a discussion of the importance of knowing oneself (4.2.24-30), Socrates then demonstrates the inadequacies of Euthydemus' understanding of good and evil (4.2.31-36) and of the nature of popular government (4.2.36-39).

The form of the two arguments is similar: Socrates has Euthydemus state his understanding of justice, leads him through various contradictions in his position, and causes him to withdraw some of his earlier assertions; Alcibiades does the same with Pericles in the discussion of law.

The purpose of the two discussions, however, is very different. Socrates' intention is to convert Euthydemus to the philosophical life by pointing out to him the emptiness of his own pretensions to

---

[19] Xenophon states that Socrates was not eager to foster skill in speaking and efficiency in affairs in his companions before they acquired prudence, "for he believed that those faculties unless accompanied by prudence, increased in their possessors injustice and power for mischief" (4.3.1, LCL tr.).

wisdom. Socrates succeeds in his intention and then begins the process of molding the character of his new companion. For Alcibiades, however, the purpose of the discussion is to demonstrate his superiority to the elder statesman. Xenophon held Pericles in high esteem,[20] and from his point of view, it would be ridiculous for the dissolute Alcibiades to attempt to mold his guardian's character. Alcibiades has simply taken over the external form of Socratic argumentation without understanding its inner purpose.

The Characterization of the Companions

The characterization of Socrates in the *Memorabilia* is achieved almost entirely through the depiction of the philosopher's relationships with his companions. He is shown guiding them in a wide variety of situations and areas of concern. While book four shows Socrates in a role similar to that of other teachers, with a fairly fixed course of instruction and students who have entered formally into that course of study, books one through three show him giving instruction on an ad hoc basis to all who will listen, and this portion of the work stresses the differences rather than the similarities between Socrates and traditional teachers. The student-teacher relationship, such as that between Socrates and Euthydemus, is to be understood only as a more intensive or more continuous form of the same relationship that Socrates has with any citizen of Athens who will listen to him.

Terminology

Xenophon avoids using the terms διδάσκαλος and μαθητής in referring to Socrates and his companions.[21] He states that Socrates never suggested that he was a διδάσκαλος of goodness or gentlemanly

---

[20] Pericles is the first citizen or guardian (προστάτης) of the state (*Memorabilia* 1.2.40); Pericles made Athens love him through the spells of his oratory (*Memorabilia* 2.6.13); Pericles was known as his country's most excellent counselor (κράτιστος σύμβουλος, *Symposium* 8.39).

[21] For studies in the use of the term μαθητής, see Karl Heinrich Rengstorf, "μαθητής," *TDNT* 4.415-60; and Michael J. Wilkins, *The Concept of Disciple in Matthew's Gospel as Reflected in the Use of the Term* Μαθητής, NovTSup 59 (Leiden, New York, Copenhagen: Brill, 1988) 11-42.

qualities (1.2.3). In 1.6.3 Antiphon the sophist calls Socrates a διδάσκαλος of unhappiness, comparing him to the διδάσκαλοι of other subjects who make their μαθηταί into imitators of themselves, but Antiphon is an opponent who does not truly reflect Socrates' own understanding. Both Xenophon (1.2.27) and Socrates (4.2.2 and 4-5) are willing to compare the philosopher's work to that of other teachers, but the distinction is carefully maintained. Apart from Antiphon's use of the term, μαθητής appears only once, in a comparison between Socrates and teachers of music (1.2.27).

The avoidance of the διδάσκαλος/μαθητής terminology is common to both Xenophon and Plato and probably originated with Socrates himself. Apparently his distaste for the term comes from its association with the sophists and their students.[22] Since both Plato[23] and Xenophon (1.6.3) use διδάσκαλος/μαθητής terminology in contexts where the teacher's fee is discussed, it is likely that the monetary side of the relationship is one reason for its rejection. An additional problem may be the association of the term with the transmission of a fixed body of knowledge. In the *Memorabilia*, διδάσκαλος is associated with music and τέχνη. The term is used of teachers of flute or lyre (1.2.27) and choirmasters (3.5.18) as well as teachers of the medical art (τὴν ἰατρικὴν τέχνην, 4.2.5) and the less worthy arts (τὰς ὀλίγου ἀξίας τέχνας, 4.2.2).[24]

Xenophon's favorite term for the followers of Socrates is συνόντες, companions, associates, or simply "those who were with him."[25] Xenophon uses the same term in the *Symposium* to refer to the guests present at a dinner (1.15) and in the *Cyropaedia* to refer to comrades in war (8.2.2). It is apparently the lack of definition in the relationship that makes the term attractive. There is no suggestion of a hierarchical relationship, structured roles, or an exclusive community.

---

[22] The students of Protagoras are called μαθηταί in Plato, *Protagoras* 315a.

[23] Plato, *Apology* 33a-b.

[24] There are also teachers of other subjects (τῶν ἄλλων ἔργων, 1.6.3) and teachers of speaking and acting (4.2.4). In the papyri, μαθητής is often used in the sense of "apprentice." For example, P.Oxy. 4.725.15, the apprentice of a weaver (Rengstorf, "μαθητής," 4.416).

[25] Forms of συνόντες occur 37 times in the *Memorabilia*. For the list of occurrences, see Mary Katherine Gloth Lander and Maria Francisca Kellog, *Index in Xenophontis Memorabilia* (New York: Johnson Reprint Corp, 1971) 82.

Whoever happens to be present at any time seems to qualify as one of the συνόντες. The term cannot be understood as a title, since it never occurs in the singular.[26]

Another term Xenophon uses for the companions of Socrates, ὁμιλητής, has a similar meaning, "one who associates with,"[27] and is most likely adapted from Polycrates, since it is first introduced in a citation of the argument of Socrates' accuser and is confined to the section discussing that charge (1.2.12; 1.2.48). Other similar terms include συνουσιασταί (1.6.1) and συγγιγνόμενοι (1.2.61).

In the long section on friendship in book two, a series of dialogues on practical affairs is introduced as advice given to alleviate the distresses of Socrates' friends, φίλοι (2.7.1). In two of the following dialogues, the partner is introduced as a comrade, ἑταῖρος (2.8.1; 2.10.1). While these specific dialogues are intended as illustrations of friendship, there is no distinction between Socrates' friends or comrades and his συνόντες. Socrates maintains that his reward for guiding his companions into virtue is the friendship that he secured from his service (1.2.7-8; cf. 1.6.9).

The particular nature of the friendship between Socrates and his companions is contained in Socrates' frequent expression of being "in love" (4.1.2). The love relationship is alluded to in the dialogue with Theodote, the courtesan, in which Socrates instructs her in the proper method for catching φίλοι (3.11). He claims to have spells and potions to catch friends and refers to his companions as φίλαι, or girlfriends (3.11.16-18). His spells and potions, which Theodote believes to be literal spells, are his conversations through which he improves the virtue of his companions.[28] Socrates begins the discus-

---

[26] See Lander and Kellog, *Index*, 82.

[27] LSJ (loc. cit.) defines the word as "disciple, scholar," but besides the *Memorabilia*, it cites only second and third century CE sources, including Philostratus' *Life of Apollonius of Tyana*, where the cited passage does not suggest such a specific meaning. LSJ (s.v. σύνειμι) similarly defines συνόντες as "followers, partisans, associates, disciples," citing the Platonic dialogues, where "disciple" is simply inappropriate. LSJ also finds a special definition of "pupil, disciple" for the use of ἑταῖρος in the *Memorabilia*. All these definitions start from the assumption that all associates of Socrates are disciples and ignore the distinction that is so important for Xenophon.

[28] Cf. the discussion of "spells" for the securing of friends in 2.6.10-14. Socrates says that Pericles possessed many spells through which he made the city

sion with Theodote with the point that Theodote should be grateful to those who have come to admire her beauty, the net in which she traps her friends, since they are in that way drawn to attend her (3.11.2-3). The analogy with Socrates is clear: Socrates owes a greater debt of gratitude to his companions for listening to his conversation than they owe to him, since through his conversation he gains their friendship.

The terminology of Xenophon consistently downplays any special relationship between Socrates and his followers. They are simply friends and companions, and his relationship to them reflects the general relationship among friends, to provide whatever service one is able to provide (2.7.1).

Lists of Associates

On two occasions, Xenophon lists men closely associated with Socrates. In 1.2.48, there is a list of Socrates' associates that Xenophon presents as a contrast to his false associates, Critias and Alcibiades. This list consists of Chaerophon, Chaerecrates, Hermogenes, Simmias, Cebes, Phaedondas, and others who are unnamed. In 3.11.17, during a discussion with Theodote about winning friends, Socrates states that Apollodorus and Antisthenes never leave him, while Cebes and Simmias come all the way from Thebes to be with him. Both these lists are introduced incidentally. The first is used to neutralize Polycrates' contention that Socrates is responsible for the deeds of Critias and Alcibiades. Xenophon counters this argument with a list of more reputable followers. The second is part of a humorous interchange with the courtesan Theodote in which Socrates is attempting to demonstrate the efficacy of his "spells and potions" for winning friends.

Those whom Xenophon names in these lists of companions do not play a significant role in the dialogues that he records. Simmias and Cebes, who appear in both lists, appear nowhere else in the *Memorabilia*, nor do Phaedondas and Apollodorus. Hermogenes reports a discussion with Socrates about the philosopher's impending trial (4.8.4-10), Chaerecrates appears in a dialogue concerning his relationship with his brother Chaerophon (2.3), and Antisthenes is

---

love him (2.6.13).

Socrates' partner in a short dialogue concerning the value of friends (2.5). Thus only three of the eight men who appear in the lists of companions are participants in the recorded dialogues. The resulting impression is that Socrates did not confine his instruction to a limited circle but rather entered into uplifting discussions with a wide cross section of the citizenry of Athens.[29]

Dialogue Partners

The variety of dialogue partners that Xenophon introduces reinforces the terminology in portraying Socrates as one who freely gave his assistance to all rather than as a teacher with a clearly defined group of students. Those like Euthydemus who received a relatively coherent course of instruction are simply a part of the larger group of συνόντες. Apart from Euthydemus, the only characters who are principals in more than one dialogue are Aristippus (2.1 and 3.8) and Antiphon (three dialogues in 1.6). Antiphon is an antagonist rather than a follower, and while Aristippus, the founder of the Cyrenaic school, is introduced as one of the συνόντες in 2.1, in 3.8 he becomes an antagonist attempting to settle accounts for his loss of face in the earlier encounter. In addition, Socrates stages a dialogue with Xenophon for the sake of Critobulus in 1.3 and engages Critobulus himself in dialogue in 2.6.

A look at the ways the dialogue partners are introduced reinforces the impression that Xenophon is seeking to minimize the sense of an exclusive group of followers. One of his dialogue partners, Euthydemus, clearly has entered into a relationship where he receives instruction from Socrates; five are introduced as his companions;[30] six are related to him as kin or by ties of friendship;[31] eleven appear

---

[29] Polycrates had charged Socrates with sinister activity carried on with his associates in secret (Chroust, *Socrates*, 93). Xenophon counters that argument directly in 1.1.10.

[30] Aristodemus apparently is to be understood as one of those with whom he passed his time daily (1.4.1-2). Aristippus is introduced as "one of his companions" (2.1.1), as is the unnamed companion guilty of neglecting a friend (2.5.1), the unnamed companion interested in the office of general (3.1.1), and Epigenes (3.12.1).

[31] Lamprocles is his eldest son (2.2.1), Chaerophon and Chaerecrates are simply brothers "who were friends of his" (2.3.1) even though they were mentioned among

without any introduction (eighteen if all those in 3.13-14 are considered);[32] two are antagonists;[33] and one has never met Socrates before.[34] The resulting impression is that Socrates' relationship with his companions is very similar to his relationship with others. He is eager to teach all people he meets how to improve or better understand the conduct of their lives.

The Individuality of the Dialogue Partners

While Socrates occasionally addresses an unnamed audience (1.5, 1.7, 2.4) or engages in a discussion for the sake of the entire group of companions then present (3.8.1), usually he directs his discussion to the specific circumstances of his dialogue partners. While in most instances Socrates himself initiates the discussion, the discussions arise from the circumstances of his partners.

Although Xenophon organizes the dialogues into groups that deal with related themes, he does not portray Socrates' teaching as a systematized body of thought on these subjects. His teaching on friendship, for example, is shown by one general discourse with no stated audience (2.4), two discourses on friendship tailored for specific individuals (2.5-6), two examples of his own activity to assist two specific friends (2.7-8), and two discourses that assist specific individuals in acquiring friends (2.9-10). Thus for Socrates, knowledge

his ὁμιληταί in 1.2.48, Aristarchus is one of his friends (2.7.1), Eutherus is "an old comrade" (2.8.1), and Diodorus a "comrade" (2.10.1). Glaucon (3.6.1) is not one of the companions, but Socrates takes an interest in him for the sake of his friends Plato and Charmides.

[32] Critobulus and Xenophon are introduced simply by name, with no indication that they are part of a Socratic group (1.3.8; Critobulus alone in 2.6.1), as is Antisthenes (2.5.1), Crito (2.9.1), Nicomachides (3.4.1), the son of Pericles (3.5.1), Parrhasius the painter (3.10.1), Cleiton the sculptor (3.10.6), and Hermogenes (4.8.4), though five of these (Xenophon, Critobulus, Antisthenes, Crito, and Hermogenes) are generally considered part of the Socratic circle. The unnamed dialogue partners in 3.2.1 and 3.3.1 are simply "a man who had been chosen general" and "a man who had been chosen leader of the cavalry." The objects of his correction in 3.13-14 are not named, nor is any relationship to him noted.

[33] The sophists Hippias and Antiphon are introduced as antagonists rather than part of his circle (1.6.1 and 4.4.5-6).

[34] Theodote and Socrates had not met before the encounter Xenophon records (3.11.1).

is not a body of abstract ideas but encompasses specific knowledge for particular situations. The generalized teaching (2.4) is only a foundation for the specific application (2.5-10).

This type of presentation is consistent with the Socratic teaching presented in 3.8. When Aristippus asks Socrates if he knows of anything good, the philosopher refuses to answer directly but instead seeks to narrow the question to the nature of the good in relation to some specific need. "If you are asking me whether I know of anything good in relation to nothing," he concludes, "I neither know nor want to know" (3.8.3, LCL tr.). He treats Aristippus' question about the beautiful (καλός) in a similar way.

The same belief is reflected in Socrates' philosophy of education. Xenophon states that Socrates "took pains to make [his companions] independent in doing the work that they were fitted for. For I never knew a man who was so careful to discover what each of his companions knew" (4.7.1, LCL tr.). The approach is illustrated forcefully in the two dialogues dealing with participation in politics (3.6-7). In the first, Socrates discourages Glaucon from his political ambitions by showing him that he lacks the requisite practical knowledge to advise the state. In the second, he encourages Charmides, Glaucon's uncle,[35] to overcome his shyness in speaking and to offer his practical wisdom to the state by entering the political arena.

The presentation of the general through the specific is a technique that permeates the *Memorabilia*. The bulk of book four deals with the relationship between Socrates and "those who customarily associated with him" (4.1.1). Chapter one discusses that relationship in general, while chapters two through three and five through seven illustrate it in particular instances. The same pattern is apparent within several of the individual chapters. Chapter three begins with a general statement that Socrates, rather than fostering skill in speaking and efficiency in affairs in his companions, taught them the need for prudence, especially for prudence toward the gods (4.3.1-2). The rest

---

[35] The specific relationship is not stated in the text although it is noted that Socrates undertook his correction of Glaucon for the sake of Plato and Charmides, suggesting that some relationship exists.

of the chapter shows how, in a specific instance, he went about fostering piety and prudence.

The *Memorabilia* itself follows the same pattern of addressing the general in terms of the specific. The charges against Socrates are stated in general terms: He is guilty of rejecting the gods and corrupting the youth. In the first two chapters, Xenophon deals with the charges in a general way. The specifics of the arguments advanced against Socrates require specific rebuttal in certain instances (e.g., the problem posed by Critias and Alcibiades), but in general, this section is more abstract than the remainder of the work. After this relatively short discussion of the charges in general terms, Xenophon turns to cataloging specific instances of Socrates' relations with his companions and his teachings about the gods. The specific instances provide proof of the general assertion made in the first two chapters.

Xenophon's stress on the individual situation of the dialogue partner is reflected in the fact that the dialogues almost are always restricted to Socrates and a single other speaker. In several situations, the individual who is the beneficiary of the discussion does not take part but simply "overhears" a discussion staged by Socrates with one of his companions, but the structure of the conversation is still quite simple.[36] There remains only one primary beneficiary and one discussion partner. The two roles in these cases are simply separated into two individuals.[37] In addition, one may consider the other companions present at a particular discussion as secondary beneficiaries.[38]

---

[36] A variation of this theme occurs when an initial statement by Socrates to one of his companions succeeds in drawing the third party into direct discussion with Socrates, such as in the discussion with Theodote (3.11.2-4). This pattern is repeated in the conversion of Euthydemus, though in that case the discussion with Euthydemus (4.2.8-39) is separated in time from the discussions for the benefit of Euthydemus (4.2.2-8).

[37] A second variation is found in the discussion with Xenophon (1.3.8-13). This discussion is staged for the benefit of Critobulus (1.3.8), but since Xenophon shares the opinion of Critobulus, the discussion becomes a reproof of Xenophon as well.

[38] In the case of the second conversation with Aristippus (3.8), the companions appear to be the primary beneficiaries (3.8.1). Aristippus' purpose is to catch Socrates in a contradiction, and Socrates does not seem to think his opponent will benefit from the discussion.

The restriction of the dialogues to the participation of two discussants cannot be attributed to a technical inability of Xenophon to portray more complex conversations, since in the *Symposium* he is able to portray a discussion with multiple participants. The direct, two-party encounters not only allow Xenophon to show how Socrates addressed the individual needs of individuals but also allow the reader to make clear judgments at the end of each dialogue as to whether Socrates in this specific instance benefited this specific person.

The extent to which Xenophon provides characterization of the dialogue partners varies considerably. At one extreme is "a man who had been chosen general" (3.2), who has no name, no lines, and no characteristics. The breezy disregard by the hedonist Aristippus of the results of his self-indulgence (2.1.8-13) and the difficulty of the gentlemanly Aristarchus in accepting the idea of his householders' working for a living (2.7.6) are believable characteristics but hardly raise them out of the category of types.[39] On the other hand, some of the dialogue partners pass beyond a typical case to become recognizable individuals. Euthydemus appears as an aloof but sincere lover of books, proud of his learning but willing to set aside his pride for the pursuit of wisdom (4.2). Theodote appears as an empty-headed beauty whose simpleminded appreciation of Socrates is the perfect foil for his ironic flirtation (3.11). While the level of characterization is spotty, it is sufficient to indicate that Socrates is matching his instruction to the individuality of his companions.

Euthydemus and the Socratic Course of Education

While 1.3 through 3.14 shows Socrates as the guide and benefactor of all with whom he associates and avoids the perception of a well-defined Socratic community, in 4.1-7 Xenophon turns to an examination of those whom Socrates led through a full course of education. Even here, however, there is no indication of a community. The reader is shown one particular individual and the typical course of study he underwent. This section is interspersed with statements about

---

[39] Aristippus' actual position was much more complex and nuanced than Xenophon has shown.

Socrates' approach to education (4.1.2-5; 4.3.1-2; 4.5.1; 4.6.1, 15; 4.7.1-10), which make it clear that Euthydemus is to be taken as a concrete example of the general approach.

Subject Matter

The subject matter that Xenophon presents in this typical course is mostly familiar to the reader: piety (4.3; cf. 1.4), justice (4.4), self-control (4.5; cf. 1.5, 2.1), clear definition (4.6; cf. 3.9), and developing in his companions ability "in the work they were fitted for" through instruction in various subjects (4.7; cf. 3.1-7, 10-11). The only new subject is justice, though Socrates' identification of justice as doing what is lawful brings to mind Alcibiades' discussion with Pericles, where the latter was unable to define law (1.2.40-46). The general identity between the subject matter of this typical course of education and that of the earlier section, in which Socrates' instruction was not confined to close associates, indicates that Socrates had no esoteric teaching. The close associates such as Euthydemus simply sought out more of the Socratic instruction that was generally available to all who were interested. This is emphasized by the fact that Socrates' teaching on justice is not illustrated by a dialogue with Euthydemus but is shown through a public debate with the sophist Hippias (4.4).

The subjects covered in this section accord well with Xenophon's apologetic intent. Socrates had been charged with rejecting the gods acknowledged by the state (1.1); on the contrary, Xenophon shows that he teaches his followers piety and identifies piety with "following the custom of the state." Socrates had been charged with corrupting the youth (1.1); on the contrary, Xenophon shows that he taught strict self-control (cf. 1.2.1-8). His accuser claimed that he taught his followers to despise the established laws (1.2.9); on the contrary, he identified justice with observance of the law (4.4.12-18). His accuser claimed he drove his followers to violence (1.2.9); on the contrary, he taught them skill in discussion so they could overcome their opponents by persuasion rather than violence (cf. 1.2.10-11). Socrates should have taught his companions prudence before politics (1.2.17); in fact, he did (4.3.1).

The Initiation of the Relationship

The way in which Socrates initiates his relationship with Euthydemus is presented as an illustration of Socrates' approach to one type of person, "those who thought they had received the best education, and prided themselves on wisdom" (4.2.1, LCL tr.), but it illustrates traits that are characteristic of the Socratic approach in general.[40] First, it is clearly Socrates who takes the initiative to start the relationship. This accords with the Socratic expression of being "in love" with his companions (4.1.2). Socrates recognizes the good dispositions of potential companions and methodically pursues his beloveds, just as he advises Theodote first to identify potential friends and then to ensnare them in her nets (3.11.9-10). Second, Socrates tailors his approach to the character of the particular person whose companionship he desires, as he has advised Critobulus that in his pursuit of friends, "The spell must be fitted to the listener" (2.6.12). Third, when Socrates has established an initial relationship with his potential companion, he demonstrates to that person the need to embark on a course of education by unmasking the potential companion's ignorance (4.2.40). Finally, the relationship is established only if the potential companion responds. Many whom Socrates forces to confront their own ignorance simply avoid him (4.2.40). Euthydemus, on the other hand, determines to improve himself and attaches himself to Socrates in order to learn from him.

Hermogenes and the Death of Socrates

The dialogue between Hermogenes and Socrates in the final chapter of the *Memorabilia* is unique in two respects. First, the subject of the conversation is Socrates, and second, Hermogenes takes the lead

---

[40] For discussions of moral conversions in the philosophical traditions, see Abraham J. Malherbe, *Paul and the Thessalonians: The Philosophic Tradition of Pastoral Care* (Philadelphia: Fortress Press, 1987) 21-28; *idem, Moral Exhortation: A Greco-Roman Sourcebook,* LEC 4 (Philadelphia: Westminster Press, 1986) 55-59; Arthur Darby Nock, *Conversion: The Old and the New in Religion from Alexander the Great to Augustine of Hippo* (London, New York, and Toronto: Oxford University Press, 1933) 164-86; *idem,* "Conversion and Adolescence," in *Essays on Religion and the Ancient World* (Cambridge, MA: Harvard University Press, 1972) 1.469-80.

in trying to influence Socrates' course of action. In a sense, Hermogenes is usurping Socrates' role as the one who leads his companion into a wiser course of action. In the previous dialogues, only Socrates' opponents attempted to take this role in dealing with the philosopher (1.6; 4.4.6).

The conversation takes place shortly before the trial of Socrates. Hermogenes' attempt to influence his mentor, while well-meaning, sadly misses the mark. He first advises Socrates to prepare for his defense, but the philosopher replies that he has been preparing for his defense all his life by doing what is right and avoiding what is wrong (4.8.4). When Hermogenes retorts that innocence does not guarantee acquittal, Socrates informs him that his δαιμόνιον has prevented him from preparing a defense to present to the jury (4.8.5). Hermogenes finds this strange, but Socrates continues that it seems better to God for him to die now, before he is subjected to the ravages of old age (4.8.6-8). The final point made by Socrates serves as a summation of the apologetic argument of the entire work. If the jury condemns him unjustly, Socrates says, its members will bring shame on themselves in the eyes of posterity, but as for himself, posterity "will ever testify of me that I wronged no man at any time, nor corrupted any man, but strove ever to make my companions better" (4.8.9-10, LCL tr.).

Though Xenophon has mentioned him as one of the true companions of Socrates (1.2.48), Hermogenes does not have the proper attitude toward his friend's impending death. Socrates himself is able to understand only through the voice of his δαιμόνον. It appears to be God's will for him to die now, and Socrates gladly aligns himself with the divine will. Xenophon does not relate Hermogenes' final reaction to his friend's pronouncements, but Xenophon himself offers the conversation as proof of the philosopher's noble attitude toward death. The companions do not understand enough to anticipate Socrates' attitude, but when it is explained, they accept and admire it.

The Founders of the Socratic Schools

The major Socratics are conspicuous by their absence from Xenophon's account of the philosopher. Aristippus is portrayed in a decidedly negative fashion, Antisthenes has a minor role, and Plato is mentioned only in passing. The effect is to distance Socrates from the Socratic schools and their founders. The teaching of Socrates, in Xenophon's portrait, is not restricted to a privileged few but is generally available to all. Thus none of the Socratics can claim a special position as the expounder of Socratic thought.

Scholarship has shown that Xenophon was aware of the writings of the other Socratics and discussed the same topics that the others had introduced.[41] This study is not concerned with that larger issue, however, but only with the portrait of the Socratics.

Aristippus

Of all the Socratic philosophers, Xenophon devotes the most space to Aristippus, the founder of the Cyrenaic school. Aristippus appears first as one of the συνόντες who is upbraided by Socrates for his lack of self-control (2.1) and later appears as an opponent, determined to even the score for his earlier defeat in argument by besting Socrates at his own game and catching him in logical contradictions over the definition of the good and the beautiful (3.8).[42] This movement from follower to opponent parallels Critias' course and is one of the few instances in which a change appears in any character. In another place, Xenophon attacks those who "after getting from [Socrates] a few trifles for nothing, became vendors of them at a great price to others" (1.2.60, LCL tr.), a clear reference to Aristippus, who charged fees in the manner of the sophists.[43]

Both of the Aristippus dialogues focus on prominent elements of Cyrenaic doctrine that Xenophon found quite offensive. The first involves the hedonistic elements in the doctrine and life style of the

---

[41] Karl Joël, *Der echte und der xenophontische Sokrates*, 3 vols. (Berlin: R. Gaertner, 1893-1901); Olaf Alfred Gigon, *Sokrates: Sein Bild in Dichtung und Geschichte* (Bern: A. Franke, 1947); Jean Luccioni, *Xénophon et le socratisme* (Paris: Presses Universitaire de France, 1953).

[42] There is a similarity with the intentions of Alcibiades in his interchange with Pericles (1.2.40-46). Both adopt the form of a Socratic challenge to self-examination and reduce it to a means of self-promotion.

[43] Diogenes Laertius states that Aristippus was the first of the followers of Socrates to charge fees (2.65).

Cyrenaic,[44] the second his claim that nothing is in itself good, but only thought to be good according to custom.[45] Clearly Xenophon wanted to distance Socrates from these doctrines, whether as part of an inter-Socratic argument over the true doctrine of the master or as part of his apologetic.

Antisthenes

Antisthenes is mentioned as a constant companion of Socrates (3.11.17) but only appears in a minor role in one dialogue concerning friendship (2.5). The discussion is staged for the benefit of a third, unnamed companion who had been neglecting a needy friend. Antisthenes serves as the straight man in the discussion, providing the intended answer to a rhetorical question posed by Socrates. One of Antisthenes' doctrines is mentioned in a distinctly unfavorable light. In 1.2.19, he attributes to "many who claim to love wisdom" the doctrine of Antisthenes that a just man can never become unjust.[46]

Plato

Plato is mentioned only once, as a friend for whose sake Socrates attempts to correct Glaucon (3.6.1). It is possible, however, that the dialogue between Pericles and Socrates' false follower Alcibiades is an attack on Plato's depiction of Socrates. In Plato, one of the primary Socratic traits is his penchant for showing the wise and powerful that they do not understand the basic concepts that they take for granted. In the *Apology*, the Platonic Socrates attributes the interest that some people found in his company to their enjoyment of "hearing me examine those who think that they are wise when they are not" (33c, Tredennick tr.), and several of the Platonic dialogues provide examples of Socrates' ability to prove how little his dialogue partners (and, indeed, he himself) know. In the *Charmides*, he shows an inability to define σωφροσύνη; in the *Laches*, he investigates courage with the same result; in the *Lysis*, friendship; in the *Euthyphro*, piety.

---

[44] For anecdotes relating to Aristippus' hedonistic lifestyle, see Diogenes Laertius 2.66-83, *passim*. The doctrinal basis for the hedonism is presented in Diogenes Laertius 2.86-92.

[45] Diogenes Laertius 2.93.

[46] Diogenes Laertius 6.105.

Xenophon's Socrates, on the other hand, has no difficulty in defining
such abstract qualities, as the chapter on definitions (4.6) shows.
Indeed, for Xenophon, the development of clear definitions was one of
the main points of a Socratic education. The discussion between
Alcibiades and Pericles, apparently a parody of Plato's dialogues,
suggests that for Xenophon, Plato, like Alcibiades, was interested only
in the superficial side of Socrates, his skill in argument, and missed the
core of what Socrates was attempting to convey to his companions.

Other Characters

In the *Memorabilia* the preponderance of the action takes place
between Socrates and his συνόντες. There are no scenes depicting
crowds either praising or blaming him. His trial is only alluded to
rather than presented in a direct account. Xenophon indicates that
Socrates challenged many people to examine their understanding of
basic virtues and that in most cases their reaction was to avoid him
(4.2.40), but no example of such an interchange is included.

Opponents of Socrates play a relatively small role. The
confrontation with Critias (1.2.31-38) shows Socrates fully in control
of his relationship with the tyrant, but it is introduced because of the
earlier association of Critias as a companion of the philosopher. In the
second interchange with Aristippus (3.8), the former companion also
has adopted the role of an opponent.

The other two opponents of Socrates who appear in the
Memorabilia are the sophists Antiphon and Hippias.[47] Antiphon (1.6)
is set most clearly in the role of an antagonist. The three discussions
that Xenophon records, all consisting of a single statement by Antiphon
and a retort by Socrates, explicate the relationship between Socrates
and his companions. In the first, Antiphon charges Socrates with being
a "teacher of unhappiness" (1.6.3), in the second he upbraids Socrates
for not accepting pay for his teaching (1.6.11-12), and in the third he

---

[47] On Xenophon's understanding of the sophists, see C. Joachim Classen,
"Xenophons Darstellung der Sophistik und der Sophisten," *Hermes* 112 (1984)
154-67.

inquires how Socrates can hope to train others for politics when he avoids politics himself (1.6.15).

In the interchange with Antiphon, Xenophon presents a distinctly unfavorable impression of the sophists. Socrates refutes the sophists' understanding of education and compares the sophists to prostitutes (1.6.13), who give their favors to anyone for money.[48] In two other places the *Memorabilia* contains attacks on the sophists. In 1.1.11-14, Socrates compares the sophists to madmen for their speculations on the nature of the cosmos.[49] Before his conversion by Socrates, the know-it-all Euthydemus had amassed a large collection of works of celebrated poets and sophists, from which he derived his false sense of his own wisdom (4.2.1). This is unmistakably propaganda against the rival understanding of education held by the sophists.

In the dialogue with Hippias (4.4), however, the sophist receives more favorable treatment. Hippias initially mocks Socrates for constantly repeating the same old themes, and Socrates chides the sophist for his obsession with the display of novelty (4.4.5-8), but then they engage in a sincere discussion of the nature of justice.[50] While the dialogue serves to show Socrates' superiority to the sophist, it also indicates his desire to assist all comers in the examination of virtue. Although Hippias begins as a good-natured antagonist, Socrates treats him as a companion, and Hippias is able to accept that role as Socrates guides the conversation.

Comparison Between Xenophon and Mark

The bulk of Xenophon's *Memorabilia* depicts Socrates in his relationships with his companions. Those relationships fall into three categories: (1) those through which Xenophon has Socrates correct

---

[48] The dialogue with Theodote (3.11) suggests that Socrates is a courtesan rather than a prostitute.

[49] There is certainly an apologetic component to this statement. The sophist Anaxagoras had been condemned to death by the Athenians, who perceived his speculations about the cosmos as an attack on the gods.

[50] For Hippias to agree to the identity of law and justice is a major victory for Socrates' debating skill, if other depictions of the sophist are to be accepted. In the *Protagoras* 337d, Plato has Hippias call law the "despot of mankind."

and distance himself from companions who might bring him into disrepute; (2) his relationships with a wide range of companions that illustrate Socratic values and his concern to serve his fellow citizens and the state, and (3) the ongoing relationship with Euthydemus that depicts a typical course of Socratic education.

Through the portrayal of these relationships, Xenophon is able to achieve his apologetic purposes. He refutes the charges that Socrates had corrupted the youth of Athens and posed a danger to the state through his teaching, and he creates a favorable portrait of the life and teaching of Socrates. Through a multiplicity of short dialogues, Xenophon depicts Socrates not as a teacher handing on a fixed body of knowledge or a systematized doctrine but rather as one who reaches out to help a broad spectrum of individuals in their particular circumstances to assist them in leading lives more productive for themselves and of greater value to the state.

Xenophon's portrayal of Socrates' companions and dialogue partners is very different from Mark's portrayal of the disciples of Jesus. Much of this difference results from the two authors' differing understandings of their own communities and of the nature of teaching. Xenophon regards Socrates' associates, among whom he includes himself, as separate individuals rather than a community. Because of the suspicion that Socrates had created a dangerous political faction, Xenophon portrays Socrates as having no fixed group of followers and the Socratic community, if Socrates and his followers can even be characterized as such, as having no structure. The lack of a Socratic school may reflect, as well, Xenophon's dislike for the organized schools of Socratics at the time of his writing.

Mark, on the other hand, is writing for a Christian community that sees itself as sharply distinguished from those outside. The portrayal of Jesus' followers reflects that separation. There is a group of twelve appointed to be with Jesus and share in his authority and work (3.13-19; 6.7-13). Of the twelve, three or four are privileged to receive special knowledge (9.2-13; 13.3-27). The disciples receive special teaching (4.10-20; 4.33-34; 7.17-23; 8.31; 9.31; 10.10-12; 10.32-34) and are told not to share their knowledge with those outside (8.30; 9.9).

The difference in the terminology used by Xenophon and Mark indicates their differing sense of community. Xenophon avoids the term μαθητής because of the special relationship between student and teacher that the term implies. Mark's use of the term reflects not so much a shift in usage[51] as a different understanding of the relationship between teacher-protagonist and his followers. For Mark, the μαθηταί of Jesus have a relationship with him that is qualitatively different from his relationship with others.

Xenophon understands teaching to mean addressing the specific concerns and needs of specific individuals. He avoids general pronouncements. The Jesus of Mark, on the other hand, makes general pronouncements but seldom addresses his teaching to the specific needs of particular individuals.[52] Even though Xenophon provides only limited characterization of Socrates' dialogue partners, it is considerably more than the Markan characterization of the disciples. The disciples are almost always presented as a group, and their characterization reflects the relationship between the group and Jesus. Only occasionally do they possess individual characteristics, such as the confusion of Peter at the transfiguration (9.6) and the ambition of James and John (10.35), but even in those cases their characterization is representative of the group. Only in the scene of Peter's denial (14.66-72) does a disciple appear as a true individual.

Mark's listing of the twelve (3.13-19), in contrast to Xenophon's lists of Socrates' associates, marks off a group that is commissioned for a specific office. Nevertheless, Xenophon's apologetic use of lists of associates suggests that Mark expected his audience to view the twelve in a favorable light. Iamblichus also uses a list of the followers of Pythagoras in a mutually reinforcing manner—the followers are good because they followed Pythagoras, Pythagoras is good because of the quality of his followers (*Pythagorean Life* 36.265-67). It would be a radical departure from the normal literary practice if Mark held a

---

[51] Plato already used the term in reference to the students of Pythagoras, *Protagoras* 315a.

[52] The rich young man (10.17-22) is one exception; the teaching occasioned by the request of James and John (10.35-45) is another. In addition, the discussion about bread (8.14-21) may be seen as addressing the particular situation of the disciples as a whole.

negative view of the disciples and yet listed them as a specially commissioned group.

Xenophon distances Socrates from the major Socratics by showing Socrates primarily in dialogue with ordinary people rather than the founders of the Socratic schools. We might expect Mark to take a similar approach if he intended to downgrade the disciples of Jesus. Instead, Mark shows the disciples to have a particularly close relationship with Jesus. Jesus does criticize the disciples, just as Socrates criticizes Aristippus, but Socrates is shown as criticizing most of his dialogue partners. His role as a moral and intellectual guide is to correct the understanding of those with whom he speaks. The distinction between Aristippus and most of Socrates' other dialogue partners is his inability to learn from Socrates. If Xenophon's strategy can be taken as a guide, Jesus' criticism of the disciples would not necessarily lead Mark's audience to a negative judgment unless it were conclusively shown that the disciples were never able to internalize Jesus' instruction. Xenophon's handling of Alcibiades and Critias also suggests that followers who were felt to be an embarrassment to a teacher would be clearly condemned. Xenophon is certainly not willing to let his audience form their own judgments about these two simply on the basis of his own characterization. They are told explicitly that Alcibiades and Critias are not true followers of Socrates. Thus the rhetorical strategies found in Xenophon lend little support to the thesis that Mark was attacking the disciples through his depiction of them in his Gospel.

IAMBLICHUS' PYTHAGOREAN LIFE

Another account of a philosopher and his followers is found in the *Pythagorean Life*, a work composed by the third and fourth century CE Neoplatonic philosopher Iamblichus that reflects the requirements of use in a formal school setting.[1] While Iamblichus was one of the leading intellectual figures of his time, very little is known of his life.[2]

---

[1] All citations from the Greek text of the *Pythagorean Life* are from the Teubner edition, *Iamblichi, De Vita Pythagorica Liber*, ed. by Ludwig Deubner (Stuttgart: B. G. Teubner, 1975). The best English translation is John Dillon and Jackson Hershbell, *Iamblichus: On the Pythagorean Way of Life: Text, Translation, Notes*, SBLTT 29, GRRS 11 (Atlanta, GA: Scholars Press, 1991). Unfortunately, this translation did not become available until this dissertation was substantially completed. Until very recently, only two English translations were available, Thomas Taylor's 1818 translation (*Iamblichus' Life of Pythagoras*, tr. by Thomas Taylor [Rochester, VT: Inner Traditions International, 1986]) and Kenneth Sylvan Guthrie's 1919 revision of Taylor's translation (in *The Pythagorean Sourcebook and Library*, compiled and tr. by Kenneth Sylvan Guthrie [Grand Rapids, MI: Phanes Press, 1987]). Both these translations are free and often misleading. Since the initial work on this chapter was completed, two new translations have appeared, Gillian Clark's *Iamblichus: On the Pythagorean Life*, TTH 8 (Liverpool: Liverpool University Press, 1989), and Dillon and Hershbell. All quotations are the author's own translations unless otherwise noted.

[2] The best discussions of Iamblichus can be found in Bent Dalsgaard Larsen, *Jamblique de Chalcis, Exégète et Philosophe*, 2 vols. (Aarhus: Universitetsforlaget i Aarhus, 1972); and John M. Dillon, *Iamblichi Chalcidensis In Platonis Dialogos Commentariorum Fragmenta*, PA 23 (Leiden: E. J. Brill, 1973). An excellent discussion of Iamblichus and the *Pythagorean Life* is now available in the introduction to Dillon and Hershbell, *Pythagorean Way of Life*, 1-30.

Most of our information comes from the biographical account in Eunapius' *Lives of Philosophers and Sophists*, a source that is often untrustworthy. The ancients placed Iamblichus in the succession of the major figures of Neoplatonic philosophy, following Plotinus and Porphyry. While the modern appraisal of his work has not been high,[3] the ancients considered him a first-class intellect. The emperor Julian believed he was a genius of the same caliber as Plato.[4]

Iamblichus' birth has recently been dated in the 240s CE,[5] and the generally accepted date of his death is approximately 325. According to Eunapius, Iamblichus studied with the philosopher Anatole,[6] who is most probably the famous Peripatetic, Anatole of Alexandria, who later became the Bishop of Laodicea.[7] Iamblichus' knowledge of Egyptian customs, which is evident in his work, *The Mysteries*, indicates that he spent a considerable period of time in Alexandria.[8] Eunapius also states that he studied with Porphyry,[9] but it is unclear whether any extended period of study was involved.[10] At some point in his career, perhaps in the 290s,[11] he established his own school in Syria, probably at Apamea or Daphne.[12]

[3] See discussion in Larsen, *Jamblique*, 1.18-21.

[4] Julian, *Orations* 4.146a.

[5] Dillon dates his birth at 245, based on the evidence of the pseudo-Julian correspondence with Iamblichus (*Iamblichi*, 3, 5-7). Larsen dates his birth about 240 (*Jamblique*, 1.34). Joseph Bidez dates his birth at 250 at the latest ("Le philosophe Jamblique et son école," *REG* 32 [1919] 32). Alan Cameron agrees with Bidez's dating ("The Date of Iamblichus' Birth," *Hermes* 96 [1968] 374-76).

[6] Eunapius, *Lives* 457.

[7] See Larsen, *Jamblique*, 1.37-38, and the citations given there for the discussion concerning the identity of Anatole; also Dillon, *Iamblichi*, 8-9.

[8] Larsen, *Jamblique*, 1.41.

[9] Eunapius, *Lives* 458.

[10] Dillon, *Iamblichi*, 10; Larsen, *Jamblique*, 1.38-40. Iamblichus was often critical of Porphyry, leading G. Mau to doubt Eunapius' report ("Iamblichos," *PW* 9.645). In the absence of more compelling evidence to the contrary, however, it seems reasonable to accept the connection between the two.

[11] So Dillon, *Iamblichi*, 11-13.

[12] According to John Malalas, p. 312, 7, Iamblichus taught at Daphne, near Antioch. Libanius, *Orations* 52.21, mentions a school of Iamblichus at Apamea, though Larsen believes this is a later Iamblichus. Praechter located the school of Iamblichus in Chalcis. Ruelle believed that Iamblichus remained in Alexandria. See Larsen, *Jamblique*, 1.40-41, for discussion and citations. See also Dillon, *Iamblichi*, 11-13.

The Pythagorean Synagoge

Iamblichus' *Pythagorean Life* can be understood properly only in the context of the larger work of which it is a part. It is the first book of a ten-book work, the Συναγωγή τῶν Πυθαγόρων Δογμάτων, and was transmitted as part of this larger work.[13] The first four books of the *Synagoge*, which are all that have survived except for fragments, are preserved together in a fourteenth century manuscript that is the archetype of all surviving manuscripts. There is no indication that the *Pythagorean Life* ever circulated independently.[14]

There is no way of accurately dating the writing of the *Synagoge*.[15] Bent Dalsgaard Larsen reasonably suggests, however, that the work was composed in Alexandria, since Iamblichus appears to have had a large library at his disposal.[16]

The term συναγωγή had been used since Plato and Aristotle to indicate a synthetic summary of doctrines, and the genre was especially important in the Peripatetic schools. A συναγωγή was used as an introductory manual, and as a genre it generally depended on the use of extracts and the mining of earlier introductions. The author of a συναγωγή was not expected to show great originality.[17]

The extant books of the *Pythagorean Synagoge* are: (1) Concerning the Pythagorean Life, (2) Exhortation to Philosophy (Προτρεπτικός), (3) Concerning General Mathematical Knowledge, and (4) Concerning the Elementary Teachings of Nicomachean Arithmetic. The nonextant books (in uncertain order) are: (5) Concerning Arithmetical Knowledge Regarding Physics, (6) Concerning Arithmeti-

---

[13] For discussion of contents, manuscripts, and fragments of the *Synagoge*, see Larsen, *Jamblique*, 1.43-47.

[14] Larsen, *Jamblique*, 1.66. The books were edited separately, which has created the impression of their being independent works.

[15] Dillon tentatively dates the *Synagoge* in the period 280-305 on the assumption that Iamblichus evolved away from his interest in Pythagoras (*Iamblichi*, 18-21), but that is hardly a compelling argument. Larsen declares that it is impossible to put the writings of Iamblichus in chronological order (*Jamblique*, 1.43).

[16] Larsen, *Jamblique*, 1.41.

[17] Larsen, *Jamblique*, 1.67-69.

cal Knowledge Regarding Ethics, (7) Concerning Arithmetical
Knowledge Regarding the Divine, (8) Concerning Geometry According
to the Pythagoreans, (9) Concerning Music According to the Pythagoreans, and (10) Concerning the Spheres [i.e., Astronomy] According to
the Pythagoreans.[18]

The bulk of the work is devoted to an exposition of the
quadrivium: arithmetic, geometry, music, and astronomy.[19] This,
along with the protreptic *Exhortation to Philosophy*, indicates that the
Synagoge served as an introductory work.   Since the fragmentary
remains of Iamblichus indicate that he wrote numerous commentaries
on Aristotle and Plato, it is most likely that the *Synagoge* served as a
preparatory step to the study of these philosophers.[20]

The *Pythagorean Life*, as the first part of this introduction to
philosophy, may have served as a student's first encounter with
philosophy in Iamblichus' school. It functions both as an introduction
to the study of the Pythagorean doctrines that follow and as an
inspiring example of the philosophical life. Significantly, it is not a
Life of Pythagoras, such as Porphyry wrote in his *History of Philosophy*, but a treatise *Concerning the Pythagorean Life*. By portraying the
rigors of the Pythagorean school and illustrating the philosophical
virtues through the example of many of Pythagoras' followers,
Iamblichus is able to provide a more general description of the
philosophic life than he could through a more narrowly focused
biography. The *Life* is largely a book of moral exhortation, and the
placement of such exhortation before the more technical books of the
Synagoge indicates that a life of virtue was considered by Iamblichus,
as it was by Pythagoras, to be both a necessary prerequisite for the
study of philosophy and the goal of the philosophical life.

[18] Larsen, *Jamblique*, 1.45-47; see also Dillon, *Iamblichi*, 19-21.

[19] Noted by Larsen, *Jamblique*, 1.69.

[20] So Larsen, who explains the quotation of Plato and Aristotle in the
Exhortation to Philosophy and *Concerning General Mathematical Knowledge* in
terms of the use of the *Synagoge* as a general introduction to philosophy
(*Jamblique*, 1.71-73, 103). On this point, however, see the discussion below on
Plato and Aristotle as Pythagoreans. Larsen also argues that the reminiscences of
Platonic passages in the *Life* suggest that the work is part of a course of education
that culminates with Plato (*Jamblique*, 91-99). See also Dillon, *Iamblichi*, 14-15.

The study of Pythagoras and Pythagoreanism was an appropriate beginning point in a Neoplatonic school such as Iamblichus' because Pythagoras was viewed as a forerunner of Plato.[21] The Neopythagorean philosophers believed that much of Plato's philosophy was derived from Pythagoras.[22] The third century BCE historian Neanthes claimed that Plato had been put out of the Pythagorean school, apparently for making public the hidden doctrines.[23] Unnamed Pythagoreans cited by Porphyry claimed that everything Plato and Aristotle said was taken from Pythagoras.[24] The author of the anonymous life of Pythagoras preserved by Photius lists Plato as the ninth in the Pythagorean succession, Aristotle as the tenth.[25] The same author states that Plato "learned his speculative and physical doctrines from the Italian Pythagoreans, his ethics from Socrates, and his logic from Zeno, Parmenides and the Eleatics. But all of these teachings descended from Pythagoras."[26]

---

[21] There was a close relationship between Neopythagorean and Neoplatonic philosophy, and in Alexandria, where Iamblichus studied, it is impossible to separate the two schools. For a discussion of this connection, see E. R. Dodds, "The *Parmenides* of Plato and the Origin of the Neoplatonic 'One,'" *ClassQ* 22 (1928) 136-40, esp., 139. For the relationship between Pythagoreanism and later Platonism, see Philip Merlan, *From Platonism to Neoplatonism*, 3rd ed. (The Hague: Martinus Nijhoff, 1968); John Dillon, *The Middle Platonists* (London: Gerald Duckworth, 1977); John Wittaker, "Epekeina nou kai ousias," *VC* 23 (1969) 91-104; *idem*, "Neopythagoreanism and Negative Theology," *SO* 44 (1969) 109-25; *idem*, "Neopythagoreanism and the Transcendent Absolute," *SO* 48 (1973) 77-86; Larsen, *Jamblique*, 1.74-79.

[22] A thorough account of the major Neopythagoreans can be found in Dillon, *Middle Platonists*, 341-83.

[23] Diogenes Laertius 8.55.

[24] Porphyry, *Pythagoras* 53. This opinion is sometimes attributed to Moderatus of Gades, but the quotation from Moderatus ends with 52.

[25] English translation in Guthrie, *Pythagorean Sourcebook*, p. 137, par. 1. The author may not have been a Neopythagorean himself. The text that has come down to us calls the Pythagorean belief in transmigration "foolish" (Guthrie, p. 138, par. 6), but this probably is a Christian interpolation.

[26] Guthrie's translation. *Pythagorean Sourcebook*, p. 138, par. 9.

A connection between Plato and the Pythagoreans is well attested outside of Neopythagorean circles. According to Diogenes Laertius, Plato studied with the Pythagoreans Philolaus and Eurytus (3.6) and mixed together the doctrines of Heraclitus, the Pythagoreans, and Socrates (3.8). Diogenes states that the doctrine of the intelligibles is from the Pythagoreans. In another passage, however, Diogenes claims two sources for philosophy, Anaximander and Pythagoras. He

Iamblichus himself seems to have accepted the idea that the teaching of Plato and Aristotle was derived from Pythagoras. In the *Pythagorean Life*, 27.131, he notes a Pythagorean doctrine that Plato appropriated in the Republic. At another point he refers to Plato and Archytas in a list of examples of Pythagoreans who offered assistance to each other (27.127).[27] In two books of his *Pythagorean Synagoge*, the *Exhortation to Philosophy* and *Concerning General Mathematical Knowledge*, he includes extensive passages from Plato, Aristotle and other non-Pythagoreans,[28] though this may be due to his apparent intention to have the *Synagoge* serve as a general introduction to philosophy.[29]

Sources

While this dissertation is concerned with the portrayal of students in extant literary works, Iamblichus' use of sources is pertinent for understanding both the way his work would be perceived and the extent to which his work reflects a more general pattern that was present in earlier centuries.

Unlike Porphyry, who cites authors thirty-one times in his *Life of Pythagoras*,[30] Iamblichus cites his sources in a much more haphazard manner. In the other extant books of the Pythagorean

---

places Socrates in the succession from Anaximander and claims it was Socrates who introduced ethics or moral philosophy (1.13-15). Diogenes quotes Satyrus as saying that Plato purchased three Pythagorean books from Philolaus (3.9) and quotes an exchange of letters between Archytas and Plato concerning Archytas' procurement for Plato of four books of the Pythagorean Ocellus (8.4.79-81). Plato himself indicates that the Pythagorean Archytas had intervened with Dionysius to save his life (*Epistles*, 7.350a-b). Different versions of the same story are found in Plutarch (*Dion* 18.1-20.2) and Diogenes Laertius (3.21-22).

For further evidence of the belief that Platonic doctrines derived from Pythagoras, see Dodds, "Parmenides," 139; Philip Merlan, "Greek Philosophy from Plato to Plotinus," in *The Cambridge History of Later Greek and Early Medieval Philosophy*, ed. by Arthur Hilary Armstrong (Cambridge: University Press, 1967) 96.

[27] See the preceding note for the connection between Plato and Archytas.

[28] Larsen, *Jamblique*, 1.104-18, 1.129-30; Dillon, *Iamblichi*, 19-20.

[29] See Larsen, *Jamblique*, 1.70-73.

[30] J. A. Philip, "The Biographical Tradition—Pythagoras," *TAPA* 90 (1959) 191.

Synagoge, Iamblichus is highly dependent on a limited number of sources and generally follows them closely.[31] For example, in the *Exhortation to Philosophy*, the second book of the work, chapter five contains an epitome of Socrates' argument from Plato's *Euthydemus*, the end of chapter five through chapter twelve is based on the lost *Protrepticus* of Aristotle, and chapters thirteen through nineteen are based on various passages from Plato.[32] Much of the material in the other books of the *Synagoge* is taken from the Neopythagorean philosopher and mathematician Nicomachus of Gerasa (active about 100-150 CE).[33]

On the basis of the style of composition evident in the other books of the sequence, one would expect the same procedure to be used in the *Pythagorean Life*. In an influential article published in the 1870s, the eminent classicist Erwin Rohde argued that the *Life* was largely derived from two sources, both now lost, a life of Pythagoras by Apollonius of Tyana, from which most of the biographical information was taken, and a life of Pythagoras by Nicomachus of Gerasa.[34] Rohde believed the similarity between Iamblichus' work and the life of Pythagoras by Porphyry resulted from their common use of Nicomachus.[35]

Recently, an alternative source theory has been put forward by J. A. Philip, who argues that Iamblichus based his life on Porphyry's work, which he expanded with a long section on the virtues on the pattern of *laudationes*.[36] Philip believes that Iamblichus did more

---

[31] Dillon, *Iamblichi*, 19-20. For Iamblichus' use of sources in book three of the *Synagoge*, *Concerning the Common Mathematical Science*, see Merlan, *Neoplatonism*, 27-28.

[32] Larsen, *Jamblique*, 1.104-18.

[33] Dillon, *Iamblichi*, 15.

[34] Erwin Rohde, "Die Quellen des Iamblichus in seiner Biographie des Pythagoras," *RheinMus* 26 (1871) 554-76; 27 (1872) 23-61. This analysis has been accepted with certain reservations by several more recent scholars. Dillon, *Iamblichi*, 19; Cornelia J. de Vogel, *Pythagoras and Early Pythagoreanism: An Interpretation of Neglected Evidence on the Philosopher Pythagoras* (Assen: Van Gorcum, 1966) 151, n. 1.

[35] Philip notes that 132 of the 816 lines of Nauck's edition of Porphyry's *Life of Pythagoras* appear in Iamblichus in almost the same words ("Biographical Tradition," 189).

[36] Philip, "Biographical Tradition," 185-94, esp., 189 and 192.

than simply string sources together and exercised much more control as an author than Rohde's hypothesis allows.[37]

While Philip's theory fails to note that the verbal similarities between Porphyry and Iamblichus are restricted to passages derived from only one or two sources and does not adequately explain the source of Iamblichus' additional material, Rohde has oversimplified the source problem. Iamblichus appears to have more than two sources, and he demonstrates a certain amount of creativity in his use of those sources.[38] Furthermore, it is impossible to determine the extent to which he borrowed from either Nicomachus or Apollonius beyond the passages cited by Porphyry and those cited by Iamblichus himself.

Structure and Purpose

Iamblichus' *Pythagorean Life* has three major divisions, a narrative account of the life of Pythagoras through the welcome that he received on his arrival at Croton (chapters 2-11), a description of his school in Croton, including his method of instruction and some of his doctrines (chapters 12-26), and a section on the virtues as taught and exemplified by the Pythagoreans (chapters 27-33).[39] In addition to these major divisions, there are a number of chapters of prefatory and concluding material.

---

[37] Philip, "Biographical Tradition," 186-87. A third discussion of Iamblichus' sources is found in G. Bertermann, "De Iamblichi vitae Pythagoricae fontibus," (dissertation, Königsberg, 1913), which I was unable to consult. Larsen states that Bertermann regards the source problem as more complex than does Rohde (*Jamblique*, 1.13, n. 21). See also the discussion in Walter Burkert, *Lore and Science in Ancient Pythagoreanism* (Cambridge, MA: Harvard University Press, 1972) 98-105.

[38] The list of miracles found in Porphyry (*Life of Pythagoras*, 23-31), apparently attributed to Nicomachus, has been dismembered by Iamblichus and introduced into various places in his account (8.36, 13.60-15.64, 15.67, 28.134-36).

[39] Iamblichus indicates a division in the text at 28.134, where he indicates that he will now write about Pythagoras' "works as they relate to the virtues." It seems, nevertheless, that the author intended to join the political activities of Pythagoras and his associates, the topic of the preceding chapter, with the works of virtue that follow. At the beginning of chapter 34 (section 241), Iamblichus states he is now turning to points that do not fall under any of the former topics.

The central section, concerning the Pythagorean school, is the most loosely organized. Chapter twelve, on philosophy, serves as a preface to the section. According to the principle of beginning with the divinities (28.134), the next chapters (13-15) describe the miraculous powers of Pythagoras that related to his school or method of teaching, and then Iamblichus takes up various other topics that concern Pythagoras' philosophical school. Both of the other major sections contain a concentration of miraculous material in the early chapters. Chapter two includes the oracles given for the founding of Samos and the birth of Pythagoras and mentions the descent of Ancaeus from Zeus and the report of Pythagoras' being the son of Apollo (which Iamblichus denies), and chapter twenty-eight includes a number of Pythagorean miracles as proof of the piety and holiness of the philosopher.

The section on the virtues is the longest of the sections (59 out of 143 pages in the Teubner edition), followed by the section on the Pythagorean school and teaching (38 pages), the narrative section (26 pages), and the concluding material (18 pages). In addition to the section on virtues, thirteen of the twenty-six pages of narrative consist of hortatory speeches delivered by Pythagoras to various groups of Crotonians, and a significant amount of hortatory and moralistic material appears in the teaching section. Thus, at least half of the *Life* is devoted to moral exhortation. This contrasts with much of the content, known or presumed, of the rest of the *Synagoge*, which is much more technical and stresses mathematical knowledge. According to Pythagorean teaching, however, technical knowledge was supposed to be in service to virtue and the divine.[40]

Iamblichus' work is much less of a coherent rhetorical argument than is the *Memorabilia*. In part this is the result of Iamblichus' use of his sources. Judging from the other portions of the *Synagoge* where the sources are available for comparison, Iamblichus makes use of extended quotation or summarization of his sources without significant

---

[40] "All these [Pythagorean] precepts, which define what should be done or not done, aim at the divine, and this is the first principle, that all of life is ordered for the purpose of following God, which is the basic rule of this philosophy" (*Pythagorean Life*, 18.86).

change. He sometimes includes conflicting information if it is included in his sources. As a result, it is probable that some of the work presents the rhetoric of Iamblichus' sources rather than a conscious rhetorical design on the part of Iamblichus himself.

It was customary to begin the study of a philosopher's doctrines with a review of his life,[41] and Iamblichus wrote the *Pythagorean Life* to provide for the requirements of a philosophical curriculum. If the teacher was sympathetic to the doctrines of a philosopher, the life would be used to praise him and to point out the coherence between his life and thought. The students would then be favorably disposed toward the philosopher as they began the study of his doctrines.

A similar rhetorical strategy, on a much smaller scale, is found in the chreia elaboration exercise in Hermogenes (*Progymnasmata* 7.10-8.10).[42] Hermogenes instructs the student to introduce the chreia and its elaboration with a short encomium of the author or subject of the chreia. Praise of the subject or author is used to dispose the audience toward a favorable reception of the thought that follows.

Some features of the *Pythagorean Life* are standard features of an encomiastic biography, such as the description of Pythagoras' ancestry, birth, and education at the beginning of the work. The list of the philosopher's successors that concludes the work is a standard feature of philosophical lives.

Because of Pythagoras' standing as a founder of philosophy, the preservation of information about him would be an important end in itself. Nevertheless, the school setting does provide a clear rhetorical context. One of the important goals of an introductory work such as the *Synagoge* is to confirm for the students the value of their studies. The placement of the *Exhortation to Philosophy* as the second book of

---

[41] Diogenes Laertius follows the pattern of biography followed by doctrines in the more extensive of his lives, e.g., the chapter on Aristippus is divided at 2.87; the book devoted to Plato is divided into life (3.1-47a) and doctrines (3.47b-109).

[42] Text and translation may be found in *The Chreia in Ancient Rhetoric: Vol. I. The Progymnasmata*, by Ronald F. Hock and Edward N. O'Neil, SBLTT 27, GRRS 9 (Atlanta: Scholars Press, 1986) 176-77. Burton L. Mack has persuasively argued that the exercise was a preparation for the study of rhetoric and that the elaboration generally follows the methods of argumentation found in the rhetorical handbooks (*Patterns of Persuasion in the Gospels*, by Burton L. Mack and Vernon K. Robbins, FFLF [Sonoma: Polebridge Press, 1989] 51-57).

the *Synagoge* testifies to the importance of this goal. The *Pythagorean Life* may itself be understood as a part of this extended presentation of the value of philosophical study.

Each of the three major sections of the *Pythagorean Life* portrays the value of a philosophical education in a different way. The first section, a chronological narrative of the life of Pythagoras through his settling in Croton, shows that Pythagoras received an education from the most prominent philosophers of his day, thus placing his accomplishments within a context of an ongoing process of education. It also shows Pythagoras as a popular preacher whose exhortations improved the morals of the people of Croton and the surrounding cities and as a leader of political reform. This indicates the value of philosophy for society as a whole and suggests that philosophers possess a moral superiority that should afford them a leading role in their communities. A student who successfully learns to philosophize acquires the mantle of moral leadership that is attributed to philosophy through the success of Pythagoras in these areas. Philosophers were often criticised for fleeing from public life in the pursuit of trifles.[43] By showing Pythagoras as a popular preacher and moral reformer, Iamblichus is able to deflect this criticism. Epictetus urged his students to face the challenges of public life (*Discourses* 1.29.36), and Iamblichus does the same through the example of Pythagoras.

The second section presents the school of Pythagoras. This serves to legitimate the study of philosophy in a school setting and to provide the historical precedent for Iamblichus' own school. The section presents the students of Pythagoras, and by implication the students of Iamblichus, as a moral and intellectual elite who are given valuable teaching that is unsuitable for the masses. Esoteric wisdom was valued for its own sake in the ancient world,[44] and the fact that the information that the students were to receive in their study of the

---

[43] See the discussion in Abraham J. Malherbe, "'Not in a Corner': Early Christian Apologetics in Acts 26:26," in *Paul and the Popular Philosophers* (Minneapolis: Fortress Press, 1989) 154-58.

[44] The prestige attached to esoteric knowledge is evident in Apollonius' pursuit of esoteric knowledge as portrayed in Philostratus' *Life of Apollonius of Tyana.* Iamblichus himself compares the secrecy surrounding the Pythagorean doctrines with the secrecy of the Eleusinian mysteries (17.75).

Synagoge was once jealously guarded esoteric knowledge would add to its perceived value.

The third section provides examples of the virtue of Pythagoras and the early Pythagoreans. This section fulfills the dual purpose of providing moral examples for the students to follow and illustrating the value of philosophy in creating excellent moral character.

The account of the destruction of the Pythagorean community, like the description of the school, points out the exclusivity of the community of philosophers. The antagonism of the depraved opponents of Pythagoras shows that philosophy cannot be understood by all, especially not by those with degenerate character, and provides a way for the students to understand those who do not appreciate their own interest in philosophy.

Iamblichus' presentation of the followers of Pythagoras varies with the specific purpose of each section of his work. In the narrative of the philosopher's life, his followers are only incidentally mentioned. The description of his school in the second section contains mostly abstract descriptions of his followers, their selection, organization, and course of study. In the section on the Pythagorean virtues, however, the followers become much more prominent. Here various incidents in their lives are used on an equal footing with those from the life of Pythagoras to illustrate the virtuous deeds of the Pythagoreans.

The Narrative Section, Chapters 2-11

The different sections of the *Pythagorean Life* are largely independent. Each exhibits a different organizational principle and presents a different kind of material. For this reason, it is necessary to make a separate examination of the rhetorical and narrative roles of students in each section.

When the narrative portion of Iamblichus' *Life* is compared with the Gospels, Xenophon's *Memorabilia*, or Philostratus' *Apollonius of Tyana*, it is striking how small a role the students of Pythagoras play in the account. In part, this may be due to the organization of the *Life*, since Iamblichus has placed his discussion of Pythagoras' school in a separate section. The school section, however, contains little narrative material and is organized according to conceptual topics. Iamblichus and his sources think of the school as a fixed entity rather than one that develops in time as a narrative would suggest.

While little is said about Pythagoras' students, considerable space is given to a description of the philosopher's own education (2.9-4.19). Two themes predominate in the account. The first is the quality of the education that Pythagoras received. The second is his ability as a student. The quality of a person's education was one of the standard topics in an encomium, and a discussion of the philosopher's education is found as well at the beginning of Philostratus' *Life of Apollonius*.

The account of Pythagoras' education fulfills dual functions in the narrative. First, it helps establish the philosopher's credentials as a wise man and to place him within the succession of philosophers. Second, it gives the students for whom the *Synagoge* was written a model for their own educational achievements. The value of education is discussed explicitly in Pythagoras' exhortation to the young men of Croton (8.42-44), where παιδεία is shown to be superior to other possible goods.

The absence of a discussion of Jesus' education in the Gospel of Mark indicates that Jesus is not to be understood as part of a succession of teachers and that his knowledge and authority are not humanly derived. The quotations of the prophets and the account of John the Baptist that begin the Gospel place Jesus in the context of sacred history, in the line of but superior to the biblical prophets.

Call Stories

One of the few accounts of Pythagoras and a follower in this section tells how Pythagoras induced a particular youth to become his student.[45] As the youth was in financial difficulty and needed money to continue his physical training, Pythagoras offered to pay him to learn lessons in arithmetic and geometry. After a time, the youth became devoted to education, and when Pythagoras protested that he could no longer afford to pay him for the lessons, the youth volun-

---

[45] This type of story, in which a philosopher tricks someone into becoming his student, also can be found in the Platonic dialogues. In the *Charmides*, Socrates begins a conversation with the youth on the pretext of helping cure him of a headache (155b-157d).

teered to pay Pythagoras instead (5.21-25). The account illustrates
Pythagoras' cleverness and reinforces the value of philosophical study
for the beginning student.

   For the most part, however, Pythagoras is not depicted as
actively recruiting students. Instead, students flock to him because of
his reputation. We are told that in Samos, "all of Greece came forward
to admire him, and the best and most philosophical came to Samos on
his account, resolved to share in his learning" (6.28). In Croton he
won an initial following through public lectures. As a result of his first
public lecture on his arrival, over two thousand men formed a
philosophical commune, living together in an immense ὁμακοεῖον, as
his school was called, and following his laws as if they were divine
counsels (6.30).[46] Pythagoras also is shown acquiring a great public
following through a series of lectures to various groups of Crotonians
(8.37-11.57).

   In the school section as well, the chapter describing the tests to
which Pythagoras subjected his initiates (17.71-79) shows Pythagoras'
followers seeking him out. The two examples of specific individuals
who sought to attach themselves to Pythagoras follow the same pattern.
Abaris saw Pythagoras during his journey through Italy, immediately
guessed that he was the god Apollo, and attached himself to the
philosopher (19.91). Similarly, Cylon of Croton, the ringleader of the
mobs that destroyed the Pythagorean community, had attempted to join
the community but had been rejected by Pythagoras (35.248). Showing
the eagerness with which students sought out Pythagoras is a way of
praising his wisdom, and the students in these accounts function as a
demonstration of enthusiasm for the philosopher.

   The absence of call stories in the *Pythagorean Life* reflects the
school setting in which philosophy was commonly taught. Students
sought out the teachers of the philosophical schools just as they sought
out teachers of rhetoric. Even accounts of conversion to the philosophical life were placed in a school setting. The famous conversion of
Polemo took place in the school of Xenocrates (Diogenes Laertius

---

[46] The text is somewhat confused in this passage, and both Deubner and Nauck
drop some of the text as an interpolation. The confusion, however, does not affect
the account of how the two thousand became followers of Pythagoras.

4.17; Lucian, *The Double Indictment* 16). Similarly, the conversion related by Lucian in his *Letter to Nigrinus* took place in the house of the philosopher Nigrinus, where the unnamed convert had come to pay his respects.

The pattern of conversion suggested by the *Pythagorean Life* is one of public speeches aimed at the moral betterment of the general population, followed by individuals seeking out the philosopher for further teaching. This is very different from the Markan pattern, in which Jesus calls specific individuals even before his public addresses have been portrayed. While Jesus' teaching is greeted with an enthusiastic response, individuals from the crowds are not shown seeking to attach themselves to Jesus. Even the rich young man who seeks Jesus' instruction is not willing to follow Jesus (10.17-22). Only those who are healed seek to follow (5.18; 10.52).

The School of Pythagoras

The description of the Pythagorean school in the narrative section (6.29-32) is largely devoted to the Pythagoreans' belief in the divinity of the sage. They received his teachings as "divine counsels" and "counted him among the gods" (6.30) or as a being intermediate between the gods and humans.[47] Here the followers serve as a vehicle for the narrator's praise of Pythagoras. Iamblichus follows up a quote from Aristotle, indicating that the Pythagoreans viewed Pythagoras as a being intermediate between the gods and men, with a recital of the philosopher's accomplishments that made the characterization apt. The rest of the chapter succinctly describes Pythagoras' school in Samos, his decision to leave for Italy, and how rapidly he gained a following in Croton.

In the chapter on political activities (7.33-34), Pythagoras' followers appear as his agents. He liberated a number of cities and established laws in the same cities through two specific followers, Charondas of Catana and Zaleucus of Locri (7.33). As in the later section on Pythagorean virtues, the followers of Pythagoras are treated

---

[47] At least part of section 30 is from Nicomachus (=Porphyry 20), and it is likely that the entire discussion of Pythagoras' divinity in this chapter is from that source.

as extensions of Pythagoras and their accomplishments are presented as being one with his.

The understanding of the disciples as agents of Jesus appears also in Mark in two conspicuous passages, the commissioning of the twelve (3.14-15) and in the mission of the twelve (6.7-13), but it is not developed in the rest of the Gospel. Since the idea occurs in the commissioning scene, it probably reflects Mark's understanding of the historical function of the twelve. It may be intended as well to confer upon Mark's listeners the status of agents of Jesus. It does not help to advance the major themes of the Gospel, however, and so the theme receives no further development.

Popular Following

While most of the *Life* is devoted to the Pythagoreans' esoteric community, the narrative portion portrays Pythagoras as a popular preacher. As noted above, half of the twenty-six pages of the narrative section are devoted to a series of public exhortations given by Pythagoras to various social groups in Croton (8.37-11.57). The series of speeches depicts an outpouring of popular enthusiasm for Pythagoras.

The general impression of Pythagoras given by the narrative section of Iamblichus' *Life* is that of a popular preacher and social reformer whose school is an association of those who were particularly devoted to the moral pronouncements that he made to the public. In this he is reminiscent Socrates in Xenophon's *Memorabilia*. In the remainder of the *Life*, however, the popular preacher disappears and Pythagoras becomes the leader of an esoteric school.

The School of Pythagoras—Chapters 12-26

The next section of the *Pythagorean Life* (chapters 12-26) describes in some detail Pythagoras' school. Even though much of the material in this section describes the relationship between Pythagoras and his students, very few students appear as individuals. Instead, Iamblichus provides a great number of generalizations. The followers of Pythagoras for the most part appear as an abstraction.

At a number of points in the description of the Pythagorean school, Iamblichus uses a statement about a particular follower or about Pythagoreans in general to make a point about the Pythagorean school. The followers in these cases appear to be more or less equivalent to Pythagoras himself, and the things they do are to be taken as normative for the Pythagorean school. For example, Lysis' condemnation of Hipparchus for divulging Pythagorean secrets is presented as a typical case, defining the Pythagorean attitude toward such a revelation (17.75).

Individual followers

Abaris. The only one of Pythagoras' followers to receive more than a passing mention in this section is Abaris the Hyperborean (19.90-93). Iamblichus introduces Abaris to illustrate the proposition that Pythagoras adapted his instruction to each student's nature and power (19.90). This was a popular theory of education that is illustrated throughout Xenophon's *Memorabilia*.[48] Clearly Iamblichus is clutching at straws to illustrate the theory. Even though the principle of individualized treatment recurs in the discussion of the Pythagorean school, the material is striking for the absence of concrete instances of interaction between Pythagoras and his students.

The account of Abaris and Pythagoras contains the clearest and most unequivocal proof of the divinity of the sage. Abaris was a wonder-worker of no mean ability and a priest of Apollo. When he sees Pythagoras, he identifies him as the god, and Pythagoras confirms his belief by showing him his golden thigh and by describing details of the temple where Abaris held office. He also states he has assumed a human form in order to improve the condition of humanity.[49]

Iamblichus does not use the story as a proof of the divinity or holiness of Pythagoras but rather introduces it as an example of how the philosopher gave individual attention to his students.[50] Earlier,

---

[48] Other examples of the theory may be found in Malherbe, *Moral Exhortation*, 50-55.

[49] This seems to have been a confession and transfiguration story much like that found in Mark 8.27-9.9 before Iamblichus placed it in its present context.

[50] The Abaris story is mentioned, though not retold in detail, in a list of miraculous deeds presented in 28.134-36 as evidence of the piety and holiness of Pythagoras. This section follows Porphyry (*Life of Pythagoras*, 27-29) almost word for word. Iamblichus would appear to have the Abaris story in two separate sources. Another version of the golden thigh story, without any mention of Abaris,

Iamblichus had denied the reports that Pythagoras was the son of Apollo (2.7-8). In that passage he states that the soul of Pythagoras came from the realm of Apollo, where he was the god's companion or was otherwise closely related. Iamblichus does not present a consistent position on the divinity of Pythagoras, and his use of this story suggests that he did not consider it an important point.

Other followers. Only a handful of other Pythagoreans appear in this section. Most of them occur as negative examples, and many are not, in fact, direct followers of Pythagoras but are rather Pythagoreans from later times.

Perillus the Thurian and Cylon the prince of the Sybarites are examples of rejected candidates (17.74).[51] A letter from Lysis (fl. 388 BCE) to Hipparchus is introduced to show the Pythagorean attitude toward those who revealed the esoteric doctrines (17.75-78). Hippasus (fourth century BCE) is mentioned as having died at sea because he revealed the method of forming a sphere from twelve pentagons (18.88; cf. 34.247). Iamblichus may have believed, however, that these Pythagoreans were contemporaries of Pythagoras. Both Lysis and Hippasus appear in a list of "those who as young men were pupils of Pythagoras in his old age" (23.104).

The one positive depiction of a follower's action is Empedocles' rescue of his host through the power of music, overcoming the host's assailant by soothing him with a song (25.113-14).[52] This anecdote parallels a similar account of Pythagoras' use of music to prevent a Tauromenian youth from murdering the youth's mistress (25.112). There is, in addition, a list of Pythagoras' followers who continued the philosopher's practice of symbolic teaching (23.104). As in the narrative section, individual followers only appear incidentally to

---

is included in a list of miracles used as evidence that the philosopher was a god (28.140).

[51] Nauck considered this passage to be a gloss. Cylon, the prince of the Sybarites, presumably is the Cylon of Croton who led the mob against the Pythagoreans (chapter 35). Unless "the prince of the Sybarites" is metaphorical, however, there is a confusion in his origin.

[52] Empedocles (fl. 444) is also listed as one of the youthful pupils of Pythagoras.

illustrate a particular point or to indicate a connection between the practices of Pythagoras and those of later Pythagoreans.

Concern for students. Although Iamblichus has very little material with which to make the point, he attempts to show Pythagoras as being concerned with his individual students. Both his insight into past lives (14.63) and his healing use of music (15.64-65) are presented in this light, and the Abaris story, as noted above, is employed awkwardly to make the same point (19.90). An abstract discussion of the individualization of his instruction also is presented (18.80).

Pythagoreans as Exemplars of Virtue

Iamblichus' style changes again in the section from chapter twenty-seven to chapter thirty-three, which is the most extensive portion of the work. Chapter twenty-seven, concerning the civic activities of the Pythagoreans, consists almost entirely of anecdotes of actions of Pythagoras and named or unnamed Pythagoreans. Chapters twenty-eight through thirty-three, which discuss Pythagorean teaching and practice relating to the major virtues, combine Pythagorean ethical teachings with examples of virtuous actions by Pythagoreans. There is no attempt to confine the accounts to Pythagoras' immediate followers; the emphasis is on the entire Pythagorean school as an embodiment of virtue.[53]

This section is the climax of the work. It is clear from the earlier section that the purpose of the Pythagorean school was to develop the virtuous character of Pythagoras' followers. The description of the school shows the method; this section shows the result and gives the students who are to read the work the clearest example for their own action. The general principles of construction and characterization are similar throughout the section. We shall examine only three chapters, those devoted to civic activity, holiness, and temperance.

---

[53] Iamblichus' sources have confused the chronology of the Pythagorean school and have described some later Pythagoreans as immediate followers. In this section, however, Iamblichus relates two incidents that took place under the rule of Dionysius in the fourth century, BCE, which could not be confused with the period of Pythagoras' own lifetime.

Civic Activity

Chapter twenty-seven, on civic activity, is not included by Iamblichus in the section on virtues and differs from the rest of the section in its lack of theoretical material. It consists of anecdotes of various types, which Iamblichus classifies as κατά τὰς πολιτεία (27.122) and presents as illustrations of Pythagoras' value in public affairs (27.133).

There is little distinction made in this chapter between the actions of Pythagoras and those of his followers. There are four anecdotes that concern Pythagoras and seven that concern Pythagoreans. Throughout the section on the virtues Iamblichus presents the Pythagorean community as a whole as the exemplar of virtue. Certainly, the virtue of his followers is intended to redound to the credit of Pythagoras himself, but the primary rationale for including so much material about Pythagoreans appears to be different. Iamblichus is writing a *Pythagorean Life* rather than a biography of Pythagoras. Pythagoras is, of course, the prototype for a Pythagorean life, but his biography in itself is only a small part of the work. The bulk of the work concerns the life of Pythagoreans within the school setting (chapters 14-26) and outside of the school (chapters 27-33). The example of the virtuous and philosophic life of the followers of Pythagoras serves as a model for the beginning students being introduced to philosophy through the *Synagoge*.

It was a common practice to offer personal examples in moral exhortation.[54] A speaker or writer might offer himself as an example,[55] or he might point to a relative of his addressee or famous examples from the past. While Iamblichus does not link the account of Pythagoras' education to an explicit exhortation to his student readers, within a school environment Pythagoras serves as a model for

[54] A brief discussion with examples is in Malherbe, *Moral Exhortation*, 135-38. See also Benjamin Fiore, *The Function of Personal Example in the Socratic and Pastoral Epistles*, AnBib 105 (Rome: Biblical Institute, 1986). For the use of Jesus as an example in the New Testament with many examples of the concept of imitation from Greco-Roman philosophy, see Hans Dieter Betz, *Nachfolge und Nachahmung Jesu Christi im Neuen Testament* (Tübingen: J. C. B. Mohr, 1967).

[55] For a discussion of Paul's use of himself as an example in the context of the use of personal examples in the moral philosophers, see Malherbe, *Paul and the Thessalonians* 52-60.

students to emulate in their own pursuit of philosophy. It was not uncommon for the use of personal examples to take the form of lists of virtuous individuals. The list of faithful persons in Heb 11.4-38 illustrates the single virtue of faith. The praise of famous men in Sira 44.1-50.21 offers examples of several virtues while praising the history of Israel.

Mark has Jesus point to his own example in the exhortation in 8.31-9.1 and the teaching in 10.42-45. The prominence of these two passages in the structure of the Gospel and the emphasis given the teaching through the disciples' misunderstanding stresses the idea of Jesus' followers imitating his suffering. Mark can also use the disciples as examples to be followed, as in their response to the call of Jesus (1.16-20; 2.14) and their successful completion of the missionary tour (6.7-13, 30), but that is not a major theme of the Gospel.

Holiness

The chapter on holiness (chapter 28) is unique in the amount of material that concerns Pythagoras himself. The chapter actually has a dual focus, "his holiness" (ὁσιότης) and "the marvelous works that proceeded from it" (28.134).

Iamblichus concentrates a great deal of his miraculous material in this chapter. Since he apparently has dismembered one of his miracle sources (=Porphyry 23-31),[56] the concentration of such material in this chapter reflects a deliberate decision rather than the structure of his sources. While Porphyry simply presents the miracle stories without comment, Iamblichus provides an interpretive framework that indicates that the miracles are a witness to the holiness of the wonder-worker.

Iamblichus states the procedure applied in this chapter in 28.147: "For it is necessary that some deed be presented as a basis for belief in what is stated." This method is confined to this particular chapter, however, and in the succeeding chapters the examples become much more sporadic. One generally finds in these chapters only a few

---

[56] In addition to the material presented in this chapter, material from the Porphyry source is found in 8.36, 13.60-15.64, and 15.67.

examples intended to exemplify in a more general way the particular virtue being discussed.

Self-control

The chapter devoted to self-control is more typical of the virtues section in its balance of theory and examples. There are considerably fewer examples here, many general statements about Pythagorean practices, and no attempt to provide examples for all the teachings.

Two previously related incidents from the life of Pythagoras are mentioned as instances of Pythagoras' concern for temperance, his persuading the Crotonians to give up relations with courtesans and his use of music to restore the temperance of a youth driven wild by passion (31.195).[57]

Iamblichus relates in great detail a story about the Pythagoreans Myllias and Timycha to illustrate "the self-control of those men [the Pythagoreans] and how Pythagoras taught it" (31.189-94). A number of Pythagoreans allow themselves to be killed rather than enter a bean field. When the tyrant Dionysius attempts to force Myllias and his pregnant wife Timycha to tell him the reason for their action, they refuse, and when tortured, Timycha bites off her tongue so that she cannot divulge the secret.

Another anecdote, concerning Archytas, is related to bolster the general assertion that no Pythagorean punished a slave or chastised a freeman while angry. Archytas tells his negligent servants that they are lucky he is angry because they have escaped punishment as a result. Iamblichus notes but does not recount a similar anecdote concerning Clinias (31.197-98).

One final incident concerns Philolaus' publishing of the Pythagorean books. This incident is presented in neutral terms in the course of a passage praising the Pythagoreans for preserving the secrecy of their doctrines (31.199).

In addition to these specific incidents, there are a number of general descriptions of Pythagorean actions and attitudes. The reader is told that the Pythagoreans maintained their bodies in a constant condition, maintained a uniformly mild joy rather than vacillating from

---

[57] The accounts appear in 9.47-50 and 25.112.

one emotional extreme to another, and would withdraw alone to heal their passions if they did fall into anger or despondency (31.196, 198). All Pythagoreans were disposed toward each other as parents toward their children, and almost all credited Pythagoras with their own discoveries (31.198). They carefully preserved the secrecy of their writings (31.199). They would often ask people why boys were taught to take a moderate amount of food if that virtue was to be abandoned in adulthood (31.203-04). They exhorted all they met concerning the danger of pleasure (31.204).

The rest of the chapter is made up of various reports of Pythagorean teachings about temperance. At the end of the chapter, the reader is told that the Pythagoreans' deeds matched their teachings and that the teachings had been received from Pythagoras himself (31.213).

Iamblichus' Characterization of the Pythagoreans

In a number of ways, the characterization of the Pythagoreans remains constant throughout this section.

One-dimensional portrayals. Although names generally are given to the Pythagorean actors, very few of them appear as more than generic Pythagoreans. The wonder-workers Abaris, Empedocles and Epimenides form a separate class, but only Abaris attains any real distinctiveness. The Pythagoreans are little more than exemplars of the various virtues.

Uniformity of tradition. Throughout the work, Iamblichus assumes a uniformity of the Pythagorean tradition, both in thought and action. The reader is told frequently in the section on virtues that the Pythagoreans believe such and such or the Pythagoreans do such and such. There is no indication of any variation in practice.

The same assumed uniformity is apparent as well in the more abstract descriptions of the Pythagorean school earlier in the book. There are, for example, some discrepancies in the dietary regulations presented in various places and major discrepancies in the two views of the Pythagorean symbola or maxims that Iamblichus presents. Occasionally, Iamblichus says some say this and some say that, but usually the two views simply are placed in different chapters, and each is presented as universally true for all Pythagoreans.[58] As a result, an account of any individual Pythagorean can stand as evidence for the entire tradition.

Individual as example. The stories of individual Pythagoreans are introduced either as examples of specific points (as in chapter 28) or as more general examples of virtues. In very few cases does any individuality survive the focus on the particular virtue to be illustrated. The examples serve the dual purposes of providing proof of the superiority of the Pythagorean way of life (and, more generally, of the philosophic life) and of being inspiring examples for the students to follow in their own lives.

Iamblichus' tendency to view stories of Pythagoras and his followers as exemplars is underscored by his adaptation of narratives that were not originally used in that manner. We have already noted how the story of Abaris is used in chapter nineteen as an example of Pythagoras' attention to the individuality of his students. The chapter on courage contains another striking example. In this chapter, Iamblichus presents an epitome of a dialogue or series of dialogues involving Pythagoras, the tyrant Phalaris, and Abaris (32.215-21).[59] Clearly, the original contains a great deal of philosophical argument on various subjects as well as a dramatic sequence in which Abaris becomes convinced that Pythagoras is a god. This extended epitome is introduced by Iamblichus, however, as the best example of Pythagoras' courage and frankness (32.215).

Pythagoreans as extensions of Pythagoras. As a result of this homogenization, the reader is led to attribute the characteristics of individual Pythagoreans to Pythagoras as well. A number of clues suggest that one is intended to do so.

---

[58] Examples of the presentation of contrasting views include the dispute about whether or not ἀκουσματικοί are Pythagoreans (18.81) and the dispute about the source of the demonstrations attached to the maxims of Pythagoras (18.87-88).

[59] Although there is no way to determine the source of this sequence, it is quite consistent with the style of Apollonius' account of the destruction of the Pythagorean community. Both are fictionalized accounts using stereotypical situations not mentioned in other extant material about Pythagoras and written with an eye to drama.

One is the linking of similar stories, one attributed to Pythagoras and the other to a follower. For example, Iamblichus advances two anecdotes as evidence that Pythagoreans were not skeptical of supernatural occurrences. The first involves Pythagoreans living some time after the death of Pythagoras: When Eurytus tells a Pythagorean companion that a shepherd has heard singing near Philolaus' tomb, the other Pythagorean asks about the harmony of the song. The second involves Pythagoras himself: When someone asks Pythagoras about the significance of his father's conversing with him in a dream, Pythagoras indicates that it has no more significance than a conversation between two living persons (28.139; cf., 28.148).[60] The same method also is found in the accounts of three clever judgments given in arbitration, the first two given by Pythagoras, the last by an unnamed Pythagorean (27.123-24), and, in an earlier section, the two accounts of Pythagoras and Empedocles preventing murders through the power of their music (25.112-14). At another point, Epimenides' calling upon the Furies to achieve the destruction of his enemies is invoked as a parallel to Pythagoras' destruction of Phalaris through the oracles of Apollo (32.220-22).

Iamblichus also uses the action of a follower to illustrate both the teaching and the character of Pythagoras. Thus Pythagoras' injunction to avoid oaths is said to show the honor in which he held the gods and is illustrated by the willingness of a certain Pythagorean to lose a large sum of money rather than take an oath (28.150). In the beginning of the holiness chapter, the miracles of Pythagoras' followers are used as evidence of the philosopher's own holiness. In the midst of a recitation of Pythagoras' miracles, introduced as examples of his holiness, it is stated that Empedocles, Epimenides and Abaris performed similar miracles (28.134). His followers' miraculous abilities thus serve as further evidence of his own.

According to Iamblichus, the Pythagoreans also regarded themselves as extensions of Pythagoras. He praises them for ascribing

---

[60] The stories were already linked before finding their way into two separate sources used by Iamblichus. Thus the tendency is by no means a peculiar characteristic of Iamblichus himself.

their own discoveries to Pythagoras rather than claiming the glory of their own works (31.198).

Concluding Material

Two of the three concluding chapters are concerned primarily with the followers of Pythagoras. Chapter thirty-five describes the destruction of the Pythagorean community.[61] Chapter thirty-six gives the Pythagorean succession and a list of followers.

Destruction of the community
The destruction of the Pythagorean community in Croton · is described in great detail. Departing from his general procedure of providing only one unattributed account of historical events, Iamblichus in this case gives three different accounts, attributed to Aristoxenus, Nicomachus, and Apollonius (35.251, 254).

According to Aristoxenus and Nicomachus, the destruction of the community was instigated by Cylon of Croton, who ardently desired to join the Pythagorean community but was rejected by Pythagoras because of his violent and tyrannical character. While Pythagoras was absent, Cylon incited his followers to set fire to a house where the Pythagoreans were gathered, and only two were able to escape (35.248-49, 251). Afterward, the surviving Pythagoreans scattered to various places and were no longer involved in public affairs. Eventually the sect died out. Many Pythagorean doctrines were lost, but some were committed to writing by the survivors and handed down to their descendants as secret books (35.250-53).

The account of Apollonius offers considerably more detail, including a trial of the Pythagoreans, a forged book of Pythagorean teachings, a pitched battle and a later repentance on the part of the Crotonians (35.254-64).

In both versions, Pythagoras was absent at the time of the destruction of the community. The accounts are intended primarily to explain the disappearance of Pythagoreanism rather than to illuminate

---

[61] This is a standard part of a life of Pythagoras (Porphyry, *Life of Pythagoras* 54-58; Diogenes Laertius 8.39-40).

Pythagorean qualities, though Apollonius' version certainly draws on an ideal model of the opposition faced by a philosopher.[62]

List of Followers

The final chapter of the book is devoted to a short succession of the Pythagorean school, an extended list of two hundred eighteen known followers according to their cities and a separate section listing seventeen female followers. Succession lists are expected in accounts of philosophers or their schools, where they serve both to indicate legitimate followers and to show the substantial following the philosopher attracted.

The listing of the twelve in Mark (3.16-19) and in the other Synoptic Gospels (Mt 10.2-4; Lk 6.13-16) would have been understood as succession lists legitimating the twelve as the authorized repositories of the traditions concerning Jesus.

Description of the School

With the few exceptions noted above, the account that Iamblichus gives of the Pythagorean school in the second section of the *Pythagorean Life* is presented in generalizations rather than as a narrative of specific events. Pythagoras' students appear as an abstract group. Although the description of the Pythagorean school does not directly further our investigation of how followers are used in the portrayal of a teacher, some features of the school as described by Iamblichus are of interest for the understanding of Mark. This section will describe the most salient features of that account. The following

---

[62] The citation of Apollonius is an epitome of what appears to have been an extended, novelistic account. Ninon's speech is clearly influenced by the accusations against Socrates recorded by Xenophon. Like Socrates, Pythagoras is charged with despising those outside the group (*Memorabilia* 1.2.51-52), quoting Homer in opposition to the common people (1.2.58), opposing the selection of officeholders by lots (1.2.9), and teaching his companions to be tyrannical (1.2.56). The Pythagorean Democedes is condemned for organizing young men to establish a tyranny. The later repentance of the people parallels the Socratic tradition as well.

description is not intended as an historical description of Pythagoras' school, which may not have followed this pattern.[63]

Esoteric teaching. The Pythagorean school carefully preserved its teachings within the group (18.82; cf., 31.193-94). Divulging doctrines to those outside resulted in ostracism by the school (17.75; cf., 34.246) and was thought to bring divine retribution (18.88; cf., 34.247).[64] The Pythagoreans felt that the doctrines could benefit only those who had purified their moral character through the discipline of the school and thus should not be given to those who had not been so purified (17.75-78, 34.246).

Symbolic teaching. Iamblichus presents two theories concerning the Pythagorean συμβολά. One explanation holds that Pythagoras and his followers taught by means of symbols to conceal the "divine mysteries from those uninitiated in their secret customs" (23.104). The other maintains that the Pythagorean maxims (ἀκούσματα) were intended as literal rules of action and originally were taught by Pythagoras with reasons and demonstrations. Since some of the students were slow, however, he taught them the maxims without giving the reasons.[65]

Selection of students. It is stressed that Pythagoras did not accept all those who sought to become his followers. He questioned them about their relations with their kin, observed their character, and

---

[63] For historical reconstructions of the actual school of Pythagoras, see Burkert, *Ancient Pythagoreanism*; Vogel, *Pythagoras and Early Pythagoreanism*; Kurt von Fritz, *Pythagorean Politics in Southern Italy: An Analysis of the Sources* (New York: Octagon Books, 1977); E. L. Minar, *Early Pythagorean Politics in Practice and Theory*, CCM 2 (Baltimore: Waverly Press, 1942); Peter Gorman, *Pythagoras: A Life* (London: Routledge & Kegan Paul, 1979); J. Philip, *Pythagoras and Early Pythagoreanism*, PSV 7 (Toronto: University of Toronto Press, 1966).

[64] But see 31.199, where Philolaus is said to be the first to publish the Pythagorean commentaries as a result of his poverty. Philolaus appears in a positive light throughout the *Life.*

[65] According to an alternative version, many of Pythagoras' associates were busy with politics and had very little time for study, so the philosopher taught them what they should do without providing the reasons (18.87-88).

There is an interesting parallel between explanations of the Pythagorean symbols and explanations of Jesus' parables. In both cases, some (such as Mark) think they masked secret teachings, while others (like many modern biblical scholars) understand them as clear teaching that was later misunderstood.

made judgments based on their physiognomy (17.71). He accepted students if they possessed an ability to remain silent, a quickness to learn, modesty, an absence of immoderate passion, gentleness, and love (20.94). The candidates had to pass through a probationary period that involved rigorous disciplines and the study of various theorems. If they were found to be dull, they would be expelled at the end of this period (17.72-74).

Probationary period. Anyone who passed the initial selection process was ignored for the next three years. After this three-year period, the candidates began a five-year term of silence. At the outset of this term, they gave all of their property to the community. If they were rejected at the end of the probationary period, they received double their property back. Rejected candidates were considered to be dead (17.72-74). The purpose of the probationary period was to purify the candidates' souls to make them worthy of receiving the Pythagorean doctrines. Their intellect needed to be unclouded as well to benefit from the philosopher's instruction (17.75-78).

Divisions of students. Students of the Pythagorean school were divided into an inner and an outer group. These generally are referred to as μαθηματικοί and ἀκουσματικοί (18.81). The μαθηματικοί were privy to the secret teachings, while the ἀκουσματικοί heard the teachings without explanation (18.81). The inner circle of students also is referred to as ἐσωτερικοί (17.72). A further distinction also is made between Πυθαγόρειοι, who held their possessions in common, and Πυθαγορισταί, who did not. The Πυθαγόρειοι may have included both μαθηματικοί and ἀκουσματικοί, though that point is contested (18.80-81). The Πυθαγόρειοι apparently are the same as a group called the κοινόβιοι, who also are defined by the characteristic of holding possessions in common (6.29-30).[66] In addition to this, there are holders of offices called πολιτικοί, who included the subgroups οἰκονομικοί and νομοθετικοί. Among their other duties, the πολιτικοί were guardians of the common property (17.72; cf., 17.74, 18.89). The proliferation of terminology undoubtedly is due to the number of different sources Iamblichus used, but the sources all

---

[66] This passage is marked as doubtful in the Teubner text. The κοινόβιοι are contrasted to the ἀκουσματικοί.

agree that the Pythagorean community was well organized and that
there were distinct levels within the community.

Use of music. In addition to teaching musical theory (26.121),
Pythagoras used music to free his students from impure passions and
to cure them of physical ailments (15.64-65, 25.110-14).

Diet. Pythagoras' students were subject to certain dietary
restrictions, but the various sources Iamblichus used differ as to the
exact nature of the restrictions.[67]

Community of property. Those who were accepted as candidates
for the Pythagorean school deposited all their property with community
trustees (17.72). Those who passed the probationary period continued
to hold their property in common. In other passages, however, it is
said that only the closer associates of Pythagoras, called Pythagoreans
or κοινόβιοι, held their property in common, while another group,
labeled Pythagorists, did not (18.81, 6.29-30).[68]

Throughout this section the Pythagorean school as presented by
Iamblichus is a tightly organized institution stressing the moral
development of the students and a closely guarded esoteric teaching.
The Pythagoreans are presented as a moral and intellectual elite who
gave unswerving allegiance to their master.

The Divinity of Pythagoras

Because of the importance of the christological issue in the
narrative of the Gospel of Mark, it will be helpful to consider

---

[67] In one place it is said that his students were ordered to abstain from all
animal food and any others that hinder the reasoning power as well as from wine
(16.68-69; cf., 6.32). In another passage, it is said that they ate herbs, maize, the
flesh of all animals that it was lawful to immolate and every food eaten with bread.
They avoided fish and drank wine only for supper and not at lunch (21.97-98). A
third passage makes a distinction between more and less advanced students. The
more advanced students were not allowed wine or animal food. The πολιτικοί
were also forbidden to eat animals. Others were permitted to eat the flesh of
certain animals, but not the heart or brains, though they were required to observe
a period of abstinence. Mallows, two species of fish and beans were also
forbidden (24.106-09).

[68] As noted above, 6.29-30 has been disputed as a later gloss.

separately the relationship between Pythagoras' followers and the discussions of the philosopher's divinity in Iamblichus' account.

Recognition of Divinity

Although the divinity of Pythagoras is asserted several times in the *Pythagorean Life*, in marked contrast to the role of christology in the Gospel accounts of Jesus, it is treated as a peripheral matter.

Several of the most prominent discussions of the divinity of Pythagoras occur in the early chapters of the work. In the account of his birth, it is asserted that the belief of Epimenides, Eudoxus, and Xenocrates that Pythagoras was fathered by Apollo must be rejected as a legend created by a certain Samian poet (2.5, 7). As a correction to this mistaken belief, it is stated that the soul of Pythagoras came from the realm of Apollo, where it was a companion of the god or otherwise closely related to him. One can discern this from both his birth and his wisdom (2.8). In the next paragraph, however, it is asserted that many people reasonably concluded that he was a son (παῖς) of a god on the basis of his beauty, majesty and temperance (2.10).

Recognition of the divinity of Pythagoras is not restricted to any particular group. A group of sailors who intend to sell the sage into slavery become convinced from his mode of life that he is a divine daemon and build an altar for him (3.14-17).

The first discussion of Pythagoras' followers is devoted largely to their belief in his divinity. They received his teachings as "divine counsels" and "counted him among the gods as a certain good and philanthropic daemon."[69] He was variously considered to be the Pythian or Hyperborean Apollo, Paeon, one of the daemons who inhabit the moon or one of the Olympian gods appearing in human form to give "the saving spark of philosophy and happiness" to mortals (6.30). According to Aristotle, the Pythagoreans recognized three classes of rational beings: god, man and a being such as Pythagoras. No particular reason is given for the Pythagorean belief, but the author

---

[69] This portion appears in Porphyry (*Life of Pythagoras* 20), attributed to Nicomachus. The following discussion, including the quotation of Aristotle, may come from Nicomachus as well, but it is not included in Porphyry's excerpt.

states that such a classification is apt because of the knowledge that Pythagoras imparted to humanity (6.31).

The Pythagoreans' belief in the divinity of their master is more focused than the general beliefs mentioned earlier, but as their opinions are so varied, they do not appear to have achieved a substantially clearer insight into Pythagoras' divine nature than did the Samians or sailors. The major difference between the two groups is the universality with which the Pythagoreans held the belief. Iamblichus shows no interest in trying to reconcile the specific claims. It seems to be enough that Pythagoras is in some sense divine.

Other discussions of the divinity of Pythagoras in later portions of the work support the conclusion that Iamblichus had no well-developed doctrine of the divinity of Pythagoras. The account of Abaris' recognition of Pythagoras as Apollo and the subsequent revelation of Pythagoras' golden thigh may have implied in its original context that the recognition of the sage's divinity was privileged information that could be discovered only by one who was himself a superhuman wonder-worker (chapter 19). In its present context, as an example of the philosopher's attention to the individual capacities of his followers, however, that implication is subordinated to the narrative's new purpose. In a later list of miracles, Pythagoras' golden thigh, the sign of his divine identity, is said to have been revealed at the games, where it would have been generally visible (28.140).

There also is very little interest in the narrative depiction of the moment of recognition. The Abaris story in chapter nineteen appears to have dramatized that moment in its original context, but Iamblichus minimizes its impact. Pythagoras' miraculous recognition of his friend's murderer is said to have caused some to consider him to be Apollo (27.133), but it is only mentioned in passing.

Miracles and Divinity

For the most part, the divinity of Pythagoras is not predicated upon the miracles he performed. The discussions of his divinity in the first six chapters do not mention any miraculous action. After the only miracle mentioned in the narrative section, the reader is told that Pythagoras' appearance, rather than the miracle, revealed his true identity (8.36).

Iamblichus' sources are inconsistent on this point, however, and he has made no effort to reconcile the different points of view. The attitude that miraculous action is proof of divinity is present in the stories of Abaris' recognition of Pythagoras (19.91-93), where the miracles confirm Abaris' recognition, and of Pythagoras' recognition of his friend's murderer (27.133), where the miracle itself induces recognition of Pythagoras as Apollo.[70] It is most overt in a list of miracle stories which are introduced as proof that the philosopher was a god (28.140).

For the most part, miracle stories are presented simply as facts. Only rarely are there reactions noted from followers or others. Iamblichus' two principal miracle sources are in the form of lists of miracles and have no narrative setting.[71] The one miracle in the narrative section is taken from one of these lists (8.38=Porphyry 25). The only miracles that seem to have come from a narrative setting are the recognition scene with Abaris (19.91-93) and one account of Pythagoras' discovery of a murderer (30.176-78).

The assertion of the divinity of Pythagoras lends weight to the study of philosophy as a holy undertaking. In the prologue, Iamblichus notes the custom of calling on the gods before undertaking the study of philosophy. This is all the more appropriate in the study of Pythagoreanism: "Since in the beginning it was transmitted from the gods, it can only be understood through the gods" (1.1). The discussion of the Pythagoreans' belief in the divinity of the sage is introduced by the observation that they received his teaching as "divine counsels" (6.30). The miracle list adduced as proof of Pythagoras' divinity is introduced with the observation that the Pythagoreans "maintain that the guarantee of the doctrines that they received is the fact that the one who first uttered them was not an ordinary person but a god" (28.140).

[70] Iamblichus includes another version of this story, however, in which the miraculous intuition does not lead to the conclusion that Pythagoras is Apollo but rather to the charge from his opponents that he had asserted that he was Apollo (30.176-78).

[71] Those sources are the miracle list in Porphyry (*Pythagoras*, 23-31), attributed to Nicomachus (in section 20, apparently intended to include the miracle list) and the list in 28.140-43.

Comparison with Xenophon and Mark

There are three distinct approaches to the depiction of Pythagoras' followers in Iamblichus' *Pythagorean Life*. In the narrative of the
philosopher's life, his followers play only a minor role. Much more
attention is given to the public works of the sage than to his relationships with his closer followers. In the description of Pythagoras'
school, his students generally are presented as an abstract body. In the
discussion of the virtues, however, accounts of individual Pythagoreans
play a major role in illustrating the virtues as embodied in the
philosophical life.

While Xenophon's ideal of philosophy as the discussion of
specific matters by concrete individuals is honored by Iamblichus'
protestation that Pythagoras tailored his teaching to the capacities of
individual students, philosophy is presented in this work as a way of
life and a system of doctrines generally applicable to the elite group
that is capable of the philosophic life. Narratives of particular
Pythagoreans are not used as much to define the character of the sage
as to provide examples of the virtues of the philosophic life.

The organization of the Pythagorean community into different
levels and the existence of specific community offices contrasts
strikingly with Xenophon's portrayal of the Socratic community, which
has no formal structure. The Jesus community of the Gospel of Mark
is similar to the Pythagorean model in its division between an inner
group of disciples who receive explanations of public teaching and the
crowds of followers who do not. It also has a leadership group, the
twelve, that has been officially appointed to office. The interchange
between Jesus and the disciples in 6.35-37 suggests that, at least in
their travels, the disciples held their property in common, but this fact
is not given any prominence in the narrative.

We might expect the rhetorical role of followers to be different
in the *Pythagorean Life* and in the Gospel of Mark simply because of
the difference in the authors' approaches to biography. According to
the classification of Friedrich Leo, there were two types of biography
in the Greco-Roman world. One was the Alexandrian type, which
combined a short chronological account of the protagonist's life with
a systematic characterization of his achievements. The second was the

Peripatetic type, which was a chronologically ordered narrative.[72] Iamblichus' *Pythagorean Life* belongs to the Alexandrian type, while the Gospel of Mark is arranged as a chronological narrative.

Since the Alexandrian type of biography does not have a sustained narrative throughout, it is less likely that a narrative role would be developed to any extent. It is not surprising, then, to find the followers of Pythagoras introduced only incidentally to support points being made about their teacher. The amalgamation of Pythagoras and his followers to exhibit a Pythagorean character in the section on the virtues is not simply an outgrowth of the style of biography. This represents more specifically the intention of Iamblichus in writing the *Life*. Since the Gospel of Mark is a chronological narrative, Mark may achieve a more sustained portrayal of the disciples. In this respect, the Gospel is much closer to Philostratus' *Life of Apollonius of Tyana*, which will be examined next.

---

[72] Friedrich Leo, *Die griechisch-römische Biographie nach ihrer litterarischen Form* (Leipzig: Teubner, 1901).

4

PHILOSTRATUS' *LIFE OF APOLLONIUS*

The next text to be considered is Philostratus' work *Life of Apollonius of Tyana*. Apollonius was an itinerant wonder-worker and philosopher who lived in the first century CE. By the early third century, when Philostratus wrote his biography, a cult had developed around Apollonius, and he had attracted the attention of the Severan emperors. Later, partially as a result of Philostratus' biography, Apollonius was put forward as a wonder-worker superior to Jesus in a book by Hierocles. Of the three Greek biographies to be examined, this work is the closest to Mark in a number of ways. It is the only one structured chronologically as a narrative of the adult life of the hero. As in Mark, the travels of the hero provide an outline for that chronology. The trial of Apollonius before Domitian plays a prominent role, similar in scope to the passion of Jesus in the Gospels. The *Life* is also similar to Mark in avoiding a systematic presentation of the doctrines of its hero, presenting instead teachings on various subjects as occasions occur in the chronological framework.

Philostratus

Relatively little is known about the sophist Flavius Philostratus, the author of *The Life of Apollonius*.[1] We can positively identify him

---

[1] For the biographical problems associated with Philostratus, see Karl Münscher, "Die Philostrate," *Philologus*, Supplementband 10 (1907) 469-558; F. Solmsen, "Philostratos 8-12," *PW* 20.1.124-77; Graham Anderson, *Philostratus: Biography*

with the author of the *Lives of the Sophists*, since he refers to his earlier *Life of Apollonius* in that work (*Lives of the Sophists* 570). In addition, he is probably the author of the *Heroicus* and the first set of the *Imagines*.[2] According to the *Suda*, Philostratus flourished under Septimius Severus (193-211), practiced in Athens and Rome, and died during the reign of Philip the Arab (244-49 CE). He may have been born in Lemnos.[3] His father may have been a sophist.[4] Most likely he came from a well-to-do family, since he studied rhetoric with four prominent sophists, Proclus of Naucratis (*Lives of the Sophists* 602) and Hippodromus of Larissa (*Lives of the Sophists* 618), both taught by students of the great Herodes Atticus; Damian of Ephesus (*Lives of the Sophists* 605-06); and Antipater from Phrygian Hieropolis (*Lives of the Sophists* 609), teacher also of the sons of Septimius Severus. He had the resources to enable him to travel widely; he claimed to have seen the western ocean himself (*Life of Apollonius* 5.2) and to have traveled most of the known world (*Life of Apollonius* 8.31). John S. Traill suggests that he may be the same Flavius Philostratus who was a hoplite general in Athens during the reign of Septimius Severus.[5]

Philostratus was part of the literary and rhetorical movement generally known as the second sophistic.[6] Much of our information

---

and *Belles Lettres in the Third Century A.D.* (London, Sidney and Dover, NH: Croom Helm, 1986), 3-7, 291-96; Glen Warren Bowersock, *Greek Sophists in the Roman Empire* (Oxford: Clarendon Press, 1969), 4-7.

[2] The *Suda*, the principal source for information about Philostratus apart from his own works, lists three Philostrati. The notices are confused and have resulted in some debate about which works belong to each of the authors. See F. Solmsen, "Some Works of Philostratus the Elder," *TAPA* 71 (1940) 557-69; Anderson, *Philostratus*, 291-96.

[3] Eunapius calls him a Lemnian (*Lives of the Philosophers and Sophists*, 454). Philostratus himself calls a younger Philostratus, a relative of his, Philostratus of Lemnos (*Lives of the Sophists* 628). The family may be from Lemnos, or Eunapius may have confused the two.

[4] The *Suda* says his father was a sophist who lived at the time of Nero, but that is chronologically impossible.

[5] John. S. Traill, "Greek Inscriptions Honoring Prytaneis," *Hesperia* 40 (1971) 324; noted with approval by Anderson (*Philostratus*, 5-6). This office was second in honor behind the eponymous archon and entailed supervision of the grain supply, the markets and shipping, as well as other civic and religious duties.

[6] For the literary background of the second sophistic, see Brian P. Reardon, *Courants littéraires grecs des IIe et IIIe siècles après J.-C.*, ALUN 3 (Paris: Les

about the movement comes from Philostratus' own *Lives of the Sophists*, and, in fact, our author is the source of the name "second sophistic" (*Lives of the Sophists* 481). The second and third century sophists were rock stars, professors, and trivia whizzes all rolled into one. Fabulously successful as rhetorical performers, they enlivened their orations with clever figures of speech, archaic Attic dialect of studied classic purity, virtuoso vocal performances, and conspicuous erudition on the most diverse subjects. The sophists generally came from upper-class families, since few others could acquire the extensive education necessary for the calling. Since they charged their pupils exorbitant sums to learn the sophists' art, however, many sophists were able to increase their wealth. As a result of these two factors, successful sophists often were among the most prominent men of their cities. The best had reputations throughout the Roman Empire, and several received favors from the emperors such as exemption from liturgies. Some were friends of emperors or were able to acquire positions in the imperial court.[7]

It is not unfair to say that the sophistic movement valued style over substance. Nevertheless, while frivolous themes might be used for rhetorical display, the sophists' rhetorical and literary skills often were turned to serious topics. Philostratus, the chronicler of the second sophistic, generally is judged to be only a second-rate practitioner of the art.

The Salon of Julia Domna

Philostratus himself indicates that he was part of the circle of philosophers and literati around the empress Julia Domna (*Life of*

Belles Lettres, 1971). For a social history of the movement, Bowersock, *Sophists*; Ewan Lyall Bowie, "The Importance of Sophists," *YCS* 27 (1982) 22-59. For other aspects, *idem*, "The Greeks and Their Past in the Second Sophistic," *PP* 46 (1970) 2-41; Glen Warren Bowersock, ed., *Approaches to the Second Sophistic: Papers Presented at the 105th Annual Meeting of the American Philological Association* (University Park, PA: American Philological Association, 1974).

[7] Bowersock, *Sophists*: Family background, 21-24; social prominence, 26-29; exemptions from liturgies, 30-42; friends of emperors, 47-50; appointments in the imperial court, 50-58.

Apollonius 1.3).[8]   Although it has been stated often that the salon of
the Empress Julia included most of the leading intellectual figures of
the time, in fact very little is known about the group.[9]   Philostratus
was a member (*Life of Apollonius* 1.3), as was the sophist Philiscus
(*Lives of the Sophists* 622).[10]   According to Dio Cassius, the empress
turned to philosophy as a diversion when the enmity of the powerful
prefect of the guard, Fulvius Plautianus, obstructed her from other
pursuits.[11]   In these early years, it is unlikely that many of the
ambitious intellectuals of the time would have felt inclined to associate
with Julia and risk the enmity of the brutal and much more powerful
Plautianus,[12] but Dio Cassius mentions the circle again late in the
reign of Caracalla,[13] at which time the empress ran the day-to-day
affairs of the empire and held power second only to that of the
emperor himself. During that period, when Philostratus was part of the
salon, association with the empress might serve well the advancement
of a literary and political career.[14]

    If Philostratus intended his *Life of Apollonius* to appeal to the
tastes of the empress, it would seem that she was much more interested
in rhetoric than philosophy.   The philosophical thought of the
Philostratean Apollonius is mostly trite and superficial.   Apollonius
surpasses the other philosophers in his philosophical life style rather
than in the depth of his thought.   A letter from Philostratus to Julia of

---

[8] For discussion of Julia Domna, see Anthony Birley, *Septimius Severus: The
African Emperor* (Garden City, NY: Doubleday, 1972); Gertrud Herzog, "Julia
Domna," *PW* 10 (1919), 926-35; Erich Kettenhofen, *Die Syrischen Augustae in der
Historischen Überlieferung: Ein Beitrag zum Problem der Orientalisierung*,
Antiquitas, Reihe 3, Band 24 (Bonn: Rudolf Habelt Verlag, 1979); Louis C.
Purser, "Court Religion at Rome in the Third Century," *PCAS* 10 (1911-12) 43-65;
Mary Gilmore Williams, "Studies in the Lives of Roman Empresses: I. Julia
Domna," *AJA* NS 6 (1902) 259-305.

[9] See discussion in Bowersock, *Sophists*, 101-09 and notes.

[10] Bowersock conjectures that the Gordian to whom Philostratus dedicates the
Lives of the Sophists might also be part of the circle, since Philostratus states that
he was in Syrian Antioch at a time when the empress is known to have been there,
but that is hardly conclusive proof (*Sophists*, 105-06).

[11] Dio Cassius 75.15.6-7.

[12] Bowersock, *Sophists*, 106.

[13] Dio Cassius, 78.18.2.

[14] See also the reservations of Miriam Griffin, Review of G. W. Bowersock,
Greek Sophists in the Roman Empire, *JRS* 61 (1971) 280.

disputed authenticity (*Epistle* 73) suggests that she had a serious interest in stylistic questions.[15]

Apollonius of Tyana

The accuracy of Philostratus' depiction of Apollonius has been discussed frequently in the scholarly sources, and no consensus has developed as to the nature of the historical Apollonius.[16]

The major sources for our knowledge of Apollonius are Philostratus and the collection of letters attributed to the sage.[17] In addition, he is mentioned in a number of other ancient writers.[18] The pre-Philostratean sources are unanimous in depicting Apollonius as a thaumaturge or μάγος. Lucian states that Alexander of Abonoteichos was a student of a student of Apollonius', who passed on to him his skill as a γόης, a wizard or charlatan (*Alexander the False Prophet*, 5). Dio Cassius includes an account of Apollonius' clairvoyant announcement of Domitian's assassination in Ephesus (67.18, cf., *Life of*

---

[15] Anderson, *Philostratus* 3. The authenticity of this letter has been questioned (e.g., Bowersock, *Sophists*, 104-05). The authenticity is supported by Graham Anderson ("Putting Pressure on Plutarch: Philostratus, *Epistles* 73," *CP* 72 [1977] 43-45) and Robert J. Penella ("Philostratus' Letter to Julia Domna," *Hermes* 107 [1979] 161-68).

[16] For summaries of the discussion, see Ewan Lyall Bowie, "Apollonius of Tyana: Tradition and Reality," *ANRW* 2.16.2.1685-92; Gerd Petzke, *Die Traditionen über Apollonius von Tyana und das Neue Testament*, SCHNT 1 (Leiden: E. J. Brill, 1970), 10-16. For various positions, Eduard Meyer, "Apollonius von Tyana und die Biographie des Philostratos," *Hermes* 52 (1917) 371-424; J. Mesk, "Die Damisquelle des Philostratos in der Biographie des Apollonios von Tyana," *WS* 41 (1919) 121-38; Johannes Hempel, *Untersuchungen zur Überlieferung von Apollonius von Tyana*, BRel 4 (Stockholm: Bonnier; and Leipzig: Voigtländer, 1920/21); F. Grosso, "La Vita di Apollonio di Tiana come fonte storice," *Acme* 7 (1954) 331-530; Glen Warren Bowersock, "Introduction," in *Philostratus, Life of Apollonius*, (Harmondsworth: Penguin, 1970); Anderson, *Philostratus*, 175-97.

[17] The letters are available in a critical edition with commentary by Robert Penella (*The Letters of Apollonius of Tyana: Critical Text with Prolegomena, Translation and Commentary*, *Mnem*Sup, 56 [Leiden: E. J. Brill, 1979]). For the discussion concerning their authenticity, see, besides Penella, the sources noted by Bowie ("Apollonius of Tyana," 1671, n. 74).

[18] Thorough discussions may be found in Petzke, *Apollonius*, 19-36; Bowie, "Apollonius of Tyana," 1671-85.

Apollonius 8.26) and elsewhere refers to him in derogatory terms as a
γόης καὶ μάγος (78.18.4). Philostratus states that the best-known
story about Apollonius concerned his capture of a vampire in Corinth
(4.25). Apollonius' biographer Moeragenes also shows him to be a
μάγος of considerable power.[19]

There are several indications that the imperial court was attracted
to the figure of Apollonius. Philostratus states that the emperor
Hadrian, who reigned twenty to forty years after the sage's death,
collected his correspondence and kept in the palace the book of
Pythagorean tenets that the sage had received at the shrine of Tropho-
nius (8.20). Philostratus notes that an earlier account of the sage had
been written by Maximus of Aegae, "a writer whose reputation for
oratory won him a position in the emperor's Secretariat" (1.12).[20] It
is not unreasonable to assume that his work, apparently little more than
a pamphlet containing accounts of Apollonius' education and wondrous
works at the temple of Asclepius, might have circulated in the court
among those whose interests were so inclined.

The Severans were particularly attracted to the sage. Septimius
Severus passed through Tyana,[21] Caracalla built a shrine to the
sage,[22] and the emperor Alexander is said to have kept a cult statue
of the philosopher as well as statues of Christ and other deities.[23]

Date and Purpose

It is generally thought that the Life of Apollonius was published
shortly after the death of Julia Domna in 217, since the work contains

[19] See the discussion of Moeragenes below, pp. 111-13.

[20] The historicity of the Maximus source is attacked by Meyer ("Apollonius von
Tyana," 401-02), but that view seems excessively skeptical and has not received
other support.

[21] Dio Cassius, 76.15.4.

[22] Dio Cassius, 78.18.4.

[23] *Historia Augusta*, Alexander Severus 29.2. In general, the *Historia* is not a
very reliable source. The account is questioned by Ronald Syme (*Ammianus and
the Historia Augusta* [Oxford: Clarendon Press, 1968], 61, 138) and Bowie
("Apollonius of Tyana," 1670, n. 71). Cf., Ramsay MacMullen, *Paganism in the
Roman Empire* (New Haven and London: Yale University Press, 1981), 92-93.

no dedication to the empress.[24] Johannes Göttsching has argued that the descriptions of good and bad rulers reflect Severus, on the one hand, and Caracalla and Elagabalus, on the other, and were intended to inspire the young Severus Alexander, yielding a date between 222 and 235 BC.[25]

Given Philostratus' general disinterest in Neopythagoreanism in the rest of his work, it is unlikely that he intended his *Life* as an apologetic for a particular philosophy.[26] In fact, the Apollonius that he presents is largely a Pythagorean in terms of his exotic life style and belief in reincarnation;[27] Apollonius also parallels Pythagoras in the types of miracles he performs.[28] Philostratus has no interest in the systematic development of Neopythagorean thought such as one finds in Nicomachus or Moderatus.[29]

If Philostratus had little interest in promoting a particular philosophy, then why did he write the *Life*? He states that the empress

[24] Wilhelm von Christ, Wilhelm Schmid, and Otto Stählin, *Geschichte der griechischen Litteratur*, 6th ed., HKA 7, 2 vols. (Munich: Beck, 1911-13), 2.2, 2.773-74; Solmsen, "Philostratos," 139; B. F. Harris, "Apollonius of Tyana: Fact and Fiction," *JRH* 5 (1969) 190; Petzke, *Apollonius von Tyana*, 5. This conclusion is questioned by Bowie, who believes the work was intended as a romance, a genre that does not usually contain dedications ("Apollonius of Tyana," 1670). A. Calderini argues for a first redaction ca. 202-05 ("Teoria e practica politica nella 'Vita di Apollonio di Tiana'," *RIL* 74 [1940/41] 213), but the suggestion has received no support.

[25] Johannes Göttsching, *Apollonius von Tyana* (Leipzig: Max Hoffmann, 1889), 74-89.

[26] So Bowie, "Apollonius of Tyana," 1672; Wolfgang Speyer, "Zum Bild des Apollonios von Tyana bei Heiden und Christen," *JAC* 17 (1974) 50.

[27] For the Pythagoreanism of Philostratus' Apollonius, see Anderson, *Philostratus*, 136-67; Thomas Gregory Knoles, "Literary Technique and Theme in Philostratus' *Life of Apollonius of Tyana*," dissertation (Rutgers, 1981), 246-54; MacMullen, *Enemies of the Roman Order*, 114-15. The elements of Pythagoreanism mentioned by Philostratus in 1.1 are the sage's former life, vegetarian diet, and abstinence from animal sacrifices and clothing made from animals, as well as the vow of silence imposed on his followers. All these elements appear in the account of Apollonius (Knoles, "Literary Technique," 246-47 and n. 35).

[28] This was first noted by Ferdinand Christian Baur (*Apollonius von Tyana und Christus, oder das Verhältnis des Pythagoreismus zum Christentum* [Tübingen: Fues, 1832], 171-227). For a summary of the parallels, see Knoles, "Literary Technique," 266-67.

[29] "The emphasis is strongly upon the trappings of the system, rather than upon its philosophical principles" (Knoles, "Literary Technique," 248-49).

commissioned him to write the account based on the notes of Damis. Philostratus may have needed no other reason than to please his royal patroness, but why would Julia have commissioned the *Life*? The answer may lie in Julia's relationship with her son, the emperor Caracalla. According to Dio Cassius, Caracalla delighted in wizards and erected a shrine to Apollonius, a "wizard and Magos in the strict sense of the word (γόης καὶ μάγος ἀκριβής)" (78.18.4).[30] Dio Cassius also reports that Caracalla "studied philosophy most of the day" even after becoming emperor, but that his training had little effect on his character, which was brutal and frivolous (78.11.3). He ordered assassins to murder his brother Geta, with whom he shared his rule, in his mother's apartment, and Geta died clinging to Julia (78.2). The murder badly strained the relationship between Caracalla and his mother, but the empress loved power too much to abandon him. Julia tried to reform her son—Dio Cassius states she gave him excellent advice—but he paid her no heed (78.18.2).

If Caracalla was enamored of Apollonius, then an account of his life would make an excellent vehicle for motherly advice. By means of the Damis source, Julia and her able assistant Philostratus were able to transform Apollonius from a wandering Pythagorean ascetic and miracle-worker into the adviser of emperors and kings.[31] Damis is, at least by implication, the source for all the reported interaction between Apollonius and his royal benefactors and antagonists. He is also, at least by implication, the source for the travelogue portions that, especially in the Indian section, closely parallel the travels of Alexander, with whom Caracalla obsessively identified himself.[32] Both the emperor and the Damian Apollonius restored shrines to Achilles.[33] Since Philostratus shared a common teacher with Caracalla, there may

---

[30] Author's translation.

[31] For a defense of the historicity of Apollonius' relations with the kings and emperors, see Steven Jackson, "Apollonius and the Emperors," *Hermathena* 137 (1984) 25-31.

[32] Conversations with Brahmans also occur in the Alexander histories and romances (Arrian, *History of Alexander* 7.2.2ff; Plutarch, *Alexander* 64; Strabo 15.1.63ff; cited by Anderson, *Philostratus*, 212 and 224, n. 95).

[33] Caracalla: Dio Cassius 78.16.7; Apollonius: *Life of Apollonius* 4.23.

have been enough goodwill between the two for the sophist to undertake his educational venture.[34]

The exhortation to moderation that makes up much of Apollonius' royal advice certainly could have been aimed at Caracalla, and many of the specific attributes for which Apollonius faults the emperor Nero were mirrored in Caracalla's degenerate life. Like Nero, Caracalla drove chariots in the arena, fought in gladiatorial contests, and learned to play the lyre. Dio Cassius states that he even begged gold pieces from the audiences at the games where he drove.[35]

Both Julia and Caracalla appear to have died before Philostratus completed the work. Afterwards the author may have published the *Life* simply to show off his literary skill, but it is equally likely that he was jockeying for position with Julia's nephews, Elagabalus and Alexander Severus, who were successively named emperors after the short reign of Macrinus. As noted above, Alexander Severus is reported to have had a great reverence for the sage. Göttsching's theory that Philostratus hoped to educate Alexander by means of the *Life* is certainly plausible.

In addition to its didactic purpose, the *Life of Apollonius* was intended to entertain as well. Significant portions, such as the travelogue sections, are developed primarily for their entertainment value. Any sophistic production served to display the literary talent and erudition of the sophist, and Philostratus' work contains a number

---

[34] Philostratus reports that Antipater reproved Caracalla for his murder of Geta (*Lives of the Sophists* 609). This passage suggests the danger inherent in the forthright approach to instructing the emperor on such matters.

[35] Dio Cassius 78.10.1-2; 13.7; 17.4. Note the interchange between Apollonius and the philosopher Philolaus concerning Nero in *Life of Apollonius* 4.36: "'And what,' said Apollonius, 'O Philolaus, are the occupations of the autocrat said to be?' 'He drives a chariot,' said the other, 'in public; and he comes forward on the boards of the Roman theatres and sings songs, and he lives with gladiators, and he himself fights as one and slays his man.' Apollonius therefore replied and said: 'Then, my dear fellow, do you think that there can be any better spectacle for men of education than to see an emperor thus demeaning himself?'" (LCL tr.). Other parallels with Nero's activity denounced by Apollonius or others include: murder of a close relative (4.38); playing the lyre (5.7, 7.12); and competing in the games (5.7). Parallels with Domitian's activity include the murder of his brother (6.32). In addition, Apollonius attacked gladiatorial contests in Athens (4.22). See further, Göttsching, *Apollonius von Tyana*, 83-86.

of themes typical of the second sophistic.[36] There also are significant parallels with features found in the romances.[37]

Whether or not Philostratus intended the imperial family to be the primary readers of his work, it is clear that he intended his work to be read and appreciated by a wider circle as well. The wider readership may not have been devotees of the Apollonius cult,[38] and the defense of Apollonius against the charges of magic (e.g., 1.2; 5.12; 7.39) suggests that he assumed that his readers would be open to such negative views.

Charles Talbert has argued for a cultic function for certain biographies of philosophers, including Philostratus' *Life of Apollonius*.[39] The *Life* may in fact have served that function, but if our argument concerning its origin is valid, it only did so in an ironic way. Because of their support for the Apollonius cult, both Caracalla and Alexander Severus could be expected to show interest in the biography, but there is no indication that Philostratus had a particular devotion to the cult of Apollonius. The work might masquerade as a cultic foundation myth, but its primary functions were instruction and entertainment. In fact, in its attack on the more extreme traditions of Apollonius' wonder-working, it appears to have transformed the image

---

[36] Göttsching, *Apollonius von Tyana*, 61-62; Anderson, *Philostratus*, 124-33.

[37] For parallels with the romances, see Anderson, *Philostratus* 229-31; Bowie, "Apollonius of Tyana," 1664-65. A number of scholars have argued that the *Life* belongs to the genre of romance, including Eduard Schwartz (*Fünf Vorträge über den griechischen Roman* [Berlin: G. Reimer, 1896], 131), William Reginald Halliday ("Damis of Nineveh and Walter of Oxford," *ABSA* 18 [1911-12] 234-380), Meyer ("Apollonius von Tyana," 377), and Bowie ("Apollonius of Tyana," 1663-67). A classification of the *Life* as an aretalogy is argued by Ferdinando Lo Cascio (*La Forma Letteraria della Vita de Apollonio Tianeo*, QIFGUP 6 [Palermo: Bruno Lavagnini, 1974]). See also the discussion of genre in Petzke, *Apollonius von Tyana*, 58-62.

[38] For evidence of the cult of Apollonius, see *Life of Apollonius* 8.31; Dio Cassius 78.18.4; Bowie, "Apollonius of Tyana," 1687-88.

[39] Talbert, *What is a Gospel?* 101-09; *idem*, "Biographies of Philosophers and Rulers as Instruments of Religious Propaganda in Mediterranean Antiquity," *ANRW* 2.16.2 (1978), 1626-46. Talbert's analysis has been criticized by David E. Aune ("The Problem of the Genre of the Gospels: A Critique of C. H. Talbert's *What is a Gospel?*" in *Gospel Perspectives: Studies of History and Tradition in the Four Gospels*, ed. by R. T. France and D. Wenham, vol. 2 [Sheffield: JSOT Press, 1981] 9-60).

of Apollonius from what was current in the cult. Nevertheless, the biography did help establish the Apollonius cult on a firmer foundation and allowed pagan propagandists such as Hierocles to set up Apollonius as an alternative to Christ.

Philostratus, Moeragenes and the Magos Tradition

Until recently the scholarly consensus held that the biography by Moeragenes that Philostratus rejects (1.3) presented Apollonius in an unfavorable light,[40] but this conclusion has been challenged effectively by Ewan Lyall Bowie and D. H. Raynor.[41] On the basis of Origen's citation of the work (*Contra Celsum* 6.41), Bowie concludes that the biography of Moeragenes was modeled after Xenophon's *Memorabilia* and presented Apollonius in a positive light as both philosopher and magician.[42] Raynor argues that the incident cited by Origen suggests a contest in which Apollonius overcomes Euphrates and an unnamed Epicurean by his magic, showing the superiority of magic and philosophy combined over philosophy unaided by magic.[43] Bowie

[40] E.g., Bowersock, "Introduction," 12; F. C. Conybeare, "Introduction," in *Philostratus, The Life of Apollonius of Tyana*, LCL, 2 vols. (London: W. Heinemann; New York: Macmillan, 1912), 1.viii.

[41] Bowie, "Apollonius of Tyana," 1673-79; D. H. Raynor, "Moeragenes and Philostratus: Two Views of Apollonius of Tyana," *ClassQ* 34 (1984) 222-26. The view of a hostile Moeragenes is defended by Anderson (*Philostratus*, 299-300).

[42] Origen says the work was four books long (like the *Memorabilia*), and he refers to it as τὰ ᾿Απολλωνίου τοῦ Τυανέως μάγου καὶ φιλοσόφου ἀπομνημονεύματα. Bowie and Raynor understand this to be the title, but it may be intended as description.

[43] Raynor, "Moeragenes," 225. The text of the passage, from the edition of Marcel Borret (*Contre Celse*, SC 132 [Paris: Éditions du Cerf, 1967]), is as follows: περὶ μαγείας φαμὲν ὅτι ὁ βουλόμενος ἐξετάσαι, πότερόν ποτε καὶ φιλόσοφοι ἀλωτοί εἰσιν αὐτῇ ἢ μή, ἀναγνώτω τὰ γεγραμμένα Μοιραγένει τῶν ᾿Απολλωνίου τοῦ Τυανέως μάγου καὶ φιλοσόφου ἀπομνημονευμάτων· ἐν οἷς ὁ μὴ Χριστιανὸς ἀλλὰ φιλόσοφος ἔφησεν ἀλῶναι ὑπὸ τῆς ἐν ᾿Απολλωνίῳ μαγείας οὐκ ἀγεννεῖς τινας φιλοσόφους ὡς πρὸς γόητα αὐτὸν εἰσελθόντας· ἐν οἷς οἶμαι καὶ περὶ Εὐφράτου τοῦ πάνυ διηγήσατο καί τινος ᾿Επικουρείου.

Raynor's translation ("Moeragenes," 222-23): "On the subject of magic, we say that anyone who wishes to examine the question whether or not even philosophers can be caught by magical means should read what Moeragenes has written in his memoirs of the magician and philosopher Apollonius of Tyana. In

suggests that the work was intended to show the superiority of Pythagoreanism over Cynicism and that Philostratus belittles the work simply because it had become the standard biography.[44] Raynor has suggested more plausibly that Philostratus seeks to undermine the work because he seeks to minimize Apollonius' role as a μάγος and the sage's wonder-working.[45]

Philostratus' attitude toward Moeragenes' depiction of Apollonius as a powerful μάγος can be discerned from his treatment of the incident reported by Origen. Not only does he make no mention of the use of magical power against Euphrates, but he goes to great lengths to distance the sage from any confrontation with his enemy. He notes that Euphrates conducted daily disputes with Apollonius' followers Menippus and Nilus but claims that Apollonius was too busy training Nilus to carry on the disputes himself (6.28). Unfortunately, this leaves Apollonius instructing Nilus by mental telepathy. One suspects this is the point in Moeragenes' narrative where Apollonius defeated Euphrates by magic and that Philostratus, in his eagerness to deny the account, has not bothered with the niceties of logic.

---

this work the author, who is no Christian but a philosopher, says that certain not undistinguished philosophers were worsted by the magic of Apollonius, although when they approached him they regarded him as a mere charlatan. Among these, I think, he included both the well-known Euphrates and a certain Epicurean."

The passage is not clear and has been translated, e.g., by Chadwick, as the two philosophers' being originally attracted to Apollonius and later abandoning him. Anderson accepts such a translation (*Philostratus*, 299). Raynor's translation, however, seems more likely philologically and fits the context much better, since Origen is arguing the vulnerability of philosophers to magic. A story depicting Apollonius in a contest with two other magicians is found in Anastasius Sinaita (*PG* 89, 524d-25b). See Robert J. Penella, "An Overlooked Story about Apollonius of Tyana in Anastasius Sinaita," *Traditio* 34 (1978) 414-15.

[44] Bowie, "Apollonius of Tyana," 1673-79. Bowie tentatively identifies Moeragenes with the Moeragenes that appears in Plutarch's *Table Talk* and an Athenian inscription, which would place the work in the first half of the second century, CE.

[45] Raynor, "Moeragenes and Philostratus," 224-26.

Moeragenes belongs to a tradition that viewed the title μάγος in a positive light.[46] Two letters of Apollonius to Euphrates (*Epistles* 16 and 17) claim the term μάγος as an honorable title in contrast to Euphrates' disparaging use of the term.[47] One of these specifically links the term with the Magi of Persia. As Dio Cassius, or his epitomator, also refers to Apollonius as "a Magos in the strict sense of the term,"[48] there appears to have been a well-developed tradition relating Apollonius to the Magi. Philostratus indicates that the testament of Apollonius, which he cites as one of his sources, contains an account of the philosopher's conversations with the Magi (1.26). Even in Philostratus, magician in the negative sense usually is denoted by the term γόης, though μάγος also appears with a negative sense.[49]

Philostratus distances Apollonius from the Magos tradition by minimizing his contact with the Magi. Since he forbade Damis to accompany him in his conversations with the Magi, there is no detailed report, and Apollonius' judgment concerning them, "They are wise, but not in all respects," places him in a position superior to them (1.26).[50] In keeping with his emphasis on Apollonius as the adviser of kings and the exemplar of fearlessness before temporal power, Philostratus has written his account of Apollonius' stay in Babylon in terms of his relations with King Vardanes rather than the Magi.

[46] The ambiguous valuation of the term μάγος is reflected also in Apuleius' *Apologia* 25-26, in which he defends magic as the knowledge of the Persian μάγοι. See the discussion in Susan R. Garrett, *The Demise of the Devil: Magic and the Demonic in Luke's Writings* (Minneapolis: Fortress Press, 1989) 12-13.

[47] Raynor, "Moeragenes and Philostratus," 224.

[48] Μάγος ἀκριβής (Dio Cassius 78.18.4).

[49] E.g., γόης is used in 4.18; 5.12; 7.17; 7.39; 8.7.2; 8.7.3. In 1.2, however, Philostratus condemns those who, because of Apollonius' association with the Magi, Brahmans, and Gymnosophs, "regard him as a μάγος and slander him as one skilled in the violent art." In the same chapter μαγεύειν and μάγῳ τέχνῃ are used in a derogatory sense. The use of the μάγος terms in this chapter is linked to the argument that Apollonius was misunderstood as a μάγος in the negative sense from his association with the Babylonian Μάγοι. Thus, Philostratus prefers the unambiguous term γόης for magician in the negative sense but can also use the term μάγος with a negative connotation.

[50] In his speech to Vardanes, Apollonius also places himself in a position to judge the wisdom of the Magi (1.32).

Sources

There has been spirited debate about the authenticity of the Damis source ever since Eduard Schwartz suggested that Damis was simply the literary creation of Philostratus, reflecting the practice of citing fictitious sources common in romance writing.[51]   There are serious problems with the historical facts presented in sections that seem to rely on the authority of Damis.[52]   These same sections also reflect a number of interests typical of a third century sophist such as Philostratus.[53] The most telling argument against the Damis source, however, is the nature of the argument mounted in favor of it by Graham Anderson, the most recent scholar to present a detailed defense. Although Anderson claims, rather unconvincingly, to have identified the historical Damis as an Epicurean philosopher who attached himself to Apollonius, he is forced by the weight of the evidence to pare down the alleged source to a collection of aphorisms accompanied by a few biographical notes such as one finds in *Secundus the Silent Philosopher* or Lucian's *Demonax*.[54]   If the Damis source consists of no more than that, the bulk of Philostratus' work still must be considered the free invention of the author.

It is most likely, however, that in the early chapters of book one

---

[51] Schwartz, *Fünf Vorträge*, 126. The theory was expanded and popularized by Halliday ("Damis," 234-38) and Meyer ("Apollonius von Tyana," 371-424). The historicity of the Damis source is accepted by Mesk ("Damisquelle," 121-38), Hempel (*Untersuchungen*, 26-32), Grosso ("Vita di Apollonio," 331-530), Petzke (*Apollonius von Tyana*), Bowersock ("Introduction"), Lo Cascio (*Forma letteraria*, 32-34), MacMullen (*Enemies of the Roman Order*, 71; 310, n. 24; 311, n.28), and Anderson (*Philostratus*). It is rejected by Solmsen ("Philostratos," coll. 149-50), Bowie ("Apollonius of Tyana," 1653-71), Robert J. Panella ("Scopelianus and the Eretrians in Cissia," *Athenaeum* 52 [1974] 295-96; *idem, Letters*, 1, n. 3), and Martin Hengel (*The Charismatic Leader and His Followers* [New York: Crossroad, 1981] 27). For summaries of the discussion, see Knoles, "Literary Technique," 9-13; Bowie, "Apollonius of Tyana," 1653-55, 1663; and Petzke, *Apollonius von Tyana*, 67-72.

[52] Bowie, "Apollonius of Tyana," 1655-62. Anderson tries to counter this argument by minimizing the amount of material that is attributed to Damis (*Philostratus*, 158-66).

[53] See above, n. 36.

[54] Anderson, *Philostratus*, 158-69 and 172-73, n. 93.

(1.4-17) Philostratus followed the work of Maximus of Aegae fairly closely. These chapters are more episodic, without the sustained narrative line of the portion of the work ascribed to Damis.[55] Also absent from these early chapters are the long dialogues and sophistic interests that pervade the rest of the work. Finally, one can note a much greater interest in the idea of converting the dissolute to a more philosophical life.[56] While there certainly are traces of the use of sources in the remainder of the book, the bulk of it appears to derive from Philostratus himself.[57]

Depiction of the Students' Role

There is very little formal description of the role of Apollonius' followers in Philostratus' *Life*.[58] This is especially noteworthy since the work is written with explicit reference to the Pythagorean tradition (1.1-2),[59] and, as is evident from the *Pythagorean Life* of Iamblichus, there was a rich tradition of description of the Pythagorean school. This lack of concern about the definition of the students' role reflects the setting for which the *Life* was produced. It is not a school or cult book but a work to entertain and enlighten the imperial family in particular and the literate public in general. In Iamblichus and Mark, on the other hand, the intended readers consider themselves followers of the particular sages whose lives are narrated and thus are concerned how to be followers. These works provide prescriptive and descriptive models after which they may pattern themselves.

---

[55] See the discussion below, pp. 137-38, on the use of Damis in sustaining a continuous narrative. Although Anderson seeks to restrict radically the amount of material attributed to Damis, the clear impression is that Damis is the principal source.

[56] Apollonius' brother in 1.13, many of "the most unrefined people" (LCL tr.) in 1.17.

[57] The work of Moeragenes may be a source for some portions, especially for the miracles of Apollonius and his relationship with Euphrates.

[58] For other discussions of Apollonius' followers in the *Life*, see Petzke, *Apollonius von Tyana*, 182-83; Robbins, *Jesus the Teacher*, 105-07, 147-55, 208-09.

[59] Especially 1.2: "For quite akin to theirs [Pythagoras' and his followers'] was the ideal which Apollonius pursued, and more divinely than Pythagoras he wooed wisdom and soared above tyrants" (LCL tr.).

Philostratus portrays Apollonius much like the description of the ideal philosopher in Dio Chrysostom's *Discourse* 32. Dio criticizes philosophers who restrict themselves to teaching in schools (32.8). The ideal philosopher is engaged with the world. He is a noble, independent soul who speaks boldly but without harshness, working for the good of humanity rather than for glory or gain (32.11-12).[60]

As with many Greco-Roman philosophers, including Socrates and Pythagoras, Apollonius' teaching is intended not so much to impart knowledge as to develop character.[61] Philosophers were not considered true teachers unless their character conformed to their instruction. This attitude is evident in the chapters on the virtues in Iamblichus' *Pythagorean Life* (28.134-33.240).[62] The emphasis on Apollonius' character rather than his knowledge reflects this understanding of a philosopher as one who has developed a true character.

The emphasis on the individual permeates the work. While Iamblichus makes use of individual Pythagoreans as exemplars of the community as a whole, reducing even the most noteworthy, such as Empedocles, to the same homogeneous status,[63] in Philostratus the emphasis is wholly on the confrontations between Apollonius and the noteworthy individuals of his time, whether kings and emperors such as Vardanes, Phraotes, Nero, Vespasian, Titus, Domitian, and Nerva, or philosophers such as Iarchus, Thespesion, Demetrius, Musonius, Dio Chrysostom, and Euphrates. While the Socrates of Xenophon was a philosopher by virtue of his instruction of all whom he met, and the Pythagoras of Iamblichus was a philosopher primarily by virtue of his instruction of his school, Apollonius is a philosopher by virtue of his superiority to the great individuals with whom he came into contact.

---

[60] For a thorough discussion of Dio's presentation of true and false philosophers in this discourse, see Abraham J. Malherbe, "'Gentle as a Nurse': The Cynic Background to 1 Thessalonians 2," *NovT* 12 (1970) 203-17.

[61] For other statements about character development as the goal of philosophy, see the excerpts in Malherbe, *Moral Exhortation*, 30-34.

[62] Other statements of this principle may be found in Malherbe, *Moral Exhortation*, 34-40.

[63] Note, for example, 28.135-36, where the miracles of Empedocles, Epimenides, and Abaris are mentioned. Abaris is the only follower to escape the homogenization process.

Call Stories

The way in which followers are shown to become adherents of their teachers reflects in significant ways the relationship envisioned between the two. Socrates is shown confronting all whom he meets with rational challenges to their own understanding of the world and carefully leads Euthydemus both by rational argument and by clever appeals to his pride to undertake philosophical study. Iamblichus includes no accounts of Pythagoras winning individual followers other than Abaris and the youth Pythagoras pays to learn mathematics. His students flock to him on the basis of an already-established reputation, and he is more concerned with driving away the unfit than with converting the reluctant.

In Philostratus' account of Apollonius, we are shown on a number of occasions individuals joining themselves with Apollonius or some other teacher. These episodes are not all of one type.

As Apollonius himself is the ideal student of philosophy, his adoption of the philosophical life serves as a model of philosophical commitment. In this way the portrayal of the philosopher parallels that of Iamblichus' Pythagoras. Apollonius is destined to possess great wisdom even before his birth. The Egyptian god Proteus, famous for his wisdom, appears to Apollonius' mother and proclaims that the child she bears will be none other than the god himself (1.4). While his father provides him with a rhetorical education, he himself seeks out philosophers of all schools (1.7).[64] He also undertakes the Pythagorean disciplines on his own initiative, since his Pythagorean teacher is a hopeless hedonist (1.7-8; 1.14). He travels to the farthest parts of the world—Babylon, India, and Ethiopia—to test his wisdom with the great sages living there. Thus, while Apollonius brings his wisdom to fruition through discipline and diligent study, this diligence in the pursuit of wisdom reflects his innate philosophical character and serves only to unfold his natural wisdom.

---

[64] Apollonius describes his adherence to Pythagoreanism as a choice from among competing philosophies rather than a conversion to philosophy (6.11). The same *topos* occurs in Justin, *Dialogue with Trypho* 2.3-6; and Josephus, *Life* 11. See Niels Hyldahl, *Philosophie und Christentum: Eine Interpretation der Einleitung zum Dialog Justins*, ATDan 9 (Copenhagen: Munksgard, 1966) 148-59.

Although the reasons why Apollonius' followers decide to follow him are rarely made explicit,[65] it is clear that philosophical character is in large part an innate quality that is developed rather than created by association with a teacher. Damis associated with Apollonius because he admired Apollonius and had a passion for travel. Upon hearing the sage's claim to know all languages without having studied them, Damis worshiped him and regarded him as a daemon (1.19). Later, in a comic scene in the Brahmans' court, Damis declares that he followed Apollonius because he desired to be a wise and educated man, to travel and become a Hellene (3.43). Damis' mixed motivation is consistent with his results as a student, since he never achieves a fully philosophical character.

Philostratus provides no motivation for Demetrius' adherence to Apollonius (4.25), but since Demetrius was an established philosopher with his own following, clearly one is to infer that he recognized in Apollonius a wisdom superior to his own. Demetrius does not follow Apollonius on his travels, and he appears only infrequently in the rest of the narrative.[66] They remain, however, good friends. The student-teacher model exemplified here is similar to the relationship between Apollonius and the Brahman sage Iarchus. Apollonius associated with Iarchus for a limited time and later remained on warm terms with him. This contrasts strongly with the Gospel of Mark, where discipleship is dependent on an intense personal relationship and is characterized by the close physical association implied by the terminology of following.

Two other conversions related by Philostratus also function as indications of Apollonius' superiority in philosophy. Menippus, one of the most prominent of Apollonius' followers in the narrative, is brought to the sage by Demetrius along with the rest of his best pupils

---

[65] The catalog of motivations in 4.1 might be considered an exception, but the people involved appear to have no special commitment to Apollonius, nor do they undertake a period of study with him. Thus they correspond to the crowds in the Gospel of Mark rather than the disciples.

[66] His warning to Apollonius on the latter's entrance into Rome to face Domitian (7.10-14) and his later concern about Apollonius' safety (8.11-15), both narrated at great length, are used to illustrate Apollonius' superior courage. Demetrius appears quite courageous in the episodes relating to Nero (4.42 and 5.19), and this earlier boldness makes his fear for Apollonius even more striking as a testimony to Apollonius' courage.

(4.25). Once again no explicit motivation is provided (4.25), but since Menippus already was committed to a philosophical life, his adherence to Apollonius is not a conversion to philosophy but reflects his judgment that Apollonius' has more to teach than Demetrius. Nilus' adherence to the sage is similar (5.12, 14-17). Nilus already was committed to a philosophical life under the tutelage of the Gymnosophs. He switches his allegiance to Apollonius after the sage bests Thespesion, the leader of the Gymnosophs, in argument. In Thespesion's own account of his life, it is clear that his choice of the philosophical life was made before he searched out the Gymnosophs, who were renowned for their wisdom (6.16). The underlying sense of competition among teachers for the best students probably reflects the attitudes of the star professors in the philosophical and rhetorical schools contemporary with Philostratus.

Timasion similarly had proved his philosophical character by rejecting his stepmother's improper advances at great cost to himself, and he joins Apollonius' group when he recognizes them to be philosophers (6.3). Earlier he had lived with the Gymnosophs (6.9). The consul Telesinus, who studied philosophy with Apollonius, was also inclined to the philosophical life and joined Apollonius through his own initiative (4.40). Similarly, the kings and emperors who value the wisdom of the sage—Vardanes, Phraotes, Vespasian and Nerva—were all predisposed to the pursuit of wisdom.

In all of these cases, philosophical commitment grows out of innate character.[67] There is no expectation that all people should be able to live the philosophical life; philosophical training simply brings out the inherent capacity of the individual. A person with only a moderate capacity for the philosophical life, such as Damis, cannot be raised to the highest levels even by a lifelong association with the greatest philosopher.

There is, however, another strain of thought that appears occasionally in the narrative, the idea that a great philosopher has the

---

[67] The attitude is also reflected in the requirements given for admission into the philosophical school of the Brahmans. Not only must the prospective student himself have an upright character, but his parents and grandparents as well must pass the character test (2.30).

power to convert even the most dissolute persons to a philosophical life. This attitude is stressed in the early chapters, which are derived from Maximus of Aegae. In these chapters Apollonius reforms his dissolute brother, though he does not convert him to philosophy (1.13), and during his stay in Antioch, we are told, "He converted to himself the most unrefined people" (1.17, LCL tr.). The conversation between Apollonius and the arrogant king at the banquet of Iarchus (3.26-33) is similar to this episode. Although Apollonius does not convert the king to the philosophical life, he does succeed in changing the king's opinion of Greeks, and the king, who initially was hostile to the sage, changes his opinion and offers Apollonius the hospitality of his palace.

Apollonius Leaves No School

In keeping with the individualistic orientation of Philostratus' depiction of the sage, Apollonius leaves no school to succeed him. Damis, his faithful follower, is told to continue to philosophize (8.28), but there is no suggestion that he taught or formed a school, and the fact that his memoirs were in the possession of a kinsman rather than a school or library (1.3) is further argument against such a possibility.[68] Apollonius' appearance to the youth who doubts immortality does take place at a school in Tyana, but the school does not appear to have any connection with Apollonius, who, after all, had not been in Tyana for many years.[69] There is no indication that Apollonius' followers ever collected the writings mentioned in various parts of the text, nor is any mention of a school made in Philostratus' discussion of his sources (1.2-3).

There are indications that Apollonius had a school during his own lifetime, but these are incidental to the main thrust of the narrative. In 1.16, a chapter derived from Maximus of Aegae, there is a short description of Apollonius' school in Antioch, part of an account of his daily schedule reminiscent of Iamblichus' *Pythagorean Life*

---

[68] If Damis is a literary construct of Philostratus, it is not surprising that he should have founded no school, but Philostratus could have created a follower who carried on a school of Apollonius.

[69] The last previous mention of Tyana is in 1.31, when Apollonius, just entering his manhood, returns home to cure the vices of his brother. Cf. Apollonius, *Epistle* 47, in which the philosopher promises to return to Tyana.

(21.96-100). School activity also is indicated in the convoluted passage by which Philostratus distances Apollonius from the disputes with Euphrates (6.28), in which the sage is said to be busy training Nilus, and in the laconic notice that "he stayed in Sicily and taught philosophy there as long as he had sufficient interest in doing so" (5.18, LCL tr.). These remain exceptions, however, part of the background for the important activities of the wise man.

The Greek philosophers Philostratus mentions—Demetrius, Musonius, Dio and Euphrates—similarly are shown acting as individuals rather than teaching in a school setting. Demetrius does have a group of followers, and Philostratus says he converted several of his companions (γνώριμοι) to Apollonius (4.25), but the other accounts of Demetrius, such as his denunciation of the Roman baths (4.42), reflect individual activity.

In contrast to the Greeks, the exotic philosophers—the Magi, the Brahmans and the Gymnosophs—are shown as having well-organized scholastic communities.[70] While this depiction undoubtedly is influenced by the traditions about these communities available to Philostratus, it does not conflict with his portrait of the ideal wise man as a lone hero. The exotics possess esoteric wisdom, and by transmitting their wisdom to Apollonius, they function in the narrative to validate the sage as the possessor of all knowledge. It is Apollonius, however, rather than the exotics, who is shown to embody the ideal of the wise man. He is clearly superior to the Magi and Gymnosophs (1.26; 6.10-32).

The exotic schools help to make another point. In depicting such faraway places, Philostratus does not have to be constrained by the facts and can create philosophical utopias. Both the Magi and the Brahmans are shown in the role of institutionalized advisers to kings. Philostratus seems to be suggesting that the Roman rulers also should rely on the advice of philosophers and sophists, such as himself.

---

[70] Note the strict criteria for admission into the Brahmans' philosophical school (2.30).

Lack of Structured Instruction

Considering the strict regimen associated with Pythagoreanism, it is remarkable how informal Apollonius' instruction of his followers is shown to be. Although the passage from Maximus of Aegae describes Apollonius' daily schedule (1.16), there is little indication that he imposed this schedule on his followers.[71] In fact, there is no indication in the rest of the narrative that Apollonius himself followed such a schedule. Similarly, he does not impose a period of silence upon Damis or any of his other followers,[72] although that was a central part of his own self-discipline (1.14-15). He does impose on Damis, at least initially, an abstinence from meat and alcohol, but later he removes the ban since it has no positive effect on his follower's character (2.7).[73]

The symbolic maxims of Pythagoras are also missing from Apollonius' pedagogy. For the most part, he teaches in a straightforward manner, with opaque sayings restricted to prophecies (5.11; 6.32), a paradoxical description of the Brahmans (3.15, 6.11),[74] and the verbal trap he lays for the border guard (1.20).[75]

---

[71] The one exception to this general lack of concern with imposing a philosophical discipline upon his followers is the notice in 5.21, "It was an essential part of [his followers'] philosophic discipline to imitate [Apollonius'] every word and action." (LCL tr.)

[72] In contrast again to the Maximus passage, which states that there were certain religious rites that "he only communicated to those who had disciplined themselves by a four years' spell of silence" (1.26, LCL tr.).

[73] It is not clear whether this is intended seriously or as a tactic to shame Damis into compliance. The readers are told that οἱ περὶ τὸν Δάμιν took to eating and drinking with enthusiasm, but it is unclear who those are and whether Damis is included with them.

[74] In both these passages, Philostratus apologizes for Apollonius' riddle. The sophist had little sympathy for this way of speaking.

[75] Jonathan Z. Smith's characterization of riddle speech as "characteristic" of Apollonius ("Good News is No News: Aretalogy and Gospel," in *Christianity, Judaism and Other Greco-Roman Cults: Studies for Morton Smith at Sixty*, ed. by Jacob Neusner, SLA 12 [Leiden: E. J. Brill, 1975], Part 1, 26, n. 16; 28) is a gross exaggeration, though it may have been more typical of the historical Apollonius than Philostratus' version. Philostratus was embarrassed by riddling language (3.15; 6.11). Eugene E. Lemcio's inclusion of 7.22 among examples of a pattern of ambiguous speech, incomprehension, critical rejoinder, and explanation ("External Evidence for the Structure and Function of Mark iv.1-20, vii.14-23 and viii 14-21," *JTS* 29 [1978] 331, n. 2) is also misleading, since Damis' concern is

While the idea of esoteric knowledge plays a significant role in the characterization of the sage, only Apollonius is privy to the esoteric secrets.[76] Damis is excluded from any contact with the Magi (1.26) as well as from hearing the occult secrets of the Brahmans (3.41).[77]

Apollonius does not instruct Damis in any orderly fashion, as we have seen in Socrates' instruction of Euthydemus or Pythagoras' instruction of his students. The dialogues between Apollonius and Damis are occasioned by the immediate circumstances of their situation. A review of the topics of conversation between the two shows, in book one, discussions of the meaning of the portent of the lioness and her cubs (1.22), the meaning of Apollonius' dream (1.23), Apollonius' opinion of the Magi (1.26), the hymns of Damophyle (1.30), the adulterous feelings of eunuchs (1.33), whether Apollonius should receive gifts from King Vardanes (1.33-34), and their desire to depart for India (1.39). Not only is this not systematic instruction, but very little of it is more than the idle chitchat of a pretentiously overeducated sophist. Only the discussion of the acceptance of gifts seems designed to develop in Damis a more philosophical character.

Nor does the quality of Damis' instruction improve in later books. In book two, Apollonius questions Damis on whether he is closer to God for being high on a mountain (2.5), and the two discuss whether it is necessary to abstain from palm wine (2.7), the nature of elephants (2.11, 2.14-15), painting (2.22), and the cleverness of King Phraotes (2.36). Once again the sophistic interests clearly predominate over the philosophical.

While the nonphilosophical nature of Apollonius' conversations with Damis reflects Philostratus' own sophistic interests, the conversa-

---

occasioned by the danger that Apollonius faces rather than his difficulty in comprehending the saying of the sage. See also the discussion of Apollonius' riddles in Petzke, *Apollonius von Tyana*, 111-16.

[76] With the exception, once again of the passage in 1.16.

[77] In spite of the fact that Apollonius published these secrets in a four-book work, περὶ μαντείας ἀστέρων. As a literary strategy, the ploy is successful in imputing to Apollonius greater knowledge than the author can convey. Philostratus expresses his own doubts about divination, and his attempt to clean up Apollonius' image is evident here in the avoidance of an explicit discussion of the "science" of divination as in the earlier exclusion of a discussion of the knowledge of the Magi.

tions indicate as well Damis' subordinate position in the narrative. Philostratus wants to show Apollonius as the instructor of kings rather than the teacher of a bumbling barbarian from Nineveh.[78] The conversations between Apollonius and the various kings and philosophers in the narrative are considerably more philosophical than those between the sage and his follower.[79]

Organization of Followers

In contrast once again with the highly structured Pythagorean school described by Iamblichus, there seems to be little or no structure among Apollonius' following. Although Damis faithfully follows his master for a period of approximately fifty years,[80] he never acquires a position of authority. Nilus and Menippus, who both possess greater intellectual ability than Damis,[81] achieves a higher status than the more senior follower, since Apollonius relies on them rather than Damis to carry on the controversy with Euphrates (6.28). Menippus also takes over for a time the role as Apollonius' chief dialogue partner (5.7; 5.14-17). This shift is primarily a literary device for providing variety in the narrative rather than a reflection of formal standing in the group, but it does show that Damis did not receive greater attention than the other followers and that Apollonius did not mediate his teaching through Damis.[82]

[78] In spite of Apollonius' extensive travels, there is a distinctly pro-Hellenic attitude in the narrative (Knoles, "Literary Technique," 237-40; Bowie, "Apollonius of Tyana," 1680-82).

[79] For citations, see the discussion below on the central role of characters other than the students, pp. 129-30.

[80] Damis accompanied Apollonius until Apollonius ended his career on earth during the reign of Nerva (96-98 CE). The two visited King Vardanes in Babylon during the third year of his reign (47 CE), shortly after Damis joined his master. Philostratus' chronology suggests that Apollonius died about the age of eighty, the earliest of the three reported ages given in 8.29 (cf. 1.4, where his age is definitely said to be over one hundred). In 1.13, Apollonius has just reached his majority, in 1.14-15 he undergoes a five-year period of silence, 1.16-17 describes his stay in Antioch after this silence, and in 1.18 he undertakes his journey to India. Thus he would have been about thirty when he undertook his journey to the east.

[81] Menippus is said to be "a qualified disputant and remarkably outspoken" (5.43, LCL tr.).

[82] As did, for example, Epictetus, who used senior students to assist in the instruction of their juniors (Epictetus, *Discourses* 1.26.13). Damis does seem to

Instability of the Group of Followers

In contrast to the Gospel of Mark, where the twelve remain with Jesus throughout most of the Gospel, or the *Pythagorean Life*, which shows Pythagoreans having a strong attachment to the community (especially 33.233-40) as well as to Pythagoras, in the *Life of Apollonius* the group around Apollonius is shifting constantly. On three occasions, the bulk of his followers abandon him in the face of difficulty or danger (1.17; 4.37; 5.43), but even in normal circumstances, the commitment of Apollonius' followers to their master is generally short-term.

In part this is due simply to the vast span of time the narrative covers. The fifty years of devotion to Apollonius that Damis displays is considerably greater than the relatively short period of discipleship depicted in Mark, although the contrast is not so great with the longevity of the Pythagorean community in Iamblichus, which seems to have existed for a considerable time.

This reflects, once again, the ideal of the wise man as a lone hero rather than a member of a community. Apollonius, who embodies the ideal, is also fleeting in his school attachments. Early in his education, he surpasses his Pythagorean teacher. He seeks out in turn the Magi, the Brahmans and the Gymnosophs, and while he identifies himself as a follower of Iarchus (6.11), he stays only a short time with him. The successful philosopher absorbs wisdom wherever he can and then moves on to practice the philosophical life on his own. This short-term commitment reflects also the practice of the philosophical and rhetorical schools, where the student received a course of instruction from his teacher and then moved on. Damis' long-term association with Apollonius may in fact be the result of his limited philosophical ability. Damis does not have the capacity to lead a philosophical life on his own and can only share in it through his association with Apollonius.

---

have seniority in 4.15, where he asserts his authority in guiding the conversation between Apollonius and the other followers. This introduces the narration by Apollonius of the events at the tomb of Achilles.

Followers as Servants

On a number of occasions, Damis and the other followers play a role that might have been filled by a trusted servant. Damis takes care that Apollonius has fresh camels and a guide (2.40),[83] and is dispatched by Apollonius to verify the portent of the three-headed baby (5.13). Menippus is left in Alexandria to spy on Euphrates (5.43). Menippus and Damis serve as couriers between Musonius and Apollonius (4.46), and Damis is dispatched as a courier to deliver Apollonius' letter to Nerva (8.28).[84]

The references in the first two books to a group that Philostratus calls "those around Damis"[85] seem to reflect as well an equation of Damis with other servants and slaves. Philostratus definitely states that none of Apollonius' followers was willing to accompany him on the journey to India and that he took with him only two attendants, a calligrapher and a shorthand writer (1.18). If the account is consistent, the phrase can only refer to the slaves of Apollonius or of Damis.[86]

In the Gospel of Mark, as well, the disciples often carry out assignments that might be given to servants. For example, they provide a boat for Jesus (3.9), secure a colt for his entry into Jerusalem (11.1-7), prepare a room for the Passover meal (14.13-16), and are charged with finding food for the crowd (7.37). As in the *Life of Apollonius*, by taking care of mundane matters, the followers can free their master for more important work. The reader's perception in the two cases, however, is quite different. For the Christian readers of Mark, subservience to Jesus was an accepted part of their religious orientation, and they could identify easily with such a level of service to their Lord. The elite readers of Philostratus, however, would not be

---

[83] This is apparently a positive action, although Apollonius himself refuses to ask for fresh camels from Phraotes and earlier had chided Damis for thinking he should accept gifts from Vardanes (1.34).

[84] "The relationship is between servant and master; it is true that Damis does more than tend to the animals, but he is in fact apparently responsible for the practical aspects of the party's existence" (Knoles, "Literary Technique," 151).

[85] οἱ ἀμφὶ τὸν Δάμιν, 1.40, 2.40; οἱ περὶ τὸν Δάμιν, 2.7, 2.29.

[86] Vernon Robbins interprets the phrase as an "open-ended reference to the number of people following" Apollonius (*Jesus the Teacher*, 122, n. 74), but there is no indication that anyone beside Damis is following Apollonius as a student at this point.

expected to identify with such an attitude. The servile depiction of Damis places him in a position inferior to that of the reader.

Damis as a Philosopher in his Own Right

Damis' role as servant of Apollonius is reinforced by the fact that he never becomes a teacher in his own right. Damis follows Apollonius for fifty years and would have been in his old age by the time of the sage's death. In spite of fifty years of training, he remained a totally unknown figure until Philostratus rescued him from oblivion. Fifty years of association with Apollonius, the perfect Attic stylist (1.7), had not even taught him to write decent Greek![87]

Apollonius indicates on a number of occasions that Damis has not succeeded in his philosophical endeavor. The sage chides Damis for not becoming closer to God in their ascent of a mountain (2.5),[88] notes that abstinence from meat and wine has not profited his follower (2.7), and later suggests that he does not expect Damis to overcome his timidity since he is a Syrian from the borders of Media, where tyrants are worshiped (7.13).

On the other hand, Damis does achieve some level of success. He is not deterred by the philosopher Philolaus' arguments against entering Rome during Nero's attack on the philosophers and is, mistakenly, concerned with the effect of this speech on the more recent adherents of the sage.[89] Apollonius' parting words to Damis encourage him to continue philosophy, even without the support of his mentor (8.28). This indicates that the sage thought he had achieved at least a basic competence in the philosophical life.

---

[87] Admittedly, Philostratus seems to be caught in his own literary dissembling at this point and probably did not realize how hopeless a student he had portrayed in his various claims about his source.

[88] Apollonius believed the Brahmans had greater wisdom because "they live in a purer daylight" and "live on the edge and confines of that thermal essence which quickens all unto life" (6.11, LCL tr.).

[89] Much later Damis is persuaded by a similar speech by Demetrius (7.13). In both instances Damis' position provides the opportunity for a demonstration of Apollonius' wisdom. His role as straight man takes precedence over the portrayal of his own education.

Followers as a Measure of Competence

Even though Apollonius is not shown primarily in a school situation and the followers of the sage play only a secondary role compared to the emperors, kings and philosophers with whom he comes into contact, the success of a philosopher, in Philostratus' view, is at least partially measured by the number and quality of his students. This attitude is evident in his *Lives of the Sophists*, where the ability of a sophist to attract students is noted with admiration (518; 606; 613). Thus Apollonius is shown several times to attract a substantial following (1.17; 4.1; 4.37; 5.43). Since Philostratus often uses Apollonius' followers to contrast with the sage's character, he runs the risk of portraying his hero as a mediocre teacher, but he avoids this by claiming the famous Cynic philosopher Demetrius as a follower of Apollonius (4.25), thus providing the sage with a famous follower.

Responsibility of Teacher for Students

Several incidents in the narrative indicate that a teacher was assumed to be responsible for the actions of his followers. When Demetrius attacked Nero while at the same time attending Apollonius, it was assumed that Apollonius had directed this attack (4.42), even though Demetrius was hardly an ordinary follower, having previously conducted a school of his own. Apollonius points with pride to the refusal of those in his following to accept gifts from King Vardanes (1.40). On the other hand, Apollonius absolves his followers from the prohibition against eating meat and drinking wine but allows them to remain in his following (2.7). There does not seem to be any intent on his part to force his followers to conform completely to his own way of life, even if that might reflect badly on himself. The followers also have responsibility for their master, as shown by Menippus' and Nilus' controversy with Euphrates on behalf of the sage (6.28).

As in the *Pythagorean Life*, the sage's followers are to some extent surrogates of their master. In both cases, certain areas are reserved for the philosopher hero. In the case of Apollonius, his gift of foreknowledge and wonder-working ability are his exclusive domain. In Iamblichus' portrait of Pythagoras, more of the sage's qualities are passed on to his followers, but Pythagoras maintains his uniqueness through his identification with Apollo and his status as the seminal thinker who founded the community.

The portrayal of followers as surrogates of their master inevitably introduces a tension into these biographical texts that aim to glorify the uniqueness of their heroes' wisdom. Iamblichus, writing a schoolbook intended to spur students to adopt the philosophical life, stresses much more the ability of students to acquire the heroic traits of the founder of the school, while Philostratus, writing for the imperial court, glorifies the uniqueness of his hero in order to endow Apollonius with the authority to advise the emperor himself.

Rhetorical and Literary Function of the Followers

The Central Role of Characters Who Are Not Students

While Iamblichus portrays Pythagoras primarily as the teacher of a close group of followers, and a description of Pythagoras' teaching and the accomplishments of his followers occupies a large portion of the *Pythagorean Life*, Damis and the other followers of Apollonius play a relatively unimportant role in Philostratus' work. The emphasis is rather on the sage's relationship with Roman emperors and foreign kings on the one hand and a number of philosophers or philosophical associations on the other.

Most of the discussions of more serious topics take place not with students but with other philosophers or kings. For example, Apollonius discusses statecraft with Vardanes (1.37); with Phraotes he discusses the nature of philosophy (2.29-30), kingship (2.34), divination (2.35-37), and justice (2.39); with the Gymnosophs, he discusses the danger of listening to informers (6.13), the nature of the gods (6.19), and the nature of justice (6.20-21). Together with Dio and Euphrates, he advises Vespasian on the best mode of ruling the empire (5.31-38).

The organization of the work also reflects the peripheral role of Damis and the other followers. While both Xenophon and Iamblichus devote a major section of their works to a description of the education of their heroes' followers, there is no part of the *Life of Apollonius* that

might be described as the education of Damis.[90] Philostratus organizes his work by geography and the royal and philosophical persons and
groups who are the main dialogue and controversy partners of the sage.
Damis mostly appears in an ancillary role, facilitating the description
of these major encounters and the travelogue portions of the work.

Philostratus intended the primary readers of the *Life* to be
members of the imperial family, and they would be expected to
identify more with the kings and emperors that populate the narrative
than with Damis, whose social role is that of a servant. Thus, the
followers do not play as important a role in this work as they do in the
Gospel of Mark or in either of the two works that examined in
previous chapters.

Damis as an Authority

Damis is fundamental to the literary strategy of the *Life of
Apollonius* in providing Philostratus with an authority through which
his account attains believability.[91] Although Bowie argues that the
use of the Damis source would indicate to contemporary readers that
the account should be taken as a romance rather than history,[92] the
ostensible purpose is to lend authority to the account. The fact that
Apollonius was put forward in later years as a pagan alternative to
Jesus indicates that contemporary readers did not understand Philostratus' work as a romance.

Philostratus stresses Damis' reliability (1.3; 1.19). In three
different places, he confirms a fact attributed to Damis by an independent source (1.23-24, letter of Apollonius to Scopelianus; 1.32, letters
of Apollonius; 3.41, Moeragenes). Two of these confirmations occur
very early in the Damis section of the narrative (beginning at 1.19) and
thus confirm early on Damis' reliability in the reader's mind.[93] As
Thomas Gregory Knoles has noted, there is a circular granting of

---

[90] Robbins argues that Philostratus shows a progression of Damis' education
through various stages (*Jesus the Teacher*, 147-55). He has constructed the
progression, however, by picking out incidents that are peripheral to the organization of the work.

[91] Knoles, "Literary Technique," 42-53.

[92] Bowie, "Apollonius of Tyana," 1663.

[93] Knoles, "Literary Technique," 49-53.

authority at work: "Philostratus becomes more authoritative for having in Damis a source contemporary with Apollonius, and Damis becomes more authoritative for having been accepted by Philostratus."[94]

On the other hand, while Philostratus gains in authority as an historian by being able to cite Damis as a source, as a narrator, he gives up any credible claim to omniscience. By relying on historical sources, he can claim only to know as much as his sources tell him. At certain times he specifically states his lack of knowledge (4.45; 8.29; 8.30), strengthening the effect of the conscientious historian.

In contrast to this, the author of the Gospel of Mark never cites the disciples as a source, even though they are the implicit source of much of the narrative. The narrator of Mark maintains a stance of thoroughgoing omniscience throughout.[95] He begins the Gospel by citing the oracles of God (1.2-3). The quotation places the events he narrates in a sacred rather than an historical plane. He does not even concede the possibility of doubt or disbelief, which the citation of sources as in Philostratus is designed to combat.[96]

Significantly, Philostratus has not used Damis as an authority, either explicit or implied, for the story of Apollonius' death and apotheosis (8.30) or for his appearance to a student after his death (8.31). By separating these events from Damis' authority, Philostratus both preserves the believability of his chief authority and adds to the believability of the miracle accounts. Since many would receive the story of the apotheosis with skepticism, it would undermine Damis' authority to claim him as an authority for the tale. Even Philostratus does not want to take responsibility for the story. Instead of presenting it as absolute truth, he says simply that some say this, but, on the other hand, some say that. This strategy allows Philostratus to narrate the miracle story, which thus becomes part of the narrative world of Apollonius, without having to defend the truthfulness of the ac-

---

[94] Knoles, "Literary Technique," 42-45; quotation from p. 45.

[95] Rhoads and Michie, *Mark as Story*, 36; Petersen, "'Point of View,'" 97-121.

[96] Luke, on the other hand, does cite his investigation of sources in his prologue (1.1-4), placing his work in the realm of history where doubt is possible and historical verification is required.

count.[97] On the other hand, by multiplying the number of authorities cited for Apollonius' miraculous deeds, Philostratus manages to increase the credibility of the miracles, at least within the narrative world, at the same time that he distances himself from them.

Function of Followers in Depicting the Character of Apollonius

The way Philostratus uses Apollonius' followers to portray the philosopher's character is very different from the ways that Xenophon and Iamblichus use the followers of their protagonists. In the *Memorabilia*, Socrates' followers function primarily to show the philosopher in his role as an intellectual and spiritual guide. In the *Pythagorean Life*, Pythagoras' followers reflect the character of their master and demonstrate the moral value of his teaching. In the *Life of Apollonius*, on the other hand, the followers serve primarily to provide contrast to the character of the sage.[98]

Apollonius is a philosopher not by virtue of a philosophical system but through his way of life. He is a Pythagorean, but Pythagorean doctrines are only incidental in the dialogues. His commitment to the Pythagorean discipline and life style, however, is mentioned frequently (e.g., 1.7-8; 1.14-16; 1.21, 1.31-32).

Three traits are most prominent in the portrayal of Apollonius' philosophical character. First is his courage in the face of danger. Second is his disdain for material wealth and royal pomp. Third is the absoluteness with which he fulfills his philosophical discipline. The three are closely related.

---

[97] Philostratus shows a similar reluctance to take responsibility for the miraculous raising of the dead girl (4.45). A similar approach to the reporting of miracles is found in Josephus, who often ends a report of a miraculous occurrence with a note to the effect that the reader is free to decide about the truthfulness of the account, *Antiquities* 1.108, 2.348, 3.81. H. St. J. Thackeray, in his notes to the *Antiquities* (*Josephus*, LCL, 9 vols. [Cambridge, MA: Harvard University Press; and London: William Heinemann, 1978] 1.52-53, n. b), adds that Dionysius of Halicarnassus had used a similar formula to conclude his description of miraculous incidents (e.g., *Roman Antiquities* 1.48.1) and that Lucian states as a general rule that historians should relate miraculous occurrences but not wholly credit them, leaving the readers to decide for themselves (*How to Write History* 60).

[98] These are the primary strategies of each author, and I do not mean to imply that the other authors never make use of either of the other strategies.

Apollonius' courage is particularly prominent in Philostratus' narrative. Philostratus states that tyranny is the best test of philosophical character (7.1), and the first three chapters of book seven argue that Apollonius showed greater courage in confronting tyranny than did any other philosopher.[99]

The theme of Apollonius' courage is contrasted throughout the work with his followers' numerous failures to display the same virtue.[100]   When the sage announces his resolve to visit the Brahmans, he is abandoned by all of his followers (1.18). Similarly, most of his followers desert him before his entry into Rome in the time of Nero (4.37) and before his journey to Ethiopia (5.43). His companions seek to dissuade him from spending a night on Achilles' grave (4.11), and Demetrius tries to dissuade him from entering Rome to answer Domitian's charges (7.11-12). While Damis accompanies him on all his adventures, he is frightened by Apollonius' dream concerning the Eretrians (1.23) and is at first persuaded by Demetrius' advice not to enter Rome (7.13).

The attitude of disdain for mundane authority, wealth, pomp, and splendor is the principal subject of the Damis portion of book one. The first two incidents reported in the journey to Babylon are parallel accounts of Apollonius' scorn for the authorities who guard the borders (1.20-21). The account of his stay with King Vardanes contains very little philosophical discussion and quite a lot of showy indifference to the power and riches of the world. He begins his stay in Babylon by refusing to worship the image of the king (1.27), follows by proclaiming to the royal representative that he has come to improve the king's character (1.28), and enters the royal court with an ostentatious display of disinterest (1.30). He then refuses to attend the king's sacrifice (1.31), refuses to lodge in the king's palace (1.33), refuses his gifts (1.35; 1.40), and belittles his wealth and ability as a judge (1.38). In contrast to Apollonius' disdain for authority, Damis worries about

---

[99] During the first century CE Cynic and Stoic philosophers played an important role in the opposition to the more tyrannical emperors. Demetrius and Musonius, who both figure prominently in the *Life of Apollonius*, were conspicuous figures in this opposition (MacMullen, *Enemies of the Roman Order*, 46-94).

[100] Cf., Knoles, "Literary Technique," 204.

offending the king and tries to persuade Apollonius to accept royal gifts (1.33).

In several instances, Damis' failings are used to underscore Apollonius' fidelity to his philosophical discipline. The sage refuses to accept gifts from King Vardanes despite his follower's urging (1.33), and he similarly refuses to drink palm wine while Damis argues that Pythagoras only prohibited wine made from grapes (2.7). When King Phraotes inquires about the state of Apollonius' camels, the sage makes no answer while Damis begs for new ones (2.40).

Damis at times takes on a comic role in his contrast with Apollonius.[101]   In a discussion about foreknowledge, Iarchus, the Brahman leader, asks Damis in jest about the follower's ability as a diviner. Damis replies with a self-deprecating joke, asserting that he had divined that association with Apollonius would be beneficial to him (3.43).[102]

Philostratus frequently uses contrasting pairs in his narrative of Apollonius. Thus good kings (Vardanes, Phraotes) are contrasted with a bad king (the arrogant king at Iarchus' banquet), good emperors (Vespasian, Titus, Nerva) are contrasted with bad ones (Nero, Domitian), good philosophers (Demetrius, Musonius, Dio) with a bad philosopher (Euphrates), a good Roman authority under Nero (Telesinus) with a bad one (Tigellinus), a good philosophical brotherhood (the Brahmans) with a bad one (the Gymnosophs). Similarly Apollonius and his followers are part of Philostratus' strategy of development through contrast.[103]

Philostratus is able to use the followers to provide contrast with Apollonius' character because of the primary readers' lack of identification with his followers. Although Damis and the other followers frequently fail, the reader does not care about their failure in the same way that the reader of Mark is concerned about the disciples' failure in that Gospel. In Philostratus, the followers' commitment to Apollonius has no ultimate significance and has little bearing on the relation-

---

[101] Cf., Knoles, "Literary Technique," 151-52.

[102] Note the difference from the Gospel tradition, in which the recognition of Jesus is often associated with revelation from God.

[103] The use of contrasting pairs was a well-established literary technique. Plutarch had used it as the organizing principle of his *Parallel Lives*.

ship between the reader and the sage. Apollonius leaves behind no school and no church, and while he teaches both the mighty and the lowly and reforms the cult in many places, his significance is not so much in what he accomplished as in who he was. He embodies the philosophical life style, and his significance to the reader lies in his example. The readers of the *Life of Apollonius* are not expected to have the same intense commitment to Apollonius that the Christian readers of Mark have to Jesus.

Furthermore, the cowardice of Apollonius' followers does not affect the sage's life, since Apollonius' power protects him from his enemies. He laughs at the idea that Domitian could cause him harm and convinces Damis of that fact by freeing himself from his fetters (7.38). Jesus, on the other hand, if he has the power to escape death, does not exercise it. In his confrontation with the authorities, he suffers and dies. Early Christians had an ambivalent attitude toward his death, summed up in the saying, "The Son of Man goes as it is written of him, but woe to that man by whom the Son of man is betrayed" (Mk 14.21). Just as Judas is culpable for his betrayal of Jesus, so also the rest of the disciples are culpable for the effect of their failures. There is no such culpability on the part of Apollonius' followers. Their failure simply reflects their own lack of character.

As a result, the reader can smile at the cowardice of Damis and the other followers of Apollonius. Since Damis is often presented as a caricature of nonphilosophical thought, and the pronouncements of Apollonius are for the most part unextraordinary, a cultured reader can identify easily with Apollonius rather than his follower. That identification flatters the reader and facilitates the reader's acceptance of Apollonius' instruction.

Followers as Dialogue Partners

The dialogues between Apollonius and his followers fulfill a number of functions in the narrative. Closely related to Damis' function in providing contrast with the philosophical character of his master is his role in providing Apollonius with a straw man for his philosophical arguments. He frequently is used to voice a nonphilosophical point of view or a viewpoint that is otherwise incorrect. In addition to the points noted in the preceding section, Damis argues incorrectly that eunuchs are incapable of feeling passion (1.33), fails to find himself closer to divinity in his traversal of a mountain (2.4), holds the wrong opinion about the skill of elephant riders (2.11), and expresses many other wrong beliefs.

On a number of occasions, Philostratus uses dialogues between Apollonius and Damis to provide the reader with insights into Apollonius' thoughts concerning his interaction with other characters. During the stay with Vardanes, the dialogue with Damis about eunuchs (1.33) establishes Apollonius' prescience in regard to the affair with the eunuch the following day,[104] and the dialogue about accepting gifts from the king (1.33-34) allows Apollonius to set forth in detail his reasons for refusing the king's offer. The dialogues with Damis and others during the trip to Rome to confront Domitian are especially important for conveying Apollonius' attitude toward this central event.[105] This function of Damis in the narrative is closely related to his function in providing contrast. The contrasting opinions and attitudes of Damis and others provide Apollonius with the opportunity to expound his own.[106]

The dialogues between Damis and Apollonius also help fill out the travelogue sections of the narrative. In the extensive travelogue

---

[104] Cf. 6.3, where Apollonius tells all his followers the story of Timasion in a show of prescience.

[105] A similar strategy is at work in Mark 8.31-33, where Jesus' rebuke of Peter tells us more about Jesus' attitude toward his impending death than it does about Peter.

[106] One can note the same dynamic at work in the *Memorabilia*. Socrates can expound his wisdom because his partners are ignorant or misguided. The absence of dialogues between Pythagoras and his followers in the *Pythagorean Life* reinforces the idealized picture of the Pythagoreans that is found there. Because Pythagoras' followers are not used to voice incorrect opinions in dialogues with the sage, they can remain in the idealized sphere of Pythagorean perfection. It is possible to convey technical information in a dialogue form without putting the student in a bad light—in the *Oeconomicus*, for example, Socrates appears as the perfect student and even guides the conversation although he is the recipient of information—but in matters that reflect on the character of the discussants, the partner receiving instruction must necessarily look bad in comparison. He or she can still win the reader's approval, however, if rapid progress and development occurs, as is the case in Socrates' instruction of Euthydemus in the *Memorabilia*.

section that fills more than half of book two (2.1-24),[107] there are several dialogues between Apollonius and Damis. They discuss whether Damis has become closer to divinity by traversing a high mountain (2.5), whether palm wine is included in the Pythagorean prohibition of strong drink (2.7), the value of elephant riders (2.11), the nature of elephants (2.14-16), and the nature of art (2.22). All of these subjects are suggested by things that they observe or encounter along the way and thus help fix the reader's attention on the exotic features of Apollonius' travel. The dialogues also convey the sense of a long journey. They extend the period of reading—almost half of this travelogue section is taken up by dialogue—and allow Apollonius to interact with his environment. This creates the illusion of a journey much more successfully than would a simple recitation of points of interest. Finally, the dialogues allow Philostratus to portray his hero as the perfect sophist, always ready to carry on erudite discussion of the most obscure topics.

Damis as a Means of Maintaining Continuity

In contrast with the episodic and topical structuring of the *Memorabilia* and the bulk of the *Pythagorean Life*, Philostratus' biography of Apollonius creates the impression of a continuous narrative. While the continuity is in part due to the organization of the work into major journeys and interactions with major partners that span several incidents and topics of conversation, Damis also plays a prominent role in creating this impression. His very appearance through the narrative creates a sense of continuity in the reader's mind, and his continuous presence provides Apollonius with a dialogue partner in the breaks between the major figures, creating a background of daily life against which the major interactions appear as highlights.

This does not mean, however, that Philostratus has wholly avoided an episodic style of thought and narrative construction. Certain sections, such as the journey through the Greek cities (4.1-34), give almost no sense of continuity. In other places, episodes are included even though they clash with the narrative as a whole.

---

[107] In the LCL edition, the travelogue occupies thirty-three pages, the visit with King Phraotes twenty-three pages.

Conspicuous among these are the two recognition scenes in which
Damis realizes the divinity of Apollonius.   After the first (1.19),
Apollonius promptly forgets his innate knowledge of all languages and
Damis promptly forgets that his master is divine. At least, he does not
bother to worship him again throughout the remaining seven and a half
books.   In the second recognition scene (7.38), Damis is struck
suddenly by Apollonius' true nature when seeing Apollonius' perform
a miracle, even though he has witnessed miracles by Apollonius several
times before and the even more marvelous feats of the Brahmans and
Gymnosophs did not move him to similar conclusions.

There is a tension in Philostratus' work between the episodic and
continuous narrative styles. His other biographical work, the *Lives of
the Sophists*, is almost totally episodic, and despite his efforts to create
continuity in the present work, the episodic style is not completely set
aside. Philostratus is most successful in creating narrative continuity
when he is composing the narrative himself without the use of sources.
When he follows Maximus of Aegae (1.4-17), the account remains
episodic or thematic. He is likely as well to have had a source for the
episodes recorded in the journey through the Greek cities. The capture
of the vampire, which occurs during that journey, is said to be well-
known story, although Apollonius attributes his elaboration of it to his
Damis source (4.25).

Damis as a Means of Creating Sympathy for Apollonius

Damis helps create sympathy in the reader's mind for the figure
of Apollonius.[108]   His lifelong devotion to his master marks the
philosopher as one who is worthy of such devotion and inspires trust
and confidence. His suggestions of concern for the well-being of
Apollonius, even though they may be misplaced from a philosophical
point of view, create a similar concern in the reader's mind. His
bumbling ordinariness helps humanize what might otherwise become
a tedious repetition of superhuman perfection.[109]   Even though the

---

[108] Cf., Knoles, "Literary Technique," 153-54.

[109] This is not the only way to humanize a narrative of perfection. Iamblichus
creates sympathy for Pythagoras through the obvious concern his followers display
toward each other.

principal identification of the primary readers is with the rulers and philosophers of the narrative, there is an identification with human emotions of Damis that induces a sympathy for Apollonius.

Damis and the Divinity of Apollonius

Damis is important in reinforcing the interpretation of Apollonius as a divine being. Wonder-working can be ascribed equally well to magic and divinity, and Philostratus explicitly defends Apollonius against the charge of magic (1.2; 6.11; 8.7). The portrayal of his wisdom and philosophical character is an implicit argument for the divine source of his wonder-working power, but Damis provides an explicit judgment that Apollonius' powers are proof of divinity (1.19; 7.38; 8.13). Because of the authority Philostratus gives to Damis as the major witness to the life of Apollonius, the reader is led to accept Damis' judgment on this matter. His verdict is echoed by the consul Tigellinus (4.44), a follower with more stature than Damis but without his longtime association with the sage.

Conclusion

We have seen in these three Greek biographies of philosophical teachers three very different ways of depicting the relationship between the philosopher and his followers. In the *Memorabilia*, Socrates is defined essentially in his role as a teacher, in both informal and relatively structured settings. Although Xenophon sets out Socratic teachings on various subjects in a more or less organized manner, one could not say that his Socrates teaches a system of knowledge. The philosopher is defined through his role as one who leads others in the pursuit of truth. His teaching is individualized and suited to the circumstances. His relationship to his closer followers is essentially no different from his more casual relationships with other Athenians. Xenophon does not justify a continued school of Socrates.

The Pythagoras of Iamblichus, on the other hand, is much more clearly a school philosopher. Pythagoras is shown to possess an organized system of knowledge. His relationships with his followers are extremely structured and essentially different from his relationships with those outside of his school. Even though the school was destroyed within Pythagoras' lifetime, the surviving followers carried on Pythagoras' traditions and adhered to his teachings as divine laws. His followers so thoroughly embodied the teaching of their master that Iamblichus can illustrate the Pythagorean virtues equally by examples from the acts of Pythagoras or from those of his followers.

The Apollonius of Philostratus is like the Socrates of Xenophon in having no organized school or system of doctrines. His teaching, like that of Socrates, is individual and circumstantial. Although he has a number of followers whom he instructs on various topics, Philostratus does not stress a school organization, nor does he indicate the presence of a structured curriculum. Apollonius' conversations with Damis are occasioned by various sites and events. Unlike Socrates, however, Apollonius is not defined essentially as a teacher. Philostratus defines the sage as the possessor of wisdom rather than a teacher of wisdom. His most essential philosophical trait is not his knowledge or his pursuit of wisdom but his fearlessness in the face of tyranny. He is one who is essentially removed from the world and its concerns.

5

THE WISDOM OF BEN SIRA

The Wisdom of Ben Sira is different from the Greek philosophi-cal biographies in both cultural background and genre.[1] The book composed by Jeshua Ben Eleazar Ben Sira[2] contains maxims and short poems about a myriad of subjects that were topics of instruction in Ben Sira's school, which is mentioned in 51.23. Unlike the biographies, the book does not focus on the life of a particular sage and contains very little narrative material. Thus it is much more difficult to secure an understanding of how Ben Sira envisions the relationship between himself and his students, and the depiction of the students plays a much less prominent role in the plan of the work. It is also different from the biographies in its lack of focus on a founding figure of heroic stature. Ben Sira considers himself to be an extraordinary mouthpiece for wisdom (24.30-33), but he is primarily a teacher and interpreter of tradition (Preface.3; 39.1-3) within a school setting (51.23).

---

[1] For the text of the Hebrew portions of Sira, see F. Vattioni, *Ecclesiastico: Testo ebraico con apparato critico e versioni greca, latina e siriaca*, PSS 1 (Naples: Istituto Orientale di Napoli, 1968). For text-critical issues of the Hebrew text, see Alexander A. Di Lella, *The Hebrew Text of Sirach: A Text-Critical and Historical Study*, SCL 1 (The Hague: Mouton, 1966). The best critical edition of the Greek text is J. Ziegler, *Sapientia Jesu Filii Sirach*, Septuaginta 12/2, (Göttingen: Vandenhoeck & Ruprecht, 1965).

[2] In order to distinguish the author from the book, the author will be referred to as Ben Sira and his writing as Sira.

The Wisdom of Ben Sira was composed in approximately 180 BCE.[3] It apparently was written in Jerusalem, since Ben Sira is identified as a Jerusalemite in the Greek text (50.27), probably a note added by his grandson in the translation, and he gives glowing accounts of the temple service and the improvements made to the city during the reign of the high priest Simeon (50.1-21).

Ben Sira and Hellenism

Although Ben Sira wrote before the conflict between the supporters of Hellenization and their opponents came to a head under Antiochus Epiphanes, the Jerusalem of his time, which had been under Greek domination for a century and a half, was already greatly influenced by Hellenistic culture.[4] Ben Sira has been seen by some as a partisan of Hellenization,[5] but his use of Hebrew and his equation of wisdom and Torah (19.20) suggest an opposition to Greek influence.[6]

---

[3] Alexander A. Di Lella and Patrick W. Skehan, *The Wisdom of Ben Sira*, Anchor Bible 39 (New York: Doubleday, 1987), 8-10 (afterward cited as Di Lella, Anchor, or Skehan, Anchor); Hengel, *Judaism and Hellenism*, 1.131; Emil Schürer, *The History of the Jewish People in the Age of Jesus Christ (175 B.C.-A.D. 135*, revised and ed. by Geza Vermes, Fergus Millar and Martin Goodman, 3 vols. (Edinburgh: T. & C. Clark, 1973-87) 3.1.202; Robert H. Pfeiffer, *History of New Testament Times with an Introduction to the Apocrypha* (New York: Harper & Brothers, 1949) 364-66; W. O. E. Oesterley, *The Wisdom of Ben-Sira (Ecclesiasticus)* (London: SPCK, 1916) 6; George W. E. Nickelsburg, *Jewish Literature between the Bible and the Mishna: A Historical and Literary Introduction* (Philadelphia: Fortress, 1981) 64. For a discussion of the problems of dating Sira, see A. Haire Forster, "The Date of Ecclesiasticus," *Anglican Theological Review* 41 (1959) 1-9.

[4] Hengel, *Judaism and Hellenism*, 1.58-175.

[5] E.g., Theophil Middendorp, *Die Stellung Jesus ben Siras zwischen Judentum und Hellenismus* (Leiden: Brill, 1973); R. Pautrel, "Ben Sira et le Stoïcisme," *RSR* 51 (1963) 535-49. Much of Middendorp's argument is refuted by Jack T. Sanders (*Ben Sira and Demotic Wisdom*, SBLMS 28 [Chico, CA: Scholars Press, 1983] 27-59).

[6] Hengel, *Judaism and Hellenism*, 1.138-53; Pfeiffer, *New Testament Times*, 370; E. P. Sanders, *Paul and Palestinian Judaism: A Comparison of Patterns of Religion* (Philadelphia: Fortress Press, 1977) 370; Alexander A. Di Lella, "Conservative and Progressive Theology: Sirach and Wisdom," *CBQ* 28 (1966) 139-46; Di Lella's Anchor commentary consistently interprets as anti-Hellenistic passages that appear to have a much more general applicability.

He was not, however, an extreme partisan of the anti-Hellenistic camp. While he draws primarily from Jewish sources, especially the book of Proverbs,[7] he states that the wise man "travels among the peoples of foreign lands/to test what is good and evil among people" (39.4, Anchor). Apparently, Ben Sira found some good things in his travels, since he draws on Theognis, Book I, for some of his material on friendship and drinking.[8] Curiously, there seems to be at least as much influence from Egyptian sources. Jack T. Sanders has demonstrated remarkable parallels between certain passages of Sira and a Demotic wisdom book attributed to Phibis.[9]

In addition, Ben Sira has made a number of significant moves that place the traditions of Israel in the context of the wider Hellenistic culture. By interpreting wisdom as Torah and the covenant as the reception of wisdom by the people of Israel, he has placed the covenant traditions within the more universally recognized sphere of wisdom. While the writings of Ben Sira in Hebrew can hardly have been intended as an apologetic aimed at non-Jews, it is certainly possible that the well-traveled sage (34.12) developed this idea as a way of presenting Judaism to a gentile audience. In any case, the idea would help the upper-class youths of Ben Sira's school, who certainly were familiar with the basic rudiments of Greek culture, to understand their own particular tradition within the context of Mediterranean civilization as a whole. The traditions of Israel can be understood as a superior version of the wider quest for wisdom, the fruit of which can also be seen in Hellenism.

[7] Di Lella, Anchor, 43-45.

[8] Sanders, *Ben Sira and Demotic Wisdom*, 30-38. While other Greek sources have been suggested, this is the only one for which there is convincing evidence of extensive borrowing.

[9] Sanders, *Ben Sira and Demotic Wisdom*, 69-101; see also, P. Humbert, *Rescherches sur les sources égyptiennes de la littérature sapientiale d'Israël*, MUN 7 (Neuchatel: Secrétariat de Université, 1929) 132-40. There are also some parallels between Ben Sira's comments on different trades (38.24-34) and an Egyptian work known as "The Satire on the Trades" or "The Instruction of Duauf," but direct dependence seems unlikely (Di Lella, Anchor, 449-50). For the text of Duauf, *ANET* 432-34.

The belief of Ben Sira that God is the source of wisdom, to be discussed in more detail below,[10] also functions to demonstrate to the reader the superiority of Israelite wisdom. The lack of traditions about human teachers contrasts positively, given this doctrine, with the well-known controversies between the Greek philosophical sects and their reverence for their founding figures. Greek knowledge with its demonstrable human sources is made to seem inferior to the God-given knowledge of Israel.

Wisdom Schools

Very little is known of the structure or curriculum of the Israelite wisdom schools.[11] Bernard Lang has argued that the primary goal of the schools was simply to instruct students in writing and that texts such as Proverbs and Ben Sira served primarily as writing exercises.[12] The wisdom lessons were piggybacked onto the writing lessons the same way that religious and moral lessons were piggybacked onto reading instruction in the *McGuffey's Readers* of the nineteenth century. It seems, however, that Ben Sira is promising more than writing lessons to his prospective pupils in 51.13-30. The rise of the synagogue as an institution presupposes a fairly widespread system of elementary instruction, since it requires the presence of a number of persons capable of reading Hebrew, which may have been a secondary language at this point.[13] Thus it seems much more likely that the wisdom schools functioned as a system of higher education to prepare young men for government service or for the priesthood.

---

[10] Pp. 162-66.

[11] Gerhard von Rad notes the "rather negative results" produced by studies of the wisdom schools (*Wisdom in Israel* [Nashville: Abingdon, 1972] 17).

[12] Bernard Lang, "Schule und Unterricht im alten Israel," in *La sagesse de l'Ancien Testament*, ed. by M. Gilbert, BETL 51 (Gembloux: Duculot; and Louvain: University, 1979) 198-99.

[13] Hengel proposes, on the somewhat shaky evidence of a saying in the Jerusalem Talmud ascribed to the late second century BCE sage Simeon b. Setah, that elementary education was fairly common in Palestine at that time (*Judaism and Hellenism*, 1.81-82). Cf., George Foote Moore, *Judaism in the First Centuries of the Christian Era: The Age of the Tannaim*, 3 vols. (Cambridge, MA: Harvard University Press, 1927-30) 1.316-17 and 3.104, note 92.

Description of Students

Jewish Particularism in Sira

While earlier products of Israelite wisdom schools had been universalistic in outlook, avoiding discussions of God's covenant with Israel, the divinely guided history of her people, or the particular requirements of the Torah, Ben Sira makes explicit the identification of wisdom with Torah (24.23; 33.2-3), recounts the history of Israel, and often refers to the persons and events of biblical history.[14] E. P. Sanders has argued cogently that Ben Sira understood wisdom as the vehicle for the election of Israel.[15] This is most clearly seen in the Wisdom hymn of chapter 24, where God commands Wisdom, "'Make your dwelling in Jacob, and in Israel receive your inheritance'" (24.8, RSV). Ben Sira intended to restrict his students to Jews who would identify with the biblical teachings.[16]

The restriction on the audience of his work is reinforced by his writing in Hebrew. Even if Hebrew had not become a purely literary language by the time of the book's composition, its use certainly would restrict readership. As one who had traveled widely (34.12) and probably served in official capacities,[17] Ben Sira would have been fluent in both Aramaic and Greek. His apparent use of a book of Demotic wisdom suggests that his language proficiency was even more extensive. Nevertheless, he chose to write in the biblical language rather than one of the international languages available to him.

This ethnic restrictiveness is in sharp contrast to the traditions of inclusiveness found in the Greek philosophical biographies and in the older Israelite wisdom tradition. While we have practically no information about the older wisdom schools and the composition of the students, the international ideal of the wisdom tradition is apparent in the story of Solomon, the archetypical wise man of the Israelite tradition, and the Queen of Sheba, who came to test his knowledge

---

[14] James L. Crenshaw, *Old Testament Wisdom: An Introduction* (Atlanta: John Knox Press, 1981) 149-56.

[15] Sanders, *Paul and Palestinian Judaism*, 329-33.

[16] Contra Di Lella, Anchor, 16.

[17] If, as is likely, Ben Sira's portrait of the scribe in 38.34c-39.11 reflects his own experience (Di Lella, Anchor, 11), 39.4 suggests this.

(1 Kings 10.1-13), and in the attribution of Proverbs 30 and 31 to men from Massa in northwest Arabia. It is also evident in the book of Job, since its hero dwelt in Uz (probably Edom) and his friends came from various places in Arabia.

In the Greek tradition, the universalistic ideal is even more apparent. Of the biographies we have examined, the *Life of Apollonius*, for all the philhellenic tendencies of its author, shows the most extensive evidence of universalism. Damis, Apollonius' lifelong follower and the putative source for much of the narrative, is a Ninevite (1.19), and Nilus, who appears as another major follower, is an Egyptian and perhaps a black (6.16). Apollonius teaches kings in both Babylonia and India and consults with the sages of Babylonia, India and Ethiopia. In the *Pythagorean Life*, Pythagoras is shown as a student of Egyptian priests and the Babylonian Magi (4.19) and attracts the Hyperborean Abaris as a student (19.90-93). The organization of the list of Pythagoreans according to their citizenship stresses the geographical breadth from which followers of Pythagoras were drawn. Twenty-nine different groups are mentioned, including the Hyperboreans, Carthaginians, and Cyrenaeans (36.267).

Upper-class Orientation

Robert Gordis, in his study of the social background of the Israelite wisdom movement, concludes that wisdom literature was the product of the upper classes and came primarily from Jerusalem.[18] There are several indications of this upper-class orientation in Sira. It is stated that freedom from toil is a precondition for the acquisition of wisdom (38.24). The reader is exhorted to be kind to the poor and oppressed (4.1-10; 7.32; 11.4-5; 34.24-25; 35.3-4), warned against ill-gotten wealth (34.32; 40.12-14), and told not to deny a worker his wages (34.27). Sira provides instructions for the proper treatment of slaves (7.20-21; 33.25-33), eating at sumptuous banquets (31.12-21), and presiding over banquets (32.1-13). His attack on merchants (26.29-27.2) suggests that his pupils came from landowning families,

---

[18] Robert Gordis, "The Social Background of Wisdom Literature," *HUCA* 18 (1943-44) 77-118. For a contrary opinion, see Victor Tcherikover, *Hellenistic Civilization and the Jews* (Philadelphia: Jewish Publication Society of America, 1959) 146-47.

but all who are overly concerned with amassing wealth come under fire (11.10). On the other hand, he extols those who are wise but poor (10.23, 10.30-11.1) and warns against the dangers of associating with the rich and influential (13.2-23; but cf. 19.28). This last instruction suggests that Ben Sira drew his students at least partially from an upwardly mobile middle class as well as the upper class.

Wisdom schools appear to have been vehicles for advancement within the temple and government structures.[19] Thus it can be assumed that in spite of Ben Sira's exhortations to seek wisdom for its own sake, most of his students would come in large part to prepare themselves for worldly success. With the advance of Hellenization, Greek education became more and more attractive as a substitute for the traditional Israelite wisdom teachings as a vehicle for success. This trend reached its culmination with the establishment of the gymnasium in Jerusalem a few years after the writing of Sira. Since wisdom had been largely a secular undertaking before the time of Ben Sira, the transition to Greek learning would be easy to justify. By emphasizing the religious character of wisdom, Ben Sira could counteract the secularizing tendency of wisdom learning and counteract the trend to Greek education with the concomitant temptation of abandoning the faith of Israel.

Student Involvement in the World

In general, there is little sense of a radical conversion or reordering of life when the student undertakes the study of wisdom. There is no separation from home and family as is required of Damis in *The Life of Apollonius*, nor is there a close-knit sectarian community that the student joins as in Iamblichus' *Pythagorean Life*. Instruction in wisdom prepares the student for a more fruitful involvement in the world as it is. The importance of a proper religious orientation is stressed throughout, but there is no intimation of a gulf between service to God and life in the world.

---

[19] Saul M. Olyan argues convincingly that Ben Sira was himself a priest ("Ben Sira's Relationship to the Priesthood," *HTR* 80 [1987] 262-65).

The Literary Portrayal of Students

In each of the philosophical biographies the readers' identification with the followers of the sage or distance from the followers has been important for the achievement of the desired rhetorical effect. In every case, there is at least a rudimentary identification between the reader and the followers, even if it restricted to both readers and followers giving respectful attention to the instruction of the sage. In Iamblichus, the identification is quite close, while in Philostratus, the reader identifies more closely with the good rulers while maintaining an attitude of ironic superiority toward Damis. Xenophon presents a much more complex case, since the reader's stance varies with the various dialogue partners.

In Sira, on the other hand, there is no character or characters who play the role of followers of a sage. His work illustrates a number of ways an author can address the role of a student in a non-narrative setting. In Sira, there are three ways in which the proper role of the student of wisdom is discussed. Ben Sira presents the reader with (1) an idealized portrait of the follower of wisdom, (2) the sage himself as a model, and (3) direct exhortation to the reader in his or her role as student or potential student. The reader is to identify closely with each of the first two figures. In the Gospel of Mark, similar strategies are used at times. Jesus presents an idealized portrait of the true follower that includes himself as a model (8.34-9.1; 10.42-45). Mark masks his exhortations to his listeners as addresses to the disciples or to the crowds, but an exhortation such as 8.34-9.1 is clearly crafted for his listening audience rather than the supposed narrative audience.

Unlike the philosophical biographies in which the portrait of the sage's followers develops as a natural part of the narrative, Sira's reflections on the student of wisdom are mostly concentrated in a few poems that deal specifically with the subject of seeking wisdom. These punctuate the observations on the multitude of subjects that make up the book. Several of them are placed at strategic places in the text, such as the beginning (2.1-18, which is the conclusion of a longer discussion on wisdom), the middle (24.1-33, which is generally understood as dividing the work in two halves), and the end (51.13-30).

The important positions accorded to these poems indicate that Wisdom and the proper pursuit of wisdom are the primary themes within which all the other, subsidiary themes are to be understood.

The Idealized Student of Wisdom

The idealized student is depicted by Ben Sira in a number of passages. In several of these, Wisdom is personified as she had been in Proverbs 8. The personification of a quality more or less equivalent to Wisdom is found also in the Greek philosophical writings. For example, in Lucian's *The Runaways*, Philosophy is personified and shown to be outraged by the behavior of charlatan philosophers of various schools. There is also a clear similarity between the exhortations of Wisdom in Sira and the tale of the testing of Heracles from Prodicus that Xenophon recounts in the *Memorabilia* (2.1.21-33), in which Virtue expresses the need of toil to achieve lasting rewards. The device, however, plays a much more significant role in Sira than in the *Memorabilia*. That corresponds with the decreased emphasis put on the human teacher in Sira.

The first of the poems depicting the ideal follower of Wisdom is found in 4.11-19. This poem is divided into three parts. The first (4.11-14) equates love of Wisdom with love of God and promises God's favor to those who pursue her. In the second (4.15-16), Wisdom herself addresses the reader with promises to bestow both wisdom and worldly favor on those who listen to and obey her.[20] The final section (4.17-19) continues the direct address of Wisdom to the reader but concentrates on the discipline that she imposes on those who follow her. Ben Sira understood discipline as a major part of the educational process: "Lashes and the discipline of wisdom are always in season" (22.6; cf. 23.2). God's mercy is understood as embodied in His "rebuking, training, and teaching, as a shepherd guides his flock" (18.13b). Fathers are encouraged to discipline their sons and break their stubbornness (7.23; cf. 30.1-3, 7-13; 41.5, 8).

A second major poem depicting the follower of Wisdom is found in 14.20-15.10. This poem speaks in general terms of the joy of finding Wisdom. The first section (14.20-27) applies various meta-

---

[20] So Hebrew MS A and Syriac.

phors to the pursuit of Wisdom, the second (15.1-6) describes the care
that Wisdom takes for those who pursue her, and the third (15.7-10)
lists various types of evil persons who cannot attain Wisdom. Much
of the poem is so generalized and metaphorical that it gives little
concrete information about the idealized student of Wisdom. He
"meditates on Wisdom" (14.20) and "ponders her ways in his heart"
(14.21, Anchor). The parallel opening of the second section equates
this with fear of the Lord and holding fast to the Torah (15.1). As
always, wisdom is a divine gift, here given by Wisdom herself.
Several specific promises of worldly reward are made to those who
pursue Wisdom. They will not be put to shame, they will be exalted
above their neighbors, and they will receive eloquence and an
everlasting name (15.4-6). Among the classes of people who cannot
attain Wisdom are fools, sinners, the arrogant, and liars (15.7-8).

   Wisdom also addresses her students in 24.19-22, a passage that
describes the rewards of learning from Wisdom with general poetic
metaphors. The sweetness of Wisdom makes her students thirst for
more (24.19-21). Those who obey her will not be put to shame or fall
into sin (24.22). This section parallels a passage later in the poem
(24.30-33) in which Ben Sira portrays himself as a channel of Wisdom
to those he instructs.

   An important portrait of the sage is found in 38.24-39.11.[21]
This poem contrasts the work of various artisans (38.25-34a) with that
of the scribe.[22]   While the artisans are to be respected for their
contributions to society (38.31-32a, 34a), only those with time for
leisurely study are able to become wise (38.24). This poem provides
the most detailed description of the role of the wise man, who is
throughout equated with the scribe of 38.24. Among the social roles
that are ascribed to the scribe/wise man are sitting on the council,

----

[21] An important study of this poem is Johannes Marböck, "Sir. 38,24-39,11:
Der schiftgelehrte Weise. Ein Beitrag zu Gestalt und Werk Ben Siras," in Gilbert,
La Sagesse, 293-316.

[22] Although this poem has been compared with the Egyptian satire, "The Satire
on the Trades" or "The Instruction of Duauf" (*ANET* 432-34), it is entirely different
in tone. In contrast to the Egyptian work, Sira shows obvious respect for the
various trades that he describes. His point is the superiority of the scribe rather
than the inferiority of the manual laborers (Di Lella, Anchor, 449-50).

filling prominent positions in the assembly, sitting as a judge, and providing instruction in wisdom (παιδεία) and law (38.32b-33). He is also said to serve the great and to be seen in the presence of rulers (39.4a). Thus all the major governmental positions, other than the high priesthood itself, Ben Sira sees as the domain of the scribe. The only nongovernmental role attributed to the scribe is that of teacher, and even here he is described as a teacher of law (κρῖμα) as well as of wisdom, rather surprisingly considering that lack of legal interest in Sira itself.

Ben Sira makes it clear, however, that the ideal scribe/wise man is not simply a governmental bureaucrat. He is primarily a scholar of both religious and secular knowledge. He studies the Law of God, the wisdom of all the ancients, and the prophecies,[23] as well as the discourses of famous men, the complexities of parables (παραβολαί), the hidden meanings of proverbs (παροιμίαι), and the enigmas of riddles (παραβολαί)[24] (38.34b-39.3). He travels widely in foreign lands (39.4b). More important than the scribe's study, however, is his piety, since wisdom is a gift of God (39.6a).[25] He prays, meditates upon the mysteries of God,[26] and boasts in the Law of the Lord's covenant (39.5-8). The scribe is rewarded with eternal fame (39.9-11).

The use of contrast between the good student of wisdom and the fool is found explicitly in 21.11-26 and implicitly in censure of the fool in 22.9-15. The first two lines of the poem of contrast remind the reader that intelligence in itself is not wisdom. Wisdom is fear of the Lord and keeping the Torah, but there is also a type of cleverness that

---

[23] Sira seems to be referring to the three divisions of the Hebrew Bible, and thus "all the ancients" really means the ancients whose writings are included in the Bible.

[24] Though παραβολαί appears twice in the list, it refers to two different forms. The term was used of a wide variety of forms in the wisdom literature.

There is a similar list in Proverbs 1.6, which includes the proverb (מָשָׁל), parable (מְלִיצָה), riddles (חִידֹת), and wise sayings.

[25] Cf. 32.14-16; 34.9-13.

[26] I take the third αὐτός of 39.7 to refer to God, so the verse reads "He (αὐτός=God) will direct his (αὐτοῦ=the scribe) counsel and knowledge aright, and he (=the scribe) will meditate on his (αὐτοῦ=God) mysteries." As well as creating a clear chiastic structure, this fits more closely the parallelism of the preceding and following lines, in which the second members contain an action of the scribe that is related to God.

increases bitterness (21.11-12).   Much of the censure of the fool
regards the impossibility of teaching the fool (21.14-15, 18-19; 22.9-
10), the fool's generalized stupidity (22.11-12), and counsel to avoid
the foolish (22.13-15). The fool is also castigated for his bad manners
(21.22-24) and is to be equated with the godless, the slanderer, the
idler, the undisciplined son, and the shameless daughter in the portion
of the poem between the fool sections (21.27-22.5). The fool is
specifically contrasted with the wise man in his ability to learn and
appreciate wisdom (21.13-15, 18-21), the value of his counsel
(21.16-17), and the manner of his counsel and talk (21.26).   The
wise/fool contrast serves to bolster the sense of belonging to a valuable
segment of society, to reinforce the value of the study of wisdom, and
to provide an incentive against abandoning that study. Although there
is no formal mechanism of banning mentioned, such as is described in
the *Pythagorean Life* (17.74), one who abandons the circle of the wise
would no doubt be classified among the fools by his former companions. The fool also appears as a negative example in 33.5, though little
specific content is given to the portrait.

The Sage as Model Student

Ben Sira presents himself as a model student of Wisdom in
several passages. In 24.30-34 (24.28-31 in NAB, which numbers
verses differently in this chapter), he speaks in the first person as a
successful follower of Wisdom who has himself become a channel for
Wisdom's self-expression. This passage is part of the great hymn to
Wisdom, 24.1-34, which is structured so that verses 13-22, in which
Wisdom herself speaks, are paralleled by 23-34, where the author
speaks in his own voice:

13-17	Garden metaphor: Wisdom compared to trees and plants
19-22	Exhortation to follow Wisdom
23-29	Garden metaphor: Torah compared to the rivers of Paradise
30-34	Ben Sira's claim to be an inspired teacher of Wisdom.

This structure suggests that the author is a vehicle for the expression of Wisdom just as is the Torah. The symbol of water is used for Wisdom (21, 29), Torah (25-27), and Ben Sira himself (30-31), while light metaphors are used for the Torah (27) and Ben Sira (32). Through the parallelism of the exhortation to followers of Wisdom and the claim of Ben Sira to be a conduit for Wisdom, Ben Sira suggests that he is himself an example of a successful follower of Wisdom. Both 13-17 and 30-34 end with imagery of labor and toil, paralleling the toil of the follower of Wisdom with the toil that has resulted in Ben Sira's ability as a teacher of wisdom.

The nature of wisdom as a gift from God is a dominant theme in the passage. This is intimated by the miraculous transformation of Ben Sira from an insignificant irrigation ditch, diverting the water from the great rivers of the Torah into his own garden in verse 30, to a river and even a sea in verse 31. The prophecy metaphor of verse 33 suggests also the direct intervention of God in making Ben Sira a successful teacher of wisdom. A second theme is the identification of the wisdom teacher with Torah and with Wisdom herself. A final theme, found in vs. 34, is the duty of the student of Wisdom to work for the benefit of the community rather than for himself alone.[27]

Ben Sira presents himself as the model student again in 33.16-18. Once again, the theme of wisdom as a blessing from God is prominent (33.17) as well as the duty of the student to work for the good of others, presented in a passage almost identical to 24.34.[28] The wisdom teacher as a vehicle for God's action is intimated by the inclusio formed by this verse with 32.14.[29] In the earlier verse, Ben Sira states, "Whoever fears the Lord will receive instruction," while in 33.18 he states that he has labored not only for himself "but for all who seek instruction." The instruction of the wisdom teacher, Ben Sira suggests, is the instruction of God.

---

[27] Patrick Skehan argues against the genuineness of vs. 34 ("Structures in Poems on Wisdom: Proverbs 8 and Sirach 24," *CBQ* 41 [1979] 376). Though the verse is doubtful, there is not sufficient evidence to dismiss it.

[28] See the preceding note. Some scholars consider 24.34 to be displaced from this passage.

[29] Skehan, Anchor, 397.

A third short autobiographical note appears in 34.9-16.[30] This
passage also shows how Ben Sira uses the example of his own life to
reinforce an abstract model of the life of a sage. The autobiographical
reference appears in the middle of a chiastic structure, a:b:b':a', in
which general statements about the wise man two bicola in length
(a, a') are paired with references to the same qualities in Ben Sira's
own life, each of which is one bicolon in length (b, b'). After speaking
in general terms about the value of travel and wide experience for the
acquisition of knowledge (34.9-11), Ben Sira puts himself forward as
an example of one who has gained knowledge through his travels
(34.12). In 34.13, Ben Sira states that he has often escaped death
because of the wide experience that he has gained. The following
bicola make the general statement that those who fear the Lord (the
same as those who are wise in Sira's thought world) do not need to
fear in times of danger because their hope is in the Lord (34.14-16).
Thus Ben Sira places his own experience as an example of what his
readers or students can expect when they attain wisdom themselves.

The final autobiographical passage is the acrostic poem at the
end of the book (51.13-30). The poem is a maze of textual and
interpretive puzzles.[31] Although James A. Sanders has argued that
the poem was not written by Ben Sira,[32] there is no compelling

---

[30] 34.9-14 in the RSV numbering.

[31] Vss. 13-19 are extant on the Qumran Psalm scroll, 11Q Pss[a]. The Hebrew
of the Genizah manuscript B appears to be a retranslation from the Syriac, in
which the acrostic nature of the poem was not recognized.

The translation of the poem is disputed in many places. Translations may be
found in James A. Sanders, "Sirach 51 Acrostic," in *Hommages à André Dupont-
Sommer*, ed. by A. Caquot and M. Philonenko (Paris: Libraire d'Amerique et
d'orient Adrien-Maisonneuve, 1971) 432-33; Patrick W. Skehan, "The Acrostic
Poem in Sirach 51:13-30," *HTR* 64 (1971) 388, 390; Celia Deutsch, "The Sirach 51
Acrostic: Confession and Exhortation," *ZAW* 94 (1982) 401-03; and in the
commentaries.

A number of attempts have been made to reconstruct the original Hebrew:
J. A. Sanders, "Sirach 51 Acrostic," 429-38; Skehan, "Acrostic Poem," 387-400.
O. Rickenbacker makes suggestions about the original Hebrew without reconstruct-
ing the entire text (*Weisheitsperikopen bei Ben Sira*, OBO 1 [Freiburg: Universitätsverlag; Göttingen: Vandenhoeck und Ruprecht, 1973] 197-213).

[32] James A. Sanders, *The Psalms Scroll of Qumrân Cave 11 (11QPs[a])*, DJD 4
(Oxford: Clarendon Press, 1965) 79-85; *idem*, "Sirach 51 Acrostic," 437. Deutsch
argues that it was not part of the original work of Sira but leaves open the question

reason to doubt it is part of Ben Sira's composition. The general tone of the passage is consistent with the rest of Sira. It contains many images that are found elsewhere in the work,[33] and it is an integral part of the literary structure. Hymns glorifying Wisdom appear at the beginning and midpoint of the book (1.1-30; 24.1-33), and this poem, expressing the author's love for Wisdom, neatly rounds out the structure. The thought of the concluding line, that God will, in His own time, grant wisdom to the person who diligently seeks it, forms an inclusio with the opening line, "All wisdom is from the Lord."

The first fourteen lines of the poem are an idealized portrayal of the author's quest for wisdom represented through the conceit of his love for lady Wisdom.[34] This section alternates between imagery of the author's desire for Wisdom (vss. 13-15, 18-19b; 21) and the rewards of attaining Wisdom (16-17, 19c-20, 22), emphasizing the growing involvement and growing reward—the more one knows Wisdom, the more one desires her. The lines that portray the attainment of Wisdom emphasize the ease of acquiring wisdom (especially vss. 16, 20b) and the nature of wisdom (here in the form of eloquence) as a gift from God (vs. 22).

The last nine lines are an exhortation to the reader to pursue wisdom by taking up lodging in Ben Sira's "house of instruction."[35] While Ben Sira may have hoped to gain students for his school by means of this "advertisement," the passage also serves to reinforce the

---

of authorship ("Sirach 51 Acrostic," 401, n. 5). Those who accept Ben Sira as the author include Rickenbacker, *Weisheitsperikopen*, 199-200; and Di Lella, Anchor, 576-77.

[33] See the lists in Deutsch, previous note, and Rickenbacker, *Weisheitsperiko-pen*, 199, following W. Fuss, "Tradition und Komposition im Buche Jesus Sirach" (Diss., Tübingen, 1963) 264-66.

[34] The sexual allusions have been exaggerated in the interpretation of James A. Sanders, *The Dead Sea Psalms Scroll* (Ithaca, NY: Cornell University Press, 1967) 112-17; *Psalms Scroll of Qumrân Cave 11*, 83; "Sirach 51 Acrostic," 428-38. Nevertheless, the hymn is clearly erotic in a psychological sense and there are sexual allusions that help to reinforce the image of passionate desire. See also, T. Muraoka, "Sir. 51, 13-10: An Erotic Hymn to Wisdom?" *JSJ* 10 (1979) 166-78.

An excellent discussion of the rhetoric of the poem can be found in Deutsch, "Sirach 51 Acrostic," 400-09.

[35] The acrostic contains 23 lines, one for each letter of the alphabet plus a פ line at the end. For an explanation of this structure, see Di Lella, Anchor, 576.

reader's continued commitment to the study of wisdom after laying down the scroll. Anyone who had read the book to this point would be expected to have a certain commitment to wisdom, and if, as is often assumed, the book was written for use within a school setting,[36] the intended reader would have been a student in a wisdom school already. The reader is not to lay the scroll aside and forget it but to return to it again and again and to seek wisdom wherever else he can (cf. 39.2-3; 6.34-36).

While the "come to my school" conceit replaces the erotic imagery in the second half of the poem, many of the same ideas are presented as in the first part of the poem. Wisdom is acquired easily:

> She is close to those who seek her,
>   and the one who is in earnest finds her (51.27, Anchor).[37]

One needs but little instruction (vs. 28) and no money (vs. 25).[38] The final verse is particularly close to the final verse of the first section with verbal echoes of giving and reward:

> The Lord has given me my tongue as a reward (vs. 22a);
> And He will give you your reward in His time (vs. 30b).

The repetition of the themes of ease of acquisition and wisdom as a gift of God reinforces the pattern of Ben Sira's experience as a model for his students that is suggested by the overall structure.

It is clear that the autobiographical sections are generally idealized, presenting a schematic view of Ben Sira as a model student. The final poem especially, based on the conceit of Ben Sira's erotic pursuit

---

[36] Lang, "Schule und Unterricht," 198-99. Di Lella suggests that the book is an edited version of Ben Sira's class notes (Anchor, 10). Wolfgang Roth proposes that Ben Sira drew on the material he used in his oral instruction in his school, "On the Gnomic-Discursive Wisdom of Jesus Ben Sirach," *Semeia 17* (1980) 75, citing Moshe Zevi Segal, *Seper Ben Sîra' Hasālēm*, 2nd ed. (Jerusalem: Bialik Foundation, 1972) pars. 18-19.

[37] This translation follows the Hebrew of the Geniza manuscript rather than the Greek, which is substantially different.

[38] The Greek of vs. 28, μετάσχετε παιδείας ἐν πολλῷ ἀριθμῷ ἀργυρίου, is defective. Skehan, "Acrostic Poem," 398.

of lady Wisdom, might be considered an idealized model rather than a truly autobiographical statement.

In addition to these passages in which Ben Sira presents himself as a model, Sira includes a passage in which Solomon appears as a model sage (47.13-18) and mentions Moses and Aaron in their role as teachers (45.5b; 45.17). All of these occur as part of the praise of famous men in chapters 44 through 50.[39] Even though sages are mentioned along with rulers, counselors, governors, composers of psalms, and self-reliant persons among the various types of persons worthy of praise in the prologue to this section (44.3-6), Ben Sira has done little to cast the heroes of Israel in the wisdom mold. Solomon is, of course, praised for his wisdom, but the traditions connecting him with wisdom were already well established. Considering the rabbinic tendency to view Moses as "our Rabbi" and Ben Sira's own conflation of Torah observance and wisdom, it is significant that there is relatively little attempt to associate Moses with the model of the sage other than the fact that he taught the covenant and the judgments of God to Israel after having received them from God (45.5). Aaron, who receives considerably more space than Moses in Ben Sira's praise of the ancestors, is also said to have received the laws from Moses so that he could teach them to the people (45.17). Both these notices are consistent with the picture of the sage in Sira as one who receives his wisdom from God and is obligated to use it for the sake of others. Thus they help reinforce the ideal model of the sage even if by themselves they are insufficient to stand as a model.

The portrait of Solomon, on the other hand, is largely drawn in terms of the model sage. Even though Ben Sira has an obvious interest in the sacrificial cult,[40] there is only passing mention of the fact that Solomon established the temple (47.13b). He is praised for his understanding (47.14) and for his mastery of the wisdom genres, enigmatic sayings (Gr., παραβολαὶ αἰνιγμάτων) (47.15), songs (שׁיר; ᾠδαί), proverbs (חיד ה; παροιμίαι), parables (משׁל; παραβολαί), and

---

[39] For an interesting analysis of the rhetoric and social function of this poem, see Burton L. Mack, *Wisdom and the Hebrew Epic: Ben Sira's Hymn in Praise of the Fathers* (Chicago and London: University of Chicago Press, 1985).

[40] Aaron, the priest, receives 32 bicola, compared to 8 for Moses, the lawgiver. Phinehas receives 10 in his role as priest, and the high priest Simeon receives 36.

interpretations (מֵלִיצָה; ἑρμηνεῖαι) (47.17). His fame is directly
connected with his wisdom (47.16), and his wealth (47.18b) is certainly
consistent with Ben Sira's view of the material rewards of wisdom.
Solomon sharply diverges from the ideal portrait of the sage given
elsewhere in Sira, however, in his shameful relationships with women
(47.19-20). Since wisdom is embodied primarily in one's way of life
rather than in intellectual agility, Solomon's lapses present a significant
problem in his value as a model. While Ben Sira ignores the problematic relationships of David (47.2-11), he is constrained to confront
Solomon's head-on. Because of Solomon's reputation as the legendary
sage of Israel, it is important that the negative side of his character be
condemned so that the reader does not draw mistaken conclusions
about the acceptable limits of a sage's behavior.

It was common for the Greek and Hellenistic philosophers to put
themselves forward as examples for their students to follow.[41] In a
similar manner, philosophical instruction within the schools often
prefaced a study of a philosopher's doctrines with an examination of
his life. As noted above, Iamblichus' *Pythagorean Life* was designed
to fulfill such a role.

What is unusual in Sira is not the author's use of himself as an
example for his readers to follow but the extent to which Ben Sira
restricts the use of himself as an example. He appears only as an
example of a successful student of wisdom. The reader is to learn
from his example only the roles of the student and the scholar.

In the parallelism that Mark establishes between Jesus and the
disciples throughout the Gospel, there is the implicit presumption that
Jesus is an example for the disciples to follow. The disciples are
commissioned and sent out to imitate Jesus' healing and preaching
mission in 6.7-13. The disciples are successful in fulfilling that
mission (6.30), although they are shown later to be imperfect in their
ability as healers (9.17-18). The disciples are later commissioned to
imitate the suffering of Jesus (13.9-13). In certain teachings the imitation motif is made explicit, such as the exhortation to take up one's

---

[41] See Chapter 3, n. 54-55.

cross (8.34) and the saying about the Son of Man coming to serve rather than to be served (10.45).[42]

The Reader as Student

Throughout the work, the reader is positioned as a student of Ben Sira's and is expected to regard him as a teacher. As the book may have been composed for use in Ben Sira's school or compiled from material used in his school, the original readers may have been, in fact, students of his.

One prominent convention Ben Sira frequently uses is the vocative "My son" or "My children" (Heb., בְּנִי; Gr., τέκνον, τέκνα) to address the reader (e.g., 2.1; 3.1, 12, 17; 4.1, 20; 6.18, 23, 32; 16.24; 18.15; 21.1). The appearance of this form of address frequently signals the beginning of a new poem or new subject. The convention was adopted from Proverbs, where it also occurs frequently (son, twenty times in chapters 1-7 and 23-27; children, four times in chapters 4-8). While one must be careful in drawing conclusions about actual relations from such a form of address, it seems reasonable that teacher-student relationships would have been conceived on the pattern of the father-child relationship.[43]

While Ben Sira always addresses the reader as a student, in some passages he directs the reader more particularly in his role as a student.

[42] These two sayings are the first and the last of Jesus' teachings concerning discipleship in the section 8.31-10.52. The inclusio formed by the two teachings that offer Jesus' own passion as a paradigm for discipleship emphasizes the importance of the idea for understanding the section as a whole.

[43] בְּנִי was the accepted mode of address by a rabbi to his student in the Tannaitic and early Amoraic periods (Louis Ginzberg, *A Commentary on the Palestinian Talmud*, TSJTSA 10-12, 21, 4 vols. [New York: Jewish Theological Seminary, 1941-61] 1.238, 1.300; cited by Gordis, "Social Background," 84, n. 9). At least one of the Tannaim, Abba Saul ben Batnith (active ca. 100 CE), was known by the honorific title Abba rather than the more usual Rabbi (Hermann L. Strack, *Introduction to the Talmud and Midrash* [Philadelphia: Jewish Publication Society of America, 1931], 112). It was a common title for a teacher in Palestine, judging from Mt 23.8-10, where Jesus forbids his disciples to use the titles Ῥαββί, πατήρ, and καθηγητής, which appear to be various honorific terms for teachers. It was also common for the Greek and Latin moral teachers to compare their relationships with their students to that between a father and his children. For references, see Abraham J. Malherbe, "Exhortation in First Thessalonians," *NovT* 25 (1983) 243-45.

In 2.1-18, he readies the reader for the difficulties that await one who comes to serve the Lord. Since wisdom is equated with fear of the Lord in Sira, it is reasonable to equate the student of wisdom with one who prepares himself for such service. The main theme is the testing to be endured by one who would serve God. He is not to be anxious in times of distress (2.2) and is to be patient in times of humiliation (2.4). The faint of heart are unable to go this difficult way (2.12-14). In addition, "those who fear the Lord" obey His words, are filled with His law, and humble themselves before Him (2.15-17).

An important exhortation to the reader is found in 3.21-24, which helps define the role of the student. In this passage, the reader is warned not to seek knowledge that has not been given by God: "Attend to what has been given [by God], what is hidden is not your concern" (3.22). The speculations of the mind only lead people astray (3.24). This warning seems to be aimed at both Hellenistic philosophies and certain branches of Israelite wisdom. The writer of Qohelet defined wisdom as the investigation of all things (Qoh 1.13), an approach that Ben Sira condemns.[44] He may well have found the speculations of Greek philosophies particularly dangerous in confusing the theological understanding of his students.[45] This is one of the few passages in Sira where the rejection of rival schools of thought is made explicit. The passage is found within a short poem praising humility, and apart from the warning against other schools of thought, the passage encourages in a general way the virtue of intellectual humility. Since wisdom is a gift from God, too great a reliance on one's own intellectual ability is dangerous in itself, no matter what a person's school of thought may be.

There is a related passage in 19.20-25, which warns against a wicked form of knowledge. The warning here is aimed more at the cleverness of the cheat than philosophical speculations. Nevertheless, as all knowledge disconnected from the fear of the Lord and the practice of the Torah is condemned, Ben Sira may have understood both types of knowledge to be essentially the same. Once again, the

---

[44] Cf. 1.2-3, 6, 8.
[45] Di Lella, Anchor, 160; Hengel, *Judaism and Hellenism*, 1.139-40.

warning implies the student must keep God in the center of his search for wisdom.

The exhortation to strive for wisdom found in 6.18-37 is similar in many respects to the autobiographical poem at the end of the book (51.13-30). It is similar in length (twenty-two and twenty-three bicola respectively, both based on the number of letters in the Hebrew alphabet) and shares with the latter poem a similar structuring of themes. Both begin with the idea of seeking wisdom in one's youth and throughout one's life (6.18; 51.13-14), an agricultural metaphor concerning the automatic ripening of wisdom (6.19a; 51.15a), and a passage that contrasts the greatness of the reward with the smallness of the labor (6.19b; 51.16). Both allude to the difficulties of pursuing Wisdom (6.24-25; 51.18), the passionate desire needed for her pursuit (6.26-27; 51.19-21), and the rewards that she gives (6.28-31; 51.20b-22). Both urge the reader to take practical steps to study wisdom (6.34-37a; 51.23, 25, 28), and both end with an exhortation to meditate on God and a promise that God will grant wisdom (6.37; 51.29-30).

The organization of the poems is so similar that they can be regarded as two variants on the same theme. The first exhorts the reader directly as a potential student of wisdom, while the second uses the author's own experience in an idealized fashion as a model for the reader to follow.

In spite of the vast difference in the goal of Jesus' disciples, the Kingdom of God, and that of Ben Sira's students, wisdom, the types of traits and attitudes that are encouraged in both are very similar. The parable chapter in Mark shares a number of themes with these passages in Sira. Both stress the importance of perseverance (Mk 4.14-20; Sir 6.18), the ability to withstand trials (Mk 4.16-19; Sir 6.20-21, 24-26; cf. 4.17-18), the importance of manifesting one's light/wisdom (Mk 4.21-22; cf. Sir 4.23; 20.30-31; 41.14b-15), the belief that some are called and some are not (Mk 4.11-12, 15-20, 25; Sir 6.20-21; cf. 15.7-8; 21.15, 18-19, 21), the expectation that the Kingdom/wisdom will grow by itself apart from the effort of the disciple (Mk 4.26-29; Sir 6.19), and the disparity between the initial and final manifestations of the Kingdom/wisdom (Mk 4.30-32; Sir 6.24-25, 29-31). In addition, one finds the παροιμία as one of the wisdom genres to which the student is to attend in the Greek version (6.35, cf. 39.2-3), though the Hebrew refers to a wise saying rather than a parable.[46]

Other specific instructions to the readers in their role as students of wisdom appear in 8.8-9. Here the readers are told not to slight the discourse of the wise (שׂיחת חכמים) and to be attentive to their maxims (חידת, παροιμίαι). In verse 9, the discourse of the elders appears in parallel with that of the wise in verse 8. The promised rewards of such study are the ability to serve princes and to know how to answer in time of need. These verses repeat themes from other parts of the work. In 6.34-36, the reader is exhorted to seek out the elders, listen to every discourse (שׂיחה) and every wise saying (בינה משׂל, also translated παροιμία by the grandson).

Lack of Examples of Imperfect Students

Ben Sira does not include examples of failure in any of his discussions of followers of wisdom. The wisdom student is only presented with an ideal, and there is no indication that in reality students may not live up to the idealized portrait with which they are presented. Only the fool is shown as a failure in his study. The only exception to this is, quite significantly, the portrait of Solomon, who is presented as profoundly flawed (47.13-20). That portrait, however, certainly would not encourage readers to accept such shortcomings in their own pursuit of wisdom. If even the great Solomon cannot escape condemnation for his faults, the reader, who is of much lesser status, can hardly expect his own transgressions to be ignored. The mention of Solomon's faults, then, tends to increase the rigor of the standard dividing the wise from the foolish.

God as the Source of Wisdom

One recurrent theme found throughout Sira is the divine source of all wisdom. Both the opening and closing words of the book make the point. The opening praise of wisdom stresses both the divine origin of wisdom in the abstract and human wisdom as a gracious gift from God.

---

[46] Ben Sira uses the term משׂל in reference to the sayings contained in his book in 50.27.

> All wisdom is from the Lord
> and is with him forever (1.1).

Only God is truly wise:

> The root of wisdom, to whom has it been revealed?
> and who knows her clever devices?
> Only one is wise, exceedingly fearful,
> seated upon his throne (1.6, 8).[47]

He gives wisdom to those who possess it:

> He has poured [wisdom] out on all his works
> Upon all humankind according to his bounty,
> but in great abundance on those who love Him (1.9-10).

The final words of the book return to the theme of human wisdom as a gift from God. After exhorting prospective students to submit to the discipline of instruction in his school, Ben Sira tells them to

> Work at your tasks in due season
> and in His own time He will give you your reward (51.30),

where the reward is clearly the sought-for wisdom. The nature of wisdom as a gift is stressed throughout, either as a gift of God (6.37) or of Wisdom herself (4.18).[48]

Not only is God the ultimate source of the revelation of wisdom, but God actively imparts wisdom to each individual, who acquires it as a gift.

> His [the wise man's] care is to rise early
> to seek the Lord, his Maker,
> to petition the Most High,

---

[47] This same attitude is found in the Markan saying that no one, not even the Son, knows the day of the Son of Man except the Father (13.32) and Jesus' rebuke of the rich young man for addressing him as good (10.18).

[48] Cf. 43.33.

> To open his lips in prayer,
>   to ask pardon for his sins.
> Then, if it pleases the Lord Almighty
>   he will be filled with the spirit of understanding
>
> (39.5-6, Anchor).

The student's primary loyalty is not to his immediate teacher or to a founding figure from the past, but to Wisdom herself. Ben Sira does not name his own teachers. Instead of placing himself in a succession of teachers, as did the philosophers of the Greek philosophical schools or the later rabbis, he understands himself to be instructed directly by God or Wisdom.[49] The praise of Wisdom with which Ben Sira begins his book is structurally analogous to the eulogy of Pythagoras and the Pythagoreans that forms the first book of Iamblichus' *Pythagorean Synagoge* and the similar biographies of philosophers that appear in introductions of their teachings.

Although Sira is the first within the extant works of Israelite wisdom to advance the active role played by God in the acquisition of wisdom as a major theme, the same belief is found in all the later works of the Jewish wisdom tradition.[50] The author of the Wisdom of Solomon says, in addressing God,

> Who has learned thy counsel,
>   unless thou hast given wisdom
> and sent thy holy Spirit from on high? (9.17, RSV).

The divine source of wisdom plays a role as well in the Greek philosophical biographies but is not such a central theme. In Xenophon, the δαιμόνιον of Socrates is mentioned (1.1.2-5; 4.3.12; 4.8.1, 5) but does not play a major role. While the piety of Socrates is stressed in the *Memorabilia*, the human aspect of the philosophical pursuit is clearly differentiated from the divine sphere. Socrates' followers are encouraged to follow their own reason in areas where

---

[49] Skehan and Di Lella read, "to my Teacher I will give grateful praise," for 51.17 and refer "Teacher" to God (Anchor, 572, 575, 577).

[50] John Coert Rylaarsdam, *Revelation in Jewish Wisdom Literature*, (Chicago: University of Chicago Press, 1946) 94-98.

there can be no doubt but to consult oracles concerning those things that can not be foreseen through reason alone (1.1.6-9; 4.7.10). For Xenophon, Socrates' philosophy occupies the realm of human wisdom. It was not divinely revealed, and while Socrates did have his own peculiar δαιμόνιον, he taught his followers to consult the gods according to the established customs.

In Iamblichus, the role of the divine is much more pronounced, but in contrast to Ben Sira, Iamblichus seems to limit the role of divinity to the revelation of the Pythagorean wisdom. Though the piety of both Pythagoras and his followers is stressed, and it is said that their wonder-working ability results from their piety (28.134-137), the gods do not appear to play such an active role in the granting of either wisdom or thaumaturgical ability as does the God of Sira. Proper understanding of the Pythagorean teaching is possible only for one who has purified his soul and its reasoning powers (16.68-70). The purification takes place through certain ascetic practices and the contemplation of theorems. Since wisdom is a characteristic of divinity, it is only possible to achieve wisdom through an assimilation of one's nature to that of the divinity, but to the extent that the students achieve that assimilation, they can expect to achieve wisdom. In Sira the acquisition of wisdom requires effort on the part of the student to purify his character and maintain a proper relationship with God, but God can freely decide whether or not to grant wisdom to the student. Ben Sira assures potential students that, in fact, God will grant the gift of wisdom to those who strive for it, but he never suggests that wisdom is the natural product of the student's effort or that God is beholden to grant wisdom to all that strive for it.

In Philostratus, there is once again a connection between wisdom and divinity. The Brahmans state that a good man is a god (3.18), and Apollonius makes the same claim in his apology before Domitian (8.5). As in Iamblichus, there is a connection between the hero's ability to work miracles and his piety (3.42; 8.7.9), and it is also clear that Apollonius enjoys the special favor of the gods (4.44; 5.12). While these passages indicate that Apollonius' foreknowledge was imparted by the gods, there is no indication that the followers of Apollonius were dependent on the gods for the acquisition of wisdom or that the gods were actively involved in the learning process. The ability of the student to learn is seen largely as dependent on his innate character. Even in those few passages where it is said that Apollonius had the capacity to convert licentious men to a philosophical way of life, it appears to be the power of the sage's character rather than the intervention of the gods that accomplishes the change.

The Gospel of Mark shares with Sira a belief in the primary importance of God in revealing the essential truths presented in the book. We have already noted the presence of many wisdom motifs in the parable chapter. Prominent among these is the much-debated theory of parables, according to which Jesus proclaims to the disciples, "To you has been given the mystery of the Kingdom of God, but to those outside all things are in parables" (4.11). Any doubt that the reader might harbor whether δέδοται is a divine passive is removed by the concluding quote from the words of the Lord found in Isaiah.

This has important implications for the reader's evaluation of the disciples' difficulty in understanding. If God plays the primary role in the acquisition of knowledge, to what extent are the disciples, or any of the other characters, culpable for their failure to understand? If we return to Sira as a model, the answer would seem to be, completely. For in Sira, even though wisdom is understood as a gift from God, the fool clearly is to be blamed for his failure to possess that gift (22.13-15). In Sira, it is clear that the student of wisdom is considered to be responsible for preparing the ground for the acquisition of the gift of wisdom through his own hard work and study (6.32-37a). In Mark, on the other hand, it is less clear whether the action of the individual is a necessary prerequisite to the acquisition of the gift of knowledge. The disciples, to whom the mystery of the Kingdom is said to be given (4.11), have fulfilled certain conditions by having responded in faith to Jesus' call to follow (1.16-20; 2.14), but the centurion, who is the first to proclaim the secret of Jesus' identity, has fulfilled no prior conditions of faith (15.39). Likewise, Bar Timaeus, who recognizes Jesus as the Son of David (10.47), has fulfilled no prior condition of faith. His following of Jesus occurs after his recognition of him as the Messiah and the subsequent healing.

Sira and Mark

While the Greek philosophical biographies are more like Mark in their structure, describing in a more or less narrative format the relations between a sage and his followers, they do not provide an ideological rationale for the difficulty that the Markan disciples have in understanding Jesus. While we can see in Xenophon and Philostratus ways in which these authors have made use of imperfect disciples to illustrate the life style, thinking, and teaching method of their philosophical heroes and to provide a negative point of comparison for the exemplary character of the sages, in both cases the sages are shown to be acting as individuals rather than as founders of philosophical schools. Their books were not intended to be used within a community that traced its origins through the followers whom their authors depict. Iamblichus, on the other hand, was addressing a community that traced its origins to Pythagoras and his followers, and in this case we find a generally idealized portrait of the disciples.

The viewpoint of Weeden and others who have seen Mark as an attack on the disciples corresponds to the expectations that would be created by biographies such as that of Iamblichus, in which there is an idealization of the philosopher's followers.

Sira, on the other hand, provides little information about the actual relationships of students and teachers in the wisdom schools and does not provide a narrative account of the interactions between wisdom teachers and their students. The book does contain, however, the seed of an ideological rationale for the depiction of the Christian communities' founding members in a less than ideal manner. In Sira, wisdom is not understood to be a human accomplishment; it is a gift from God. While Sira assures the seeker after wisdom that his efforts will be rewarded, it is up to God to provide the reward "in His own time" (51.30). A lag is expected between the effort of the wisdom seeker and the bestowal of wisdom by God. Such an understanding of wisdom would allow for a period of misunderstanding on the part of those who later became the leaders of Christianity.

PART II

THE GOSPEL OF MARK

6

CALL STORIES

Mark introduces his Gospel as "the good news of Jesus Messiah, Son of God" (1.1). The beginning of the Gospel places Jesus within the grand sweep of sacred history, God's promises to Israel recorded in Scripture (1.2-3), the prophets of old (1.2), and a latter day prophet, John the Baptist, who testified to the coming of Jesus (1.4-8). Mark's introduction identifies Jesus as the beloved Son of God (1.11), portrays him as one who overcame Satan (1.13), and connects Jesus with the listening audience, those who have been baptized with the Holy Spirit (1.8). The prologue presents the divine reality of Jesus, not Jesus as seen through human eyes. Even John the Baptist, who testifies to the coming of Jesus and later baptizes him, does not recognize Jesus or interact with him in any way other than the baptism.

After a quick summary of the preaching of Jesus (1.14-15), Mark introduces the first disciples. At this point the narrative of Jesus decisively enters the human sphere. Now the listener can discover how the human world will react to the Son of God. By placing the call stories as the first of the narrated interchanges between Jesus and other human characters, Mark emphasizes their importance in representing the human reaction to Jesus. They are the first people who interact with Jesus, the ones to whom Jesus addresses his command, applicable to all, that they come after him and catch people rather than fish. Throughout the Gospel the disciples remain the ones who interact with Jesus on the most significant level, who receive most completely his

171

teaching, who grapple most deeply with the question of his identity, who follow him most loyally, and who betray him most shamefully.

The Pattern of the Markan Call Stories

The three call stories in Mark, the call of Peter and Andrew (1.16-18), of James and John (1.19-20), and of Levi (2.14), all show marked similarity in structure and wording, as indicated by the synopsis on the facing page (Figure 6.1). The similarity of the stories is underscored by the juxtaposition of the first two and the close proximity of the third to the earlier pair. The repetition of the common wording and structure suggests that the stories are to be taken as typical of Jesus' call and a disciple's response. The stories have seven parts: (1) a participle indicating Jesus' motion to the location of the call, (2) the verb εἶδεν and the names of the disciples, (3) a participle indicating a characteristic activity of the disciples' occupations, (4) a verb of address,[1] (5) a quotation of the words of calling (missing in the second story), (6) a participle indicating the disciples' leaving their earlier situation, and (7) a statement that they followed Jesus.

Mark introduces pericopes with verbs of motion with almost mechanical regularity,[2] the change of location serving to indicate to the listener the beginning of a new episode.[3] The motion is used to bring Jesus into a new situation or to bring a different character into contact with Jesus. Thus it is not surprising to find the same technique at work here. The effect of the constant motion is to fragment the narrative, since each episode introduces a new location

---

[1] Robbins argues that the use of καλεῖν rather than εἰπεῖν or λέγειν makes the second call significantly different from the first ("Mark 1.14-20," 231-34). It seems rather that ἐκάλεσεν αὐτούς is synonymous with εἶπεν αὐτοῖς, Δεῦτε ὀπίσω μου, and the variation is intended only to relieve monotony in the immediate repetition of nearly identical episodes.

[2] E.g., in chapter one, 1.9; 1.12; 1.14; 1.21; 1.29; 1.35; 1.40. In addition 1.4-8 begins by locating John in the wilderness (1.4) and follows with a verb of motion (1.5).

[3] John Drury notes, "Topographical movement such as going into a house or over water, leaving a place or arriving at one, divides [Mark's] narrative text much as paragraphing divides ours" ("Mark," in *The Literary Guide to the Bible*, ed. by Robert Alter and Frank Kermode [Cambridge, MA: Belknap Press, 1987] 406).

Figure 6.1
Synopsis of the Call Stories

```
A  καὶ παράγων        παρὰ τὴν θάλασσαν τῆς Γαλιλαίας
B  καὶ προβὰς ὀλίγον
C  καὶ παράγων [2.13: παρὰ τὴν θάλασσαν]

A  εἶδεν Σίμωνα                  καὶ 'Ανδρέαν τὸν
                                      ἀδελφὸν Σίμωνας
B  εἶδεν 'Ιάκωβον τὸν τοῦ Ζεβεδαίου καὶ 'Ιωάννην τὸν
                                      ἀδελφὸν αὐτοῦ,
C  εἶδεν Λευΐν     τὸν τοῦ 'Αλφαίου

A                           ἀμφιβάλλοντας ἐν τῇ θαλάσσῃ·
                                  ἦσαν γὰρ ἁλιεῖς.
B  καὶ αὐτοὺς ἐν τῷ πλοίῳ καταρτίζοντας τὰ δίκτυα,
C                         καθήμενον ἐπὶ τὸ τελώνιον,

A  καὶ         εἶπεν    αὐτοῖς ὁ 'Ιησοῦς,
B  καὶ εὐθὺς ἐκάλεσεν αὐτούς.
C  καὶ         λέγει    αὐτῷ,

A  Δεῦτε ὀπίσω μου, καὶ ποιήσω ὑμᾶς γενέσθαι ἁλιεῖς
                                      ἀνθρώπων.
B
C  'Ακολούθει μοι.

A  καὶ εὐθὺς ἀφέντες τὰ  δίκτυα
B  καὶ        ἀφέντες τὸν πατέρα αὐτῶν Ζεβεδαῖον ἐν τῷ
                                  πλοίῳ μετὰ τῶν μισθωτῶν
C  καὶ        ἀναστὰς

A  ἠκολούθησαν   αὐτῷ.
B  ἀπῆλθον ὀπίσω αὐτοῦ.
C  ἠκολούθησεν   αὐτῷ.
```

and new characters as well as new events. This reduces the causal connection of events within the narrative world and forces the listener to make the connections based on his or her own perception from a position external to the narrative. Since the rhetorical thrust of the Gospel is often more coherent than the narrative, the fragmentation of the narrative focuses the listener's attention upon the rhetorical rather than the narrative level. It also focuses the listener's attention upon Jesus, who is the one thread of continuity between the episodes.[4] The isolation of the call stories through change in location has the effect, at least in the initial pair, of accentuating the lack of motivation that is provided for the disciples' response to Jesus, since the disciples apparently have no information on which to base their decisions other than the information included within the episodes.

The εἶδεν clauses combine with the verbs of motion to indicate that the calls are not based on extended interchanges. Jesus came; he saw; he called. In 1.20 this is emphasized further by the insertion of εὐθύς. Jesus saw James and John, and *immediately* he called them.[5] Once again the lack of preparation is emphasized.

The mention of the disciples' occupations has a somewhat different effect in the different episodes. In the call of Levi, it underlines Levi's disreputable character. For the fishermen, it sets up the fishing for people metaphor and the fishermen's abandonment of their occupation following the call. With James and John, the abandonment of their past life is accentuated by the fact that they abandon their father as well as their livelihood. We have seen in the other literature a great deal of variation in the follower's relationship to his or her old way of life. In the *Memorabilia*, it is stressed that Socrates addressed each person within his or her own situation. The duties toward one's family are upheld (1.2.55; 2.2-3). The organization of the Pythagorean community, on the other hand, required a radical break with one's former life (*Pythagorean Life* 16-17).

The minimal content of the call is unusual. Jesus simply tells Levi, "Follow me," and not even that abrupt command is recorded in the call of James and John. The promise given to Peter and Andrew is devoid of

---

[4] This can be contrasted to the more continuous narrative of Philostratus, which allows characters other than Apollonius to be developed more fully.

[5] Although Mark uses εὐθύς so often that the word eventually loses some of its force, it continues to suggest a rush of events, and the three prior uses of εὐθύς, in 1.10, 12, and 18, all retain their full force as indicators that no time elapsed between the reported incidents.

content within the narrative world. It is only with the benefit of hindsight that the listener knows how these disciples became "fishers of persons."

Meaning of "Fishers of Persons"

In spite of some scholars' efforts to define more precisely the background and meaning of the "fishers of persons" metaphor,[6] the meaning of the promise can only be deduced from the context. The uses of the metaphor of fishing are too varied to assume that any one biblical or non-biblical example lies behind the Markan usage.[7] The flexibility of such a metaphor is evident in the *Memorabilia*, where Xenophon uses very similar metaphors of hunting to describe the occupation of the courtesan Theodote[8] as well as that of Socrates, who implies that he is more successful as a hunter of friends than is the courtesan.[9]

The narrative context, however, gives the listener very little help in understanding the metaphor. The listener can equate the fishing of persons with following Jesus, but any clearer understanding seems elusive. The disciples are never shown gathering people. When Jesus gives them a specific mission, it is to preach repentance, exorcise and heal (6.7-13). Given the various usages of the fishing metaphor elsewhere, it would be reasonable to construe the preaching of repentance as fishing for persons, but the sending out of the twelve is too far removed from the call stories to provide the listener with help in the present context. It is certainly possible, however, to construe Jesus' own activity in the call narratives as fishing for persons,[10] and thus the

---

[6] E.g., Jindrich Manek, "Fishers of Men," *NovT* 2 (1958) 138-41; Charles W. F. Smith, "Fishers of Men: Footnotes on a Gospel Figure," *HTR* 52 (1959) 187-203.

[7] For a survey of various ways in which the metaphor was used in Greek, Jewish, and Near Eastern texts, see Wilhelm H. Wuellner, *The Meaning of "Fishers of Men"* (Philadelphia: Westminster Press, 1967) 64-133.

[8] Θηρᾶν, 3.11.6-8; Socrates as a συνθηρατής, 3.11.15; the use of dogs, 3.11.8; and nets 3.11.8-10.

[9] Socrates refers to his followers as θῖλαι in 3.11.16. In this portion of the dialogue, Xenophon changes the metaphor from hunting to magic. The logic of the interchange, however, is based on the hunting metaphor. Socrates can offer Theodote advice and assistance in catching friends because he is a better hunter of friends than she is.

[10] Noted by Benoît Standaert, *L'Évangile selon Marc: Commentaire*, LirB (Paris: Éditions du Cerf, 1983) 46.

176 *Follow Me!*

listener might take the metaphor to mean that the disciples will do (in the future) what Jesus is doing now, calling people to follow. Within the narrative, however, they do not call anyone to follow either themselves or Jesus.

Given the important location of the call stories, the use of an opaque metaphor to describe the role of a disciple would be quite inept. It is more reasonable to assume that Mark expected his listeners to understand the content of the metaphor from their own knowledge of the subsequent activity of Peter and Andrew. Since the post-Easter missionary activity of the disciples could be described aptly as fishing for persons, and as this activity roughly corresponds to Jesus' activity in calling the disciples, it is most likely that Mark's audience would take this activity rather than anything described in the narrative itself as the referent of "fishers of persons." Thus the listener would understand the call of discipleship to involve the missionary activity of the church, however that might have been understood within the Markan community.

While Mark's listeners can infer the content of "fishers of persons" from the disciples' later activity, the fishermen in the narrative do not have the benefit of hindsight. Thus within the narrative world, the content of the call remains a riddle, and it cannot be seen as providing motivation for the fishermen's response. The call is parabolic in the Markan sense. It is metaphorical language that requires interpretation and simultaneously obscures and reveals the truth hidden within a description of mundane reality.[11] The listeners have the key to interpreting the parable, but the fishermen do not.

Rhetorical Functions of Call Stories

A review of the call stories in the philosophical and wisdom literature shows that they can be adapted to a variety of rhetorical functions. As the following discussion indicates, the stories may simultaneously fulfill more than one of these functions.

Protreptic. One important function of such stories is protreptic.[12]

---

[11] This will be discussed in more detail in the two following chapters.

[12] On the nature of protrepsis and several examples, see Malherbe, *Moral Exhortation*, 122-24; Stanley Kent Stowers, *The Diatribe and Paul's Letter to the Romans*, SBLDS 57 (Chico, CA: Scholars Press, 1981) 48-78; Mark D. Jordan,

Protrepsis is generally understood as an exhortation to follow the philosophical life or the pursuit of wisdom. A protreptic call story is designed to show the advantages of the philosophical life or the pursuit of wisdom. It often includes a protracted exposition of the advantages of the philosophical life or of the doctrines of a specific school. Euthydemus' conversion by Socrates in the *Memorabilia* (4.2) is the best example of such a call story in the works that we have examined. Other examples include Plato's protreptic dialogues and Lucian's *Nigrinus*. In other cases, the argument is extremely compressed, as in the story of the conversion of Xenophon related by Diogenes Laertius:

> The story goes that Socrates met him in a narrow passage, and that he stretched out his stick to bar the way, while he inquired where every kind of food was sold. Upon receiving a reply, he put another question, "And where do men become good and honourable?" Xenophon was fairly puzzled; "Then follow me," said Socrates, "and learn." From that time onward he was a pupil of Socrates.[13]

Socrates has cleverly compressed a protreptic argument into two simple questions. The argument itself is left unspoken, but it can easily be supplied by the reader: It is certainly as important to become good and honorable as it is to secure physical sustenance; you should devote yourself to the development of your character as well as to the enjoyment of physical pleasures. The two questions leave Xenophon convicted of directing his energy toward the less important aspects of life.[14]

To illustrate the superiority of one teacher or school. Since protreptic conversion stories argue for the superiority of a particular way of life or thought, they may indicate the superiority of that way to various competing systems. The call of Euthydemus in the *Memorabilia* (4.2),

---

"Ancient Philosophic Protreptic and the Problem of Persuasive Genres," *Rhetorica* 4 (1986) 309-33. For protreptic in the Platonic dialogues, see Konrad Gaiser, *Protreptik und Paränese bei Platon*, TBA 40 (Stuttgart: Kohlhammer, 1959).

On the protreptic use of call stories with citations of several examples, see Malherbe, "'Not in a Corner'," in *Paul and the Popular Philosophers*, 161-63.

[13] Diogenes Laertius 2.48 (LCL tr.).

[14] For the importance of bringing a convert to the realization of his or her errors as a strategy of philosophical conversion, see Malherbe, *Paul and the Thessalonians*, 21-28.

for example, indicates the superiority of Socrates' wisdom over the wisdom contained in the books in which Euthydemus takes so much pride. In the New Testament, a similar use of a conversion story is found in Acts 19.1-7. Paul converts a number of followers of John the Baptist in Ephesus, and the speedy acceptance of Christian baptism by these Johannine sectarians suggests that the sect is simply an imperfect form of Christianity.[15]

Similar stories are also found in encomiastic passages, which praise the subject without intending to convert the reader or hearer. In Philostratus, Nilus' conversion (6.12) shows Apollonius' superiority over the Gymnosophs. Similarly, Demetrius' conversion (4.25) shows Apollonius' superiority over Cynicism. Diogenes Laertius includes a long list of followers whom Stilpo drew away from other schools, noting, "So far did he excel all the rest in inventiveness and sophistry that nearly the whole of Greece was attracted to him" (2.113-14, LCL tr.).

Call stories may also indicate the superiority of a teacher by showing the quality of followers that the teacher attracted. Demetrius' conversion in the *Life of Apollonius* (4.25) is a good example of such an approach. The philosopher Demetrius was well known in his own right, and so his decision to follow Apollonius, besides showing the superiority of Apollonius' teaching to that of the Cynics, is a testimony to the value of the philosopher's thought. In a more general way, the strict requirements placed on those who sought to become followers of the Brahmans (*Life of Apollonius* 2.30) or of Pythagoras (*Pythagorean Life* 17.71-74) indicates the quality of the students whom these teachers could attract.

To characterize the teacher, the student, or the relationship between the two. While all narrative episodes involve some measure of characterization, call stories, because they generally serve to introduce followers to the readers or listeners, often have a particularly important

---

[15] So Ernst Käsemann, "The Disciples of John the Baptist in Ephesus," in *Essays on New Testament Themes* (Philadelphia: Fortress Press, 1982) 136-48; Ernst Haenchen, *The Acts of the Apostles: A Commentary* (Oxford: Basil Blackwell, 1971) 549-57. The preceding episode, recounting the baptism of Apollos, probably makes the same point, but it is less clear if Apollos was associated with the baptist sect. In any case, the conversions show the superiority of the apostolic church to the imperfect forms of belief from which Apollos and the followers of John were converted.

role in characterization.[16] For example, Euthydemus' character is established in the initial protreptic dialogue of the fourth book of the *Memorabilia* (4.2), and it remains essentially unchanged through the ensuing dialogues.

The characterization of Damis in the *Life of Apollonius* (1.19) is particularly interesting in its disappointment of reader expectations. Since call stories are used so often for protreptic or apologetic ends, the audience expects to hear an argument for the value of the teacher's wisdom or a demonstration of either the teacher's or the student's extraordinary ability, power, or wisdom. Students are expected to be overwhelmed by a teacher's wisdom and to be motivated by a desire for the good and the true. The confounding of such expectations makes the characterization of Damis very effective. Damis' decision to follow Apollonius because of his love of adventure marks him from the beginning as a disciple of dubious quality. The episode defines Damis as a man more concerned with adventure than with philosophy and more impressed with wondrous powers, such as Apollonius' alleged ability to understand all languages, than with thought.

Independently circulating call stories may gain currency because of their power to characterize a teacher-hero. The conversion of Xenophon quoted above, which seems to have been an independent chreia,[17] is especially effective as a characterization of Socrates, showing his brashness, his wit, his ability to point out people's ignorance of basic moral understanding, and his dedication to the pursuit of the good and the honorable.

The same chreia provides a good example of a call story as a characterization of the relationship between a teacher and a follower. It is a particularly concise and memorable example of the Socratic teaching method, the use of questions to elicit an intended self-discovery from the dialogue partner.

---

[16] Robbins, *Jesus the Teacher*, 93.

[17] It is totally unrelated to any of the other information that Diogenes provides about Xenophon, is completely self-contained, and has a greater impact as an independent episode than it does in its current place in Diogenes Laertius. Diogenes makes frequent use of self-contained chreia with minimal, if any, attempt to integrate them into a narrative or logical structure.

To illustrate the dedication of the student. One common variant of the call motif, which often serves primarily to characterize the student rather than the teacher, is found in those stories in which the potential student actively seeks out his teacher. Pythagoras' pursuit of teachers (*Pythagorean Life* 2.9-4.19) is an example of this type, and serves to show the philosopher's dedication to learning. The story of the young Jesus in the temple (Lk 2.41-51) also contains elements of this type. Passages that show a philosopher attending a number of teachers, such as the account of Apollonius' education in Philostratus (1.7) and the description of Menedemus in Diogenes Laertius (2.125-26), similarly show the dedication of the philosopher-student. Most rabbinic call stories fit this model.[18]

Another group of such stories might be termed book conversions. In this type, the potential student is converted through a philosophical writing and then seeks out the writer of the work or a substitute teacher. In Aristotle's fragmentary dialogue *Nerinthos*, both Axiothea and Nerinthos seek out Plato after reading one of his dialogues, and Zeno leaves Phoenicia after hearing a reading of the *Apology*. According to Diogenes Laertius, Zeno became a follower of Crates after reading Xenophon's *Memorabilia*. When he inquired of the bookseller where men like Socrates were to be found, the bookseller told him to follow Crates.[19] These stories illustrate both the greatness of the teacher (the power of Plato's writings, the testimony that Crates was like Socrates) and the eagerness of the potential student.

As an occasion for a miracle. Conversion may also be based on, or confirmed by, a miraculous sign or power. Abaris followed Pythagoras after the philosopher revealed to him his golden thigh, signifying that he was indeed the god Apollo (19.91-92). Damis' decision to follow Apollonius is based in part on Apollonius' claim to understand all languages without instruction (1.19). In these stories the conversion of the follower replaces the more commonly found response of the crowd in underlining the exceptional nature of the miracle.

---

[18] Rengstorf, "μαθητής," 4.444; Hengel, *Charismatic Leader*, 31-32; Robbins, *Jesus the Teacher*, 101-03.

[19] Aristotle, *Fragments* (ed. V. Rose, 1886) 74; Diogenes Laertius 7.3; both cited by Hengel, *Charismatic Leader*, 28.

To show the power of the teaching to achieve a moral conversion.
A very different approach to a conversion story is the conversion of a
morally disreputable person that shows the marked change in character
that the hero's teaching is able to achieve. Such conversions are found
in both protreptic and encomiastic passages. Apollonius' conversion of
his brother in Philostratus' work (1.13) is an example of the encomiastic
type. Iamblichus ends two of Pythagoras' public discourses with notes
about how much his audience's conduct improved after hearing his
speech (9.50 and 11.56-57). Here the passages function both to influence
the reader's conduct and to praise Pythagoras.

The most famous such account is that of Polemo's conversion by
Xenocrates.[20] One version of the conversion is preserved in Diogenes
Laertius:

> In his youth he was so profligate and dissipated that he actually
> carried about with him money to procure the immediate gratification
> of his desires, and would even keep sums concealed in lanes and
> alleys.... And one day, by agreement with his young friends, he burst
> into the school of Xenocrates, quite drunk, with a garland on his head.
> Xenocrates, however, without being at all disturbed, went on with his
> discourse as before, the subject being temperance. The lad, as he
> listened, by degrees was taken in the toils. He became so industrious
> as to surpass all the other scholars, and rose to be himself head of the
> school in the 116th Olympiad.[21]

A second century account of the radical change of character
brought about by philosophical exhortation is found in Lucian's protreptic dialogue *Nigrinus*:

> For [Nigrinus] went on to praise philosophy and the freedom that it
> gives, and to ridicule the things that are popularly considered
> blessings—wealth and reputation, dominion and honour, yes and
> purple and gold—things accounted very desirable by most men, and

---

[20] For discussions of moral conversions in the philosophical traditions, see
Chapter 2, n. 40.

[21] Diogenes Laertius 4.16 (LCL tr). Other accounts of Polemo are found in
Lucian, *The Double Indictment* 17; Horace, *Satire* 2.3.253-57; Epictetus,
Discourses 3.1.14; 4.11.30.

till then by me also. I took it all in with eager, wide-open soul, and at
the moment I couldn't imagine what had come over me; I was all
confused. Then I felt hurt because he had criticised what was dearest
to me—wealth and money and reputation,—and I all but cried over
their downfall; and then I thought them paltry and ridiculous, and was
glad to be looking up, as it were, out of the murky atmosphere of my
past life to a clear sky and a great light.[22]

Even in such stories, however, the opinion was often expressed
that the underlying character of the future student had to be good for the
philosophical ideas to take hold. Thus Epictetus says of Polemo, "That
is why the words of Xenocrates laid hold even of a Polemo, because he
was a young man who loved beauty. For he came to Xenocrates with
glimmerings of a zeal for the beautiful, but was looking for it in the
wrong place" (*Discourses* 4.11.30 (LCL tr.).[23] The same attitude is
expressed by the narrator of *Nigrinus*, who notes, "Not all who listen to
philosophers go away enraptured and wounded, but only those who
previously had in their nature some secret bond of kinship with philosophy" (Lucian, *Nigrinus* 37, LCL tr.).[24]

To show the value of intellectual inquiry. Another important
attraction of philosophy was the joy of intellectual inquiry, and conversion to the intellectual life might also be the subject of a call story. A
good example is the story told of Pythagoras, who paid a lad to learn
mathematical lessons until the student became so entranced with the
subject that his teacher was able to extract payment for the lessons
(*Pythagorean Life* 5.21-25).

Narrative functions. Call stories may have primarily narrative
rather than rhetorical functions. Damis' decision to follow Apollonius is
an important part of Philostratus' narrative. Since Philostratus attributed
most of his information concerning Apollonius to this fictitious follower,
it was necessary for the coherence of the narrative to introduce Damis

---

[22] Lucian, *Nigrinus* 4 (LCL tr.).

[23] The context is a discourse on cleanliness in which Epictetus states that it is
easier to teach philosophy to those who pay attention to the grooming of their hair
(such as Polemo, who was a dandy) than to those who neglect it, since the former
are at least searching for beauty.

[24] Lucian states in the *Double Indictment* 17 that Polemo "was not naturally bad
or inclined to Intemperance" (LCL tr.).

early in the story. Characterization might be included under this heading as well, but characterization often serves rhetorical ends in didactic and propagandistic writings such as we have examined.

Peculiarities of the Markan Call Stories

Lack of Motivation

Given the typical functions of call stories to expound the values of a life of wisdom or to demonstrate the power or superiority of a teacher, the Markan call stories are peculiar in the lack of motivation provided for the fishermen's decision to follow Jesus. These first call stories occur before any report of Jesus' mighty works and before any detail has been given about the content of his teaching. The four fishermen do not appear to have heard Jesus' preaching. In the first case, Simon and Andrew are simply instructed to follow Jesus and given the ambiguous promise that they will become fishers of persons. In the second case, the call of James and John, the content of Jesus' call is not even recorded.[25]

There is no example of such an unmotivated call story in any of the other literature examined in this dissertation. In Xenophon, Euthydemus becomes an associate of Socrates only after extended wheedling and long discussions about the benefits to be achieved from such an association (*Memorabilia* 4.2). Damis becomes a follower of Apollonius because of his desire to travel and Apollonius' claim to supernatural power (*Life of Apollonius* 1.19). Apollonius' other followers join him because of his reputation or his superior ability as a thinker (4.25; 4.40; 5.12, 14-17; 6.3). The first followers of Pythagoras in Croton join him after his public teaching (*Pythagorean Life* 6.29), and his later followers are attracted to a teacher with an established reputation. Abaris becomes a follower of Pythagoras after identifying him as the god Apollo (19.91-92). Ben Sira

---

[25] Ernest Best suggests that Mark would have included the call stories among "the wonderful events or miracles in his Gospel" because they "took place without psychological preparation and as a result only of Jesus' simple word to [the disciples]" ("The Miracles in Mark," in *Disciples and Discipleship: Studies in the Gospel According to Mark* [Edinburgh: T. & T. Clark, 1986] 181). This judgment is accurate if one considers only the narrative level of the Gospel, but the rhetorical function of the stories within the Gospel diverts the listeners' attention from the narrative level, as shown below.

exhorts the reader to follow wisdom by showing the benefits to be gained on both the material and spiritual level (4.11-16; 6.28-31; 14.20-15.6; 24.19-22; 51.20-22).

Luke, who follows the biographical pattern more closely than the other Gospel writers, seems to have found the lack of motivation in the Markan call stories problematic. He records several instances of Jesus' preaching and healing activity and the enthusiastic acceptance of the crowds (4.14-44) prior to the decision of the first disciples to follow Jesus. In the Lukan order, Peter has already witnessed the healing of his mother-in-law (4.38-39) as well as the miraculous catch of fish (5.1-10a) before becoming a disciple (5.11). The writer of John also provides motivation for the first disciples, who hear John the Baptist's testimony to Jesus (1.35-36). In this case, the disciples recognize Jesus immediately as the Messiah, and Simon follows Jesus because his brother has testified that Jesus is the Messiah (1.40-42; cf. 1.45).

Only Matthew follows Mark in leaving the call of the disciples unmotivated. Unlike Mark, however, he moves from the call stories to a summary passage about Jesus' preaching and healing and the enthusiastic response of the crowds (4.23-25). As a result, the listener hears the call stories in Matthew as specific incidents within a general summary report that stretches from 4.12 to 4.25, and the call of the disciples is perceived as a specific instance of the activity reported in the summarizing passages. Mark, on the other hand, by placing the call stories first in a series of specific instances of Jesus' activity, presents them as the first of a chronologically ordered series of events. This makes the stories stand on their own as self-contained units, leaving the hearer without a clear sense of probable causation.

The lack of probable causation on the narrative level leads the listener to find causation on the discourse level, as suggested by the order of the narration. The central thrust of the prologue is to establish Jesus as the beloved Son of God. The two short reports that intervene between the baptism, in which Jesus' status as the beloved Son is proclaimed, and the first call stories serve to reinforce Jesus' identity as the Son of God: As the Son of God he overcomes the temptation of Satan (1.13); as the Son of God he proclaims the coming of his Father's kingdom (1.14-15). As the Son of God he calls disciples. The hearer knows that the disciples respond to Jesus because he is the Son of God. The lack of psychological motivation serves to emphasize the more essential, spiritual motivation. The ignorance of the disciples themselves of this essential causation within the narrative is another instance of the well-known split between reality and human perception that pervades the Gospel. This split becomes an essential component of the relationship between Jesus and the disciples in chapters four through eight.

The lack of motivation in the call stories also serves to generalize the stories and thus facilitate the hearer's identification with the disciples. The Gospel was composed for a Christian audience[26] that, because of their self-identification as followers of Jesus, would readily identify with the disciples who are called to follow.[27] The succinct narration of the stories—setting, call, and positive response—allows all listeners to experience the disciples' call as their own call within the rhetoric of the narrative. Any argumentation may meet with listeners who fail to

[26] At a number of points the rhetoric of the Gospel presupposes Christian belief. The nature of the Markan call stories provides evidence that Mark intended his Gospel to be heard by a Christian audience. The lack of motivation in the stories, the lack of argument for the value of following Jesus, and the lack of details showing the benefit derived from following Jesus would make the stories inappropriate for an evangelical discourse in which the call of the disciples would function as a model for those who had not already made a similar commitment.

[27] See Robert C. Tannehill, "The Disciples in Mark: The Function of a Narrative Role," *JR* 57 (1977) 392-93. The identification between hearer and disciples generated by the initial call stories, however, does not necessarily create an identification with the disciples in all succeeding incidents. The Gospel operates on the level of historical narrative, in which the distinction between the listeners and the disciples is clear, as well as on the rhetorical level, in which there is sometimes but not always an identification between the listeners and the disciples. While the listener can easily experience generalizable utterances of Jesus, such as the demand to follow or the naming of Jesus' followers as his true relatives (3.33-35), as direct address to themselves, the narration of historically specific incidents, such as the feeding stories, allow the listener more distance from the disciples. Tannehill acknowledges that listeners' understanding of the identity of Jesus creates an ironic distance between the listener and the disciples when the disciples fail to understand this point (400), but he minimizes the significance of that distance. The Christian listeners know the outcome of Jesus' ministry and possess an understanding of its salvific significance withheld from the disciples. They also possess the advantage of familiarity with the unexpected teachings of Jesus that catch the disciples by surprise. The ironic distance between the listeners and the disciples requires the interpreter to consider the rhetoric of each episode with care before a judgment can be made concerning the extent of the listeners' identification with the disciples.

experience the disciples' call as their own call within the rhetoric of the narrative. Any argumentation may meet with listeners who fail to identify with the argument, but the reliance on implied argumentation, as in Mark, allows every Christian listener to respond. Paradoxically, the lack of motivation at the narrative level universalizes motivation at the discourse level. Thus the listener is led, at the very outset of the narrative, to reaffirm his or her commitment to following Jesus, and in this way the Gospel does not allow a disinterested hearing of its message.

Characterization of Jesus I: Authority

The lack of protreptic argumentation in the first call stories is illustrative of another major concern of Mark, the authority of Jesus. It is appropriate for Euthydemus to be swayed by Socrates' logical arguments since, according to Xenophon, Socrates believed that the proper course of human life was in large part to be determined through rational examination. Only those questions that could not be decided rationally were to be submitted to the gods (*Memorabilia* 1.1.6-9). Thus Socrates only dealt with those issues that were amenable to rational decision making. As a guide to the process of rational investigation, Socrates could only have authority because of his superior powers of rational analysis, powers that he sought to share with his followers.

Jesus' message, on the other hand, is not amenable to rational analysis. How is one to determine whether the Kingdom of God is at hand? No rational proof is offered, and given Mark's parabolic view of the world, in which the publicly accessible meaning is a mask for true meaning,[28] none is possible. The truth of the statement is dependent on the authority of the one who delivers it. Is Jesus the authorized herald of God or not?

Because of this, Jesus' authority, rather than his rational powers, is central to many of the teaching and controversy episodes. In the first episode describing Jesus as a teacher, those who hear him are amazed at his teaching because he teaches "as one possessing authority" (1.22), and after the expulsion of the demon they again describe his teaching as κατ'

---

[28] This will be discussed in more detail below. An excellent discussion of Markan epistemology and its underlying view of the world can be found in Joel Marcus, "Mark 4:10-12 and Markan Epistemology," *JBL* 103 (1984) 557-74.

ἐξουσίαν (1.27).[29]   The first controversy between Jesus and the authorities is also linked explicitly to his authority. The scribes charge Jesus with blasphemy because he claims for himself the authority to forgive sins, an authority that only God possesses (2.7). In reply, Jesus does not provide rational argumentation but rather heals the paralytic, "so that you might know that the Son of Man has authority on earth to forgive sins" (2.10). Similarly, the question of plucking grain on the Sabbath is argued on the basis of authority.   While Jesus provides a scriptural warrant for allowing his disciples to break the Sabbath law, the conclusion of the argument does not concern the legitimacy of the Sabbath law but rather Jesus' authority to abrogate it: "The Son of Man is lord even of the Sabbath" (2.28).[30]   The controversy over Jesus' exorcisms also is concerned explicitly with his authority: Does Jesus derive his authority over the demons from the prince of demons (3.22) or from having defeated Satan (3.27)?[31]

While much of the ensuing narrative concerns the question of Jesus' authority, for Mark's listener the authority of Jesus has already been clearly established. The listener has already heard John's testimony to Jesus (1.7-8), God's proclamation of Jesus as His beloved son (1.10-11), and the endurance of Jesus through the temptation of Satan (1.13). The pre-existing inclination of Christian listeners to accept the proclamation of Jesus as authoritative has been reinforced by the authority granted

---

[29] I understand this phrase to refer to the teaching rather than the command to the demon, but it makes little difference in the present discussion.

[30] Mark consistently uses the term "Son of Man" as a self-designation for Jesus, and there is no reason to interpret it as a circumlocution for "human being" in this case.

The intervening controversies, concerned with ritual matters of eating with unclean persons and fasting, are implicitly concerned with authority as well, since Jesus is claiming the authority to establish new ritual standards.

[31] Other major controversy stories center on the question of authority. Jesus questions the authority of the traditions of the elders (7.1-13). The high priests, the scribes, and the elders demand to know on what authority Jesus is acting (11.27-33). In addition, Jesus claims the authority to set aside the Mosaic law (7.19; 10.2-12). Kingsbury cites the issue of authority as the "critical issue" of the conflict between Jesus and the religious authorities (*Conflict in Mark: Jesus, Authorities, Disciples* [Minneapolis: Fortress Press, 1989] 65-75, esp. 66-67.

to Jesus in the narrative.[32] Since the listener experiences the proclamation of Jesus as authorized by God, the proclamation increases the
experience of Jesus' authority. Jesus is not only the Son of God in some
indefinite sense. He is the one authorized to proclaim the imminent
coming of the Kingdom.

Thus while the narrative provides no psychological motivation for
the disciples' response, it does provide motivation for the listener to
respond to the call of Jesus. The listeners respond to the narrated
authority of Jesus as the Son of God and the one who overcame Satan.
They also know that a response to Jesus' call is a response to the
Kingdom. Thus the listeners do not notice the disciples' lack of motivation within the narrative as strange, since, in identifying with the disciples' response to Jesus, they project their own motivation into the
fishermen's decision. At the same time, the disciples' unmotivated
response reinforces the experience of Jesus' authority. The disciples
respond simply because Jesus has authority. Although the disciples are
deprived of the listener's understanding of why Jesus has authority, the
listener approves of their unquestioning response to that authority.

The centrality of authority to the Markan portrait of Jesus is also
apparent in the appointment of the twelve, where Jesus transfers his
authority, rather than a body of teaching, to the disciples. The twelve are
constituted so that they might be sent out to proclaim in Jesus' stead and
to have authority to cast out demons (3.14-15).[33] The content of the

---

[32] It is doubtful, however, that the narrated events are sufficient to establish
Jesus' authority for a listener not predisposed to accept the narrative claims at
face value.

[33] Κηρύσσειν in Mark generally retains its primary meaning of proclaiming
(as a herald) the message of another. John the Baptist, who proclaims (κηρύσσειν) a baptism of repentance (1.4) and a greater one coming after himself
(1.7), is sent out (ἀποστέλλειν) by God to prepare the way (1.2). His authority comes from God (clearly implied in 11.29-33). Jesus acts as the herald of
God, proclaiming (κηρύσσειν) the gospel of God (the reading τὸ εὐαγγέλιον
τῆς βασιλείας τοῦ θεοῦ in many manuscripts is an obvious "correction"),
where God is the source of the good news as well as its content (1.14). When
Jesus sends out the twelve, he sends them out κηρύσσειν; when the twelve
report on their own activity, they report what they taught (διδάσκειν). There
are two occurrences of κηρύσσειν in which the proclaimer is not, at least by
implication, one who is sent by another. These both refer to the proclamation of
a healing of Jesus by those who were specifically ordered to keep the healing
secret (5.20; 7.36). Here κηρύσσειν is used for the reporting of a momentous

proclamation is not even mentioned. The narrative of the sending out of the twelve follows much the same pattern. Mark states that Jesus "began to send them out two by two, and he gave them authority over the unclean spirits" (6.7). Jesus then gives them specific directions about what to take, where to stay, and what to do if the people will not listen (6.8-11). It is only then, in describing the disciples' activity, that Mark mentions the activity of proclamation, and the only content of the proclamation is "that they might repent" (6.12).[34]

Such a transfer of authority is quite alien to the philosophical and wisdom material we have examined. Both Pythagoras and Apollonius might be described as possessing a miraculous authority over spirits or natural processes, but they do not transfer that authority to their students. Although several of Pythagoras' followers possess miraculous abilities (*Pythagorean Life* 28.135-36), they possess them as a result of their own piety. The unreported conversations between Apollonius and the Brahmans (*Life of Apollonius* 3.41) convey certain powers to Apollonius through the transfer of esoteric knowledge, but there is no suggestion that authority could be conveyed apart from the teaching.[35]

---

event, another of the traditional functions of a messenger. The translation of κηρύσσειν as "to preach" distorts the meaning of the term in Mark.

Mark generally uses κηρύσσειν when the message is considered to be a unitary proclamation (the baptism of repentance, 1.4; the coming of a greater one, 1.7; the gospel of God, 1.14; the gospel, 14.9; the activity of Jesus 5.20, 7.36) and διδάσκειν when the message is understood as a collection of individual teachings (ἐδίδασκεν αὐτοὺς ἐν παραβολαῖς πολλά, 4.2; ὅσα ἐδίδαξαν, 6.30; ἤρξατο διδάσκειν αὐτοὺς πολλά, 6.34; the teaching in the temple, 12.35, 14.49). The one possible exception is the proclamation of the healed leper in 1.45, ἤρξατο κηρύσσειν πολλά, but there πολλά appears to be adverbial, since the content of his proclamation is the single fact of his healing.

[34] Ἵνα in this verse is more likely to indicate purpose rather than content. In that case, there is no content indicated.

[35] On two occasions Mark provides instruction on the performance of miraculous deeds. In 9.29, Jesus indicates that a certain type of spirit can only be driven out through prayer. In 11.23-25, he gives more general directions on the connection between faith, prayer, and miracle. These episodes, however, are later in the narrative; Jesus grants the disciples authority to cast out demons in 3.15 and 7.7. In 7.13, when Jesus explicitly directs the twelve to perform exorcisms, they are successful. In 9.18, when the disciples are unsuccessful in exorcising an unclean spirit, they seem to be operating on their own, at human request rather than at Jesus' direction.

Characterization of Jesus II: Jesus as the Founder of a Community

It is common for the first scenes in which a character appears to be used to define that person's essential traits. This is true in Mark as well as in other narrative works. For example, the first mention of Judas Iscariot (3.19) indicates that he handed Jesus over to the authorities, the act that is constitutive of Judas' identity in Christian consciousness. Collective characters also receive their essential traits at their first appearance. Thus, in the first scene involving the crowd, the people are amazed at Jesus (1.27), and in the second crowd scene, they flock to Jesus to receive healing (1.32). The scribes (representing the larger collective of Jewish authorities) are introduced as grumbling and charging Jesus with blasphemy (2.6). The motivationless call stories are consistent with the later characterization of the disciples as ones who follow Jesus without the benefit of understanding.

Mark's placement of the call stories at the very outset of Jesus' ministry designates the gathering of disciples as an essential component of Jesus' earthly identity.[36] The first episodes involving Jesus define his spiritual identity as the Son of God (1.9-11) who has overcome Satan (1.12-13). The next episodes define his earthly identity as one who proclaims the Kingdom of God (1.14-15), gathers a community of disciples (1.16-20), teaches (1.21-22), casts out demons (1.23-28), and heals (1.29-34). The first thirty-four verses of the Gospel provide the reader with an understanding of Jesus' identity that remains essentially unchanged throughout the first half of the Gospel. The only important modification of the characterization of Jesus in the first half of the Gospel is the intensification of the wonder-working power of Jesus as one who has power over the elements of nature (4.35-41). The first half of the Gospel is basically an investigation of the relationship between the identities of Jesus defined in these first thirty-four verses. In the second half of the Gospel, on the other hand, the discourse is radically altered by the introduction of the third identity of Jesus, the one who was crucified and resurrected (8.31).

The existence of disciples is much more central to the identity of the Markan Jesus than it is for any of the other teachers whom we have

---

[36] Cf. John R. Donahue, *The Theology and Setting of Discipleship in the Gospel of Mark*, PMLT 14 (Milwaukee: Marquette University Press, 1983) 19.

treated. Xenophon depicts Socrates as one who teaches everyone, and only incidentally and late in the *Memorabilia* does he show the relationship between Socrates and Euthydemus, the only one of the dialogue partners who is shown in an extended relationship with Socrates.[37] None of the biographies we examined introduces the gathering of students so early in the description of the hero. Iamblichus establishes Pythagoras' credentials as a wise man (1-14) before discussing his school (15-27), even though the community of the Pythagoreans rather than Pythagoras himself appears to be the true subject of the work. Similarly, Philostratus demonstrates Apollonius' wisdom (1.1-15) before introducing students, and the presence of students remains somewhat peripheral to Apollonius' central identity, since many of the primary dialogues take place between Apollonius and men who cannot accurately be termed students, such as the Brahmans (3.18-26, 34-37, 42-49), the Gymnosophs (6.13, 19-21), and the various kings and emperors (1.37; 2.29-30, 34-37, 38; 5.31-38). The wise man of Ben Sira is only secondarily a teacher, and Wisdom is Wisdom whether she has followers or not. The early introduction of Jesus in his role as the creator of a community indicates that this is an important aspect of his Messianic office.

Importance of Personal Attachment

It is striking that the creation of community has primacy over both teaching and christological confession in the Gospel of Mark. The first disciples have received no teaching from Jesus and make no christolo-

---

[37] *Pace* Robbins, who terms the Socrates of Xenophon a "disciple-gathering teacher" (*Jesus the Teacher*, 60) and consistently refers to the followers of Socrates as "disciples." Besides its inappropriateness in relation to Xenophon's Socrates, the use of the term "disciple-gathering teacher" by Robbins prejudges the question of whether or not the disciples of Jesus were in fact similar to the students of other teachers, since the term "disciple" in English is so closely associated with the disciples of Jesus. In general usage, the Greek term μαθητής means student or apprentice and does not have the same connotations as the English word "disciple." See Rengstorf, "μαθητής," 4.416-26; Wilkins, *Concept of Disciple*, 11-42. Although the term could be applied to the followers of a philosopher, Xenophon avoids using the term (see above, Chapter 2, pp. 46-49). It does not appear in Ben Sira, and both Iamblichus and Philostratus prefer other terms to describe the followers of their heroes.

gical confession until much later.[38] At least in part, this results from
the strong element of personal attachment in the relationship of the
disciples and Jesus. Discipleship is primarily an attachment to Jesus and
only secondarily involves learning from him. The same primacy of
attachment over learning is repeated in the rhetorical organization of the
Gospel. The listener is led in the initial call stories to reaffirm his or her
attachment to Jesus, but it is only in chapter four that the listener is
presented with any explicit teaching of Jesus.

This is in sharp contrast to the portrayal of students in the
philosophical and wisdom literature. Students of philosophers are shown
to have a strong commitment to their teachers, but the commitment is
based on the value of the philosophers' teaching.[39] In the *Memorabilia*
(4.2), Euthydemus makes a commitment to intellectual inquiry. Socrates
proves himself a better guide than the books that Euthydemus has read,
and thus he wins the young man's allegiance. Jesus' disciples, on the
other hand, are not called to attach themselves to Jesus' teaching or to an
intellectual or spiritual process in which Jesus acts as a guide. They are
specifically called to attach themselves to the person of Jesus, to "come
after me." Their assignment, similarly, is not to teach but to gather
others, to become "fishers of persons."

The account of the choosing of the twelve also stresses the personal aspect of the disciples' mission. Jesus forms the twelve "so that they
might be with him, and he might send them out" (3.14b-15). The twelve
are also to proclaim an unspecified message. Κηρύσσειν here clearly
retains its primary meaning of proclaiming as a herald, since the apostles
are those sent out by Jesus to make a proclamation.[40] Thus the proclamation of the twelve is relational as well, since the twelve are to represent

---

[38] Cf. John 1.41, where the first disciples follow because they recognize
Jesus as the Messiah. In Luke, Simon Peter recognizes Jesus as a divine
emissary before he is called. He addresses Jesus as "Lord" and becomes
conscious of his sinfulness, saying, "Depart from me, for I am a sinful man"
(Lk 5.8, RSV).

[39] Malherbe points out the strong intellectual and emotional attachment the
narrator in Lucian's *Nigrinus* has for his teacher (*Moral Exhortation*, 57).
Porphyry reports a story that Pythagoras' followers, when caught in a burning
building with their master, threw themselves into the fire to make a bridge for
Pythagoras' escape (*Life of Pythagoras*, 57).

[40] Cf. n. 33, above.

Jesus as his heralds. The transfer of authority over the demons to the twelve suggests that the twelve are representatives of Jesus.

The relational aspect of the disciples' calling is further emphasized in 3.31-34, in which Jesus refers to the crowd around him as "my mother and my brothers." The familial relationship to Jesus is generalized beyond the immediate crowd with the explanatory statement that "whoever does the will of God is my brother and sister and mother," but in the context of the incident "the will of God" is equated with being with Jesus, since Jesus makes no distinctions within the crowd between those who are his mother and brothers and those who are not.

Jesus' family members also seek to be with him, but they attempt to reverse the mandated relationship. Rather than seeking to follow Jesus, they seek for him to follow them. Jesus' demand for a reversal of roles between himself and his mother must be read in the context of the strongly hierarchical family structure of the time.[41] In that context the demand appears shocking.

The appropriation of the role of the parent is suggested as well, though not so clearly, in the call of the sons of Zebedee, who leave "their father Zebedee...with the hired hands" while "they followed [Jesus]" (1.20). The detail of the hired hands remaining with Zebedee balances the sons' leaving with Jesus, thus emphasizing the switch in the primary loyalty made by the sons.

The relational emphasis of discipleship is apparent also in the final charge to the disciples given through the young man at the tomb (16.7). The disciples are not given a commission as in Matthew but instead are given a promise of the renewal of their relationship with Jesus. He is still going before them; they will see him again.

Because of the priority of personal relationship over christological, dogmatic, or ethical concerns in the Markan portrayal of discipleship, the response of the first disciples is an ideal response that cannot be equaled by the listeners. The first disciples respond only to Jesus' personal authority without knowing his identity or his important role in the divine drama of the end of the age. The listeners' response is always colored by

---

[41] Jesus himself comes down strongly in favor of the authority and rights of parents in his dispute with the Pharisees and the scribes over Corban (7.9-13).

their knowledge of Jesus' identity, which makes impossible a completely personal response.

Lack of Moral Criteria for Following

In each of the call stories, the Christian listener tends to identify with the disciples who are addressed by Jesus, but the surrounding narrative gives a very different meaning to the listener's experience of responding to Jesus' call at different times. The first pair of call stories is imbedded in a narrative environment in which Jesus' authority is paramount. The third call story (2.14), on the other hand, while it closely follows the form and wording of the first two, is heard in a narrative environment that focuses on sin, forgiveness, and the healing of sin. It follows the healing of the paralytic (2.1-12), which is the last of the series of healings and exorcisms found in 1.21-2.12 and the first of the series of controversies found in 2.1-3.6. In the earlier episode located in the synagogue at Capernaum, the worshipers recognized Jesus' teaching and exorcism as signs of authority. In the episode of the paralytic, also located in Capernaum, Jesus explicitly claims his healing as a sign of his authority to forgive sins (2.10).[42] The authorities, through their unstated charge of blasphemy, helpfully point out to the listener that this is a divine authority, one that must be granted by God Himself (2.6-7).[43] Clearly, there is an escalation of authority claimed for Jesus at this point, for this is the first time the religious officials object.

The call of Levi, then, occurs in a context concerned with the forgiveness of sins. In many ways, this episode serves to universalize the first call stories. If, as seems most likely, the first disciples occupied an

---

[42] The passive voice of ἀφίενται leaves the role of Jesus ambiguous. William L. Lane understands Jesus to be making a declaration concerning the action of God (*Commentary on the Gospel of Mark*, NICNT [Grand Rapids, MI: Eerdmans, 1974] 95-96). The scribes, however, understand Jesus to be claiming authority to forgive sins. The scribes may have objected to Jesus' claiming prophetic authority, as Lane argues, but he offers no evidence that the claim to prophetic authority could be equated with blasphemy. It is even questionable whether the claim to Messianic authority was blasphemous.

[43] The question of the scribes, "Who is able to forgive sins except the one God?" does not necessarily equate Jesus with God, but does mean that God has granted him an authority previously reserved for God Himself and has thus elevated him above all other human beings.

elevated position in the symbolic world of the intended listeners,[44] this may have created resistance to a complete identification with their response. In that case, the call of the tax collector Levi would allow listeners who were mindful of their own sin to identify more easily with the call. If, on the other hand, the listeners viewed themselves as blameless, the call of Levi would force them into a reexamination of that self-image. Immediately following the call of Levi, the Pharisees attack Jesus for eating with tax collectors and sinners. The consistently negative portrayal of the religious authorities indicates that they were negatively valued within the intended audience's symbolic world, and even first-time listeners would not want their own thought to conform to that of Jesus' opponents. Finally, Jesus' authoritative declaration, "I did not come to call righteous people, but to call sinners" (2.17), clearly places the listeners, who share a self-understanding as those who have been called by Jesus, in the category of sinners.

Thus while both sets of call stories create an identification between the listeners and the disciples, the effect of the stories is different. The first serves primarily to reaffirm the listeners' commitment to follow Jesus through the presentation of the idealized response of important community leaders, while the second leads the listener to confront his or her sinful condition and reception of forgiveness by presenting the call of an otherwise unknown sinner.[45] It is significant that the structure and wording of the call stories is so similar for leaders and sinners alike.

[44] Even those who argue that Mark's Gospel is a polemic against the disciples generally assume that Mark's intended audience had a positive evaluation of the disciples that the Gospel was meant to subvert (e.g., Weeden, *Traditions in Conflict*, 162; Werner H. Kelber, *Mark's Story of Jesus* [Philadelphia: Fortress Press, 1979] 93). As noted above, the promise made to Peter and Andrew, that they shall become "fishers of persons," is only intelligible if the audience associates it with the later missionary activity of the disciples. Since the promise is given by Jesus, it is hardly possible that the audience could then give a negative evaluation to the disciples' promised mission.

[45] It has long puzzled Markan commentators why Levi does not appear in the list of the twelve in Mark, since his call corresponds so closely to that of the first four disciples. Although we cannot know with certainty whether or not Levi was known to Mark's original audience, the choice of an obscure follower may have been intentional. In any case, Levi is clearly characterized as disreputable in contrast to the initial four, who do not share his disreputable occupation.

In both the philosophical biographies and Ben Sira, the emphasis has been on the teacher's attraction of those who were already philosophically inclined to become students of philosophy or wisdom. In Ben Sira, the dichotomy between the wise and the foolish is clear and unequivocal. The fool cannot benefit from a teacher's instruction (21.14, 15b, 18-19; 22.9-10). In Iamblichus, only those with the most pure character are allowed to join the philosophical fellowship (*Pythagorean Life*, 17). In Philostratus, the Brahmans examine not only the character of a prospective student but also the quality of his forebears for three generations (2.30), and the disciples of Apollonius are for the most part attracted from those who are already committed to philosophy. In these cases, the quality of the followers reflects positively on the teacher.

Lack of Moral Change

There also is a tradition of philosophical conversion that stresses the radical change of character undergone by a convert. It is quite striking, in comparing the call of Levi to the philosophical anecdotes of the conversion of the dissolute, that Mark makes no effort to demonstrate a change in the convert's life. Levi does not provide the reader with a demonstration of the power of Jesus' teaching to alter faults of character, nor does he provide a model for the listener's own moral conversion. The only change indicated in Levi's life is that he followed Jesus. Since he physically left the tax office in order to follow Jesus, the listener may infer that he gave up his unsavory profession as well, but it is not explicitly stated. Nor is it indicated that he experienced any change of heart concerning the worthiness of his profession.[46]

Mark's lack of concern about changed life style also is evident in the following verses (2.15-16), where Jesus' associates are referred to as tax collectors and sinners in the present tense rather than reformed sinners or those who had been sinners.[47] Even Jesus' reply to the Pharisees (2.17) leaves the question of change of life style ambiguous at

---

[46] Cf. the similar story in Luke 19.1-10, in which the tax collector Zacchaeus gives half his goods to the poor and offers restitution to anyone whom he might have defrauded.

[47] Elsewhere, Mark does use tenses to indicate a change in status. In 5.18, he uses an aorist participle to designate the one who had been possessed by a demon.

best. The medical imagery that he employs was used frequently in the philosophical literature in reference to the philosophers' power to cure a person of wrong attitudes and behaviors,[48] but in the Markan context, it is unclear whether it carries that meaning. The narrative environment of the saying gives no indication of Jesus effecting changes in anyone's character. In the preceding episode, the healing of the paralytic (2.1-12), the paralytic's sins are forgiven, and the dispute between Jesus and the scribes concerns Jesus' authority to declare sins forgiven. There is no discussion of the nature of the paralytic's sins or whether he refrained from similar sins after his encounter with Jesus. Jesus does not exhort him to refrain from sin in the future.[49] The disputes with the authorities that follow on the saying about calling sinners show Jesus widening the range of accepted behavior beyond the norm established by the religious authorities rather than bringing people into conformity with moral norms. The rhetorical point made by the stories is not the norms of acceptable behavior to which the Christian must adhere but rather Jesus' authority to establish the norms of ritual activity such as fasting and the limits of permissible behavior on the Sabbath.[50] Since the narrative environment is concerned with Jesus' authority in matters of divine prerogative, and since the immediately preceding episode deals with Jesus' authority to forgive sins, it is more natural to hear the medical metaphor in terms of forgiveness rather than as effecting a change in behavior.

There is also no mention of standards of character or of change in character in the naming of the twelve. This lack of moral demand is underlined particularly by Mark's note that Judas was the one who betrayed Jesus (3.19). Since Jesus' extraordinary powers of perception of the internal state of characters has already been established (explicitly in 2.8; implicitly in 3.1-6), the listener must wonder whether Jesus consciously selected someone with such a flawed character to be one of

---

[48] Abraham J. Malherbe, "Medical Imagery in the Pastoral Epistles," in *Texts and Testaments: Critical Essays on the Bible and Early Christian Fathers*, ed. by W. E. March (San Antonio, TX: Trinity University Press, 1980) 19-35.

[49] Cf. the story of the woman caught in adultery found in some manuscripts of the Gospel of John, where Jesus tells the woman, "Go, and from now on do not sin any more" (8.11c, NAB).

[50] Cf. Powell on the parallel pericopes in Matthew (*What is Narrative Criticism?* 41-42).

his representatives. Other passages that reflect surprise on Jesus' part (e.g., 4.13; 6.6) allow for the interpretation that Jesus did not know that Judas would betray him, but given the ancient belief in the static nature of character, we must assume that Judas' character is flawed even now. Certainly the notice in an account of the naming of the twelve shows that no transformation of character was envisioned as accompanying the call to follow Jesus.

It is only later in the Gospel, especially in the teaching of chapters eight through ten that Jesus begins to place moral demands upon the disciples, and then the demands are to a great extent connected with the disciples' relationship to Jesus.

7

PARABLES AND BREAD

The disciples' lack of understanding, which has drawn so much attention in the discussion of Mark, is first developed as a major motif in the section of narrative between 4.1 and 8.26.[1] Within this section several incidents concerning the disciples' understanding are interrelated by verbal and thematic similarities that suggest that the listener should interpret all the specific episodes as one unified theme. The specific episodes include (1) the disciples' failure to grasp the veiled meaning of the parables (4.1-34), (2) the stilling of the storm (4.35-41), (3) the feeding of the five thousand (6.30-44), (4) the walking on water (6.45-52), (5) the failure to understand the saying about defilement (7.14-23), (6) the feeding of the four thousand (8.1-10) and (7) the discussion in the boat about bread (8.14-21).

These episodes fall into two distinct groups, episodes that concern parables (4.1-34; 7.14-23) and episodes that primarily concern miracles (4.35-41; 6.30-44; 6.45-52; 8.1-10; 8.14-21). Mark suggests that the miracles may be understood by analogy to the parables by the repetition in 8.17-18 of language from the Isaiah passage used to portray the outsider's lack of understanding of the parables in 4.12.

---

[1] The thematic unity of incomprehension in this section has been noted by many scholars. See, e.g., Weeden, *Traditions in Conflict*, 26-32; Kelber, *Mark's Story of Jesus*, 30-42; Madeleine Boucher, *The Mysterious Parable: A Literary Study*, CBQMS 6, (Washington: The Catholic Biblical Association of America, 1977); Frank J. Matera, "The Incomprehension of the Disciples and Peter's Confession (Mark 6,14-8,30)," *Bib* 70 (1989) 153-72.

Nevertheless, the two types of misunderstanding are distinct and for the sake of clarity should not be treated as an undifferentiated group.

The most important incident concerning the disciples in this section that does not form part of the misunderstanding motif is the mission of the twelve (6.7-13, 30), which forms a frame around the discussion concerning the identity of Jesus and the death of John the Baptist. This episode is much like the call stories in showing the twelve obediently fulfilling the commission given them by Jesus.[2] Since Mark frequently uses the framing technique to suggest connections between the intercalated episodes,[3] the association between the disciples' successful completion of their mission and John's death, which serves as a type for Jesus' own passion, suggests that the disciples, like John, may be required to give up their lives and will be successful in facing that mission as well, albeit outside the narrative scope of the Gospel.

The organization of the first two sections (1.1-8.21), then, shows an interpenetration of the commissioning and response theme with the lack of understanding theme. The interpenetration of themes is the way Mark indicates simultaneity within the limitations of his episodic narrative style, while episodes belonging to a single thematic progression are separated from each other to indicate continuation through a period of time. Rather than a linear scheme of commissioning and degeneration, there is an overlap. Jesus continues with his progressive commissioning of the disciples in spite of their incomprehension.[4]

---

[2] Robert M. Fowler argues on the basis of later episodes that the twelve did not adequately fulfill the commission (*Loaves and Fishes: The Function of the Feeding Stories in the Gospel of Mark*, SBLDS 54 [Chico, CA: Scholars Press, 1981] 117-19), but he overlooks the episodic nature of the Markan narrative.

[3] Jesus' kinsfolk and the Beelzebul controversy (3.20-35); the withering of the fig tree and the cleansing of the temple (11.12-25); Peter's denial and the trial of Jesus before the Sanhedrin (14.53-15.1). The significance of the intercalations have been discussed by many scholars. For a listing and discussion of intercalations, see John R. Donahue, *Are You the Christ? The Trial Narrative in the Gospel of Mark*, SBLDS 10 (Missoula, MT: Scholars Press, 1973) 58-63. For a recent treatment, see James R. Edwards, "Markan Sandwiches: The Significance of Interpolations in Markan Narratives," *NovT* 31 (1989) 193-216.

[4] Commissioning scenes continue throughout the Gospel of Mark. Mark 8.34, "If anyone desires to come after me, let him deny himself and take up his cross and follow me," serves both as a generalized call to discipleship and a redefinition

The parable and miracle theme is more complex than the calling theme examined in the previous section, and the parallels with the philosophic and wisdom literature are less direct. We shall proceed with our investigation of the theme of incomprehension in this section of the Gospel by first examining some of the individual episodes in relation to the philosophical and wisdom parallels and then studying the theme as a whole.

Parables

The Parable Discourse

The interpretation of the parable discourse, and especially the parable theory in 4.11-12, is one of the most hotly contested issues in Markan scholarship.[5]

The importance of the discourse has been set up through the frequent references to Jesus' teaching in the first three chapters (1.14-15, 21-28, 38-39; 2.13). In spite of this emphasis on proclamation and teaching in summary passages, Mark does not present the content of Jesus' teaching anywhere in the first three chapters other than the initial one-sentence summary. Instead, the listener is

---

of the disciples' commission. The farewell discourse of chapter thirteen provides instructions for the future, to watch (13.33, 37), to endure (13.9-20), to beware of deceivers (13.5-6, 21-22), and to preach the gospel to all nations (13.10). The resurrection scene also has a commissioning-like aspect, since the disciples and Peter are to go to Galilee to renew their relationship with Jesus. The disciples do not appear to understand these commissions at the time that they receive them, but the same can be said of their initial call to follow Jesus or to become fishers of persons. There is a progressive commissioning of the disciples in the Gospel that at every step goes beyond the disciples' current understanding.

[5] One of the principal divisions being between those who see the parable theory as central to the Markan message (e.g., Boucher, *Mysterious Parable*; Marcus, "Marcan Epistemology;" Werner H. Kelber, *The Oral and the Written Gospel: The Hermeneutics of Speaking and Writing in the Synoptic Tradition, Mark, Paul, and Q* [Philadelphia: Fortress Press, 1983] 117-29) and those who see the parable theory as inconsistent with the Markan narrative as a whole (e.g., Weeden, *Traditions in Conflict*, 138-58; John C. Meagher, *Clumsy Construction in Mark's Gospel: A Critique of Form- and Redaktionsgeschichte*, TST 3 [New York and Toronto: Edwin Mellen Press, 1979] 87). A recent review of scholarship is available in Beavis, *Mark's Audience*, 69-86.

presented with Jesus' healings and exorcisms and his conflict with various Jewish authorities and his family.[6]

The central thrust of the discourse, however, is not the content of Jesus' teaching but the nature of that teaching, the fact that he taught in parables. The disciples' role is secondary to the main thrust of the discourse, the teaching in parables. This is clear from the structure of the discourse (Figure 7.1, next page).[7]

---

[6] While those conflicts give the listener some insight into the teaching and practice of Jesus, they are presented in terms of Jesus' reacting to his opponents rather than as a synopsis of Jesus' teaching. So also Donald H. Juel, *Mark*, ACNT (Minneapolis: Augsburg, 1990) 65-66.

[7] The structure given here is very close to that proposed by Joanna Dewey (*Markan Public Debate: Literary Technique, Concentric Structure, and Theology in Mark 2:1-3:6*, SBLDS 48 [Chico, CA: Scholars Press, 1980] 147-52). She points out the chiastic pattern of 4.2b-20 but sees the entire discourse as a chiasm, with the "sayings material" of vv. 21-25 as the center member (150-52). While there is some justification in seeing the seed parables of vv. 26-32 reflecting the seed parable vv. 2b-9, vv. 10-20 is commentary, and it is unlikely any audience would hear it reflected in the concluding parables. An alternative reading of the structure of the discourse, which sees the interpretation of the parable of the sower as the center of a chiasm encompassing the entire parable discourse has been proposed by J. Dupont ("La transmission des paroles de Jésus sur la lampe et la mesure dans Marc 4,21-25 et dans la tradition Q," in *Logia: Les Paroles de Jésus—The Sayings of Jesus: Memorial Joseph Coppens*, ed. by J. Delobel, BETL 59 [Louven University: Peeters, 1982] 206, n. 12). This proposal is followed by both Joel Marcus (*The Mystery of the Kingdom of God*, SBLDS 90 [Atlanta: Scholars Press, 1986] 220-23) and Greg Fay ("Introduction to Incomprehension: The Literary Structure of Mark 4:1-34," *CBQ* 51 [1989] 65-81). A similar structure is proposed independently by John R. Donahue (*The Gospel in Parable: Metaphor, Narrative, and Theology in the Synoptic Gospels* [Philadelphia: Fortress Press, 1988] 30-32). This proposal has the strength of pointing out the similarity in theme between the parables of vv. 21-25 and the commentary of Jesus in vv. 11-12, but ignores the chiastic pattern in vv. 2b-20. Dewey, Dupont, and Donahue all base their analyses in part on anachronistic distinctions between "parables" (vv. 2b-9; 26-32) and "sayings" (vv. 21-25), in spite of Mark's understanding of all the material as parable. Another alternative calls 4.10-23 the "first interpretation" of the sower parable and 4.24-32 the "second interpretation" (Tolbert, *Sowing the Gospel*, 149).

Burton L. Mack has produced a curiously strained reading of the discourse in terms of the chreia elaboration pattern found in Hermogenes *Progymnasmata* (7.10-8.10, text and translation may be found in Hock and O'Neil, *Chreia in Ancient Rhetoric I*, 176-77). According to this reading, 4.1-2a correspond to an encomium, 4.24-25 corresponds to the citation of an authority, 4.26-29 is a personal example, 4.30-32 is *the* analogy (παραβολή), 4.33-34 is an exhortation,

* *Figure 7.1*
Structure of the Parable Discourse

4.1-2a		introduction: teaching in parables	1.5 verses
	4.2b-9	parable of the sower	7.5 verses
	4.10	disciples request explanation	1 verse
	4.11-12	parable theory	2 verses
	4.13	Jesus rebukes disciples	1 verse
	4.14-20	explanation of the parable	7 verses
	4.21-23	parable of the lamp	3 verses
	4.24-25	parable of the measure	2 verses
	4.26-29	parable of the seed growing automatically	4 verses
	4.30-32	parable of the mustard seed	3 verses
4.33-34		summary: teaching in parables	2 verses

The fact of Jesus' parabolic teaching is mentioned at the beginning and the end of the discourse (4.2; 4.33-34), forming an inclusio around the teaching material itself. The parable of the sower and its explanation (4.3-20), which take up more than half of the entire discourse, are structured to emphasize the parabolic nature of the teaching. This portion of the discourse has a very clear chiastic structure,[8] with the parable (4.3-9) and its explanation (4.14-20) forming the outer members. The separation of the parable and its explanation gives the listener time to ponder the meaning of the parable, or, more accurately, to notice its lack of a self-evident

and 4.11-12 is an explanation of the parable of the sower (*Patterns of Persuasion*, 152-58).

[8] The importance of chiasm for indicating to the audience the meaning of a passage has been argued by John W. Welch ("Introduction," in *Chiasmus in Antiquity: Structure, Analyses, Exegesis*, ed. by John Welch [Hildesheim: Gerstenberg Verlag, 1981] 9-16), Augustine Stock ("Chiastic Awareness and Education in Antiquity," *BTB* 14 [1984] 23-27), and Paruniak ("Oral Typesetting," 158-60).

meaning, since all the intervening material underscores the difficulty of understanding the parable. The disciples' inability to understand is mentioned in verse 10 and reemphasized in verse 13. The parable theory, which occupies the place of emphasis at the center of the chiasm,[9] stresses the purpose of the parables in concealing the Kingdom of God from those outside. The opaque nature of the parables is also emphasized in the summary at the end of the discourse, which stresses once again the division between the disciples, for whom Jesus explained everything, and those outside, who hear as they are able to hear.

The structure of the second half of the parable discourse reinforces the same point. Four parabolic statements occur in rapid succession.[10] The first one ends with the admonition, "If anyone has ears to hear let him hear!" The second begins with a similar warning, "Watch what you hear!" Both warnings serve to remind the listener of the quotation from Isaiah that provides the rationale for speaking in parables. The rapidity with which the parables follow each other prevents the listener from interpreting them adequately as individual

---

[9] John Welch, *Chiasm in Antiquity*, 10.

[10] Although some modern definitions of parable would exclude some of these, Mark treats them as parables. The term παραβολή was extremely flexible in antiquity, covering proverbial expressions as well as illustrative stories, allegories and riddles (see Marsh H. McCall, Jr., *Ancient Rhetorical Theories of Simile and Comparison* [Cambridge, MA: Harvard University Press, 1969]). The Hebrew *mashal* and the Aramaic equivalent, *mathla*, were even more inclusive. Joachim Jeremias lists sixteen separate forms covered by the terms (*The Parables of Jesus*, 2nd rev. ed. [New York: Charles Scribner's Sons, 1972] 20). See also Boucher (*Mysterious Parable* 86-89) and the literature cited there.

One might count four separate parables in verses 21-25, making a total of six for the second half of the discourse, but it seems better to suppose that the Markan divisions, indicated by the introductory formulas, "and he said," or, "and he said to them," separate units that he considered separate parables.

Dewey maintains that Mark understood "the difference in form between proverbial material and a true parable" in spite of his use of παραβολή for both categories (*Markan Public Debate*, 151). It is more likely, however, that Mark's language reflects the pattern of his thought and that he did not think in terms of the form-critical category "parable."

James G. Williams has recognized that these sayings are parables and has applied the term "sayings parables" to them and others like them (*Gospel Against Parable: Mark's Language of Mystery*, BLS 12 [Bradford on Avon: Almond Press, 1985] 148).

entities. Parables, according to Ben Sira, are something that the scribe dwells upon (ἐν αἰνίγμασι παραβολῶν ἀναστραφήσεται, 39.3b). The mind cannot tease out their meaning instantaneously. Even if all the parables in the discourse were self-evident in meaning, which they are not, or if the audience had previous knowledge of their proper interpretation, which is much more likely, the listeners can hardly keep up with the kaleidoscope of images presented.[11]

It is a common Markan technique to illustrate characteristic behavior by presenting a number of similar episodes in succession. For example, there are four healings and a summary of healings in 1.21-2.12 and five controversies between Jesus and the Jewish authorities in 2.1-3.6, concluding with a statement of the murderous antagonism of those authorities toward Jesus. In the overall structure of the narrative, those complexes of healings and attacks by the authorities establish characteristics of central importance for the narrative as a whole, while the particulars of the healings and controversies are much less important.[12] Here also the succession of parables, in conjunction with summary statements about teaching in parables, follows the same pattern. The parables are illustrative of the summary statement, which is programmatic for the next several chapters, if not for the Gospel as a whole, while the meanings of the individual parables are less important for the narrative.

The casual way in which Mark inserts a private dialogue between Jesus and his disciples in the midst of his public teaching indicates also that the important point is the double meaning of the parables and the distinction between insiders and outsiders.[13] Since

---

[11] This is one of the points where the oral presentation of the Gospel has a significant effect on its interpretation. Scholarly interpretations of the parable discourse generally have dwelt on the meaning of the individual parables and sought to find the significance of the discourse by finding patterns in the meanings derived from the individual parables. Such a method presupposes a leisurely study of the parables rather than an oral presentation.

[12] The questions involved in most of the controversies—association with sinners, fasting, and Sabbath observance—play no direct role in the condemnation of Jesus, although they do imply the authority of Jesus that is implicit in his identity. Only the charge of blasphemy in 2.7 is reflected in the charges at the trial.

[13] Dewey (*Markan Public Debate*, 147) and Lane (*Mark*, 164) see 4.21-32 as addressed to the crowd and only vv. 10-20 as private teaching. Marcus (*Mystery*

the crowd is still present and Jesus is still in the boat in 4.36, the private audience could not have taken place within the narrated time. Mark simply ignores the narrative level in order to make the rhetorical point that is essential for understanding the development of the narrative as a whole.

All the references to the disciples in the discourse serve to demonstrate the enigmatic nature of the parables. The request for an explanation (4.10) indicates that the parables are not self-explanatory and is used to introduce the parable theory and the interpretation. Jesus' rebuke of the disciples' lack of understanding (4.13) reinforces the listener's awareness of the difficulty of understanding and generalizes that difficulty from the individual parable to "all the parables."[14] The summary passage (4.33-34) emphasizes both the

---

of the Kingdom, 140-41) and Donahue (*Gospel in Parable*, 31-32) see vv. 10-25 as private teaching and vv. 26-32 as addressed to the crowd. Other commentators see all of 4.11-32 as addressed to the disciples (Werner H. Kelber, *The Kingdom in Mark: A New Place and a New Time* [Philadelphia: Fortress Press, 1974] 28-41; Rudolf Pesch, *Das Marcusevangelium*, 2 vols., HTKNT 2 [Freiburg, Basel, and Vienna: Herder, 1976] 1.225-28, 266-67), but that is untenable, given the fact that Jesus dismisses the crowd in 4.36. Most of these interpreters underestimate the extent to which Mark ignores the narrative level and constructs the discourse to be rhetorically effective for his own audience. Only the discussion of 4.10-20 takes place in private. 4.21-23 is clearly a parable in Mark's understanding since it concludes with the formula, "If anyone has ears to hear, let him hear," and thus, according to the logic of the summary in 4.33-34, it must be addressed to the crowd. The reading of Marcus and Donahue results from the application of anachronistic form-critical categories that distinguishes the material of 4.21-25 from that of 4.26-32.

[14] Tolbert, Williams, and Paul J. Achtemeier ("Mark as Interpreter of the Jesus Traditions," in *Interpreting the Gospels*, ed. by James Luther Mays [Philadelphia: Fortress Press, 1981] 120-21) have suggested that this saying establishes the parable of the sower as a key to all the parables. Tolbert sees the parable of the sower as a summary of the typology of chapters one through ten (*Sowing the Gospel*, 127-230, esp. 128) and interprets 4.13 as "another, even more blatant, signal of its significance" (*Sowing the Gospel*, 151). Williams, citing this verse, says, "The sower parable is so crucial that if the disciples could understand it, they would be able to comprehend all the parables." He calls this parable "the *master parable*" (*Gospel Against Parable* 41). It is more likely, however, that the disciples' failure to understand the hidden meaning of the parable indicates to Jesus an inability to comprehend the meaning of parables in general. The parable of the sower has no particular significance for the disciples' understanding of the following parables. It is simply the first parable of the discourse in which the use and importance of parables is presented. Because of its position in the discourse,

difficulty of understanding the parables and the privileged position of the disciples who receive private explanations.[15] The disciples' inability to unravel the parables on their own has no effect on their role as insiders.[16] What they cannot accomplish on their own they receive as a gift.

Such a presentation of the disciples is fully consistent with the characterization presented in the call stories. Just as the call stories indicate that the disciples do not owe their position to their own inherent moral superiority, the parable discourse and the ensuing misunderstandings in chapters four through eight show that their position is not dependent on superior mental qualities. The mystery of the Kingdom is a gift.

The Parable about Purity

An examination of the parable and explanation in 7.14-23 shows that here also the primary point is the distinction between the disciples

---

it is the parable through which Mark demonstrates his understanding of parables and the significance of the parabolic for understanding the gospel. The parable of the sower is particularly effective for this purpose because of its length (twelve lines in the UBS text compared to seven lines each for the parables of the seed growing secretly and the mustard seed), which lends appropriate narrative weight to the presentation; because of the presence of an interpretation; and because the interpretation includes five individual interpretations that emphasize through repetition the existence of hidden meanings.

[15] Weeden ascribes the theory of secret teaching to "Mark's *theios-aner* opponents" (*Traditions in Conflict*, 147). Although 4.34 is a summary passage, Weeden argues that it belongs to pre-Markan tradition: "If 4:34, asserting that Jesus taught only in parables, is Markan redaction, then Mark must have either been a very careless, inconsistent writer or very feebleminded thinker. For even a cursory reading of the Gospel shows that Jesus did not teach *only* in parables" (*Tradition in Conflict*, 140). This statement reflects the worst excess of redaction-critical thinking in its assumption that Mark is responsible only for his own redactional insertions rather than for his Gospel as a whole. It also reflects a narrow, twentieth-century, form-critical definition of parables. According to Mark's own, broader understanding of the term, Jesus is portrayed as teaching primarily, although not exclusively, in parables. More important, Weeden overlooks the deeper implications of the parabolic structure of thought discussed below, including the clear association between the hermeneutics of parable and of miracle.

[16] Marcus suggests that the disciples' questioning should be understood as a faithful response to the parables (*Mystery of the Kingdom*, 91).

as insiders and those who are outside.[17] The parable and explanation are part of an extended complex concerning the interpretation of the law that begins at 7.1. The complex presents three different groups in interaction with Jesus. The disciples appear in 7.2 as the object of the Pharisees' and scribes' attack. They reappear in 7.17 requesting an explanation of the parable presented in 7.14-16. Jesus' defense of the disciples against the opponents' attack suggests that the disciples' action in 7.2 is correct, but their later inquiry about the parable suggests that they do not understand completely why their action is correct. The Pharisees and scribes appear entirely in a negative light. Jesus attacks them as hypocrites (7.6) and, rather than answering the specific objection that they have raised as he did in the debates in chapter two, he rejects their entire legal system as an illegitimate substitution of human traditions for God's commandments (7.8-13). As in chapter four, the crowd receives Jesus' parabolic teaching (7.14-16), but does not receive an explanation.

Unlike the parable discourse, however, this complex does not focus on the parables themselves. The subject of the complex is the proper understanding of purity, and Jesus uses invective, scriptural citation, and examples as well as the parable to make his point. The parable helps establish a hierarchy of insiders and outsiders. The Pharisees and scribes are established as hopeless outsiders in their interaction with Jesus. Jesus dismisses them as hypocrites, and they show no indication of listening to him. As in chapters two and three, the opponents seek to discredit rather than learn from Jesus.[18]

---

[17] While this saying does not fit the form-critical criteria for parables, Mark calls it a parable, indicating that it is to be understood in relation to the other parables in the Gospel.

[18] Juel's attempt to characterize the debates between Jesus and the religious authorities as harmless differences of opinion such as the opinions of Shammai and Hillel codified in the Mishna (*Mark*, 50-51) reflects a form-critical tendency to treat the episodes as isolated pericopes and does not do justice to the way the episodes function in Mark. In Mark, the authorities are introduced as accusing Jesus of blasphemy, the offense for which they later condemn him to death (2.6-7). In 3.2, the Pharisees are characterized as testing Jesus so that they might accuse him. In 3.6, the Pharisees and Herodians plot to kill Jesus. In 3.22, the authorities claim that Jesus is in league with Beelzebul. In 3.28-30, Jesus declares that the authorities have committed an unforgivable sin in their attacks on him. In the passage under consideration here, Jesus dismisses the authorities as hypocrites.

The summoning of the crowd is unexpected. Jesus has not taught the crowd since the parable discourse of chapter four. Mark's note that Jesus summoned them "again"[19] suggests that he had in mind the earlier discourse in which the distinction between the crowd and the group of insiders was established. The linguistic similarities between the two episodes also suggest they were formed from a common pattern.[20] These similarities are indicated in Figure 7.2 on the following pages.

The repetition of the same pattern suggests that this passage is to be interpreted along the same lines as the parable discourse, as an indication of the disciples' privileged position over against the crowd. This is especially true as there is no indication of an intensification of Jesus' rebuke for the disciples' lack of understanding. In each case Jesus seems to have expected the disciples to understand the parable, but while he expresses disappointment, he immediately provides an explanation. He gives as a gift what the disciples should have achieved on their own. Once again the disciples' inability to understand underscores the general difficulty in understanding.

The entire complex reiterates in summary form the roles established in the first four chapters. The opponents attack Jesus and

---

The controversy stories in the Markan context are not so much debates as attacks by the authorities. For a perceptive discussion of the way in which Mark's narrative setting transforms the meaning of isolated stories, see Kelber, *Oral and Written Gospel*, 109-111.

[19] The alternate manuscript reading of πάντα is derived from the πάντες later in the verse.

[20] A similar comparison of the pattern of these two passages appears in Willi Marxsen, "Redaktionsgeschichtliche Erklärung der sogennanten Parabeltheorie des Markus," *ZTK* 52 (1955) 259. Lemcio describes the pattern as diatribe, ambiguity, incomprehension, surprised/critical rejoinder, and explanation, and he examines several parallels from Ezekiel, Zechariah, and Jewish Apocalyptic. He indicates that the pattern can imply true blame for incomprehension, but does not necessarily do so ("Structure and Function of Mark iv. 1-20," 323-38). David Daube has proposed a pattern of misleading public pronouncement followed by private teaching in the rabbinic writings ("Public Pronouncement and Private Explanation in the Gospels," *ExpT* 57 [1945-46] 175-77; *New Testament and Rabbinic Judaism* [London: University of London, Anthone Press, 1956] 141-50). His examples, however, are significantly different from the Markan passage, since the misleading public pronouncements are aimed at hostile questioners and the true explanation is independent of the public pronouncement.

Figure 7.2
Synopsis of 4.3-20 and 7.14-23

4.3a   ἀκούετε· ἰδού[21]
7.14   ἀκούσατέ μου πάντες καὶ σύνετε

4.3b-8   parable
7.15   parable

4.9   ὃς   ἔχει ὦτα ἀκούειν, ἀκουέτω
7.16   εἴ τις ἔχει ὦτα ἀκούειν, ἀκουέτω[22]

---

[21] Although the introductory particle ἰδού is so familiar in biblical writings that its use in specific instances is rarely remarked upon, it is used only seven times by Mark (compared to sixty-three occurrences in Matthew and fifty-five in Luke), and one of these occurrences is in a scriptural quotation (1.2). In five of the other occurrences, it retains its literal force as a command to look, and the following statement refers to something that can be perceived visually by the addressee (3.32: Look! Your mother and brothers are outside seeking for you; 10.28: Look! We have forsaken everything; 10.33: Look! We are going up into Jerusalem; 14.41: Look! The Son of Man is being betrayed into the hands of sinners; 14.42: Look! The one who is betraying me has drawn near). There is also significant manuscript evidence for reading ἰδού in 13.23, ὑμεῖς δὲ βλέπετε· ἰδού· προείρηκα ὑμῖν πάντα, where ἰδού parallels the earlier injunction to take heed, ὑμεῖς δὲ βλέπετε. If this reading is original, it parallels the use of ἰδού in 4.3 as a warning to attend closely to Jesus' words.

[22] Although manuscript evidence is divided on the inclusion of this verse, its omission is largely restricted to Alexandrian manuscripts, and there is much more widespread evidence for its inclusion. The reasoning of Bruce Metzger, "It appears to be a scribal gloss (derived perhaps from 4.9 or 4.23), introduced as an appropriate sequel to ver. 14" (*TCGNT*, 94-95), suggests that the verse is an arbitrary addition to parabolic material rather than part of a pattern of Markan usage. Judging by the appearance of similar imperatives in other early Christian writings, there is little reason to expect a scribe to add a gloss in a manner consistent with Markan usage. Matthew has the imperative to hear at the end of the interpretation of the parable of the tares (13.43) and at the conclusion of the proclamation that John is Elijah (11.15). Luke has it at the end of the parable about salt with which he concludes a discourse on discipleship (15.35). In Revelation, the saying is used to conclude each of the seven letters to the churches (2.7, 11, 17, 29; 3.6, 13, 22), and in 13.9, it apparently introduces a commentary on a portion of the vision in which it is imbedded. The Gospel of Thomas uses the imperative to hear six times to introduce or conclude parables or sayings (logions 8, 21, 24, 63, 65, 96), but the choice of logion to which it is attached appears to be arbitrary. The imperative appears with a number of minor linguistic

Figure 7.2, continued

4.10 καὶ ὅτε ἐγένετο   κατὰ μόνας,   ἠρώτων
7.17 καὶ ὅτε εἰσῆλθεν εἰς οἶκον ἀπὸ τοῦ ὄχλου, ἐπηρώτων

4.10 αὐτὸν οἱ περὶ αὐτὸν σὺν τοῖς δώδεκα τὰς παραβολὰς
7.17 αὐτὸν οἱ μαθηταὶ αὐτοῦ   τὴν παραβολήν

4.11-12 explanation of speaking in parables

4.13 οὐκ οἴδατε τὴν παραβολὴν ταύτην, καὶ πῶς πάσας τὰς
                                        παραβολὰς γνώσεσθε;
7.18a οὕτως καὶ ὑμεῖς ἀσύνετοί ἐστε;   οὐ νοεῖτε...;

4.14-20 the meaning of the parable
7.18b-23 the meaning of the parable

are in turn rejected by him. The crowd hears Jesus but does not understand. The disciples hear Jesus and are given the understanding that they cannot achieve on their own.

Mark's episodic narrative functions as much through the accumulation of incidents as it does through linear development. The position of Jesus' opponents, for example, does not develop within the narrative. They are introduced as accusing Jesus of blasphemy (2.7). By the beginning of chapter three, they have already determined to kill him (3.6). Although the controversy in chapter seven generalizes the

variations. The use of the conditional clause is unusual. The form occurs in Mark 4.23, but outside of Mark, it occurs only once, in Revelation 13.9. The use of the infinitive ἀκούειν to modify ὦτα is also Markan. Luke includes it, but Matthew and Revelation do not. It is very unlikely, then, that a scribe would have used a Markan form of the imperative. Even if he looked up the Markan form from chapter four, it is unlikely that he would have chosen the conditional form of the imperative (4.23) rather than the more familiar participial form (4.9), which occupies a place more prominent in the parable discourse and is more analogous to the present situation, in which the parable is followed by an interpretation. Luke omits the imperative after the parable of the lamp, where Mark includes it, so there is a precedent for Matthew's omission of the imperative after the parable about defilement. The sporadic use of the imperative to hear outside of Mark suggests that its inclusion was generally considered a stylistic matter and that it was not considered an integral part of particular sayings.

earlier disputes, it does not add significantly to the development of the opponents' position or to Jesus' reaction to them. It is unlikely, then, that the disciples' question should be understood as an intensification of their earlier lack of understanding. It simply reiterates the characterization from chapter four. The complex does clarify, however, the respective positions of the three groups—opponents, crowd, disciples—by indicating their respective responses on a single theme, the purity system of the scribes and Pharisees.

The Parables and the Esoteric Teaching of the Philosophers

In each of the three philosophical biographies and the Wisdom of Ben Sira, the hero of the biography or the wise person possesses knowledge that is not generally shared by the mass of humanity. By definition, a sage must possess superior knowledge or understanding. The nature of the superior knowledge, however, varies widely in the different works. For Xenophon, Socrates' knowledge, apart from the promptings of his daemon, was generally accessible to human reason (1.1.2-9), and Socrates sought to bring all men and women to share that knowledge through the guided use of their powers of reasoning. One of the central points Xenophon makes is the absence of an esoteric knowledge restricted to Socrates' followers (1.1.10-16; 1.2.50). Socrates' knowledge is available to all, and people are limited in acquiring it only by the limitations of their own character and capacity to reason (1.2.61).

The teaching of a similar type of generally accessible wisdom is portrayed as part of the activity of each of the sages. Pythagoras publicly teaches moral precepts to the people of Croton before he establishes his esoteric school (8.36-11.57). Apollonius' teaching of Damis is generally accessible, if not commonplace, wisdom, and his teaching of the various kings and emperors falls in the same category. The character of his listeners determines whether this public teaching is accepted or rejected. The wise and good are receptive, the foolish and arrogant are not. Ben Sira's precepts are similarly accessible. Ben Sira warns the wise person not to waste time trying to teach the fool (22.13-15), but only because the fool is unteachable (21.14).

On the other hand, each of these three works depicts an esoteric type of wisdom that the hero possesses in addition to the wisdom that he teaches to the public. In the *Pythagorean Life*, this esoteric knowledge is only available to those who have passed through a strenuous course of study and discipline (17.75-78; 34.246), and it is guarded jealously from those on the outside through the use of symbolic sayings (23.104). Apollonius' esoteric wisdom is even more rarified. Apollonius is only once shown to transmit the esoteric wisdom in his possession to any of his followers, in a short note in the pre-Damis part of his narrative dependent on Maximus of Aegae (1.16), but he is shown to learn esoteric wisdom from the Magi (1.26) and the Brahmans (3.41). Apollonius occasionally speaks in riddles (3.15), but the riddles usually are oracles (as 4.24; 4.43; 6.32), which are traditionally ambiguous, and not bearers of esoteric wisdom. The esoteric understanding of the wise man of Ben Sira is not as pronounced, but the ideal scribe is able to seek out the hidden meanings of parables, ἀπόκρυφα παροιμιῶν ἐκζητήσει καὶ ἐν αἰνίγμασι παραβολῶν ἀναστραφήσεται (39.3).[23]

In two of these works, no esoteric wisdom is presented to the reader. In Apollonius of Tyana, the reader is told that Apollonius had discussions of esoteric wisdom with the Magi and Brahmans (1.26; 3.41), but the content is not narrated. In Sira, there are no examples given of the riddles and conundrums that the wise man is able to understand. In the *Pythagorean Synagoge*, on the other hand, a great deal of the supposedly esoteric material is presented. Iamblichus only presents short lists of the precepts taught to the ἀκουσματικοί in the *Pythagorean Life* (18.82; 23.105), and he omits the explanations presented to the inner circle. In the second book of the *Synagoge*, however, the *Exhortation to Philosophy*, Iamblichus provides explanations for thirty-nine of the Pythagorean symbols, and the following eight books provide explanations of Pythagorean doctrines that, at least by implication, derive from the secret teaching. Since Iamblichus took his material from previously published works, the material was hardly a well-preserved secret in his own day. The previous secrecy, however, does lend prestige to the material. Furthermore, by postpon-

[23] In the book of Daniel, generally dated some fifteen to twenty years after the composition of Sira, the wise man's ability to unravel conundrums (6.24) is linked to a body of allegedly esoteric knowledge (12.4).

ing the inner explanations to the second book, Iamblichus is able to present a certain appearance of esotericism that reinforces the historical account of secrecy.

Jewish apocalyptic works often use a similar strategy of feigned secrecy to add weight to their accounts (Dan 12.4; 2 Esdr 14.44-48; *Jub.* 1.26-28; *1 Enoch* 82.1-3; *2 Enoch* 33.9-12). In this case the secrecy helps make plausible the connection between ancient patriarchs and sages and the material in the books, but a delight in the revelation of hidden secrets pervades these works. Secrecy is valued for its own sake. Truth is portrayed as something that is necessarily hidden. The same principle is also applied to history. Behind the rise and fall of empires, there is an inner history guided by God, and the dire circumstances of the present are often seen as a mask for the approaching triumph of God and his people.

The presentation of an esoteric interpretation in the parable discourse falls within the same pattern. The content of the interpretation of the parable does not appear to be the kind of carefully guarded secret knowledge that must be kept from common people. On the contrary, it is a straightforward description of the reception of any sectarian teaching. It might be described as pseudoesoteric, since there appears to be no reason for keeping it secret, and it is hidden only to the extent that the parabolic method of presentation purposefully obfuscates the teaching.

The pseudoesoteric nature of the hidden meanings of the parables suggests that here also the secrecy is used for the prestige it lends to the teaching. That prestige is more importantly to be associated with the primary secret of the Gospel, Jesus' hidden identity. As in Jewish apocalyptic, the secrecy also points to the nature of the world that is reflected in the structure of apparent meaning covering an inner truth. The parables themselves are a parable of the structure of reality, the disjunction between appearance and meaning, the necessity of searching for truth hidden and yet revealed by the publicly accessible events in the world.

It is very curious, in the light of the other examples of esoteric teaching, that Jesus takes the disciples to task for failing to grasp the hidden meaning of the parables. In Apollonius, Damis is taken to task for not possessing the proper philosophical character (2.5; 2.7; 7.13), but the sage does not expect his follower to grasp the esoteric teaching. That teaching is not presented in any form to his unworthy follower. In Iamblichus, the novitiates are presented with the symbolic teaching (23.104; or, alternatively, with the conclusions without the reasoning, 18.87-88), but there is no indication that they are expected to unravel the mysteries for themselves.

Ben Sira's ideal scribe provides a closer parallel. There is a significant overlap in the themes of this depiction and the parable discourse of Mark.[24] The wise man is able, with the grace of God, to unravel the meanings of parables. The unraveling of parables, however, is one of the characteristics of the wise man, the one who has already successfully pursued the acquisition of wisdom. Ben Sira does not fault those who do not possess that ability, nor does he show the student of a wise man being presented with riddles to solve.

Ben Sira does share with Mark a belief that understanding (in Sira, wisdom; in Mark, the mystery of the Kingdom of God) is a gift of God. In Sira, this is expressed in 1.1-10; 6.3-7; 39.5-6; 51.30; in Mark, it is expressed through the divine passive of 4.11.

In keeping with the depiction of the disciples in the call stories, Mark does not indicate that the mystery of the Kingdom of God has been given to the disciples because of any superiority in their character. In all the other examples of esoterica it is largely the quality of the students' character that qualifies them to receive the esoteric teaching. Even for Ben Sira, who stresses the nature of wisdom as a gift of God, the quality of the students' character is an important prerequisite for the reception of that gift (39.5-6; 51.30). Mark, on the other hand, simply divides people into two groups, "you" and "those outside." As in the saying about Jesus' true family (3.34-35), the two groups are determined by the nature of their association with Jesus. That contrasts sharply with the status of Damis, the loyal student of the philosopher in the *Life of Apollonius*. He never qualifies to receive esoteric teaching in spite of his lifelong association with Apollonius. Just as doing the will of God in 3.35 appears from the context to be equivalent to associating with Jesus, the "mystery of the Kingdom of

---

[24] See above, Chapter 5, pp. 161-62.

God," which has already been given to "those around him," is given on the basis of association with Jesus.

Parabolic Miracles

The Stilling of the Storm (4.35-41)

A second programmatic idea for the Gospel section 4.1-8.26 is found in the episode of the stilling of the storm. This episode reiterates the connection between Jesus' miraculous activity and the mystery of his identity suggested in 1.27, 2.10, and 3.23-27. As with the parables, the miracles do not present a clear meaning on their surface. Their meaning must be teased out.[25] The last verse (vs. 41) especially functions to call the listener's attention to the link between Jesus' miraculous activity and the question of his identity. It is directly parallel to the crowd's response after the first exorcism performed by Jesus (Figure 7.3, next page).

These two responses appear to be variations on a set pattern in Mark's storytelling repertoire and serve the same function, to link Jesus' miraculous activity to the question of his identity. The shift in speakers from the crowd to the disciples indicates that the question of identity is now to be concentrated in the relationship between Jesus and his disciples.

In the first three chapters, the disciples are not greatly involved in Jesus' miraculous activity. The healing of Peter's mother-in-law does occur in private (1.29-31), but the disciples are not mentioned in the other healings.[26] The crowds make acclamations in some of the healings stories (1.27 2.12), but the group most closely associated with

---

[25] For Mark's parabolic understanding of miracles, see also Boucher, *Mysterious Parable* 69-80; D. E. Nineham, *The Gospel of St. Mark*, PGC (Baltimore: Penguin, 1963) 181-82.

[26] In the first exorcism (1.21-28), the disciples are only suggested by the plural form εἰσπορεύονται in the introductory verse. The first mass healing (1.32-34) takes place at the house of Simon and Andrew, but the disciples are not mentioned. In the cleansing of the leper (1.40-44), the healing of the paralytic (2.1-12), and the healing of the man with the withered hand (3.1-6), the disciples are not mentioned at all, though the house in Capernaum in 2.1 may be the house of Simon and Andrew, where healings had occurred earlier.

Figure 7.3
Synopsis of 1.27 and 4.41

1.27 καὶ ἐθαμβήθησαν ἅπαντες
4.41 καὶ ἐφοβήθησαν φόβον μέγαν

1.27 ὥστε συζητεῖν   πρὸς ἑαυτοὺς λέγοντας
4.41 καὶ   ἔλεγον πρὸς ἀλλήλους

1.27 τί   ἐστιν τοῦτο
4.41 τίς ἄρα οὗτός ἐστιν

1.27 διδαχὴ καινὴ κατ᾿ ἐξουσίαν

1.27   καὶ τοῖς πνεύμασι τοῖς ἀκαθάρτοις ἐπιτάσσει
                             καὶ ὑπακούουσιν αὐτῷ;
4.41 ὅτι καὶ ὁ ἄνεμος καὶ ἡ θάλασσα ὑπακούει   αὐτῷ;

the healings is the Jewish authorities. In 1.22, Jesus' teaching authority is contrasted with that of the scribes, and the subsequent action links Jesus' teaching authority to his authority over demons. In 1.44, the cleansed leper is told to show himself to the priest and make an offering as a testimony. The episode of the paralytic includes a debate between some of the scribes and Jesus concerning Jesus' authority to forgive sins (2.6-12). Jesus heals the man with the withered hand in spite of the Pharisees' displeasure, and the healing sparks a plot between the Pharisees and the Herodians to eliminate Jesus (3.1-6).[27] This section also includes a debate between Jesus and the scribes from Jerusalem concerning the meaning of Jesus' exorcisms (3.22-29).

In chapters four through eight, however, the disciples become most prominently involved with the miracles, especially with the sea and bread miracles. The opponents entirely disappear from the miracle

---

[27] The indefinite "they" of 3.2 refers back to the Pharisees, the opponents of the previous episode. The final verse, 3.6, indicates that the Pharisees went out from the synagogue and took counsel with the Herodians, who had not been present.

episodes, the only link between the opponents and the miracles being the Pharisees' incongruous demand for a sign from heaven (8.11).

The repetition of the question of Jesus' identity (1.27; 4.41) indicates that the disciples' response to Jesus' miracles in chapters four through eight is to be understood in relation to the response of the crowds and the opponents in chapters one through three. Although the disciples have difficulty understanding Jesus' identity on the basis of the miracles, the opponents have concluded that Jesus is demon-possessed (3.22), a blasphemer (2.6), and a defiler of the Sabbath (3.2-5) who ought to be killed (3.6) on the basis of similar evidence. The crowds, while they respond positively to Jesus, never progress beyond their initial inquiry concerning Jesus' identity.[28]

The opponents' negative response in chapters one through three gives a context for interpreting the disciples' confused response in chapters four through eight and significantly mitigates the listeners' possibly unfavorable response to the disciples' distress. As with the parables, the disciples understand the miracles with difficulty, but eventually they do make a proper, though incomplete, identification of Jesus (8.29). They do not possess an inherent superiority of insight, but through Jesus' persistence they receive insight as a gift.

The First Feeding Miracle

In the first feeding story the disciples establish for the listener the magnitude of the miracle that Jesus performs. They bring to Jesus' attention the problem of the crowd's hunger, and in response to Jesus' request that they feed the crowd, they indicate the impossibility of solving the problem through ordinary means. Given the nature of miracle stories, this role is not at all unexpected.[29] We can find a

---

[28] The initial query of the crowd about the meaning of Jesus' teaching and exorcism is another instance of discourse overwhelming narrative. The query functions at the discourse level to alert the listener that Jesus' authoritative teaching and healing point beyond themselves, but at the level of narrative, the query sets up a false expectation that the crowd's interest in the matter will be decisive in the development of the narrative events.

[29] There is a clear correspondence between the function of the disciples here and the following typical motifs of healing miracles listed by Rudolf Bultmann: the length of the sickness, the dreadful or dangerous character of the disease, the ineffective treatment of physicians, and the contrast of the master and disciples

roughly equivalent situation in *Apollonius of Tyana*, where Damis establishes the magnitude of the miraculous element in the episode in which Apollonius frees his foot from a fetter (7.38). There Damis' despair sets up the audience for Apollonius' show of supernatural authority, and Damis' response underlines the magnitude of the miracle. Even closer parallels are found in two biblical feeding stories that may have served as models for shaping the Markan episodes. In those stories, a servant of Elisha (2 Kings 4.43) and Moses himself (Num 11.21-23) protest the impossibility of feeding a large group of people, only to see God miraculously provide for the group.[30]

The interchange between Jesus and the disciples also serves to shift responsibility for the procurement of bread away from the crowd and thus establishes the need for the ensuing miracle.[31] In Mark, there is a clear tendency to show Jesus performing miracles only in response to a request or when faced by a specific situation requiring action, such as the demons' making his identity known.[32] In order

---

(*The History of the Synoptic Tradition* [New York: Harper & Row, 1963] 221). All of these motifs function to establish the magnitude of a healing miracle, just as the disciples in this case establish the magnitude of the feeding miracle.

[30] Noted by Matera, "Incomprehension of the Disciples," 155-56.

[31] Fowler's reading of the interchange as an indication of the disciples' "antagonism to Jesus" (*Loaves and Fishes*, 116) results from a severe overinterpretation of the episode and from a misperception of the central focus. In the philosophical and wisdom material, the portrayal of a teacher's students is generally used to give information about the teacher. There must be quite compelling reasons for approaching a passage in terms of what it says about the disciples rather than what it says about Jesus. I see no reason to read the feeding story as anything other than an account of a miracle performed by Jesus. Fowler's judgment that "the heart of 6:30-44 is the controversy over bread and money between Jesus and the Twelve (6:36-38)" is quite strained (*Loaves and Fishes*, 117). Nor can I agree that 6.36-38 should be read as a controversy. The disciples' suggestion that the crowd be dismissed so they can find food (6.36) is perfectly consistent with Jesus' own compassion for the crowd (6.34). The disciples' question to Jesus, "Should we go out and buy two hundred denarii worth of bread?" is phrased as a deliberative subjunctive, suggesting that they are simply trying to clarify the rather surprising request that they feed the crowd themselves. If the disciples were challenging the direction given by Jesus, a syntactical form requiring a negative response would be more appropriate.

[32] There is only one exception to this principle earlier in the Gospel, the healing of the man with the withered hand (3.1-6), in which the healing is presented as a point of conflict between Jesus and the Jewish authorities. In the context of Mark, it is not unreasonable to assume that the presence of the man was itself a request

to maintain the principle that Jesus did not perform public miracles on his own initiative, Mark establishes a need for the miracle through the interchange with the disciples that demonstrates the impossibility of the crowd's being fed through natural means.[33]

At least among the educated, from whom most of the literary remains are derived, there was a strong current of distrust for shows of miraculous power. In Philostratus, the Brahmans reject the ostentatious display of miracles (3.15), as does Thespesion, the Gymnosoph, whose own production of a miraculous sign (ἀποσημαίνειν) occurs in a tirade against the Brahmans designed to discredit Thespesion himself rather than the object of his attack (6.10). Apollonius violates the principle with his public disappearance from the court of Domitian accompanied by a claim of immortality (8.5), but in general, the sage is restrained in his exercise of miraculous power.[34]

---

for aid. In the healing of the paralytic (2.1-12), Jesus offers the healing as proof of his authority to forgive sins, but the paralytic and his friends have come to seek healing, not forgiveness.

There are two miracles later in the Gospel that Jesus initiates. Both are seen only by the disciples. The first is the walking on the water (6.45-52). The curious note that Jesus meant to pass the disciples by (6.48) may be meant to suggest that Jesus did not intend to be seen by the disciples and that they caught him, in an unguarded moment, with his divinity showing. The second is the withering of the fig tree (11.12-14, 20-25).

[33] The suggestion of Kingsbury that the disciples should have performed the miracle themselves (*Conflict in Mark*, 98-99) overlooks the similarities with other miracle stories noted above. Nor can it be sustained by the narrative of Mark. Mark creates an important distinction between Jesus, who possesses authority in his own right as the Son of God, and the disciples, who possess only derivative authority given to them by Jesus. Jesus gives the twelve authority over the demons (3.15), and when they are sent out, the twelve successfully exercise that authority (6.13). There is no suggestion that Jesus has given the disciples authority to multiply bread.

[34] The distrust of ostentatious miracle-working is especially clear among the historians. Suetonius relates that Vespasian gained authority in his role as emperor through the miraculous healing of two men, one blind and the other lame (*Vespasian* 7). In this account, the men first approach the emperor with their request, and Vespasian is shown to be reluctant to attempt the healing, agreeing to do so only at the continued urging of his friends. On the other hand, Diodorus Siculus portrays King Eunus, the leader of a second century BCE slave revolt, as a trickster making an ostentatious display of feigned miraculous power (34.2.4-14). Josephus tells of three first century Jews who called people to witness their miraculous power (Theudas, *Antiquities* 20.97-98; a prophet from Egypt, *Antiquities*

The disciples also function in the story as mediators between Jesus and the crowd (6.41). The disciples distribute the bread that Jesus has broken. This is particularly significant if, as seems likely, the story was understood as a type for the Eucharist.[35] In that case, the disciples would be portrayed as mediating the Eucharist in spite of the fact, mentioned in the following episode, that they did not understand about the loaves (6.52).

Walking on Water

In the walking-on-water episode, the disciples function primarily as the audience who observes and reacts to the miracle.[36] Once again, the disciples' reactions, first fearfully mistaking Jesus for a ghost and then being amazed at the miracle, are fairly typical elaborations in the miracle genre. Here, however, Mark begins to establish a pattern in the disciples' reactions. The disciples are amazed, he tells the listener, "because they did not understand about the loaves, but rather their hearts had been hardened" (5.52).[37] The passive most likely indicates divine activity.[38] This is consistent with the suggestion of

---

20.167-72 and *War* 2.261-63; Jonathan the Sicarius, *War* 7.437), all of whom he dismisses as impostors. This evidence suggests that the public display of miraculous power was likely to give rise to the charge of fakery.

[35] Among those who have suggested linking the stories with the Eucharist are Bastiaan van Iersel, "Die wunderbare Speisung und das Abendmahl in der synoptischen Tradition," *NovT* 7 (1964) 167-94; Alkuin Heisig, *Die Botschaft der Brotvermehrung*, StutB 15 (Stuttgart: Katholisches Bibelwerk, 1966) 61-67; Quentin Quesnell, *The Mind of Mark: Interpretation and Method through the Exegesis of Mark 6,52*, AnBib 38 (Rome: Pontifical Biblical Institute, 1969); and Jean-Marie van Cangh, *La multiplication des pains et l'Eucharistie*, LD 86 (Paris: Éditions du Cerf, 1975). Fowler criticizes the view, insisting that the feeding stories cannot be read in terms of the Last Supper, which occurs later in the narrative, as if Mark's original audience heard the narrative in a total vacuum (*Loaves and Fishes*, 138-47).

[36] A detailed study of the pericope can be found in John Paul Heil, *Jesus Walking on the Sea*, AnBib 87 (Rome: Biblical Institute Press, 1981), 67-75; 118-45.

[37] For a summary of proposed interpretations of the disciples' lack of understanding in this text, see Boucher, *Mysterious Parable*, 69-73.

[38] So also Matera, "Incomprehension of the Disciples," 157-59, who supports this point with a study of the idea of hardening in the New Testament. Similarly, Camille Focant, "L'Incompréhension des disciples dans le deuxième Évangile," *RB* 82 (1985) 167; Nineham, *St. Mark*, 181.

a divine intention to prevent perception in the parable theory (4.11-12) and the portrayal of knowledge as a divine gift.

The Second Feeding Miracle

The disciples' role in the second feeding story is essentially the same as in the first, although it is somewhat truncated. In this episode, it is Jesus rather than the disciples who raises the question of the crowd's hunger, and the disciples' role is limited to indicating the difficulty of procuring food (8.4) and distributing the broken bread (8.6). The repetition of such a similar episode, however, raises the question of why the disciples react in the same manner when confronted with the problem of feeding the crowd. Surely they could have remembered the earlier miracle!

The explanations offered for this phenomena have varied as the understanding of Mark's Gospel has changed. When the Gospel was regarded as essentially an historical account, various psychological explanations were put forward.[39] For the form critics, who regarded the Gospel as a loosely organized collection of essentially independent episodes, the repetition, with only minor variations, of the feeding story was considered to be primarily a matter for source criticism. The two episodes, in their basic similarity, were understood to make the same point. The repetition of the disciples' query was evidence of a doublet in the tradition rather than an incident to be interpreted within the narrative of the Gospel.[40]

---

[39] Several are noted by Fowler (*Loaves and Fishes*, 93; 213, n. 2) and Vincent Taylor (*The Gospel According to St. Mark: The Greek Text with Introduction, Notes, and Indexes*, 2nd ed. [London: Macmillan, 1966] 359). John Calvin, with a less optimistic view of human nature than most modern commentators, notes, "There is not a day on which a similar indifference does not steal upon us; and we ought to be the more careful not to allow our minds to be drawn away from the contemplation of divine benefits" (*Commentary on a Harmony of the Evangelists, Matthew, Mark, and Luke*, CalC 16 [Grand Rapids, MI: Baker Book House, 1979] 2.274).

[40] Taylor provides a good example of this approach (*St. Mark* 629-30). Taylor cites other supporters of the doublet hypothesis on page 359. See also Paul J. Achtemeier, "Toward the Isolation of Pre-Markan Miracle Catenae," *JBL* 89 (1970) 265-91; idem, "The Origin and Function of the Pre-Markan Miracle Catenae," *JBL* 91 (1972) 198-221.

The appearance of narrative criticism, accompanied by the assumption of a high degree of authorial control, has transformed the repetition of the query into evidence for Mark's theological concerns. Thus Robert M. Fowler has taken the repetition of the query as evidence of the Markan polemic against the disciples.[41] Frank J. Matera sees it as underlining the disciples' incomprehension, which he attributes to a motif of hardening used to express the mystery of Jesus.[42] Robert C. Tannehill, though he argues against the polemical view of Markan opposition to the disciples, states that the disciples' reaction in the second story "suggests a perverse blindness that must disturb the reader."[43]

This approach, however, misjudges the nature of the Markan narrative, applying standards of linearity and character development that are not applicable to Mark. Mark's narrative style is in large part cumulative rather than linear.[44] That is to say, the narrative is built from essentially independent episodes that maintain their independence in their specific details while producing their effect through the accumulation of their independent impact.[45] Ancient audiences did not expect from historically based works the kind of linear development that modern readers assume from their experience of modern fiction.[46] None of the philosophical biographies examined in this

---

[41] Fowler, *Loaves and Fishes*, 93-99.

[42] Matera, "Incomprehension of the Disciples," 161.

[43] Tannehill, "Disciples in Mark," 399.

[44] For a somewhat different discussion of the nonlinear character of the Markan narrative, see Dewey, "Oral Methods," esp. 37-42; *idem*, "Interwoven Tapestry," 221-36.

[45] For a different view of Markan episodic narrative, see Cilliers Breytenbach, *Nachfolge und Zukunftserwartung nach Markus: Eine methodenkritische Studie* (Zurich: Theologischer Verlag, 1984) 82-84; *idem*, "Das Markusevangelium als episodische Erzählung," in *Der Erzähler des Evangeliums*, ed. by Ferdinand Hahn, StutB 118/119 (Stuttgart: Verlag Katholisches Bibelwerk, 1985) 139-69; *idem*, "Gospel of Mark as Episodic Narrative," *Scriptura* (special issue 4, 1989) 1-26.

[46] The comments of Welch on this point are quite pertinent: "It should be apparent that ancient rhetoric and modern prose do not strive to achieve the same ideals. Modern style demands, for example, that an author write more or less linearly, following a line of syllogistic or dialectical reasoning, or developing a continuous flow of ideas. Circuitousness and repetitiveness are shunned in most circumstances. In many ancient contexts, however, repetition and even redundancy appear to represent the rule rather than the exception. Parallelism thrived. Indeed,

work maintains a continuous narrative throughout.[47] Only the *Life of Apollonius* makes any pretense of doing so, and even in that work large sections are almost totally episodic, with unrelated events being cataloged according to a supposed chronological or geographic order (e.g., 4.1-34).

In such a cumulative narrative, it is more likely that the verbal similarities between the two feeding stories, of which the repetition of the disciples' query is only one, are intended to function together to make the listener aware of the repetition of a similar incident. The fact that Jesus performed two miraculous feedings is significant for the narrative. Jesus later takes the disciples to task for failing to understand the two feedings (8.17-21), but he does not berate them for having inquired a second time where to find food in the wilderness. Instead, he questions them about the amount of leftover pieces they collected and condemns them with language earlier associated with failure to understand the hidden meaning of parables.

The disciples' nearly identical response in the two feeding stories is one more instance of Mark's creating coherence at the discourse or rhetorical level of the Gospel at the expense of coherence at the narrative level.[48] The repetition of the feeding underscores for the

---

repetition once served several valuable purposes. It had express pedagogical functions, and double structures carried moral implications for the ancient mind as well: 'For God speaketh once, yea twice, yet man perceiveth it not' (Job 33:14)." *Chiasmus in Antiquity*, 12.

The constraints of oral delivery, which tended to keep writing closer to the model of oral literature, also made repetition a valuable compositional tool. For the use of repetition in oral narrative, see Bennison Gray, "Repetition in Oral Literature," *JAF* 84 (1971) 289-303.

[47] Even more extreme than the cases examined in this dissertation is the type of biography exemplified by much of Diogenes Laertius, where independent chreiae are juxtaposed without any semblance of overall narrative continuity.

[48] James A. Notopoulos has noted how oral compositions are tolerant of a great deal of inconsistency between individual episodes ("Parataxis in Homer: A New Approach to Homeric Literary Criticism, *TAPA* 80 [1949] 21). This tolerance for inconsistency results from the audience's concentration on single episodes as they are being presented. The same tolerance may be expected in written compositions intended for oral delivery, such as the Gospel of Mark, if the writer was close to the oral traditions or was himself an oral tradent.

Kelber has argued that Mark was hostile to the oral tradents (*Oral and Written Gospel*, esp. 90-139). I find that argument unconvincing, but space does not allow a refutation of the argument here. In spite of his theory of Markan hostility to

listener the importance of these miracles for understanding Jesus' identity. The disciples' response in each feeding story functions at the episodic level to indicate the magnitude of the miraculous display of power.[49] At the level of the macro-narrative, however, only the discourse or rhetorical level of the individual feeding episodes contributes to meaning, while the repetition of the similar response becomes incoherent.

This incoherence underscores the formulaic nature of Mark's narrative technique. Even in the relatively small number of episodes that we have examined, we have frequently noted similarities in phrasing and narrative sequence, suggesting that Mark follows relatively fixed patterns in the construction of similar episodes. While this repetition often has been cited as evidence of the existence of doublets in the tradition[50] or of Mark's having constructed one episode on the model of a preexisting one,[51] these explanations posit fixed verbal forms that are inconsistent with oral traditions[52] or with the free adaptation of written tradition that we find in the other synoptic Gospels.[53] The repetitive nature of the Markan narrative is more likely to be the result of Mark's compositional technique. Oral

---

orality, however, Kelber argues cogently for the oral-like nature of Markan redaction (*Oral and Written Gospel*, 64-70).

[49] Tolbert suggests that Mark's audience feels superior to the disciples at this point, because "while the disciples cannot fathom how Jesus will be able to feed the four thousand..., the audience knows he will do it, just as he earlier fed the five thousand" (*Sowing the Gospel* 223). It is more likely that the exchange reminds the audience that they also cannot fathom how Jesus is able to feed the four thousand, even with the knowledge that he did it.

[50] E.g., the scholars cited above in n. 40.

[51] E.g., Fowler, *Loaves and Fishes*, 68-90.

[52] Kelber, *Oral and Written Gospel*, 30, relying on the works of Milman Parry and Albert B. Lord cited on 34, n. 5-6. These studies describe oral epic poetry, but the findings appear to hold true for other extended oral narratives. The studies are not applicable to short sayings, which may well have been transmitted in fixed forms, as proverbs, for example, generally are. For an analogy between the transmission of jokes and narrative episodes of the Gospel, see Meagher (*Clumsy Construction*, 3-15).

[53] The fluidity of the written tradition is emphasized by L. W. Hurtado ("The Gospel of Mark: Evolutionary or Revolutionary Document?" *JSNT* 40 [1990] 17-18).

storytelling relies heavily on such verbal and narrative formulas.[54] It is very likely that Mark was an oral storyteller as well as the writer of a Gospel. In any case, his unsophisticated technique is similar in many ways to that of oral composition.[55] The repetition of the disciples' query indicates that the query was a fixed part of his formula for relating a feeding miracle, a formula that most likely was influenced by the biblical precedents that included such expressions of the impossibility of the task.[56]

The Discussion about Bread (8.14-21)

In the discussion about bread in the boat, Mark explicitly brings together the two threads of parable and miracle that have been developed in this part of the Gospel.[57] Jesus addresses a parable to the disciples (8.15);[58] the disciples fail to understand, as they have consistently failed to understand the parables; Jesus rebukes them with terminology clearly reminiscent of the parable theory (8.17b-18), but then, instead of offering an explanation of the parable, he interrogates them about the details of the feeding miracles (8.19-20). As in 6.52, hardening language is used to describe the disciples (8.17c). In the earlier passage the listener is told that the disciples' hearts had been

---

[54] Kelber presents an excellent discussion of the formulaic composition of Markan episodes (*Oral and Written Gospel*, 44-89). He attributes this formulaic style to "Mark's oral legacy," however, and minimizes Mark's responsibility for this aspect of the compositional style of the Gospel. His thesis of a radical discontinuity between the oral transmission of traditions and the written Gospel leads to a treatment of the oral-like character of Markan language in terms of "the pre-Markan mode of language" (*Oral and Written Gospel*, 45) rather than as the Markan mode of language.

[55] For an exposition of some of those techniques, see Dewey, "Oral Methods," 32-44.

[56] 2 Kings 4.43 and Num 11.21-23, as noted above.

[57] For recent discussions of this pericope, see Drury, who focuses on the number symbolism ("Mark" 414-16); Matera, who sees the identity of Jesus 1 as the point the disciples fail to understand ("Incomprehension of the Disciples," 161-65); N. A. Beck ("Reclaiming a Biblical Text: The Mark 8:14-21 Discussion about Bread in the Boat," *CBQ* 43 [1981] 49-56); and L. Wm. Countryman ("How Many Baskets Full? Mark 8:14-21 and the Value of Miracles in Mark," *CBQ* 47 [1985] 643-55).

[58] As always, I am using the term parable in the Markan sense rather than as a modern form critical category.

hardened in relation to the feeding miracle. Here Jesus expresses surprise and dismay at that fact.

In the two earlier parable episodes, Mark has established a pattern of parable, incomprehension, rebuke, and explanation. This leads the listener to expect that here also the disciples' lack of understanding will be overcome. That, however, does not happen within the confines of the episode itself. Instead of providing an explanation, Jesus widens the discussion to include the bread miracles. Through Jesus' interrogation of the disciples, Mark confronts his listeners with the need to interpret the meaning of the feedings. The references to the Pharisees and Herod in the parable further expand the scope of material requiring explanation. The Pharisees and Herod play prominent roles as villains in the only two episodes between 4.1 and 8.26, other than the sending out of the twelve, that do not concern parables or miracles. It is natural then that the listeners should understand "the leaven of the Pharisees and the leaven of Herod" in terms of these episodes.[59] If that is so, then the listener is confronted in this episode with a demand to interpret the entire section of the Gospel from 4.1 to the present point.

Although it is difficult to judge the original audience's competence for interpreting specific points, it seems likely that they could be expected to interpret successfully the meaning of the feeding miracles. The linking of the bread and sea miracles with Peter's confession in the tradition prior to Mark is suggested by the appearance of a similar cycle in John.[60] The other synoptic Gospels also maintain the close

---

[59] The interpretation of the Gospels always confronts one with the problem of determining the extent and type of outside knowledge that the intended listener could be expected to draw upon. Clearly, the Gospels are not entirely self-contained narratives unrelated to the world known by the listeners. It is likely, however, that the listeners must rely heavily on the Markan narrative and other Christian traditions for their understanding of the Pharisees and of Herod. The fact that Mark takes pains to explain some of the practices of the Pharisees in 7.3-4 suggests that the Markan audience was not familiar with them from their own experience. It is also unlikely that a Roman audience would have had any familiarity with a Judean king living forty years earlier other than the information contained in Christian traditions.

[60] Feeding of the five thousand (John 6.1-14); walking on the water (John 6.15-21); discussion about the significance of bread (John 6.22-59); the confession by Peter (6.69). The absence of the second sea miracle and feeding complex in

association of the bread and sea miracles with Peter's identification of Jesus as the Messiah.[61] The probable linking of the episodes in the tradition suggests that there was a body of interpretation concerning the interrelationships between the episodes that Mark could expect his audience to understand.

In that case, the missing explanation would be found not in the present episode but in the following section, Peter's confession, the teaching about the passion and the transfiguration.[62] The feeding

---

Luke, who moves directly from the feeding of the five thousand (9.10-17) to Peter's confession (9.18), may also be explained in terms of his recognition of the sea miracle/feeding/confession complex, which he decided to include in a single rather than a double version.

The existence of this complex in John suggests the existence of such a complex in the tradition even if John was familiar with Mark's Gospel, since John usually feels no compulsion to include episodes related in the synoptics or to follow the synoptic order.

[61] Breaking of bread and recognition of Jesus are also linked in the Emmaus story in Luke 24.30-31. Gerd Theissen's contention that the eschatological interpretation of Jesus' miracles found in the Q sayings material is absent in the narrative tradition (*The Miracle Stories of the Early Christian Tradition* [Philadelphia: Fortress Press, 1983] 281) is defensible only if one adopts the position that there is no connection between eschatology and Jesus' identity as the Messiah or the Son of God.

[62] Several scholars have suggested that the point of Jesus' questioning of the disciples is not his identity but the inclusion of the gentiles in the Christian community. This position is based on the understanding of the second feeding as a gentile feeding (e.g., Kelber, *Kingdom in Mark*, 45-65; *idem, Mark's Story of Jesus*, 40-41; Beck, "Reclaiming a Biblical Text," 49-56; Howard Clark Kee, *Community of the New Age: Studies in Mark's Gospel* [Philadelphia: The Westminster Press, 1977] 95; David J. Hawkin, "The Incomprehension of the Disciples in the Marcan Redaction," *JBL* 91 [1972] 495). This interpretation, however, fails to take account of the thematization of incomprehension in the three boat scenes in 4.35-8.21. In the first, the miraculous stilling of the storm leads to a query concerning Jesus' identity (4.41). In the second, the disciples' lack of understanding of the loaves is stressed and linked to their amazement at Jesus' walking on the water and the second calming of a storm. The repetition of the calming motif, in identical language (καὶ ἐκόπασεν ὁ ἄνεμος, 4.39; 6.51), and the fear motif (which in the earlier episode is explicitly linked to the question of identity, 4.41) bring the earlier episode to mind and suggest that here also the reason for the disciples' amazement (6.51) is their failure to understand Jesus' identity. The theme of identity is further emphasized by Jesus' self-identification, "ἐγώ εἰμι, do not be afraid" (6.50). In the third scene, Jesus' query, οὔπω νοεῖτε οὐδὲ συνίετε; πεπωρωμένην ἔχετε τὴν καρδίαν ὑμῶν; (8.17), is clearly reminiscent of Mark's comment on the disciples in the second scene, οὐ

miracles point to Jesus' hidden identity as Messiah (8.29) and Son of
God (9.7).[63] In both cases, the statement of Jesus' identity is followed

---

γὰρ συνῆκαν ἐπὶ τοῖς ἄρτοις, ἀλλ᾽ ἦν αὐτῶν ἡ καρδία πεπωρωμένη
(6.52), indicating a resumption of the identity theme.

The numbers of baskets of fragments, twelve and seven, which has been cited
in favor of this interpretation (e.g., Kelber, *Mark's Story of Jesus*, 39, 41) is hardly
conclusive. Seven is an extremely common symbolic number in Middle Eastern
folklore, and especially in Jewish and Christian traditions because of its connection
to the seven days of creation (see K. H. Rengstorf, "ἑπτά, ἑπτάκις,
ἑπτακισχίλιοι, ἑβδομάς, ἑβδομήκοντα," *TDNT* 2.627-35). It is hardly
plausible to interpret Mark's use of the number seven on the basis of the seven
leaders of the Hellenists in Acts 6.3, a later composition. Haenchen cites Str-B
2.641 for the fact that Jewish town councils consisted of seven men and suggests
the seven Hellenists may be patterned on such a council (*Acts of the Apostles*,
263).

Nor is it clear from the geographical references that the second feeding was
a gentile feeding. It apparently takes place in the Decapolis, since that is the last
location given by Mark (7.31), but there was a significant Jewish population in the
Decapolis before the revolt of 70 CE (thirteen thousand Jews were massacred in
Scythopolis at the beginning of the revolt, Josephus, *War* 2.466; Gadara took part
in the revolt and had to be subdued, *War* 4.413-18; Hippos and Gadara are
mentioned among the chief locations from which a captured Jewish army of nearly
forty thousand men had been raised, *War* 3.542). The objections Jesus makes to
the request of the Syrophoenician woman (7.27) suggests that healing is to taken
as an exception rather than part of a pattern.

The suggestion by Quesnell that the disciples are rebuked for not having a
fully developed theology of the Eucharist, including salvation through the cross,
the union of the Christian community, and Jesus' future return (*Mind of Mark*, 232)
goes well beyond what the text can support. The explicit connection Mark makes
between misunderstanding the bread and amazement at Jesus' walking on water
does not suggest that any of those things are at issue. One can understand bread
as a symbol of salvation through the cross and still be amazed that Jesus can walk
on water. Similar objections confront Williams' somewhat less ambitious proposal
that the object of the disciples' misunderstanding in the miracles of the loaves was
Jesus' sacrificial death as the offering of the new covenant (*Gospel against
Parable*, 48).

[63] A number of scholars have suggested that Peter's confession is defective.
The idea was argued by A. Meyer ("Die Entstehung des Marcusevangeliums," in
Festgabe für Jülicher zum 70. Geburtstag [Tübingen: Mohr, 1927] 35-60).
Summaries of such views may be found in Matera (*What Are They Saying?* 25-46)
and Jack Dean Kingsbury (*The Christology of Mark's Gospel* [Philadelphia:
Fortress Press, 1983] 25-33). Since Mark begins his work by attributing the title
Messiah to Jesus (1.1) and later has Jesus accept the title (14.62), it is difficult to
see how it could be incorrect here. While the disciples' understanding of the title
may be incomplete, it is hard to see how the disciples' attribution of the title to
Jesus could be anything other than an advance in understanding within Mark's

Follow Me!

by a command to secrecy (8.30; 9.9), suggesting that his identity is to be handled as a mystery (cf. 4.11). The pattern of incomprehension, rebuke and explanation is preserved but expanded in scope to encompass several episodes.[64]

By his references to the prior feeding episodes and the parable discourse in the interchange in the boat (8.14-21) Mark leads his listeners to reflect upon multiple episodes. Further evidence that Mark intends the listener to consider multiple episodes at this point is found in the parable about the leaven of the Pharisees and the leaven of Herod (8.15). Taken in isolation, the parable has eluded interpretation, but previous and following episodes provide the listener with both context and interpretation.[65]

---

narrative world (similarly, Hawkin, "Incomprehension of the Disciples," 499). For an extensive refutation of the idea that Mark understood the title Messiah to be defective, see Kingsbury, *Christology of Mark's Gospel*.

[64] It should be noted that the pattern functions at the level of episodic impact rather than at the level of detail. There is no narrative explanation of how the disciples, who are totally uncomprehending in 8.17-21, are able to identify Jesus properly as the Messiah in 8.29, unless one takes the healing of the blind man as a symbolic explanation.

The conclusion that the disciples' incomprehension functions rhetorically in this section much as it does in the episodes involving the interpretation of parables parallels Matera's opinion: "The theme of the disciples' incomprehension in 6,14-8,30 serves the Christological function of heightening the mystery of Jesus' identity," ("Incomprehension of the Disciples," quote from 172).

[65] Even in the first century the meaning of the parable was not obvious. Matthew's interpretation of the leaven as teaching (Mt 16.12) is clearly Matthean rather than Markan. Luke interprets the leaven as hypocrisy (Lk 12.1). Taylor follows Israel Abrahams (*Studies in Pharisaism and the Gospels*, first series [Cambridge: The University Press, 1917] 52-53) in understanding the leaven as the evil impulse (*St. Mark*, 365). Henry Barclay Swete understands Mark to distinguish between the leaven of the Pharisees and the leaven of Herod. The first is, following the synoptic interpretations, either their teaching or their hypocrisy. The second is "the practical unbelief which springs from love of the world and the immoralities to which in a coarser age it led" (*The Gospel According to St. Mark: The Greek Text with Introduction Notes and Indices* [London and New York: Macmillan, 1905] 169-70). Eduard Schweizer understands the verse as a blunder by Mark that disrupts the episode and suggests the yeast symbolizes "the evil desire of sin" (*The Good News According to Mark*, [Richmond: John Knox, 1970] 160-61). Lane takes a multi-episodic approach, though one more limited than the one proposed here, interpreting the saying in terms of the request for a sign in 8.11 as "the disposition to believe only if signs which compel faith are produced" (*Mark*, 281). Melbourne similarly sees the parable as meaning that "the disciples

The adjacent episode involving the Pharisees concerns their demand for a sign from heaven (8.11-12). A number of explanations of the episode have been advanced,[66] but it seems most natural to understand the demand as ironic.[67] At the crucifixion, Mark portrays Jesus' tormentors as making an ironic confession of Jesus' identity,[68] and it would be in keeping with that narrative style to have the Pharisees at this point ironically sum up the meaning of the miracles as signs from heaven. In that case, the leaven of the Pharisees might

---

were to beware of false Messianic expectations and of a Messianism based on signs" (*Slow to Understand*, 153). Kee understands it to refer to the political postures of the Pharisees (passive acquiescence to Roman rule) and the Herodians (active collaboration), though he indicates nothing from the context to suggest a political reading (*Community of the New Age*, 97-98). Juel comes closest to the interpretation presented here, linking the saying to the episodes in 7.1-13 and 6.14-29 (*Mark*, 114).

[66] Best suggests that Mark includes the episode at this point to indicate "that the miraculous element within [the miracles] is not to be stressed" ("Miracles in Mark," in *Disciples and Discipleship*, 182). Best interprets the miracles in terms of a wide variety of pastoral lessons that he derives from them. Lane points to the earlier dispute about exorcisms (3.22-30) as evidence that the Pharisees saw Jesus' miracles as ambiguous actions and are here seeking an unambiguous sign. Mark is rejecting the reliance on such an unambiguous sign (*Mark*, 276-79, but on the ambiguity inherent in the term σημεῖον, see p. 235 and n. 69, below). Swete similarly sees a demand "for σημεῖα of a higher order than the miracles" (*St. Mark*, 167). Schweizer sees a distinction between a sign freely given by God, which is acceptable, and a sign given in response to human demand, which is not (*Good News*, 158-60). Taylor sees Jesus rejecting a "test of signs" but also understands the pericope as pointing to the quality of the feeding as a sign (361-2). Theissen sees the refusal of a sign as "punishment for unbelief" but sees the sign as something other than the miracles (*Miracle Stories* 296).

[67] Juel points out that the parallel request for a sign after the miraculous feeding in John (6.30-31) is clearly ironic (*Mark*, 113). In John, it is Jesus who introduces the discussion of signs by chastising the crowd for understanding the feeding only in term of the satisfaction of their hunger (6.26). When the crowd asks, "What should we do to be doing the works of God?" Jesus states that the work of God is to believe in him, making explicit the connection between sign and belief (6.28-29). The crowd then stupidly asks for a sign, pointing to the manna the Israelites ate in the desert. Since the parallel between the manna and the miraculous multiplication of loaves is unmistakable, the request underscores the sign quality of the miracle previously narrated.

[68] Donald Juel says irony is the "most prominent feature of the passion story" (*Messiah and Temple: The Trial of Jesus in the Gospel of Mark*, SBLDS 31 [Missoula, MT: Scholars Press, 1977] 47). For other examples of irony in Mark see Rhoads and Michie, *Mark as Story*, 59-62.

be understood as the inability to perceive the hidden meaning of revelatory events, or in Jesus' terms (8.12) to be given a sign.[69] This is precisely the error that the disciples display in the discussion, an inability to understand the feeding miracles.

The reference to Herod, however, indicates that more is at stake than the comprehension of divine signs, since the episode involving Herod, like the dispute with the Pharisees in 7.1-23, does not involve signs. In 7.8, Jesus charges the Pharisees with abandoning God's commandments to follow human traditions. The listener is not given an explicit judgment concerning Herod, but the beheading of John shows him placing his human standing with his daughter and his guests above the inner promptings of his heart, which recognizes John as a holy and just man (6.20, 26). Put more generally, both Herod and the Pharisees think and act according to human judgments rather than the judgment of God. The inability to discern signs is the epistemological aspect of the failure to think the thoughts of God. The beheading of John and the establishment of false traditions reflect the moral aspect of the same failure. Thus the Markan interpretation of the parable of the leaven can be found in Jesus' rebuke of Peter in 8.33 for "thinking human thoughts rather than the thoughts of God." The episodes

---

[69] The only other use of the term σημεῖον in Mark occurs in the farewell discourse. In the introduction of the discourse, the disciples ask for the sign that will indicate the end time (13.4). Here the sign is clearly something that is not intelligible in itself. The disciples require special instruction in order to recognize it. In 13.22, Jesus indicates that false messiahs and prophets will perform signs and wonders. "Signs and wonders" is a fixed phrase that does not carry the same meaning as "sign" by itself. If the phrase is admitted as evidence of the Markan understanding of "sign," however, the possibility of false signs shows once again that there is no necessary connection between the outward manifestation of the sign and its meaning.

Boucher indicates that Jesus refuses the demand for a sign because the Pharisees have already been given a sign in the loaves. She argues that there are two interpretations of σημεῖον at work in the episode. For the Pharisees, a sign is an absolute proof, while for Mark it indicates a veiled revelation (*Mysterious Parable*, 76). Augustine Stock also notes that the demand for a sign "demonstrates once again that miracles, like parables, have a deeper level of meaning which can be missed. The Pharisees stand among 'those outside' who will not see" (*The Method and Message of Mark* [Wilmington, DE: Michael Glazier, 1989] 222).

involving Herod and the Pharisees provide negative examples of living according to human judgments.[70]

Miracle and Identity in the Philosophic Biographies

All three of the philosophers whose biographies we have examined were noted for their supernatural abilities. Socrates was led by the promptings of his δαιμόνιον, while both Pythagoras and Apollonius are credited with numerous miraculous achievements. In none of these biographies, however, is the ambivalent nature of the miraculous developed to the degree that it is in Mark.

Xenophon's handling of Socrates' supernatural power contrasts sharply with the way in which the other authors treat their heroes' miracles, primarily because Socrates' δαιμόνιον plays no essential role in defining his identity. For Xenophon, Socrates' essential identity is found in his ability to lead people to deeper understanding through dialogue. The δαιμόνιον plays little or no role in narrative depiction of Socrates as an intellectual and moral guide. Xenophon is aware of the ambivalent attitude toward supernatural power. Socrates' δαιμόνιον is the basis of one of the charges against the philosopher, that of bringing in new gods (1.1.2). Thus Xenophon carefully argues for its legitimacy at the beginning of his work (1.1.2-5). Since the δαιμόνιον plays little role in defining Socrates' identity, however, Xenophon is able to deal with the ambivalent nature of his supernatural power by adopting a rhetorical strategy of minimizing the extraordinary character of the δαιμόνιον.

Philostratus is also well aware of ambivalent attitudes about his hero's supernatural powers.[71] He states that Apollonius had been

---

[70] The connection between the epistemological and ethical dimensions of failure to think the thoughts of God is further suggested by Jesus' remark, "Elijah has come, and they did to him as they pleased." The failure to understand John's hidden nature, that he stood in the position of Elijah, leads to the moral failure of killing him.

[71] On the hostile interpretations of miraculous power and attempts to defend various miracle workers against the charge of magic, see Anitra Bingham Kolenkow, "A Problem of Power: How Miracle Doers Counter Charges of Magic in the Hellenistic World," in SBLSP 1976, 105-10; Anton Fridrichsen, *The Problem of Miracle in Early Christianity* (Minneapolis: Augsburg Publishing House, 1972); Harold Remus, *Pagan-Christian Conflict Over Miracle in the Second Century*, PPFPM 10 (Cambridge, MA: Philadelphia Patristic Foundation, 1983); Eugene V.

denied initiation to the Eleusinian mysteries because the hierophant regarded him as a wizard (γόης, 4.18) and that the priests of Tropho-nius tried to block his access to the shrine for the same reason (8.19). He also indicates that wizardry was one of the principal charges Domitian brought against Apollonius (7.17). He takes pains to refute the idea that Apollonius was a μάγος (1.2), denies that Apollonius was a γόης because of his ability to forecast the future (5.12), argues at length that the sage's ability to free himself from his fetters was not a result of wizardry (7.39), and has Apollonius defend himself against the charge of wizardry in his speech prepared for delivery before Domitian (8.7.2, 9).

In spite of Philostratus' acute awareness of the ambiguous implications of Apollonius' miraculous powers, however, the recognition scenes involving the sage's miracles (1.19; 7.38; 8.13) include no hint of ambiguity.[72] The certainty with which Damis moves from Apollonius' supernatural power to identifying him as a superhuman

---

Gallagher, *Divine Man or Magician? Celsus and Origen on Jesus*, SBLDS 64 (Chico, CA: Scholars Press, 1982).

[72] J. Z. Smith interprets 1.19 as a misunderstanding, suggesting that Apollonius' claim to understand all languages was not meant literally but indicated instead "that the discussions they would have required no translation because human speech was inadequate for the matters to be discussed" ("Good News is No News," 26-27). I see no reason, however, for not taking the claim at face value, even though it is not followed up later in the work. In the following chapter we are told that Apollonius understood the language of animals, which is a further elaboration of the same theme. The claim that he understood language through the practice of silence is similar to his statement that his power of foreknowledge was the result of his diet (8.7.9). Both diet and the period of silence are means of purification (cf. 3.42). Since the Brahmans state that those who practice divination become θεῖοι (3.42), it is not unreasonable for Damis to conclude from a similar supernatural power that Apollonius was a daemon. Apollonius does later ridicule Domitian for mistaking him for a daemon (7.32), but in the same audience, he also ridicules the emperor for trying to imprison one whom he thought was a wizard and thus capable of escape from prison (7.34), even though Apollonius later demonstrates this capability on two occasions (7.38; 8.5). The confusion about the nature of Apollonius' identity results from Philostratus' indifference to the question. He uses the motif for narrative decoration according to the opportunities raised in each individual episode, but there is no deliberate attempt to create ambiguity. The birth and death narratives provide the only points where the ambiguity appears intentional, and Smith rightly points out that ambiguous birth and death narratives had become a convention ("Good News is No News," 27).

being helps to dispel the ambiguity for the reader. Damis provides a model for the reader's own positive evaluation of the sage's powers. For Damis, the miracles provide a transparent view of Apollonius' nature. Apollonius' miraculous disappearance from the courtroom following his trial (8.3) is interpreted by both Apollonius and Philostratus as a transparent sign of his identity.[73]

Iamblichus includes two lists of Pythagoras' miracles in one chapter, one as evidence of Pythagoras' pious character (28.134-37), the other as proof of his divine identity (28.140-43). Iamblichus has made little or no effort to harmonize his sources, and the conflicting points made by the two miracle lists no doubt reflect the conflicting points of view of his source material. The first list includes a number of miracles performed by followers of Pythagoras, suggesting that the ability to work miracles is the common property of those who have an exceptionally pious character. The second list confines the miracles to Pythagoras and claims them as proof of divinity. Both lists, however, are predicated upon an understanding that miracles function as straightforward evidence of some characteristic of the sage. The phrase Iamblichus uses is τεκμήρια τῆς εὐσεβείας (28.137). In Aristotle, τεκμήριον indicates a certain proof, while σημεῖον indicates a sign used as a probable argument.[74] It is likely that Iamblichus, who was trained in Aristotelian philosophy, used the term in this technical sense. Aristotle's distinction appears to follow the general sense of the common meaning of the words. Τεκμήριον is used only once in the New Testament, in Acts 1.3, where Luke indicates the

---

[73] Theissen's interpretation of the interchange between Apollonius and Domitian (7.34) as a refusal to give a sign (*Miracle Stories*, 296) is untenable. Apollonius points out to the emperor the inconsistency of trying to confine a wizard with chains. The emperor boasts that the only way Apollonius will go free is to use his supernatural power to escape. Apollonius, in turn, refuses to do so until he has finished pleading his case, because of the obligation he has to those who had been implicated with him. At the completion of the trial, Apollonius quotes from Homer the words, "I tell thee I am not mortal," and vanishes into thin air. Philostratus specifically states that Apollonius intended this act as a sign of his identity: "And he thought that he would best effect his end if he left no one in ignorance of his true nature, but allowed it to be known to all to be such that he had it in him never to be taken prisoner against his own will" (LCL tr.).

[74] *Prior Analytics* 70a.11, 70b.2; *On Sophistical Refutations* 167b.9; *Rhetoric* 1357a.33, 1357b.4, 1402b.19; cited in LSJ.

positive proof Jesus gives that he is alive after the resurrection. The sense of ambivalence and hiddenness found in Mark is thus completely lacking in Iamblichus' miracle lists.[75]

In both Xenophon and Philostratus the ambivalence of the hero's miracles is expressed through alternative explanations of the miraculous activity. The issue in the *Life of Apollonius* is the source of the sage's miraculous power: Is he a wizard, a practitioner of black magic, or is divine power working through him? Xenophon indicates there were two unflattering interpretations of Socrates' δαιμόνιον. His defense of the reliability of the counsel of the δαιμόνιον (*Memorabilia* 1.4-5) indicates that some believed that Socrates was a charlatan who simply made up his prophecies. The charge of bringing in strange deities, which Xenophon traces to the counsel of the δαιμόνιον (1.1-2), implies that the δαιμόνιον was a false or illegitimate power.[76]

---

[75] J. Z. Smith claims that the lack of interpretation given to the miracle lists in Iamblichus signifies ambiguity ("Good News Is No News," 32), but both lists are given clear, though conflicting, interpretations. His statement, "They are hints; but they do not serve to prove or to demonstrate," is contradicted by Iamblichus' own terminology.

Smith claims for the Pythagoras of Iamblichus an ambiguous divine identity parallel to that of the Markan Jesus. He backs his claim by abstracting the miraculous elements and the various pronouncements concerning Pythagoras' identity that are scattered throughout Iamblichus' work and constructing from them a myth of a misunderstood son of god ("Good News Is No News," 28-35). While Iamblichus wants to claim a divine origin for Pythagoreanism, and thus for philosophy in general, he is unconcerned about defining specifically the nature of that origin. Pythagoras' identity is not a major theme of the work, and the ambiguity that is apparent in the birth stories, where Iamblichus seems consciously to address the issue, is intended to defuse speculation on the philosopher's divine nature. The ambiguity created by the artificial juxtaposition of fragments from diverse portions of the work reflects Iamblichus' known lack of criticism in the use of diverse source materials and his lack of concern about creating a coherent theme of identity. There was clearly a great deal of ambiguity concerning Pythagoras' identity in the underlying traditions, but ambiguity due to the accretion of traditions is quite different from ambiguity as a quality consciously portrayed.

[76] Howard Clark Kee summarizes the general ambiguity surrounding the miraculous as follows: "In this epoch, both champions and critics of miracle-workers are agreed as to what the basic issues are: are miracles evidence of divine wisdom and power, of demonic power and wizardry, or of fraud and chicanery?" (*Miracle in the Early Christian World: A Study in Sociohistorical Method* [New Haven: Yale University Press, 1983] 273). The Markan ambiguity reflects this general ambiguity but interprets it on an epistemological level.

In Mark, however, there is an additional ambivalence. Jesus' opponents interpret his power as demonic (3.22), much as do the opponents of Socrates and Apollonius. The disciples, on the other hand, do not put forward a hostile interpretation. Their problem is incomprehension. They seem to have no interpretation at all. Even the hostile reaction that Jesus receives at his hometown (6.1-6) does not consist of a false interpretation but rather a refusal to make an interpretation. Jesus' fellow townsmen reject his miraculous power because their familiarity with his ordinary humanness makes them reject the implications of his miraculous power. For them, he can only be the carpenter, the son of Mary, the brother of James and Joses and Judas and Simon. There can be no hidden level, no parabolic reality. Mark had earlier linked the concern of Jesus' family with his opponents' hostility through the intercalation of the episodes in 3.20-35. Here also, the rejection that Jesus receives at his hometown suggests the more general rejection of the Jewish people. The term πατρίς, which refers to Jesus' hometown in 6.1, also means native land, and in Jesus' saying in 6.4 it can be understood in that wider meaning.

Mark, then, has turned the *topos* of the miraculous recognition scene on its head. Instead of the typical recognition scene, he presents a number of nonrecognition scenes that are only later resolved in recognition, and the disciples provide the principal narrative vehicle for this transformation.

The unambiguous recognition scenes in the philosophical biographies portray a hero whose divine nature is hidden but can be revealed at will to those whom he chooses. Mark, on the other hand, portrays Jesus as a divine being whose attempts to reveal himself meet with frustration through a significant portion of the narrative. The irritation that Jesus expresses at his disciples' obtuseness (4.13, 40; 7.18; 8.17-21) and his amazement at the disbelief he encounters in his hometown show a being much less in control of events than the philosophical miracle-workers. To some extent Jesus' frustrated expectations can be attributed to the difference between those expectations and God's purpose, since the use of the passive voice in 6.52 to describe the hardening of the disciples suggests the agency of God,[77] but the parable of the tenants (12.1-12) suggests that God's will is frustrated as well.

The inability to recognize the divine power at work in miracles has parallels in the traditions of the Hebrew Bible, such as Pharaoh's refusal to acknowledge God's power displayed through the plagues visited upon Egypt (Exodus 5-14), the Israelites' persistent disbelief during the Exodus and wandering in the wilderness in spite of repeated miracles, and the miraculous defeat of the prophets of Baal by Elijah, which results not in the acceptance of Elijah but in his flight from Israel (1 Kings 18.17-19.3). The closest parallel is the Israelites' disbelief during the Exodus and the years in the wilderness. The Israelites, like the disciples in Mark, are God's chosen ones who are relatively sympathetic to the protagonist, but they lose faith repeatedly in the face of miracles of great power. Like the Markan Jesus, both God and Moses show definite signs of irritation at the stubbornness of their charges (e.g., Ex 32.7-10, 19-20). Mark may have been conscious of the model of the Israelites in the wilderness, since the disciples' nonrecognition is concentrated on the feeding miracles, which often have been seen as parallel to the miracle of the manna in the wilderness. On the other hand, he may only have been influenced by the belief implied in the Pentateuch that God saves in spite of, rather than because of, the moral qualities of those he saves.[78]

The Role of Miracles in Narrative Development

Mark is the only one of the works we have examined in which the miracles play a prominent role in the development of the narrative. In Xenophon, Socrates' δαιμόνιον is absent from most of the work, appearing only in an argumentative section at the very beginning

---

[77] There are other indications throughout the Gospel of a distinction between Jesus' expectation or understanding and that of God. The cry of dereliction from the cross (15.34) clearly suggests that Jesus had not expected to be forsaken by God, and the prayer in Gethsemane (14.35-36) shows that while Jesus was willing to die if necessary, he was not convinced of the necessity of his death. The limitations of Jesus' knowledge of specific aspects of God's plan for the future is expressly stated in 13.32.

[78] Cf. Williams, *Gospel Against Parable*, 60.

(1.1.2, 4) and the discussion of the trial and execution at the end (4.8.1, 5). Iamblichus confines most of the miracles he relates to the lists in non-narrative portions of the work (28.134-37, 140-43). There are only a few rather incidental miracles in the narrative portion (an oracle preceding his birth, 2.5-7; an unexpectedly calm sea voyage, 3.16; Pythagoras' miraculous knowledge of the number of fish in the Crotonians' nets, 8.36), and the proportion of the entire text given over to miracles is extremely small.

Apollonius' miracles are more prominently featured by Philostratus, with clusters of supernatural occurrences at the sage's birth (1.4-6) and death (8.30-31). There is also a claim of miraculous power associated with the introduction of Damis into the narrative (1.19) and a miraculous escape from the court of Domitian (8.5) culminating the trial scene, which is the most significant single event in the narrative. The recognition scene in prison, in which Apollonius removes his leg from the fetter (7.38), is also important for the development of the report of the imprisonment and trial, assuring the reader beforehand that Domitian has no ultimate power over the sage. Apollonius' prediction of the epidemic at Ephesus (4.4) and his subsequent cure of the plague (4.10) is further developed in the narrative as one of the principal charges against the sage in the confrontation with Domitian (7.10; 8.5; 8.7.8). Many of the other miracles, however, are isolated episodes, unconnected to the development of the narrative as a whole. While Philostratus uses miracles as narrative devices at significant places within the narrative, the miracles only become a major focus of the story in the conflict with Domitian.

For Mark, on the other hand, Jesus' miracles and the reactions of various groups to them is one of the most important themes in the first half of the Gospel. Jesus' identity is the central focus of the Gospel, and for Mark, that identity is defined not by Jesus' capacity as a teacher but in his supernatural identity as the Messiah, the Son of God. While Pythagoras and Apollonius are portrayed as supernatural beings, their supernatural identity functions to legitimate their teaching.[79] In Mark, Jesus' teaching is largely subordinate to his

---

[79] J. Z. Smith's claim that in Iamblichus' *Pythagorean Life* "we encounter an essentially contentless revelation" ("Good News Is No News," 36) would be a remarkable revelation indeed to the readers of the nine books of Pythagorean

divine identity. Apart from the disputes about the law, the teaching is concerned mostly with the proper attitude toward Jesus or the events that his appearance has set into motion.[80] Even the disputes about the law largely hinge on Jesus' authority, which is directly related to his divine identity,[81] and within the context of the Gospel, the teaching about the law tends to legitimate Jesus' identity as much as his divine identity legitimates the teaching. The authority with which he makes legal judgments is one more sign of his identity.

The concern with Jesus' identity, and especially the hiddenness of that identity, moves the miracles from the periphery to the center of the narrative. Mark has made the miracles symbolic of Jesus himself. Like Jesus, the miracles represent the infusion of divine power into the mundane world. The miracles are the sign of divine power working in Jesus, but for Mark Jesus' divinity is hidden and veiled. Thus the miracles also become hidden and veiled in their meaning if not in their manifestation. The parabolic nature of the Markan miracles makes them capable of narrative development. Mark does not simply provide a list of miracles, as does Iamblichus, or a few isolated miraculous recognition scenes, as are found in Philostratus. Instead, he forces the listener to dwell upon the meaning of the miracles and uses the ambiguity of supernatural power manifested in the miraculous to signify the hiddenness of Jesus' identity.

---

doctrine that followed the *Life* in the *Synagoge*. The claim is equally specious with respect to Philostratus' *Life of Apollonius*. The fact that Apollonius' "philosophy, as represented by Philostratus, consists of neo-Pythagorean and Stoic commonplaces that may be found in any doxographical handbook" ("Good News Is No News," 28) does not mean that Apollonius' divine identity was more important to Philostratus than his teaching. It reflects only Philostratus' lack of philosophical originality. Banalities, after all, can profit just as much from divine sanction as can profundities and may be more in need of their support.

[80] While some passages may be capable of various interpretations, I would place in this category 1.15; 1.38; 2.17; 2.19-22; 2.25-28; 3.23-35; 4.2-32; 8.31-9.1; 9.11-13; 9.33-50; 10.13-45; 11.27-12.11; 12.35-37; 13.3-37; 14.6-9; 14.22-25.

[81] Each of the disputes in 2.1-28, all of which are in some sense legal disputes, involves the identity and authority of Jesus. The teaching on divorce in 10.1-12 hinges on Jesus' authority to supersede the law of Moses, as does Mark's interpretation of the saying about purity, in which Jesus declares all foods clean (7.14-23).

Incomprehension and the Unexpectedness of the Miraculous

The difficulty that the disciples have in coming to terms with Jesus' miraculous power plays a major role in the listener's understanding of the place of miracle in the narrative world of the Gospel. While both Iamblichus and Philostratus report miracles, the portion of the narrative devoted to them is vastly greater in the Gospel of Mark.[82] The relative scarcity of Q-type teaching material in Mark makes that Gospel much more miracle-dense than the other Synoptic Gospels. In such a miracle-dense narrative there is a risk of making the miraculous the norm for the narrative world, thus undermining the sense of awe that a single miracle story is able to evoke and destroying the ability of the miracle to function as a parabolic sign of divine reality. Early Christian literature exhibits a wide range of approaches to the miraculous, with some works, especially among the later, noncanonical literature, depicting a miracle-laden world as the Christian norm, if not the norm for the world as a whole. In such a world, the power of the divine becomes openly manifest, while in the Markan world, the divine reality overlaps the mundane world through the person of Jesus, but the divine remains hidden. The miracles are unexpected flashes that point to that reality.

Mark maintains the miraculous as an unexpected in-breaking of power.[83] It is the opponents of Jesus who relate his exorcism to the natural structure of the world, the hierarchy of demons and the power of one demon over another (3.22). That rationalization of the miracles is clearly and unequivocally rejected (3.28-30). By associating Jesus' miracles with the parables through Jesus' language in 8.18, Mark indicates that the miracles are, like the parables, incomprehensible on the level of common understanding. They are, like the parables, pointers to hidden meaning. As signs of the hidden reality of Jesus,

---

[82] Theissen counts sixteen miracles in Mark (*Miracle Stories*, 295) compared with ten in the much more massive *Life of Apollonius* (*Miracle Stories*, 294, n. 26). Miracles make up more than a quarter of the literary bulk of Mark according to Best ("Miracles in Mark," in *Disciples and Discipleship*, 181) and Etienne Trocmé (*The Formation of the Gospel According to Mark* [Philadelphia: Westminster Press, 1975] 45-47).

[83] Theissen notes the stress on the unexpected in the individual Christian miracle traditions (*Miracle Stories*, 284).

the miracles cannot be swallowed up in the expected. They must reflect the unexpectedness of Jesus' identity.

Mark is able to maintain the unexpectedness of the miraculous throughout his narrative in spite of the routinization of healing and exorcism in the first few chapters primarily through two devices. The first is the escalation of the miraculous between the first three chapters and chapters four through eight. Simple exorcism becomes the exorcism of two thousand demons at a time, healing becomes revivification, and nature miracles are introduced. Thus the same wonder that greeted the first exorcism ("What is this?" 1.27) can be repeated with the introduction of the first nature miracle ("Who is this?" 4.41). The second device is the continued surprise expressed by the disciples who have been witnesses to all the miracles. This may appear either as a reaction after the fact (4.41, 6.51-52), a lack of expectation before the fact (6.37, 8.4), or the failure to interpret Jesus' words in terms of his miraculous power (5.31).

The attempt to maintain the unexpectedness and extraordinary character of the miraculous is related to Mark's understanding of the miracles as parabolic indicators of Jesus' identity as the Son of God. In works where the miraculous is not understood as an indicator of identity, the miraculous may be purposefully portrayed as part of the ordinary activity of the world. Xenophon, for example, portrays the promptings of Socrates' δαιμόνιον as essentially equivalent to accepted means of divination (*Memorabilia* 1.1.2-4).

The understanding of miracles as proofs of a pious character, as in parts of Iamblichus (28.134-37), also suggests that miracles, while unusual, are within the realm of the ordinary structure of reality (cf. 28.138-39). Other pious Pythagoreans, for whom no special hidden identity is suggested, share the master's ability to perform miracles as a result of their own achievements of piety. The under-standing of miracles as proof of piety within the natural order of reality is reflected in the structure of this section, which is essentially a list of miracles performed by Pythagoras and his followers. The rapid recitation of a number of miracles provides cumulative evidence. As a result of the lack of narrative setting, the expressions of awe and questions about meaning that commonly accompany the Gospel miracles are absent, leaving the readers without narrative incitements to their own feelings of awe.

Philostratus makes the most elaborate attempt to explain miraculous powers as part of the natural order. The Arabians' gift of understanding the language of birds is ascribed to their eating the heart or liver of serpents (1.20). The gift of foreknowledge is related by the Brahmans to purity of soul and the amount of ether it contains (3.42). Apollonius states that Pythagoras' ability to know his past lives was the result of his diet and refusal to wear clothes from animals (8.7.4) and claims his own prophetic ability is the result of his diet, which has caused his senses to be preserved by the ether (8.7.9). This materialistic explanation of Apollonius' powers portrays him as superior while denying divine intervention.

Social Aspects of Parabolic Understanding

Boundary Definition

The approach to boundary definition exemplified by the call stories in the Gospel of Mark differs from those in the philosophical biographies and Sira. The call of the disciples lacks the protreptic argumentation found in most philosophical call stories and centers on the disciples' reaction to the person of Jesus rather than the acceptance of a body of doctrine or a specified way of life. The disciples are not distinguished from others in terms of superior character, and there is no emphasis given to a radical moral reformation. The centrality of Jesus' person for in-group/out-group definition is underscored in the first three chapters by the contrast between the disciples and the Jewish authorities, who are characterized by their opposition to Jesus. While the disciples accept Jesus' authority by responding to his call, the Jewish leaders reject his authority to forgive sins (2.1-12), to redefine eating and Sabbath practices (2.15-3.6), and to drive out demons (3.22-30). The crowds occupy an intermediary position, reacting positively to Jesus' teaching and healing but not submitting to his authority.

This account reconfirms the Christian sectarians in their view of the world, in which Jesus is the Son of God and their relationship with him is central, but it fails to account for one troubling fact of sectarian existence. Why, if Jesus' status was so clearly shown through his healings and exorcisms, did the Jewish authorities remain so blind to their significance? Why do the sectarians in their own day continue to face such widespread incomprehension?[84]

All of the works we have examined have been sectarian in some sense. They either represent an elite community possessing special knowledge (*Pythagorean Life*, Wisdom of Ben Sira), or their hero is one who is rejected by many (*Memorabilia*, *Pythagorean Life*, *Life of Apollonius*). We can see in these works two basic approaches to the universal sectarian problem of why the sectarian community, its understanding of the world, or its defining hero is rejected by the world. The works either deny the sectarian nature of their groups or heroes, or they ascribe their special status to their superior character or to their having passed through special disciplines.

Xenophon wrote the *Memorabilia* to prove that Socrates was not a dangerous sectarian. He argues that Socrates did not form a group separated from society. Socrates was only interested in the common Athenian pursuit of truth and goodness. He was devoted to the gods and reserved no special teaching for his closer associates. The hostility to Socrates results from misunderstanding and his opponents' malevolence. Xenophon writes as if the hostility to Socrates can be overcome through improvement in the public's understanding.

---

[84] A number of scholars have suggested that early Christians used the parable theory to explain the rejection of Jesus by the Jews, including Taylor (*St. Mark* 257); Hawkin ("Incomprehension of the Disciples," 497-98); C. H. Dodd (*The Parables of the Kingdom*, revised ed. [New York: Charles Scribner's Sons, 1961] 4); Matthew Black (*An Aramaic Approach to the Gospels and Acts*, 3rd ed. [Oxford: Clarendon Press, 1967] 214). Williams also sees the theme of the hidden Messiah as addressing the rejection by the Jews, but links the theme more closely with the suffering servant imagery than the parable theory (*Gospel Against Parable* 55). What I am arguing here, in contrast to that view, is that the parable theory does not address an historical question—why Israel rejected Jesus—but a pressing question in the social life of Mark's Christian contemporaries and the plausibility of their belief structure. A similar view is argued by Marcus ("Marcan Epistemology," 572-73) and Lewis S. Hay ("Mark's Use of the Messianic Secret," *JAAR* 35 [1967] 16-27, esp. p. 26).

The perceived connection between the rejection of Jesus and the later rejection of the Christian community is most clearly expressed in 1 John 3.1, "The world does not know us because it did not know him." In Mark it is found in the saying about taking up one's cross to follow Jesus (8.34).

The *Pythagorean Life*, on the other hand, revels in the sectarian nature of the Pythagorean community. The Pythagoreans are set apart by superior character (17.71-73; 20.94-95) and severe intellectual and moral disciplines (16.68-17.73). The opponents still possess malevolent motivation (35.248-49), but their understanding of the sectarian nature of Pythagoreanism is not disputed.

The *Life of Apollonius* combines both these strategies. On the one hand, it shows Apollonius as a nonsectarian. He is shown only once to teach esoteric knowledge to his followers, in the summary statement in 1.16. He founds no enduring school and teaches an unexceptional moral code to kings and emperors. On the other hand, Apollonius himself possesses esoteric knowledge that he has acquired through his exceptional character and discipline. Once again the opponents are dismissed as malevolent.

Sira is the least sectarian of the writings. For Ben Sira the wise are a group set apart by their superior understanding, but he portrays the wise as an elite rather than a sect. The wise have superior character (21.11-26), have been devoted in their pursuit of wisdom (4.17-19; 14.20-27; 24.19-22, 30-34; 38.34-39.3; 51.13-21), and have been blessed with the leisure to undertake that pursuit (38.24). They also have received their wisdom as a gift from God (1.1; 24.30-34; 33.17; 39.6; 51.30). The wise are opposed by fools rather than enemies (21.11-26; 22.9-15).

Neither of these strategies is possible for Mark's Christian sectarians. They understand themselves as a people set apart by their allegiance to Jesus, so they cannot deny their sectarian character. They are not set apart by superior moral character or intellect. Like Ben Sira, they understand their special knowledge is a gift from God, but that gift is no longer understood to be dependent on their own superiority or effort.

The in-group/out-group definition is approached through another direction in 4.1-8.26. In the first three chapters, the in-group is defined by their positive reaction to Jesus' command, "Follow me." The Christian listeners experience the call as a direct address to themselves and, by responding positively through an internal recommitment to follow Jesus, reaffirm their membership in the group that follows Jesus. The next section is dominated by another slogan placed on Jesus' lips and experienced by the Christian listener as direct address: "To you has been given the mystery of the Kingdom of God, but for those outside everything is in parables" (4.11). This promise reaffirms the nature of membership in the group as a gift rather than the result of the member's superior character. It also addresses the central problem of why those outside do not see or understand. In the philosophical and wisdom material, the primary explanation for the division between insiders and outsiders is the superior intellectual and moral character of those who can understand philosophy and wisdom. Even in Sira, where God plays a very active role in the bestowal of wisdom, He does so on the basis of character and effort. In Mark, God is shown to play a much more active role. He gives to some, to others He leaves everything in parables.[85]

A second level of explanation the slogan offers is the distinction between apparent and real meaning. In the parable discourse itself, this distinction is illustrated through the allegorical interpretation of the parable of the sower, but the wider application of the distinction becomes clear when Mark uses the language of seeing and hearing, originally introduced in relation to the parables, in Jesus' sharp questioning of disciples concerning the feeding miracles (8.17-21). The miracles also have a meaning beyond what is apparent to the physical eyes.[86] History itself has meaning beyond the apparent tragedy of the events experienced by Jesus' beleaguered followers, as is made clear in Jesus' farewell discourse. For those who know the key (13.28-29), the events indicate a reality quite different from that

---

[85] The general theme of the Christians' possession of privileged revelation and the inability of outsiders to comprehend is common in many New Testament texts. See Quesnell, *Mind of Mark*, 183-87.

[86] The association between miracle stories and missionary activity stressed by Theissen suggests that the miracle stories were understood as transparent proofs or signs of Jesus' identity (*Miracle Stories*, 259-64). This accurately reflects the understanding of miracle expressed in Acts, with its triumphalistic tone about the spread of Christianity, and may well be true for isolated miracle stories in the oral tradition. In Mark, however, where the miracles have been interpreted as parabolic signs, they serve to reinforce faith within the community. The parabolic interpretation suggests a disappointment in the effectiveness of the miracle stories as missionary propaganda and a belief that the Christian understanding of Jesus' miracles was apparent only to the eyes of faith.

apparent to the uninitiated eye. Jesus himself is parabolic in the Markan sense of possessing a reality both hidden and disclosed by its outward form. Jesus is the Son of God, as Mark announces in the opening of the Gospel (1.1) and reiterates through the two pronouncements from heaven (1.11; 9.7), but the heavenly reality is masked by his ordinary appearance. The miracles, which disclose the heavenly reality, are subject to misinterpretation (3.22-30) or blind incomprehension (8.17-21). God's judgment is hidden by human judgment (8.33).[87]

---

[87] Williams has also suggested a connection between parable and the Markan view of the world (*Gospel Against Parable*, 193-99). We differ, however, on the nature of the Markan understanding of reality. Williams understands that reality as "mystery": "...the union of these two 'worlds' or dimensions of reality [reflected in parables] is always just beyond our grasp within human existence" (*Gospel Against Parable*, 193). I see Mark's view as similar to that of apocalyptic. The hiddenness of the divine reality is the essential point. In apocalyptic, the hidden divine reality is often, though not always, perfectly comprehensible, and the writers of apocalyptic often claim to understand it. For Mark, the hidden reality of Jesus seems to be summed up adequately in the confession that he is the Messiah, the Son of God.

John R. Donahue has described Mark as a narrative parable of Jesus, based on alleged literary qualities of parables (as defined by form-criticism rather than Mark), especially the tendency of parables to overturn conventions ("Jesus as the Parable of God in the Gospel of Mark," *Int* 32 [1978] 369-86). What I am proposing here is something more restricted than that, simply that the parable with its two layers of meaning is a sign of the structure of reality as Mark understands it, with the apparent simultaneously concealing and revealing reality.

Both Kelber (*Oral Gospel* 123-29, 211-20) and Donahue (*Gospel in Parable*, 194-99) have suggested that the parable is the controlling genre of Mark, based on similar literary analyses of parables. Elizabeth Struthers Malbon sees the structures of both myth and parable (using a similar literary analysis of parable) as basic to the Gospel ("Mark: Myth and Parable," *BTB* 16 [1986] 8-17). My suggestion is also more restricted than these proposals, as it is concerned with the Markan view of the world and does not address the question of genre. It seems to me that the Gospel as a whole is not parabolic in the Markan sense, since the primary hidden meaning, that Jesus is the Messiah and Son of God, is clearly stated. Parable is not an adequate genre for portraying parabolic reality, since the portrayal of that reality requires the presentation of both levels of meaning, the apparent and the real. Parable, on the other hand, presents only the apparent level of meaning, and the reader or listener is required to supply the level of essential meaning.

The idea that parable as a literary genre subverts the accepted understanding of reality was proposed by John Dominic Crossan (*The Dark Interval: Towards a Theology of Story* [Allen, TX: Argus Communications, 1975] 54-62). For Mark, however, the parables function to bridge the contradiction between the apparent and the real, the function of myth in Crossan's typology.

There is a rhetorical shift in the presentation of the disciples beginning in chapter four that corresponds to the new emphasis on the parabolic nature of reality. Up to this point, the presentation corresponds to the ideal-disciple type exemplified by the followers of Pythagoras in Iamblichus, the student of Wisdom in Ben Sira, and the responsive followers of Socrates, such as Euthydemus, in Xenophon. In chapters four through eight, the portrait of the disciples is dominated by their lack of comprehension. Our study of the philosophical biographies suggests that such lack of comprehension is to be expected whenever the underlying reality is understood to be different from the apparent reality that can be perceived with the senses.

Philostratus offers a clear example of such lack of comprehension. When Apollonius reveals his real identity to Damis by miraculously removing his leg from the fetters (7.39), it is clear that Damis has been uncomprehending up to that moment. Given the number of miracles Apollonius performed previously in the presence of his companion, one cannot help but feel that Damis has been slow in catching on. On reflection, however, one can see that incomprehension is a natural, if not entirely necessary, by-product of an extended narrative portrayal of a hidden divine personality. The parabolic presence of a divine personality in human form necessarily undermines narrative coherence based on ordinary plausibility, since the ordinary is understood as a mask for the real.

The narration of a single epiphany, which requires only a one-time shift between the apparent and the real, may be perfectly plausible within the story world of the narrative. The simultaneous presentation of two different levels of reality, however, places much greater strains on narrative plausibility. The hidden reality must be apparent enough to be grasped by the audience yet hidden enough to be kept from the

---

On the other hand, my suggestion is broader than Boucher's statement that Mark "has...taken what is essential to the parable, the double-meaning effect, and made it the starting point of a theological theme concerning the audience's resistance to hearing the word" (*Mysterious Parable*, 83), since I understand Mark's parabolic view of reality to go well beyond Jesus' words and miracles. The conscious reflection on parable may be restricted to those areas, but the parabolic view of reality is pervasive.

other actors in the narrative. The audience must know more than the narrative actors, and as a result the narrative actors appear slow.

When, as in Mark, the mask of reality is understood as parabolic, simultaneously revealing and concealing the underlying reality, the level of apparent incomprehension can become acute. One strategy for such a narrative depiction is to distinguish in-groups who perceive and out-groups who do not, as Mark has done in the first three chapters. That in itself, however, does not convey the universal hiddenness of parabolic reality. The meaning hidden in the apparent is accessible only as a divine gift. There cannot be a group to which it is naturally accessible as a simple in-group/out-group presentation would imply. The depth of the mystery, and the corresponding greatness of the gift, is depicted through the difficulty with which even those in the in-group receive understanding.

Within the sectarian frame of reference from which Mark and his audience view the world such lack of comprehension is not unexpected. For the sectarian, lack of comprehension is the norm. There is only a small group of believers to whom reality has been revealed. That is quite different from the nonsectarian viewpoint, in which it is assumed that most people share a common, and accurate, view of reality, and the lack of understanding of that reality is viewed as deficient. In a relatively new sect, such as early Christianity, there are many who have themselves experienced the transition from incomprehension to comprehension, according to the sectarian viewpoint. While sectarians may be hostile to outsiders' incomprehension, the presence of many converts who have themselves experienced this shift of understanding fosters a tolerance for the previous incomprehension of those now within the sect. Paul's pre-Christian career as a persecutor of the church, for example, is not hidden by either Luke or Paul. On the contrary, Paul's conversion has for centuries stood, in its very radicalness, as a symbol of the more general spiritual reorientation experienced in conversion.

The theme of incomprehension dominates the Gospel of Mark much more than the *Life of Apollonius* because the question of identity is so much more central to the Gospel. For Philostratus, the question of Apollonius' hidden identity is peripheral to his central interests, such as kingship, fortitude, and travel trivia. Apollonius is largely a vehicle for Philostratus' discussions of these subjects. The question of identity does not influence the basic structure of the biography, and the episodes that deal with it (1.19; 7.38; 8.13) are poorly integrated into the overall narrative. For Mark, on the other hand, the question of identity and the parabolic nature of reality are central to the plot and structure of the narrative. Miracles function for both Mark and Philostratus as the windows through which the hero's hidden reality is revealed, but while Philostratus relates only a handful of miracles performed by Apollonius in a much larger work, in Mark a considerable portion of the work narrates Jesus' miraculous activity. This focus on the question of identity produces an intensification of incomprehension. While Damis appears somewhat slow in having overlooked a few miracles, Jesus' disciples maintain their incomprehension through a litany of miraculous activity designed to leave the listener with no doubt about Jesus' divine power.

Iamblichus' non-narrative approach to the biography of Pythagoras reduces his followers' apparent slowness in understanding his identity. If Abaris' recognition of Pythagoras as Apollo (19.91-92) is understood to be in a narrative relationship with the rest of the account, one would be required to conclude that the rest of his followers failed to understand his identity. There are a number of reasons, however, why the reader does not make such a negative valuation of the followers. One of the primary reasons is the disjointed nature of the portion of the *Life* in which the Abaris episode appears. It is a single narrative episode in a non-narrative framework, used to portray Pythagoras' teaching style. The revelatory point of the episode is suppressed by the framework that stresses an incidental aspect of the story, the special consideration given to Abaris. This leads the reader to consider the episode as an isolated piece of information that reveals Pythagoras' character without implicating the other characters in the *Life*. Pythagoras does not expect his followers to discover his identity, nor does Iamblichus feel it is important that they do so.

The more important the question of identity becomes in an account, the more forcefully the rhetoric pushes the narrative in the direction of noncomprehending followers. A single identity-related episode leaves the reader/listener with information about the identity of the hero, but it does not push the reader rhetorically to accept that information or to value it as particularly important. In fact, the isolated identity-related episodes in Iamblichus exist within a work that is ambivalent about the claims made in those episodes (2.5-8).

Within the narrative strategy of the Gospel as a whole, the disciples' incomprehension may be understood by looking at the analogous hardening of Pharaoh in the Exodus story of the ten plagues. In that story, the narrator is faced with the problem of making plausible Pharaoh's failure to acknowledge God's power, which is to be demonstrated to the listeners through the recital of the plagues. Each plague is an independent demonstration of God's power and the fact that God's power is arrayed on the side of the Israelites. The reiteration of that demonstration through ten plagues is extremely effective, but it taxes the narrator's capacity to maintain the credibility of Pharaoh's failure to grasp the point himself. The only way to maintain both God's unlimited power, as demonstrated to the dullest listener in the recital of the plagues, and God's apparent inability to convince Pharaoh is to ascribe Pharaoh's stubbornness to God. Pharaoh is not withstanding God; he is an unwitting tool in God's demonstration of power.

Similarly in Mark, the use of hardening language to describe the disciples' inability to comprehend, and especially the use of the divine passive (6.52; 8.17) that indicates the work of God, helps to provide an explanation for the disciples' apparent dullness.[88]

The Disciples as Non-comprehending Foils

The primary rhetorical purpose for the disciples' noncomprehending response is the depiction of the parabolic nature of Jesus' earthly career. The portrayal of the disciples is a result of that depiction of parabolic reality. In their lack of comprehension, the disciples represent the general human condition rather than a perverse reaction of an especially corrupt group.

Nevertheless, the philosophic biographies suggest that such a rhetorical strategy is not consistent with all understandings of discipleship. It contrasts especially with Iamblichus' idealized portrayal of Pythagoras' followers. Iamblichus is the one author who considered

---

[88] Matera, "Incomprehension of the Disciples," 157-59.

himself to be a member of the philosophical hero's school and to be in the line of succession transmitted through the followers whom he describes. Philostratus' use of Damis as a foil to Apollonius comes closest to Mark's use of the disciples in this section to represent the gap between Jesus and the rest of humanity, but Damis is purely a narrative device without historical reality and certainly without ties to an existing school. Mark cannot be as free in his narrative depiction of the disciples as Philostratus is in his depiction of Damis because Mark is dealing with historical personages who have had great influence in the development of Christianity. While the rhetorical purpose of Mark's portrait of the disciples may be to portray the reality of Jesus, Mark must present the disciples also in a way that is consistent with his view of the historical disciples.

Thus the question arises again whether Mark's portrait of the disciples would be understood in a positive or negative light by his Christian audience. Here the call stories are most helpful, because they most directly reflect the audience's own self-understanding. There is a direct identification of the listener with the disciples in the call stories, and the call stories are used within the rhetoric of the Gospel to reaffirm the listener's own allegiance to Jesus. In comparison to the philosophical and wisdom material, the call stories are conspicuously free of positive attributions of character either before or after the call is accepted.

The incomprehension theme of chapters four through eight develops the earlier characterization of the followers of Jesus (including the Christians of Mark's audience) as ones who need not be of superior character to be called to follow or to be accepted by Jesus. In sharp contrast to the philosophical literature, there is no portrayal of a radical character change even when those with deficient character answer Jesus' call. The incomprehension theme expands the theme of association with Jesus as an unearned gift by making it clear that the disciples have not earned the Kingdom through extraordinary insight. It is neither character nor understanding, but rather the nature of their relationship to Jesus, that determines their position as insiders.

The contrast with the philosophical and wisdom literature is clear. For Iamblichus, Pythagoras' followers had to meet strict standards of character, and their mental insight was developed through years of training before they were allowed access to the esoteric teachings. In Philostratus, Damis, whose loyalty and obedience to Apollonius are unquestionable through a lifetime of service, is never given access to the esoteric lore of Apollonius, nor does Damis receive anything for his years of devoted service other than the improvement of his character that association with the philosopher has produced. Similarly, in both Xenophon and Ben Sira, association with the philosopher or wise man has no reward other than the improvement of character and insight that results from that association.

The eschatological orientation of the Gospel of Mark, on the other hand, foresees a good to be derived from association with Jesus that is separable from such present benefits. The goal for the follower of Jesus is the Kingdom of God rather than wisdom or the development of good character. That shift of orientation makes the term teacher as a primary designation for Jesus inappropriate. While Jesus does teach, the goal of the disciples and of the listeners is something other than learning a system of thought or a way of living. The goal is inclusion in the elect community of those who will be gathered by the angels at the end of time (13.27). Thus the primary designation for Jesus is Messiah, with its royal connotations.[89] A king has a communal function of defining the community.

Even when Jesus begins to make moral demands on the disciples, the primary emphasis remains on inclusion within the community. The informational content of his teaching is minimal. The severity of the demand, on the other hand, is extreme. The followers must abandon all else in their devotion to Jesus.

---

[89] The royal christology of Mark is especially apparent in the passion. See Frank J. Matera, *The Kingship of Jesus: Composition and Theology in Mark 15*, SBLDS 66, (Chico, CA: Scholars Press, 1982).

8

OPPOSITION TO THE PASSION

Call stories and the recognition through a miraculous sign are typical scenes in the accounts of the lives of philosophers and of divine heroes, and Mark has used variations of these *topoi* in his characterization of Jesus. Another *topos* used by Mark is the opposition of a hero's followers to the death or endangerment of the hero. Peter's rebuke of Jesus following the first passion prediction (8.31-33) has close analogies in the philosophical material, though Mark's account has its own distinctive traits. As with the call stories, the philosophical parallels will be examined first to determine ways in which the episode may be expected to function within the narrative rhetoric, and then the distinctive features of the Markan episode will be considered.

Parallels to Peter's Rebuke

The Socratic Material

Although Xenophon's *Memorabilia* was written as a defense of Socrates against the accusations for which he was put to death, there is little material that directly relates to the death itself. The scenes that Xenophon does include show a clear contrast between Socrates' attitude and that of his followers, represented by Hermogenes (4.8.4-11). Hermogenes' expressions of concern for Socrates are rebuffed repeatedly with witty aphorisms culminating in the philosopher's explanation of why it is opportune for him to die at this time. Xenophon's account comes at the end of the *Memorabilia* and provides

a striking instance of Socrates' nobility and the consistency with which
he lived according to the dictates of his reason and the guidance of his
daimonion.   Xenophon repeats the same story in the *Apology* and
includes, as well, other material in the same vein (*Apology* 27-28).

The opposition between Socrates' attitude of acceptance toward
his own death and his companions' concern was a firmly established
feature in accounts of the philosopher's last days. It can be found not
only in Xenophon but in the Platonic accounts and in isolated chreia
as well.[1]   Plato made Socrates' trial and death the subject of three
dialogues.   In the *Crito*, Plato portrays the interchange between
Socrates and a friend seeking to help him escape from prison. Crito
seeks to persuade Socrates to escape even though he is already aware
of his friend's attitude toward death (43c). Socrates accepts Crito's
concern and makes it the occasion for a discussion of his obligation to
uphold the laws. The accounts in the *Memorabilia* and the *Crito* of
Plato exhibit the same basic pattern. A follower of Socrates is anxious
about the philosopher's life and suggests practical steps to be taken for
his safety.   Socrates rebuffs his friend's advances and explains the
philosophical basis for his own course of action. The friend appears
to acquiesce since he offers no further arguments.

At the end of the *Apology*, Socrates addresses those of the jury
who voted for his acquittal "in order to reconcile [them] to the result"
(39e, Tredennick tr.). The Platonic Socrates anticipates his supporters'
sorrowful reaction and shows concern for their feelings, and Plato
skillfully uses this device to address the reader's own concern about
the wisdom of Socrates' decision.

The final dialogue dealing with Socrates' death is the *Phaedo*.
The *Phaedo* relates a discussion between Socrates and several of his
followers on the day of his execution. In this dialogue, the followers

---

[1] One of the exchanges Xenophon records is found as an example of a chreia
in both Theon's *Progymnasmata* (207) and Doxapatres (2.265.16-20). Diogenes
Laertius records this and other witty exchanges concerning his death (2.5.35). The
spurious epistle of Aeschines to Xenophon continues the tradition but is dependent
on Xenophon and Plato (Abraham J. Malherbe, *Cynic Epistles: A Study Edition*,
SBLSBS 12 [Missoula, MT: Scholars Press, 1977] 252-59). Another letter in the
same collection has Aristippus remark that Socrates "should have been saved in
any way possible" and suggests that Socrates' action was "wrong and foolish"
(Malherbe, *Cynic Epistles*, 262-63).

do not seek to deter Socrates from his course, but they do persist in reacting inappropriately to his death.

At several points in the dialogue, there are references to emotional reactions to Socrates' impending death (59a-b; 60a; 84d; 116a-d; 117c-e).[2] Taken together these incidents serve three functions within the dialogue. First, they serve to remind the reader that with the death of Socrates, Athens lost a great man. The emotion of Socrates' friends evokes a similar emotion in the reader. Second, they underline the reality of death, the subject of the dialogue, and thus help keep the dialogue from becoming an abstract discussion of the subject. In connection with this, they provide the occasion for the discussion. Finally, the incidents serve to emphasize Socrates' own equanimity in the face of death. The contrast between the followers' reaction and Socrates' serves to accentuate the greatness of the hero.

For the Platonic Socrates, his friends' discomfort is the occasion for a philosophical discussion that is aimed at reducing their sorrow as well as establishing philosophical truth. The function of the argument as a consolation is stated explicitly in the *Phaedo* (115d) and the *Apology* (39e). Socrates is not particularly surprised, nor does he show serious irritability at his friends' feelings. Their reaction is expected though not correct, and he is not able to change that reaction completely. While he does get his friends to keep their emotions in check, he

---

[2] The bulk of this material is concentrated by Plato at the beginning and end of the dialogue and thus serves as a frame for the intellectual content. The beginning and the end reflect each other, both containing an account of the emotional state of the philosophical friends of Socrates, including a special mention of Apollodorus (58e-59b and 117c-e), and an account of the emotional reaction of someone not within the philosophical circle (Xanthippe [60a] and the jailer [116c-d]). The incident concerning Simmias toward the middle of the dialogue is of a different type, reflecting the followers' concern for Socrates' own emotional state.

The beginning and end display a concentric arrangement:

a   mention of the death of Socrates
b   the emotional state of his philosophical friends
c   the emotional state of a nonphilosophical friend
d   the body of the dialogue
c′   the emotional state of a nonphilosophical friend
b′   the emotional state of his philosophical friends
a′   the death of Socrates.

does not convince them fully of his position. They still break down and cry when he drinks the poison (117c-e).

Although the Socratic pattern and the scene in Mark share common features, the attitudes of Socrates and Jesus are quite different. While Socrates' friends are well aware of his understanding of his own death, at least in the *Crito* and the *Phaedo*, the disciples in Mark are unprepared for the sudden announcement of their master's death. Nevertheless, while Socrates retains his gentle humor in the face of the repeated inability of his followers to accept his death, Jesus' rebuke of Peter is by far the sharpest that he addresses to any of the disciples.

The Life of Apollonius of Tyana

Philostratus' *Life of Apollonius* contains a number of incidents analogous to Peter's reaction to the passion prediction. At several points Apollonius' followers react with fear or concern when the hero undertakes a strenuous or dangerous mission. These incidents primarily serve to illustrate Apollonius' exemplary character through the negative contrast with his followers.[3]

The consistency with which the philosopher's followers react with fear or concern every time he begins a dangerous or strenuous undertaking suggests that Philostratus is mechanically applying a well-worn *topos* of contrast between the fortitude of a sage and the fearfulness of ordinary people represented by the followers. When the sage announces his resolve to visit the Brahmans, all of his followers abandon him (1.18). Similarly, most of his followers desert him before his entry into Rome in the time of Nero (4.37) and before his journey to Ethiopia (5.43). His companions also seek to dissuade him from spending a night on Achilles' grave (4.11). Finally, when Demetrius tries to prevent him from entering Rome to face Domitian, Damis, Apollonius' lifelong follower, is persuaded by Demetrius' arguments that the project is a mistake (7.10-14).

In all of the incidents in the *Life of Apollonius*, the main point is Apollonius' character: his fearlessness, his prescience, his ability to deal with the dead. For the most part, the characterization of the follower or followers is incidental. Sometimes they are fearful for their

---

[3] Cf., Knoles, "Literary Technique," 204.

own safety; sometimes they are concerned about Apollonius. The variety of motivations helps avoid monotony in the repetition of basically similar scenes. Even Damis and Demetrius, who are much more fully developed than any of the other followers, show no consistency of attitude. Both display considerably more bravery during the first visit to Rome under Nero than they do during the later visit under Domitian.

Acts of the Apostles

A similarly structured story is found in Acts 21.10-14. There the prophet Agabus prophesies that the Jews of Jerusalem will bind Paul and deliver him to the gentiles. Paul's associates beg him not to go to Jerusalem. Paul sternly rebukes them and declares his willingness to die for the Lord's name, and his associates reluctantly give in. This interchange is found in one of the we passages, and the narrator includes himself among those who react with dismay at the prophecy of Paul's imprisonment.

Since this is a Christian story, it may have been influenced by the incident at Caesarea Philippi. The Acts story takes place in Caesarea at the house of Philip, and the location suggests that there was a connection between the two incidents. Luke, however, omits from his Gospel the trading of rebukes between Jesus and Peter, and thus his hand is not at work in creating the parallel. He includes the story for its dramatic value and its usefulness in depicting Paul's determination. In this case, the narrator includes himself among those who begged Paul not to go to Jerusalem, indicating that the audience is not to judge too harshly the concern that Paul's associates express about the calamity that is to occur.

This evidence suggests that a first century reader would be familiar with the *topos* of followers protesting the impending death of a teacher-hero.[4] In each of these writings the primary literary function

---

[4] A satirical variant of the *topos* is found in Lucian's account of the death of the Cynic philosopher Peregrinus. Lucian shows Peregrinus relying on the pleas of a sympathetic crowd to provide an excuse for reneging on his promise to burn himself alive. A portion of the crowd does call on Peregrinus to preserve his life, but another part unexpectedly calls on him to fulfill his promise (*Passing of Peregrinus* 33). In this case, Peregrinus's Cynic companions support his resolve (26) but show signs of grief at his death (37). The philosopher's public suicide

of such incidents is to illuminate the character of the philosopher-hero. The specific functions of the incidents include: (1) to provide an occasion for exhibiting the exemplary behavior of the hero; (2) to provide an occasion for developing the characterization of the hero; (3) to provide a negative example as a contrast to the exemplary behavior of the hero; (4) to provide the occasion for the teaching of the hero or for a witty aphorism; (5) to help the reader come to terms with the action of the hero; (6) to anchor a discussion about death in the reality of death; and (7) to suggest the magnitude of the loss the world suffered with the death of the hero.

The types of followers who offer inappropriate responses to the impending death or dangerous undertaking of a philosopher or spiritual leader run the gamut from highly sympathetic to totally unsympathetic characters. They include the anonymous followers of Apollonius introduced only for the sake of their cowardly reactions, the bumbling but lovable and loyal Damis, Demetrius the philosopher, the character-less figures of Xenophon, the generally round and sympathetic characters of Plato, and the narrator of Acts.

Peter's Rebuke of Jesus in Mark

Mark presents the trading of rebukes between Peter and Jesus quite succinctly (8.32-33). The content of Peter's objection is not included, suggesting that the particular content is not important. The term ἐπιτιμᾶν that Mark uses for both rebukes is the same term he generally uses in exorcism scenes (1.25; 3.12; 9.25), but he uses it in other contexts as well. The strongest association in Mark is not with exorcism but with silencing (1.25; 3.12; 4.39; 8.30; 10.48; both occurrences in the present scene; and perhaps 9.25).[5] Nevertheless, the conjunction of ἐπιτιμᾶν with the use of the name Satan suggests that Mark may have considered Jesus' reply to Peter to be either a literal or a figurative exorcism of the chief disciple.

---

and Lucian's account of it, however, are both influenced by Christianity. According to Lucian, Peregrinus had held a position of influence in the Christian church at an earlier point in his life.

[5] The only clear exception to this pattern is 10.13, where the disciples rebuke those bringing children to Jesus, and their intent is to prevent an action.

While the first part of Jesus' rebuke is quite clear—"Get behind me, Satan!"—the second can have of a range of meanings. Φρονεῖν may mean think, understand, or purpose, and the vague objects, τὰ τοῦ θεοῦ and τὰ τῶν ἀνθρώπων, are appropriate for all three senses of the verb. Thinking, understanding, and willing are related in Mark, and it is possible to let φρονεῖν retain all three connotations. In the section of the Gospel leading up to this scene, however, the emphasis has been on the disciple's understanding. Thus the closest approximation of the meaning is, "You do not understand the things of God but the things of men (and therefore you do not think as God thinks or have the same purpose as God)."[6]

The continuation of the scene clearly suggests that the primary issue is one of understanding. The phrase προσκαλεσάμενος plus an object and a form of λέγειν is a formulaic pattern used six times by Mark (3.23; 7.14; 8.1; 8.34; 10.42; 12.43). In four of those cases (3.23; 7.14; 8.34; 10.42), it occurs within an extended controversy to introduce Jesus' contribution to the controversy or to indicate a change in his audience. In two others it introduces Jesus' observation on or reaction to a scene he has observed (8.1; 10.42). In all but one of these cases, the formula introduces pronouncements by Jesus that explain the correct understanding of the preceding situation.[7]

A comparison of Peter's response to the first passion prediction with the analogous incidents in philosophical material suggests a number of points about the interpretation of the incident. First, it is unlikely that the listeners would have been surprised by Peter's resistance to Jesus' announcement of his impending death. Even without considering the philosophical analogies, it is hard to suggest an alternative response on the part of the disciples. "And Peter said, 'Good; it's about time that you died,'" is grotesque. "And Peter said,

---

[6] The RSV translation, "For you are not on the side of God, but of men," is much too sweeping. The issue is Peter's thinking in the immediate context, while the RSV suggests that Peter is categorically opposed to God. The translation also suggests that God and men are opposed to each other rather than that their thinking or intentions differ.

[7] The exception is 8.1, where the formula introduces Jesus' reaction to the previously described hunger of the crowd.

'That's right, Teacher; it is only by losing your life that you can gain it,'" reverses the roles of teacher and disciple.[8]

One credible alternative would be something along the lines of, "They did not understand the saying, but they were afraid to ask him about it," which we find in 9.32, after the second passion prediction, but even that reflects less favorably on the disciples than some expression of concern for their teacher's life or mission. Moreover, that response provides no opening for the subsequent teaching section that links the disciples' fate and attitude to Jesus'.

Another alternative would be to move directly from passion prediction to teaching material, but then the importance of the teaching material would be diminished. Peter's objection underscores the fact that the teaching is contrary to common sense, and the intensity of the interchange helps focus the listener's attention. Luke leaves out the trading of rebukes (9.21-27), and in his Gospel the teaching section that follows appears to be just one of many teaching sections.

A final alternative would be a simple request for an explanation for the passion, similar to the requests for explanations of the parables in 4.10 and 7.17. That approach would allow for an explanation but would inappropriately leave Jesus' death in the realm of intellectual understanding. The announcement of Jesus' death ought to spark an emotional as well as an intellectual response.

Second, in all the philosophical analogies, the primary function of the incidents is either to illuminate the character of the philosopher-hero or to provide an occasion for teaching. The characterization of the followers is secondary. Philostratus seeks to introduce some variety into his accounts by varying the character of the ones who offer objections. Many of these characters are introduced only for the sake of their objections, and the reader has only minimal interest in them as characters. Others are major characters, but even Damis and Demetrius

---

[8] While there are positive responses to death in the martyrologies, the situation there is hardly analogous. The heroic mother of Second and Fourth Maccabees can urge her seven sons to bravely face the most excruciating deaths (2 Macc 7.21-23, 27-29; 4 Macc 16.6-25) because they are faced with a clear choice between breaking the law of God or dying. They share a common loyalty to the Torah and thus can encourage each other to choose death. The purpose for Jesus' death is unclear. Jesus simply announces that it is necessary.

are of interest mostly for the way they illuminate Apollonius' character. Thus we can expect that the primary functions of the incident in Mark are similar. What the incident tells the listener about Peter is secondary. The use of the προσκαλεσάμενος formula to introduce explanatory material suggests that Peter's objection here, like the disciples' queries concerning the meaning of the parables in 4.10 and 7.17, serves primarily as a transition, in this case joining the passion prediction and the explanation.

Third, judging by the range of characters who display inappropriate responses in similar circumstances, there is nothing in the fact of Peter's response that would reflect negatively upon Peter.[9] The audience must judge Peter according to other data given in the Gospel. This is especially true since the audience is not informed of the content of Peter's objection. The audience could be expected to react negatively if Peter abandoned Jesus at this point, as do Apollonius' followers, or if the content of his objection displayed a bad character, but the simple fact of his objection, judging from the philosophical material, would be neutral. The audience knows only that the response is inappropriate. In the Platonic accounts, Socrates' disciples persist in such inappropriate responses to the philosopher's death long after he

---

[9] Norman Perrin states, "Peter is presented as one who cannot accept the idea of a suffering Messiah even when that suffering culminates in resurrection," citing 8.31-32 as his proof text (*What is Redaction Criticism?* GBS [Philadelphia: Fortress Press, 1969] 54), but the passage indicates only Peter's initial reaction. After the second passion prediction, the disciples' reaction is confusion rather than rejection of the idea (9.32). The disciples' fear on the road to Jerusalem (10.32) suggests that at that point they believed that Jesus' death was going to occur, just as he had predicted. The request of James and John after the third passion prediction, to sit on the right and left hand of Jesus "in your glory," while clearly inappropriate, seems to accept the two-stage schema of Jesus presented in 8.38, in which glory is postponed to a future time after the present period of persecution. Mark only uses the term δόξα three times, and the other two occurrences (8.38 and 13.26) are clear references to the divine glory of Jesus at the parousia. At the Last Supper, Peter reacts to Jesus' prediction of suffering not by opposing it but by protesting his own willingness to suffer with Jesus if need be (14.29-31). Peter and the disciples appear convinced throughout of the fact that Jesus is the Messiah even if he suffers, and that conviction is more relevant to the story than the fact that they had not miraculously appropriated the church's later reflection on the passion before the fact.

has made his own position clear, but readers are generally sympathetic to the depiction of his followers.

Peter's rebuke of Jesus and Jesus' counterrebuke are to be heard within a larger context that would include the discussion of Jesus' identity, the passion prediction, the trading of rebukes, the teaching section, and the transfiguration. In the transfiguration narrative (9.2-8), it is clear that Jesus' earlier rebuke of Peter has not affected Peter's position as the central disciple. He is included in the group of three privileged to experience Jesus' hidden glory, and he maintains his position as spokesman for the inner group. His incompetent reply and the Markan note, "For he did not know what to answer, for they were afraid" (9.6), suggests that he was expected to speak for the disciples and felt some pressure to fulfill that role. The stability of Peter's role as the chief disciple shows that the identification of Peter with Satan refers only to the content of his rebuke and does not describe his character as a whole.

The lack of concern for Peter's character *per se* is emphasized by the fact that the content of Peter's rebuke is not presented. The listener can only speculate whether Peter is concerned with his own life, Jesus' life, or the establishment of the Kingdom of God. Jesus' teaching in 8.34-9.1 addresses all three concerns. So even after the teaching the listener is unsure of the exact content of Peter's concerns.

Finally, there is nothing in the philosophical material that parallels Jesus' association of Peter with the demonic powers. While Socrates and Apollonius judge their followers' reactions in terms of the ideal character and behavior that their philosophical understanding leads them to adopt for themselves, Jesus understands his own death in terms of a struggle between God and Satan. Peter's negative reaction to Jesus' announcement of his impending death does not elicit a judgment on Peter's character but a characterization of Peter as Satan and a charge that his judgment has put him at odds with God's divine judgment and has placed him on the wrong side of the cosmic struggle. The equation of Peter with Satan in his objection to the passion communicates very clearly to the Markan audience the seriousness of a proper understanding of this point.

Comparison of Specific Functions

The analysis of the functions of the analogous scenes in the philosophical literature suggest a number of possible functions for Mark's account of Peter's rebuke.

To Provide an Occasion for Teaching

The analogies from the philosophical literature suggest that Peter's inappropriate response may elicit teaching from Jesus to correct his understanding. This is generally the case in the Socratic material and sometimes, though not always, with Apollonius. One listening to Mark might expect the same thing from earlier incidents where the disciples express a lack of understanding, such as in the parable discourse (4.10-20) and the saying about clean and unclean (7.14-23).

The content of Jesus' teaching (8.34-9.1) concentrates once again upon a parabolic epistemology, the split between apparent meaning and true meaning. In this discourse, life itself is presented as parabolic.[10] Life understood humanly is a mask for life in God's understanding. The attempt to save one's life from a human perspective leads to the loss of one's life from God's perspective. The parabolic nature of "life" is clearest in the pair of rhetorical questions in 8.36-37 that point to "life" as the thing of supreme value. "Life" in these sayings can be

---

[10] Stock says of this discourse, "Even though Jesus is addressing the people, ostensibly 'those outside,' he does not here speak in parables (cf. 4:11,34)" (*Method and Message of Mark*, 239). This reflects the common exegetical practice of substituting a form-critical definition of parable for Mark's understanding of parable. The saying in 8.35 is extremely similar to the saying in 7.15 that Mark specifically calls a parable (7.17). Both are structured as antithetical parallelisms. Both contain elements that need clarification. In 7.17, the meaning, as presented by Mark, hinges on the recognition that "the things that go out from a person" do not refer to bodily substances (which appear to be irrelevant in 7.19) but to evil actions and attitudes (7.20-23). Since evil attitudes do not literally "go out" from a person, the interpretation further hinges on seeing ἄνθρωπος in the second member of the saying as referring to the heart (7.21), that is, the essential person. Thus ἄνθρωπος changes meaning from the first member to the second. Ἄνθρωπος in the first member is the physical person; ἄνθρωπος in the second member is the essential person. Similarly, the meaning of the parabolic saying in 8.35 hinges on the dual referent of life. In each member, the first reference to life refers to physical life while the second refers to essential (divinely understood) life.

understood from a human perspective, leading the listener to destruction, or from a divine perspective, leading the listener to salvation.[11] While life from God's perspective is not clearly defined, its content is suggested by the final antithesis of 8.38. Human "life" is connected with the present adulterous and sinful time while divine "life" is associated with the future time when Jesus, the Son of Man, will come in the glory of his Father. Furthermore, divine life is associated with connection to Jesus. The one who is ashamed of Jesus and of whom Jesus is consequently ashamed does not possess the divinely understood life. The one who is ashamed in 8.38 stands as the antithesis of the one who follows in 8.34. Once again, relationship with Jesus is seen as being of primary importance. The teaching is not a lesson on the value of self-sacrifice in general but concerns the importance of the relationship with Jesus upon which true "life" is seen to depend. The understanding of "life," however, is pivotal for the decision to follow, since following Jesus may entail the apparent, that is, humanly understood, loss of life.

The teaching section reverses the previous order of public teaching followed by private explanation found in chapters four and seven. In this case, Jesus explains publicly the private teaching about his death.[12] There is no indication, however, that in reversing the earlier pattern Mark is suggesting a reversal of insiders and outsiders. The teaching on life is parabolic. It will not necessarily be understood by the crowd. The hermeneutical key, the distinction between the judgment of God and the judgment of humans (8.33), is given only to

---

[11] Ernest Best notes that the interpretation of the verses hinges on the meaning given to "life" but opts for a reading of life equivalent to "himself" throughout ("Discipleship in Mark: Mark 8:32-10:52," in *Disciples and Discipleship*, 9). He sees the ambiguity of the term as a problem for interpretation rather than one of the central points of the discourse.

Bultmann claims that the two sayings make very different points, the first that "riches are of no avail at death," the second that "life is the highest good" (*History of the Synoptic Tradition*, 83), but his reading of the first is problematic. The first saying, just as the second, reflects an exchange, the person gains the whole cosmos and loses his life. The point of the saying is precisely that such an exchange is a bad bargain because life is the highest good.

[12] Ernest Best notes the distinction between this scene and the usual Markan pattern of secret teaching (*Following Jesus: Discipleship in the Gospel of Mark*, JSNTSS 4 [Sheffield: JSOT, 1981] 31).

the disciples. The crowd is also ignorant of the passion, which is the subject of the discourse and gives concrete meaning to the vague references to losing one's life and taking up the cross.

While Mark has the form of a narrative, it is primarily a rhetorical or ideological work, and at several points in the Gospel the rhetoric overwhelms the narrative form.[13] We noted earlier the confusion about the apparent audience in the parable discourse, where Mark narrates the private explanation of the parable of the sower in the middle of a public discourse.[14] In 8.34-9.1, Jesus' discourse is unintelligible to the supposed listeners within the narrative because the real audience for the discourse is Mark's audience rather than the crowd of the Gospel. The crowd is called only to indicate the teaching has general validity beyond the immediate group of disciples.[15]

[13] Cf. Quesnell, *Mind of Mark*, 232.

[14] Dewey notes also problems with the apparent disappearance of characters in the healing of the paralytic 2.1-12 (*Markan Public Debate*, 75-76; 222, n. 34) and suggests, "If the parable discourses and the healing of the paralytic are any indication, perhaps it was not important for a first century popular author to account for changes in the internal audience of a narrative" (*Markan Public Debate*, 147).

[15] It is also problematic where the crowd would have come from, since Jesus and his disciples appear to be alone (Lane, *Mark*, 306). Matthew has Jesus address only the disciples, and Luke replaces the crowd with a more ambiguous πρὸς πάντας.

Ernest Best suggests that the disciples represent the church while the crowd represents "the unevangelised mass outside" (*Mark: The Gospel as Story* [Edinburgh: T. & T. Clark, 1983] 84-85). This misrepresents the dynamics of Mark's rhetoric by reducing these collective characters to allegorical representations (cf., Elizabeth Struthers Malbon, "Fallible Followers: Women and Men in the Gospel of Mark," *Semeia* 28 [1983] 47). Since the entire Gospel is addressed to believers, the address to the crowd is addressed to believers as well. This speech especially addresses believers in explicating the meaning of following Jesus, a theme of no interest to non-believers but vital to those who define themselves as followers of Jesus, and is one of those instances where Mark's audience is most likely to hear Jesus' words as direct address to themselves. Best's contention that Mark is attacking the idea of esoteric teaching by having Jesus address the crowd (*Gospel as Story*, 85) ignores the fact that the crowd cannot understand the teaching since they have no knowledge of the passion, which the speech presupposes.

Follow Me!

To Introduce Consolation

The Platonic Socrates notes in the *Phaedo* that his discussion of
the nature of death is intended to console his followers and prevent
them from mourning his death (*Phaedo* 115d).[16] Although it is not
stated explicitly, the argument in Mark 8.34-9.1 functions in a similar
way. The revelation of the parabolic nature of life and death and the
distinction between divine and human understanding of the matter
function in the same way as the Socratic speculations on the nature of
death to free the followers from the sorrow caused by their limited
understanding. The final assurance about the imminence of the
Kingdom of God serves to allay the other probable cause of concern
for the disciples, that the death of Jesus will prevent the establishment
of the Kingdom.

Jesus' discourse also serves as consolation for the audience
listening to the Gospel, since it addresses as well the possible
difficulties they might face as followers of Jesus and puts those
difficulties, even the possible loss of life, into a divine perspective.[17]
All difficulties are shown to be insignificant compared to the supreme
value, true life, which comes from loyalty to Jesus. The promise of the

---

[16] On the philosophical consolation and its use in early Christianity, see Mary
Melchior Beyenka, *Consolation in Saint Augustine*, CUAPS 83 (Washington: The
Catholic University of America, 1950); Robert C. Gregg, *Consolation Philosophy:
Greek and Christian Paideia in Basil and the Two Gregories*, PPFPM 3
(Cambridge, MA: The Philadelphia Patristic Foundation, 1975); Charles Favez,
La consolation latine chrétienne (Paris: Libraire Philosophique J. Vrin, 1937).
Some of the same strategies of consolation found in the philosophers were used in
funeral orations and Latin consolation poetry. Both philosophical and poetic
consolations are discussed by Mary E. Fern, *The Latin Consolatio as a Literary
Type* (St. Louis: St. Louis University Press, 1941). For Greek funeral orations,
see Theodore C. Burgess, "Epideictic Literature," *UCSCP* 3 (1902) 146-57.

[17] The genre of consolation was used by the philosophers to address both the
death of a loved one and the difficulties the addressee faced in life. Many of the
same arguments were used in both situations. According to Cicero, the Greek
rhetoricians cataloged consolation *topoi* for poverty, inability to achieve fame,
exile, the ruin of one's country, slavery, infirmity, blindness, and "every accident
upon which the term disaster can be fixed" (*Tusculan Disputations* 3.34.81, LCL
tr.). There are extant consolations from Seneca written to his mother on the
occasion of his own exile (*To Helvia*) and to a friend whose slaves had run away
(*Moral Epistles* 107).

imminence of the Kingdom assures the listeners that their own difficulties will be short-lived.

A discussion of the strategies of consolation employed by the philosophers is found in Cicero's *Tusculan Disputations* (3.31-34). According to Cicero, there are three steps in giving consolation: (1) to show that there is either no evil or very little; (2) to discuss the common lot of life, i.e., that no one is free from sorrow; and (3) to show that there is no possible advantage to being overcome by sorrow (3.32.77). Mark does the first by making a distinction between physical life, the loss of which is insignificant, and eternal, divinely understood life, which is of more value than the entire universe.[18] He does the second by connecting the community's sufferings to the sufferings of Jesus and by indicating that suffering, the bearing of one's own cross, is a requirement for all who follow Jesus. The third point is achieved not through argumentation but through the sharpness of the rebuke given to Peter. Concern about physical life is consigned to the realm of Satan and the inappropriate thinking of human rather than divine thoughts. The rebuke is performative language that "exorcises" worldly anxiety, banishing it from the realm of appropriate concern for the followers of Jesus.

Cicero further states that the different philosophical schools had different approaches to consolation: Cleanthes argued that the evil has no existence; the Peripatetics that the evil is not serious; Epicurus sought to withdraw the attention to what is good; the Cyrenaics believed that grief arose from unexpected circumstances and thus argued that nothing unexpected had taken place; Chrysippus concentrated on convincing the mourner that mourning was not an obligatory duty (3.31.75-76). This list overlaps Cicero's own three-step strategy, which was purposefully eclectic, but includes some additional

---

[18] The philosophers often use arguments about the nature of death in consolation. None of them is as radical as Mark, however, in redefining life and death. Positive depictions of the afterlife are advanced by pseudo-Plutarch (*To Apollonius* 120b-c), Plutarch (*Consolation to his Wife* 611d-612b), and Seneca (*Moral Epistles* 24.18; *To Marcia* 24.4-26.7). Refutations of fearful presentations of the afterlife are also used by Seneca (*To Marcia* 19.4). Lack of suffering among the dead is a common theme, generally phrased in terms of a number of possible afterlife states (Dio Chrysostom, *Orations* 30; pseudo-Plutarch, *To Apollonius* 107d-108e; Seneca, *To Polybius* 9.2-3; *Moral Epistles* 24.18; 99.30).

arguments. Once again, similarities with the Markan discourse are
apparent. Mark draws attention away from the difficulties of his
audience by closing with a reference to the imminence of the Kingdom
of God (9.1).[19] By making the believers' suffering a requirement for
following Jesus (8.34), he implies that their suffering is to be expected.
The rebuke of Peter (8.33) releases the listener from an obligation to
mourn Jesus or others who have suffered from their faith in him.

The discourse is quite challenging to the disciples, but that is
often the case with philosophical consolations as well, since they
challenge the common-sense view of reality.[20] Their whole purpose is
to challenge the normal human reaction to loss or suffering. The
philosophical conceptions that they advance, such as the Stoic doctrine
that most of the misfortunes of life are matters of indifference to a true
philosopher, could be very difficult to put into practice.

---

[19] The position that 9.1 refers to the transfiguration rather than the parousia
(e.g., Lane, *Mark*, 313-14 ; Stock, *Method and Message of Mark*, 242; C. E. B.
Cranfield, *The Gospel According to Saint Mark*, CGTC [Cambridge: Cambridge
University Press, 1959] *ad. loc.*) is untenable. Cranfield argues, "The Transfiguration points forward to, and is as it were a foretaste of, the Resurrection, which in
turn points forward to, and is a foretaste of, the Parousia." This interpretation,
however, ignores the pervasive theme of the hidden identity of Jesus. The
transfiguration is not an indicator of the future but a revelation of the present. The
three disciples are allowed to see Jesus' hidden identity. They are presented with
both sides of the parabolic reality of Jesus, but that reality has been present all
along.

The interpretation of the saying in terms of the transfiguration also ignores the
rhetorical function of the discourse in 8.34-9.1 as an address to Mark's listeners.
The reference to the Kingdom coming in power is in the future while the
transfiguration is in the past. Jesus promises that "some of those standing here"
would see the Kingdom having come in power while all of Mark's audience are
told of the transfiguration and none of them saw it. If Mark's audience was to
understand Jesus as referring to the transfiguration, then Mark would be ending this
discourse by suddenly slamming closed the possibility of its reference to the
present. It is highly unlikely that Mark intended to do that. The discourse is much
more germane to Mark's own audience than to the narrative audience, since the
crowd had not even heard of the crucifixion, and neither the disciples or the people
in the crowd were faced immediately with the prospect of losing their lives for the
sake of Jesus.

[20] The consolations tended to be ineffective for this very reason. See Cicero,
Tusculan Disputations 3.30.73-74; Seneca, *Moral Epistles* 1.12, 5.16.

A significant difference between this discourse and the philosophical consolations, however, is the nature of the release from sorrow that is offered. Both see sorrow as the result of faulty understanding and seek to shape the understanding of the addressee. In doing so, both operate at the level of the individual. There is, however, an additional communal aspect to the consolation in Mark. For Mark, the guarantee of true life is provided by the individual's connection with Jesus. Thus the consolation is restricted to those who follow Jesus and helps reinforce the boundary between the believing community and those outside.

Another distinctive aspect of the consolation is the underlying parabolic understanding of reality and the central importance of parabolic speech in the argument. While the philosophical consolations attempt to secure a change in attitude through clear rational argumentation, the Markan argument is essentially esoteric. It is coherent only for those who understand the parabolic nature of the central rhetorical questions and the true meaning of life that is presented through the juxtaposition of statements.

To Illustrate the Exemplary Behavior of the Hero

The analogous scenes in the philosophical material generally serve to show the resolution of the hero in facing danger or death, and this is the case in the Markan scene as well. It is important for Mark's characterization of Jesus not only that he goes the way of suffering and death but also that he actively chooses to go that way. The passion prediction itself is neutral in this regard. It simply presents the passion as necessary (δεῖ). There is nothing that indicates that Jesus has chosen the way of suffering himself. Peter's rebuke brings in the element of choice. Whatever the content of the rebuke, the listener must assume that Peter believes Jesus has a choice in the matter, and Jesus' reply shows that Jesus shares this view. His reply is not, "I have no choice," but that Peter is thinking incorrectly in wanting him to choose against suffering. The vehemence of Jesus' reaction indicates the vehemence of his choice.

Jesus' rebuke of Peter shows his determination to follow the way of God but also suggests that he has some difficulty in making that choice. Earlier in the Gospel, Satan has played the role of tempter

(1.13), and the identification of Peter with Satan indicates that Peter's objection presents a new temptation to Jesus.[21] Jesus is not immune to human understanding, thinking, and judgment. He does not have a complete understanding of God's plan and ways, as shown by his statement that only the Father knows the day and hour of the final judgment (13.32) and, more poignantly, by his painful surprise at being abandoned by God on the cross (15.34). The inner conflict that Jesus experiences in the face of the passion is most clearly portrayed in the prayers at Gethsemane (14.33-36).

Jesus' rebuke of Peter functions at one level within a rhetoric of consolation and exhortation as a direct rebuke of Mark's audience that releases his listeners from their obligation to mourn for Jesus, and possibly for members of their own community who may have lost their lives for the sake of Jesus. The rebuke shocks Mark's listeners out of their anxiety over the possibility of suffering violence because of their belief. On the narrative level, however, the forceful "exorcism" of Peter/Satan by Jesus suggests that Jesus experiences Peter's objection as a threat to his own resolve. The suggestion of such an inner tension is foreign to the spirit of the philosophical accounts. There the heroes remain unperturbed in the face of death or danger.

The narrative portrayal of Jesus provides a model for the listeners, who are to pick up their own crosses and follow. Thus the vehemence of Jesus' rebuke is also a model for the listeners' own vehemence in denying their human judgments and understanding and holding fast to their understanding of divine purpose hidden within the course of apparent events. If, as suggested by the content of 8.34-9.1 and 13.9-13, Mark's community knew persecution firsthand,[22] they would have experienced quite starkly the conflict between the apparent

---

[21] Jesus' language here is very similar to that in the third temptation scene in Matthew 4.10, where Jesus dismisses Satan with the phrase ὕπαγε, Σατανᾶ followed by an explanatory clause. A number of manuscripts contain the exact wording of Mark, ὕπαγε ὀπίσω μου, Σατανᾶ. Matthew makes explicit Peter's role as tempter in the present scene by Jesus' words to Peter, σκάνδαλον εἶ ἐμοῦ (Mt 16.23). Cf., Stock, *Method and Message of Mark*, 237-8.

[22] Many scholars have argued that Mark was written for a persecuted community (e.g., Perrin, *What Is Redaction Criticism?* 52; Tolbert, *Sowing the Gospel*, 304; Stock, *Method and Message of Mark*, 9-12; Lane, *Mark* 12-170). For a contrary position, see Juel, *Mark*, 20.

difficulty of their situation and the inner course of history presented to them by their faith. Mark provides a model of faith and obedience that does not deny the difficulty of sustaining that attitude.

To Develop the Total Characterization of Jesus

Jesus' expressions of frustration or disappointment at the failure of people to understand and respond to his word are common in Mark. Frustration with the disciples is part of a Markan formula for moving from misunderstood teaching or action to explanation that appears in 4.13, 7.18, and 8.17-18, as well as the present episode. Jesus' disappointment, however, reaches far beyond his inner circle. In 3.5, he is angered by the hardheartedness of his opponents. In 6.6, he is amazed at the lack of faith he finds in his hometown. In 9.19, he condemns his entire generation as faithless and expresses frustration at having to endure its responses to his mission. Thus the disciples' failures are part of a general human failure.[23] The parable of the tenants (12.1-9) suggests that God himself is surprised by the murderous reaction that greeted his son.[24]

As noted earlier, the disciples' incomprehension of Jesus' miracles is closer to the model of the Israelites' disbelief in the Exodus and wilderness narrative than to the reactions to miracles found in the philosophical biographies. Those narratives also provide a model for the disappointed surprise of God and the divinely appointed savior to the people's inadequate response.

While the attitudes of the philosophers toward humanity in general varied greatly, the expressions of dismay in the philosophical biographies examined in this dissertation tend to be much more restricted than Jesus' general condemnation of his generation in 9.19. As with Ben Sira (21.13-21), there is a belief that the world is

---

[23] Elizabeth Struthers Malbon has stressed that the disciples are similar to the crowds and other individuals and groups that made up Jesus' following in their inability to fully understand Jesus and fully implement his teaching ("Fallible Followers," 29-48; *idem,* "Disciples/Crowds/Whoever: Markan Characters and Readers," *NovT* 28 [1986] 104-30). For a contrary reading, which sees in the crowds and minor characters of the Gospel a proper reaction to Jesus, see Tolbert, *Sowing the Gospel,* 127-230.

[24] Mary Ann Tolbert stresses the role of the parable of the tenants as a summary of the Markan plot, *Sowing the Gospel,* 231-99.

populated by the wise and the foolish alike, and there is no expectation
in these works of a universal or even general acceptance. Socrates is
willing to enter into dialogue with anyone, but he is not annoyed by his
rejection. He accepts with equanimity even the most vicious attacks
that culminate in his death. Iamblichus shows Pythagoras teaching the
masses in Croton (8.37-11.57), but only a few are expected to qualify
to receive the secret teachings (17.71-74; 20.94). Apollonius is quick
to condemn evil, but does not expect many to qualify as his followers
(5.43). General condemnations of humanity are found with some
Cynics, but the Cynics do not expect everyone to respond positively to
their teaching and pride themselves on being unmoved by rejection.

To Present a Negative Example

Although Peter's objection does not necessarily lead the listener
to make a negative judgment about Peter's character as a whole, his
objection does provide a negative contrast to Jesus' behavior. The
contrast between Jesus and Peter, however, is not a simple one between
good and bad. As is often the case in the philosophical literature, the
objection represents the ordinary, not the degenerate. Both Jesus and
Peter have their attachments to human affairs. Both must struggle to
overcome them if they are to be obedient to God. Nevertheless, Mark
puts the contrast in starkest terms: While Jesus is the Son of God,
Peter is identified with Satan. This points out the centrality of the
difference. Everything hinges on the choice of obedience.

To Anchor the Discussion in the Reality of Death

Mark does not allow Jesus' death to become a cheerful slogan
or mythic event from the past. More than any of the other Gospel
writers, he conveys the excruciating reality of the crucifixion of the
Son of God. Theological reflection on Jesus' death is not allowed to
dominate the pain.

The casual way in which Mark refers to Jesus' dying "for many"
without offering any explanation (10.45; 14.24) indicates that his
audience was aware of at least one understanding of the value of Jesus'

death as a ransom or sacrifice.[25] Mark's audience did not consist of the original followers of Jesus, who had experienced his execution firsthand, but the second- and third-generation believers for whom the remembrance of the crucifixion was a ritual act filtered through theological reflection.[26] It would be easy for such an audience to regard Jesus' death as an abstraction, a mythic event, or the pseudo-death of a divine being.

Mark disallows that too-easy acceptance of Jesus' death. Peter's objection to the passion prediction is one more way in which the listener is reminded of the reality of that death. Peter's objection is quite correct according to human judgment. The ensuing teaching drives home the point by making the listeners understand Jesus' death in terms of the more existentially compelling situation in their own community. Jesus' followers, like Jesus himself, have to deny the demands of human concerns. They have to transcend concern for their lives, understood humanly, to save their lives. It is by understanding their own dilemma that the listeners are able to understand the dilemma of Jesus. If they succeed in being obedient to the demand that God places on them, not to be ashamed of Jesus and his word, then they can understand Jesus' own decision. Rather than explaining Jesus' action through logical argumentation, Mark challenges his listeners to understand it through their own situations.

To Suggest the World's Loss from the Death of the Hero

Here Mark differs from the analogies in the Socratic literature. For Mark, Jesus' death is counterbalanced by his resurrection (8.31) and imminent return in glory (9.1). Jesus is only temporarily absent. Even in death, he functions as the head of the Christian movement (8.34; 16.7). He will exercise his role as judge only in the future

---

[25] Barnabas Lindars points out that δοῦναι τὴν ψυχὴν αὐτοῦ in 10.45 does not necessarily mean the loss of one's life (cf. Acts 15.26, where παραδεδωκόσι τὰς ψυχὰς αὐτῶν refers to Paul and Barnabas, who are very much alive) ("Salvation Proclaimed VII. Mark 10[45]: A Ransom for Many," *ExpT* 93 [1982] 294). In Mark, where the saying appears in close proximity to the third passion prediction, however, it must refer to the passion.

[26] The second mention of the value of Jesus' death "for many" is found in the institution of the Lord's Supper (14.24).

(8.38). For Xenophon and Plato, Socrates was primarily a teacher, one who led his associates through personal conversations to a better understanding of proper conduct. For Mark, on the other hand, Jesus is only incidentally a teacher.[27] In spite of the frequent references to Jesus as a teacher and the use of the term μαθητής, or student, for his disciples, Jesus' role as teacher is secondary to his role as Messiah and Son of God. To the extent that Jesus' role as teacher is publicly accessible through his adoption of the social forms associated with that role, the role belongs to "human things," the outward form that veils the inner reality. Jesus is truly understood in his role as teacher only when his primary identity as Messiah and Son of God is understood, for what Jesus teaches his followers is not a system of thought and action in some general sense, but the proper thought and action to be adopted as followers of the Messiah and Son of God.[28] While Socrates can no longer function as a teacher after his death, Jesus continues to function in his primary roles as Messiah and Son of God.

Peter's Rebuke and Θεῖος Ἀνήρ Christology

Theodore Weeden has argued that Mark wrote in opposition to a faction of the church holding a θεῖος ἀνήρ christology,[29] that he presents Jesus as a wonder-worker in the first half of the Gospel only

[27] Although Robbins exaggerates the importance of Jesus' role as a teacher and the similarities between Jesus and the comparable Greek and Jewish models for teacher-student relationships in *Jesus the Teacher*, Paul Achtemeier overstates the opposite case when he suggests that Mark wrote, among other things, to combat the understanding of Jesus as a teacher or philosopher ("Mark as Interpreter," 115, 127).

[28] The presentation of Jesus as a teacher who teaches about himself is one of the reasons for the relative paucity of teaching material in Mark. The sayings of Jesus that present general ethical and religious material are largely irrelevant to the portrait of Jesus Mark presents.

[29] The existence of a fixed type associated with the term θεῖος ἀνήρ in the first century has been questioned by the investigations of several scholars, notably Wülfing von Martitz ("υἱός," *TDNT* 8.338-40); David L. Tiede (*The Charismatic Figure as Miracle Worker*, SBLDS 1 [Missoula, MT: Scholars Press, 1972]); and Carl R. Holladay (*Theios Aner in Hellenistic Judaism: A Critique of the Use of This Category in New Testament Christology*, SBLDS 40 [Missoula, MT: Scholars Press, 1977]). For a summary of the critique of the concept and further references, see Kingsbury, *Christology of Mark's Gospel*, 33-37.

to show that portrait to be incorrect in the second half, and that Peter objects to the passion prediction because of his θεῖος ἀνήρ christology.[30] Since Apollonius of Tyana is one of the sources on which the modern construction of the θεῖος ἀνήρ type is based,[31] the analogous incidents in Philostratus' biography have a significant bearing on such a theory. In the *Life of Apollonius* there are a number of instances in which Apollonius' followers object to his undertaking a dangerous project, but the discussions surrounding Apollonius' entry into Rome to face Domitian (7.10-14) provide the closest parallel to the account of Peter's rebuke. In that case, Apollonius' well-meaning friend and his chief follower seek to dissuade him from entering Rome, but he rebuffs their arguments. Damis accompanies Apollonius to Rome, where the philosopher is imprisoned by Domitian (7.22). Apollonius remains quite cheerful in prison, while Damis falls into despair. The philosopher reassures him, "No one is going to kill us," and to show Damis there is no need for concern, he removes his leg from his fetters (7.38).

> Damis says that it was then for the first time that he really and truly understood the nature of Apollonius, to wit that it was divine and superhuman (θεία τε εἴη καὶ κρείττων ἀνθρώπου), for without any sacrifice,—and how in prison could he have offered any?—and without a single prayer, without even a word, he quietly laughed at the fetters, and then inserted his leg in them afresh, and behaved like a prisoner once more (LCL tr.).

---

[30] Weeden, *Traditions in Conflict*. See especially 64-66 for the place of the trading of rebukes in Weeden's argument. Weeden understands Peter's rebuke of Jesus (9.32) as a "rebuke of Jesus' christological claims" (*Traditions in Conflict*, 40, n. 34).

Perrin, following Weeden, claims that Peter interprets Jesus as a "divine man," and goes on to say, "Here, therefore, the Lord reflects this understanding of Christology in the most explicit terms possible: 'Get behind me Satan! For you are not on the side of God, but of men' (8.33). The conclusion is inevitable: Mark presents a false understanding of Christology on the lips of Peter, a true understanding on the lips of Jesus" (*Redaction Criticism* 56).

[31] Bieler says, "Den ausführlichsten Bios eines göttlichen Menschen hat uns Philostratos in seinem Apollonios van Tyana gegeben" (ΘΕΙΟΣ ΑΝΗΡ, 1.7). Bieler includes twelve citations under Apollonios von Tyana in the index, more than for any other figure except Pythagoras.

Clearly, Damis' earlier objections to Apollonius' submission to Domitian in Rome resulted from a mistaken understanding of Apollonius' divine nature. He was worried about his master's safety because he failed to understand Apollonius' miraculous power. Had he understood Apollonius' nature as a θεῖος ἀνήρ, he would not have been concerned.

It would seem to be very difficult for Damis to comprehend the nature of his companion, because we find him once again despairing of Apollonius only a few days later (8.11-12). "Shall we ever behold, O ye gods, our noble and good companion?" he laments to Demetrius as they wait to hear the outcome of the philosopher's trial (LCL tr.). Apollonius has already made his unseen entry and pops into the open to reassure his follower. Once again, the follower's concern about his master's plight results from a lack of faith in Apollonius' divine power.

This evidence suggests that a θεῖος ἀνήρ christology would lead Peter to be confident that Jesus would transcend death. On the contrary, Peter does not seem to hear the prediction of Jesus' resurrection, and the disciple's inability to comprehend Jesus' resurrection is explicitly noted in 9.10. Thus if a mistaken christology were the cause of Peter's rebuke, his mistake would be his failure to understand Jesus' divine glory rather than an overvaluation of his wonder-working ability.

Teaching on Discipleship: 9.30-10.45

We shall not undertake a detailed study of this section of the Gospel. Nevertheless, since Mark clearly links the teaching of 8.27-10.45 through the repetition of the three passion predictions, and the entire section is often taken as a unified presentation of one segment of the relationship between Jesus and the disciples,[32] it is necessary to indicate in general terms the rhetorical function of the disciples in the remaining part of the section. Those interpreters who believe that Mark is presenting a polemic against the disciples

---

[32] E.g., Weeden, *Traditions in Conflict*, 32-38; Kelber, *Mark's Story of Jesus*, 43-56; Kingsbury, *Conflict in Mark*, 104-10; Tannehill, "Disciples in Mark," 400-02; Norman Perrin, *The New Testament: An Introduction* (New York, Chicago, San Francisco, and Atlanta: Harcourt Brace Jovanovich, 1974) 155-58.

generally stress the disciples' misunderstanding as the primary development of the plot in this section.[33] Those interpreters who see Mark's presentation of the disciples as pastoral, on the other hand, tend to stress the content of the teaching rather than the misunderstandings of the disciples with which the teachings are often introduced.[34]

In the pastoral understanding, the failures of the disciples in this section are generally seen as common Christian failings that are used to introduce teaching for the benefit of the Markan audience.[35] Ernest Best has noted that it is common in philosophical literature for the failure of a follower to function primarily as a vehicle for teaching.[36] In Xenophon, Socrates' dialogue partners are for the most part characterless ciphers or one-dimensional types that have no interest for the reader other than as vehicles for teaching. While Philostratus fleshes out Damis' character more fully, Damis still functions within the dialogues primarily as the one who is taught. His presence, his actions, and his comments provide the narrative structure for the presentation of Apollonius' teaching and erudition. In both cases, the moral failures of dialogue partners frequently provide an occasion for teaching. For example, Damis sees in the palm wine of India an opportunity to evade the Pythagorean prohibition of wine (*Life of Apollonius* 2.7). Socrates corrects Critobulus for kissing Alcibiades' son (*Memorabilia* 1.3.8-13), Lamprocles for ingratitude toward his mother (2.2), and Chaerophon and Chaerecrates for quarreling (2.3). Thus the philosophical literature supports the possibility that the disciples' failures in this section are only vehicles for Jesus' teaching and have no importance for the development of the narrative apart from that function.

On the other hand, teaching in Mark is often subordinated to the development of the narrative or rhetorical effect. In the controversy

---

[33] Weeden, Perrin, Kelber in the previous note.

[34] Best, "Discipleship in Mark;" Augustine Stock, *Call to Discipleship: A Literary Study of Mark's Gospel*, GNS 1 (Wilmington, DE: Michael Glazier, 1982) 140-48.

[35] Best, *Following Jesus*; Karl-Georg Reploh, *Markus—Lehrer der Gemeinde: Eine redaktionsgeschichtliche Studie zu den Jüngerperikopen des Markus-Evangeliums*, SBM 9 (Stuttgart: Katholisches Bibelwerk, 1969).

[36] Best, *Gospel as Story*, 47.

section of 2.1-3.6, the content of the controversies is subordinated to the fact of the controversies, which establishes the antagonism of the authorities toward Jesus.[37]   Similarly, the content of the parables in the parable discourse is subordinated to the fact that Jesus taught in parables. Teaching is occasionally subordinated to plot development in Philostratus as well. For example, the dispute between Apollonius and the Gymnosophs (6.10-11) establishes the contrast between the Brahmans (the ideal philosophical brotherhood) and the Gymnosophs (the faulty philosophical brotherhood). It also is linked to the intrigues of Euphrates (6.13) that lead to Apollonius' arrest (7.36) and thus serves as an important part of the plot development. Similarly, the disputes between Apollonius and Domitian (7.32-33; 8.4-10) are more important as narrative, in showing Apollonius' defiance of the evil emperor, than as teaching.

Both strategies—narrative subordinated to teaching and teaching subordinated to narrative—are part of the rhetorical repertoire of the didactic and ideological narrative of the time, and one cannot establish either reading by an appeal to parallels in ancient literature.[38]

The misunderstandings in 8.27-10.45 fall into two distinct groups, and it is necessary to treat them separately if we are to understand correctly how they function in the Markan rhetoric. The first group consists of misunderstandings that are noted in narrative comments or elicit Jesus' condemnation. The second group consists of failures of the disciples that lead to teaching by Jesus.

Mark often gives his listeners clear indications concerning the proper understanding of sections of material through narrative statements, sometimes in the form of concluding summaries at the end of those sections. Thus the series of controversies between Jesus and the authorities in 2.1-3.6 ends with the statement that the Pharisees took counsel with the Herodians on how to destroy Jesus (3.6). The

---

[37] Cf. Kelber, *Oral and Written Gospel*, 111.

[38] Weeden's contention that ancients would have been trained to understand Mark in terms of the presentation of character (*Traditions in Conflict*, 12-19) leads him to an assumption that the teaching in this section is subordinate to the narrative development of character, while Best's appeal to philosophical parallels overlooks the cases in which teaching is subordinate to narrative and character development in that literature.

listener knows from this concluding statement that the controversies represent the authorities' antagonism toward Jesus. They do not function within the narrative as a compilation of rules about ritual matters. Similarly, the parable discourse concludes with a summary concerning Jesus' use of parables in teaching (4.33-34), thus focusing the listeners' attention on the use of parables in the discourse rather than on their content. In developing the misunderstanding theme in 4.1-8.21, Mark relies largely on Jesus' words rather than narrative statements, but the narrative explanation in 6.51b-52, linking the disciples' astonishment at Jesus' walking on water with their failure to understand about the loaves, contributes decisively to the listeners' understanding of the theme.

In 8.27-10.45, three statements by the narrator concern the disciples' inability to understand. After Peter's proposal to build booths on the Mount of Transfiguration, the narrator states, "For he did not know what to say, for they were afraid" (9.6). After Jesus' command to the disciples that they should not tell anyone about the events on the mountain until after his resurrection from the dead, the narrator indicates that the disciples did not understand the resurrection, stating, "And they observed this command, disputing among themselves what rising from the dead is" (9.10).[39] Finally, after the second

---

[39] Although πρὸς ἑαυτούς is often taken as modifying ἐκράτησαν rather than συζητοῦντες (e.g., RSV and NAB: "So they kept the matter to themselves, questioning…"), out of six occurrences of συζητεῖν in Mark, three others, including two in close proximity to 9.10, are modified by either πρὸς ἑαυτούς (1.27, in most manuscripts) or πρὸς αὐτούς (9.14; 9.16). Of the other two occurrences, one has a dative object (αὐτῷ, 8.11), and only one is used intransitively (12.28). Mark uses κρατεῖν to refer to the arrest of Jesus (12.12; 14.1, 44, 46, 49, 51) and John (6.17) and the attempt of Jesus' relatives to seize him (3.21). He also uses the phrase κρατήσας τῆς χειρός, "taking someone's hand," three times (1.31; 5.41; 9.27). All these cases involve a physical taking. The only other use of κρατεῖν with a nonphysical object occurs in 7.3, 7.4, and 7.8, where the object is τὴν παράδοσιν, the traditions of the elders, and the sense is keep or observe (RSV: "observe" 7.3, 7.4; "hold fast" 7.8). Similar usage is found in 2 Thes 2.15 (with παράδοσις) and Rev 2.14, 15 (with διδαχή), but in these cases the sense is more believe or maintain faith in. Λόγος has to refer to the saying of Jesus, the command to silence, rather than the transfiguration (as "the matter" of the RSV implies), since the rising from the dead in the participial clause directly echoes the wording of the command.

passion prediction, the narrator states, "They did not understand this saying and they were afraid to ask him about it" (9.32).

Peter's confusion at the transfiguration of Jesus (9.6) continues the earlier theme of the inability to comprehend the significance of the manifestations of power in 4.1-8.21. It is likely that here also the confusion is linked to an inability to grasp Jesus' identity even when confronted by wondrous signs. The voice from the cloud identifying Jesus as the beloved Son of God provides the correct interpretation of the event that the disciples have witnessed.

The other two failures to understand concern predictions of the passion and resurrection. All three of the passion predictions are associated with some expression of the disciples' confusion. The first is followed by Peter's rebuke (8.32), the second is followed by the statement that the disciples did not understand (9.32), and the third is preceded by the statement that they were amazed and afraid at Jesus' approach to Jerusalem (10.32). This clear pattern of confusion associated with the predictions of the passion and resurrection is similar to the patterns of noncomprehension concerning the parables and the bread miracles in 4.1-8.21. The statements about Jesus' death are quite straightforward, and the disciples seem to understand them, as evidenced by Peter's rebuke (8.32) and the fear the disciples experience at the approach to Jerusalem (10.32). What causes confusion is the meaning of the resurrection (9.10) and the necessity of the passion. The disciples do not understand the true life that is distinct from life understood humanly.

The interchange between Peter and Jesus in 8.32-33 serves to underline the surprising nature of Jesus' announcement, and the repetitive pattern of fear and lack of understanding associated with each prediction of Jesus' passion or resurrection serves a similar function. The inability to understand the prediction of the passion also justifies the repetition of the predictions. The repetition structures this section in a way that focuses the listener upon the upcoming passion and its meaning. Just as the disciples' inability to recognize Jesus' identity in his wondrous miracles allows Mark to draw out the recognition scene in order to give it its proper narrative weight, the disciples' inability to understand the passion predictions allows a repetition of the predictions and a more extensive discussion of the meaning of the passion, thus giving added narrative weight to the presentation of the passion. The disciples' inability to understand the passion connects the passion with Jesus' identity as mysteries that are unintelligible to outsiders and helps explain for Mark's audience why those outside regard this important part of their belief system as a folly or scandal.

The failures of the disciples that give rise to teachings of Jesus in 9.30-10.45, on the other hand, are not given prominent places in the narrative structure. Unlike the controversies in 2.1-3.6, where there is a consistent portrayal of the Jewish authorities' opposition to Jesus, in this section there is teaching that is precipitated by the questioning of the Pharisees (10.2-12) and by the young man seeking eternal life (10.17-31) as well as teaching arising from the failures of the disciples. Between the second and third passion predictions (9.33-10.31), more than half of the narrative is devoted to episodes in which teaching is precipitated by someone other than the disciples (twenty-seven verses compared to twenty verses for episodes in which a failure of the disciples initiates teaching). In both of the episodes precipitated by non-disciples, the disciples are presented rather positively.[40] In contrast to the controversy and parable sections, there is no consistent presentation in this section of the theme of misunderstanding.

In 4.1-8.21, where lack of understanding is the focus of the narrative, Mark clearly indicates the importance of that theme in the climactic episode that concludes the section, the controversy in the boat in which Jesus repeatedly points out the disciples' lack of understanding (8.14-21). The concluding words of the controversy, "Do you not

[40] In 10.10, the disciples ask for further clarification of the teaching on divorce. The structure of this part of the episode is similar to the earlier requests for explanations of parables and suggests that Mark understood the saying in 10.9 to be parabolic. Here, however, there is no rebuke of the disciples for lack of understanding. Thus the privileged position of the disciples in receiving information is stressed rather than their lack of understanding.

In the episode of the man seeking eternal life (10.17-31), the disciples, who have given up their families and homes to follow Jesus, contrast favorably with the man who is unable to give up his riches. The contrast is very important in putting the disciples' failures in perspective. If they are not perfect, they are considerably closer to the ideal than are others.

yet understand?" clearly indicate that the disciples' lack of understanding is central to the narrative at this point.

The culmination of the series of teachings in 8.31-10.45, on the other hand, points to the connection between the teachings and the passion of Jesus. The Son of Man came to serve and to give his life as a ransom for many (10.45).[41] Here the content of the teaching is emphasized rather than the disciples' inability to understand it.

Another indication of the primacy of teaching content in this section is the similarity of content in the teaching introduced by the rich man seeking eternal life (10.17-31) and teaching given in response to the disciples. The demand placed on the rich man to sell all his possessions, give the proceeds to the poor, and follow Jesus (10.21) and the saying about giving up houses, fields, and relatives for the sake of Jesus (10.29-31) echo the demand for a life of service in 10.42-45 and the demand of suffering for sake of Jesus in 8.34-9.1. They are also related to the egalitarian teachings of 9.33-50, since in giving up their wealth Jesus' followers would lose their social position as well.

Finally, the narrative's progression in the following section, 11.1-12.44, suggests that the teaching section is concerned more with the passion than with the disciples' failures. The major theme of chapters eleven and twelve is the conflict between Jesus and the authorities that leads to his arrest and execution. The disciples here are portrayed as loyal followers.[42] If the main point of 8.27-10.52 were the failure of the disciples, the sudden shift in their portrayal in the following chapters would be inexplicable. If the point of the section, on the other hand, is to prepare the listeners for the passion through the passion predictions and to illuminate the meaning of the passion for the listeners' lives through the teaching material, then the rhetorical development between the two sections is coherent.

---

[41] Cf. John R. Donahue, who states that this saying summarizes the theology of 8.27-10.52 ("Temple, Trial, and Royal Christology (Mark 14:53-65)," in *The Passion in Mark: Studies in Mark 14-16*, ed. by Werner Kelber [Philadelphia: Fortress Press, 1976] 77.

[42] Weeden ignores this section in the development of his portrait of the disciples. His description of the three stages in the disciples' relationship to Jesus jumps from chapter 10 to 14.10 (*Traditions in Conflict*, 38).

Teachers' Responsibility for Their Students' Character

Ernest Best has argued, following David Daube's work on the responsibilities of teachers and students,[43] that Mark could not have portrayed the disciples as failures because Jesus, as their teacher, would have been held accountable for their failure.[44] In support of that claim Best cites the charge against Socrates that he corrupted the youth of Athens. The analogy is not very accurate, however, since the assumption on which the charge is based is not that Socrates' followers were failures as followers but that they were failures as citizens. The charge assumes that the followers of Socrates represent the values taught them by the philosopher.

The *Memorabilia* was written primarily to defend Socrates against the charge of corrupting the youth of Athens, and Xenophon's approach to the charge is more complex than Best's argument allows. Xenophon uses three distinct strategies in refuting the argument. The first is to present the teaching of Socrates as morally uplifting and generally in accord with the mores of the city. The second is to present Socrates' followers and dialogue partners as, for the most part, solid Athenian citizens. The third strategy is to depict certain followers of Socrates as unsuccessful followers. Xenophon discredits Critias and Alcibiades (1.2.12-48), whom Polycrates singled out in his accusation, and Aristippus (2.1; 3.8), whose teaching Xenophon rejected.

Those scholars who argue that the Gospel of Mark is a polemic against the disciples might point to Xenophon's discrediting of Critias, Alcibiades, and Aristippus as a precedent. There is, however, a great difference between discrediting a few of a teacher's followers who have gone astray from the values taught by their teacher and discrediting a teacher's entire following. The discrediting of Socrates' three disreputable followers is a successful strategy for Xenophon only in conjunction with a defense of the bulk of his followers.

There is a precedent for the wholesale failure of a leader's followers, however, in the Hebrew Bible. The story of the Exodus

---

[43] David Daube, "Responsibilities of Master and Disciples," 1-15.

[44] Ernest Best, "The Role of the Disciples in Mark," in *Disciples and Discipleship* 122-23.

provides the most prominent example. The Israelites as a whole repeatedly fall into grumbling and disbelief. Even Moses' brother Aaron joins them in abandoning God and Moses to build the golden calf (Exodus 32). God's failure to hold his followers, the Israelites, together is a theme repeated frequently throughout the Hebrew Bible. Yet the Bible is hardly designed to discredit God. If an author can claim access to the divine viewpoint, it is possible to portray a perfect leader, such as God, as abandoned, betrayed, and misunderstood by everyone. In this case the intent of the narrative is pastoral rather than polemical, however. The Hebrew Bible, after all, was adopted by the descendants of the faithless Israelites as their national scripture; it was not written by Israel's opponents. The suggested narrative in life beyond that in the text is that now, through God's perseverance, the people of Israel will, at long last, become true followers of God.

A partial failure on the part of a teacher's followers, on the other hand, is a feature of all three of the philosophical biographies we have examined. Apart from Socrates' three disreputable followers discredited by Xenophon, the dialogue partners in the *Memorabilia* display a range of responses to Socrates' teaching, some being more successful than others. The progressive initiation into the Pythagorean community described by Iamblichus (*Pythagorean Life* 17.71-78) suggests a substantial failure rate among those accepted for the initial phase. In addition, a limited number of renegades are mentioned (17.74-78; 18.88), including the leader of the anti-Pythagorean riots that destroyed the community in Croton (35.248-51). Damis is only mildly successful as a student of Apollonius, and at the time of Apollonius' final entry into Rome to face Domitian both Damis, his most loyal follower, and Demetrius, his most prominent follower, suffer from a failure of nerve (7.10-14). Ben Sira does not describe unsuccessful wisdom students other than the totally unteachable fool, but his is a presentation of the ideal rather than a portrait of a particular teacher and his followers. He does, however, describe Solomon, the most prominent student of Wisdom, as being significantly flawed (47.19-21).

On the other hand, the quality of a teacher's students could be used as evidence of the quality of the teacher. Philostratus adds the philosopher Demetrius to Apollonius' following in order to provide him with a famous and respected student, Xenophon provides a list of creditable followers of Socrates to counterbalance the distaste with which Alcibiades and Critias were regarded (*Memorabilia* 1.2.48), and Iamblichus provides many examples of the creditable actions of Pythagoras' followers (*Pythagorean Life*, esp. 27.122-33.240).

Thus, while a teacher is held partially responsible for his followers' actions, that responsibility is limited, except in those cases where it is assumed that the followers are adhering to the teacher's practice. A good teacher is expected to improve the character of his followers but is not held responsible for everything that they do.

Reliability of the Disciples as an Implied Source

John Drury, who holds that Mark had "a certain animus" against the disciples, detects a contradiction between Mark's portrayal of the disciples and their role as purveyors of tradition: "Indeed, he presents them as so obtuse and wrongheaded that it is extremely difficult, within Mark's own terms, to account for his having any coherent or dependable tradition to use at all."[45] Unlike Luke, who explicitly claims to be following the traditions of eyewitnesses (Lk 1.2), and John, who claims the beloved disciple as the guarantor of the reliability of his narrative (Jn 21.24), Mark does not claim explicitly that the disciples provided the source material for his account. Nevertheless, by presenting an account of events in history, Mark implies to his listeners that he has trustworthy sources for the events he narrates.

Mark's use of an omniscient narrator[46] allows him to provide an authoritative interpretive frame for publicly perceivable events. The omniscient stance of the narrator implies that Mark is providing a reliable interpretation of those events. Still, the omniscient narrator of Mark cannot dispense with implied sources. The omniscient stance implies infallibility in sifting and interpreting sources. At the same time it implies that the Markan sources themselves are reliable if not infallible.[47] In the Markan worldview, the events of the Gospel are

[45] Drury, "Mark," 404.

[46] Petersen, "Point of View;" Rhodes and Michie, *Mark as Story*, 35-44.

[47] The ancient perception of the reliability of the Markan sources is suggested by Luke's prologue, which states that many had composed narratives of the Gospel events "just as those who were eyewitnesses from the beginning and ministers of

parabolic, with the report of externally observable events requiring a reliable source, while the omniscient narrator provides the interpretation of the true meaning.

Because of Mark's two-level view of reality, in which human perception is distinguished from meaning, the disciples' difficulties do not impugn their reliability in reporting events that are open to human perception. If Mark understands the disciples' difficulties as illustrative of the human condition in general and the necessary difficulty one faces in understanding Jesus' meaning within the divine framework, then the disciples' difficulties serve to validate the interpretive stance of the Gospel. Those difficulties imply to the audience that Mark's interpretation of the hiddenness of Jesus' identity is not his own innovation but reflects the experience of his implied sources.

---

the word have handed them down to us" (Lk 1.2). Since Luke made use of Mark in his own composition, he must have included Mark among those who had composed reliable narratives. The perception of Mark's reliability would be enhanced if his audience were already familiar with a significant amount of the Gospel material.

9

CONCLUSION

Each portrait of a teacher and his followers examined in this study is unique in many ways. Each represents a different understanding of the teacher's role, fulfills different rhetorical purposes, and uses different rhetorical strategies. Like the others, the portrait of Jesus and his disciples in the Gospel of Mark is unique in many respects. Mark shares with the other writers, however, a common pool of narrative and rhetorical strategies that were part of the culture of his time. Mark's choices from among those strategies, both those he adopts and those he does not, are indicative of his understanding of the world and his purposes for writing. The way he has adapted those strategies in his narrative suggests Jesus' distinctiveness in his understanding.

Unlike the descriptions of philosophers and wisdom teachers, in which there is also a connection between the teaching figure and the divine, the Gospel of Mark makes the issue of Jesus' divine identity a central focus of the presentation. The divine connection is not used simply to establish the validity of Jesus' teaching and way of life. Instead, the teaching is subordinated to the issue of identity.

Mark's Gospel is a portrait of Jesus as the Messiah and Son of God. To make that portrait convincing, the Gospel must persuasively show Jesus to be the Son of God and at the same time account for the fact that the world is not persuaded. Mark does this by creating a two-level narrative world, in which there is a pervasive distinction between the apparent and true meaning. The disciples play a vital role in the creation of this world.

Unlike the followers of philosophers and wisdom teachers, the disciples of Jesus are shown to have no apparent merit. While other teachers draw their students from an intellectual and moral elite, Jesus gathers an undistinguished group, and Mark emphasizes the inclusion of the tax collector Levi among them (2.14-17). Yet the audience knows that this seemingly undistinguished group, because of its connection with Jesus, is the real elite, part of the elect of God whom the Son of Man will gather from the four winds when he returns from heaven (13.26-27). The disciples' real identity, like that of Mark's listeners, is hidden from ordinary perception.

The disciples are particularly important in presenting the hidden nature of Jesus' identity. The disciples form a privileged group to whom the knowledge of Jesus' identity can be at least partially revealed while it remains hidden from the world at large. Without such a group, the parabolic nature of Jesus' identity would be greatly vitiated. What Mark portrays is not a sequence of hiddenness and later revelation, which would fit a Jesus whose identity is generally acknowledged, but a simultaneity of hiddenness and revelation, which matches the still generally unacknowledged nature of Jesus' identity.

The difficulty the disciples have in identifying Jesus indicates the general difficulty of penetrating the outward mask of parabolic reality and serves at the same time to underscore the importance of understanding that identity. A quick recognition would suggest that the identity is of only minor significance for the Gospel. The audience will perceive the recognition to be important only if the theme is given prominence through the placement of material dealing with it and through the weight of extended narration.

Mark generally uses repetition of similar scenes or sayings as a means of emphasis. He repeats healings in chapter one, disputes in chapter two, and parables in chapter four. A rhetorical strategy of repetition is problematic for the theme of recognition, however, since repeated recognition scenes would undermine the portrayal of Jesus' hidden identity by suggesting that Jesus' identity could be grasped easily. Nevertheless, Mark has been able to incorporate a limited repetition into the disciples' recognition of Jesus by relating two types of recognition scenes involving Jesus and the disciples, Peter's confession (8.27-30) and the revelation of Jesus' identity on the mountain (9.2-8). In the first, Peter discovers Jesus' identity himself. In the second, Jesus' identity is revealed. The variation in title from Christ to Son of God not only reflects different aspects of the Markan confession of Jesus as the Christ, the Son of God, but allows for the credible repetition of recognition.[1]

Mark is able to augment this limited repetition by making the disciples' recognition a matter of narrative tension in the section of the Gospel spanning chapters four through eight. The impatience that the listener may experience waiting for the disciples to understand Jesus' identity emphasizes the importance of that identity in the listener's mind. In effect, Mark stretches out the recognition scene for four chapters and thereby gives it the narrative bulk necessary to indicate its importance within the story.

In the teaching sections of chapters eight through ten, Mark uses the disciples to underscore the split between the apparent and the hidden reality revealed by Jesus' teaching. When Peter reacts with concern to the announcement of Jesus' impending death (8.32), Jesus teaches the hidden reality, that those who appear to be saving their lives are losing their lives at a more fundamental level (8.34-9.1). When the disciples grasp for position (9.33-34; 10.35-45), Jesus teaches the hidden reality, that those who serve and appear to have lowly positions are the ones who are first (10.42-45).

Mark provides his listeners with an authoritative identification of Jesus as the Son of God in the prologue (1.11), and much of the plot hangs on the ironic distance between the listeners who know that identity and the characters in the narrative who do not. Excluding Jesus himself, most of the human actors in the Gospel fall into three

---

[1] In addition to the recognition scenes involving the disciples, Mark repeatedly narrates secret recognitions in the world of the spirit. The baptism scene, which functions as a public recognition in both Matthew and John, functions in Mark as a recognition scene for the audience but not for the characters in the narrative world. The recognition by the demons functions the same way. Demons proclaim Jesus to be the Holy One of God (1.21), the Son of God (3.11, indicating the customary response of the demons), and Son of the Most High God (5.7). The proclamation of the demons, like much in the Gospel, functions only on the rhetorical level. Within the narrative, no one but Jesus hears them. The crowd at the synagogue responds to Jesus' teaching and his authority over the demon but not to the demon's proclamation of his identity (1.27).

categories: the opponents, the disciples and single-scene characters. Single-scene actors include both the crowds, who appear to be different groups in each scene, and the individual characters who interact with Jesus in single scenes, most often to ask or receive healing.

These three groups represent three different and unequal human responses to Jesus. The opponents represent unthinking hostility and rejection. The crowds generally represent enthusiastic acceptance of Jesus' healing and interest in his teaching. The reaction of both groups, however, is superficial. Neither grapples with the true nature of Jesus. The opponents are blinded. The crowds have neither understanding nor commitment. The single-episode characters, while they may display a self-interested faith in Jesus' ability as a healer, rarely show deeper insight into Jesus' nature or commitment to him or his teaching.[2]

The disciples, on the other hand, provide a sympathetic human perspective seriously engaged with Jesus and his meaning. The difficulty that the disciples experience in understanding Jesus, in spite of their positive orientation and commitment, makes the hiddenness of his identity a reality for the listener. The disciples' difficulty in understanding the way of the cross points up the uniqueness and difficulty of the teaching. The tragedy of Peter's recognizing his own cowardly denial of Jesus makes real the tragedy of humanity's denial of Jesus. The disciples represent the best human reaction to Jesus. It is that which brings their failures home so tellingly to Mark's listeners.

The incomprehension of the disciples represent the inability of the world to penetrate the mask of the mundane to comprehend the reality of Jesus. Only the angels and the demons, both of whom dwell in the realm of spirit, can easily penetrate the mask. Even the disciples, those who were closest to Jesus and most supportive of him, comprehend only with the greatest difficulty who Jesus is.

---

[2] The two who show insight into Jesus' identity are blind Bar Timaeus (10.47-48) and the centurion at the cross (15.39). Only the Gerasene demoniac (5.18) and Bar Timaeus (10.52) attempt to attach themselves to Jesus.

Bibliography

I. ANCIENT TEXTS AND TRANSLATIONS

For most Greek and Latin authors, the texts, translations, and titles of the Loeb Classical Library have been used. In addition, the following have been used:

Ancient Near Eastern Texts Relating to the Old Testament. Ed. by James B. Pritchard. 2nd rev. ed. Princeton: Princeton University Press, 1955.

Anonymous Prolegomena to Platonic Philosophy. Ed. and tr. by L. G. Westerink. Amsterdam: North-Holland Publishing, 1962.

Biblia Hebraica Stuttgartensia. Ed. by Rudolf Kittel. Stuttgart: Deutsche Bibelstiftung, 1977.

The Chreia in Ancient Rhetoric: Volume I. The Progymnasmata. Ed. by Ronald Hock and Edward N. O'Neil. SBLTT 27. GRRS 9. Atlanta: Scholars Press, 1986.

The Cynic Epistles: A Study Edition. Ed. by Abraham J. Malherbe. SBLSBS 12. Missoula: Scholars Press, 1977.

Ecclesiastico: Testo ebraico con apparato critico e versioni greca, latina e siriaca. Ed. by F. Vattioni. PSS 1. Naples: Istituto Orientale di Napoli, 1968.

The Greek New Testament, ed. by Kurt Aland, Matthew Black, Carlo M. Martini, Bruce M. Metzger, and Allen Wikgren. 3rd ed. New York: American Bible Society, 1975.

Iamblichus. *De Vita Pythagorica Liber.* Ed. by Ludwig Deubner. Corrected ed. by U. Klein. Stuttgart: B. G. Teubner, 1975.

_____. *On the Pythagorean Life.* Tr. by Gillian Clark. TTH 8. Liverpool: Liverpool University Press, 1989.

_____. *On the Pythagorean Way of Life: Text, Translation, Notes.* Tr. by John Dillon and Jackson Hershbell. SBLTT 29. GRRS 11. Atlanta: Scholars Press, 1991.

_____. *Pythagoras: Legende, Lehre, Lebensgestaltung.* Tr. by Michael von Albrecht. Zürich and Stuttgart: Artemis, 1963.

The Letters of Apollonius of Tyana: Critical Text with Prolegomena, Translation and Commentary. Ed. by Robert J. Panella. *Mnem*Sup, 56. Leiden: E. J. Brill, 1979.

Lives of the Later Caesars: The First Part of the Augustan History, With Newly Compiled Lives of Nerva and Trajan. Tr. and introduction by Anthony Birley. Harmondsworth: Penguin, 1976.

Novum Testamentum Graece. Ed. by Eberhard Nestle, Kurt Aland, et. al. 26th ed. Stuttgart: Deutsche Bibelstiftung, 1979.

The Old Testament Pseudepigrapha. Ed. by James H. Charlesworth. 2 vols. Garden City: Doubleday, 1983.

Origen. *Contre Celse.* Introduction, text edited and translated by Marcel Borret. SC 132. Paris: Éditions du Cerf, 1967.

Philostratus. *Life of Apollonius.* Tr. by C. P. Jones. Ed. and introduction by G. W. Bowersock. Harmondsworth: Penguin, 1970.

Porphyry. *Life of Pythagoras.* Translation by Morton Smith. In *Heroes and Gods: Spiritual Biographies in Late Antiquity* by Moses Hadas and Morton Smith (New York: Harper & Row, 1967) 105-28.

_____. *Vie de Pythagore, Lettre a Marcella.* Ed. and tr. by Édouard des Places. Collection des Universités de France. Paris: Société D'Édition "Les Belles Lettres," 1982.

The Psalms Scroll of Qumrân Cave 11 (11QPs^a). Ed. by James A. Sanders. DJD 4. Oxford: Clarendon, 1965.

Pythagorean Sourcebook and Library: An Anthology of Ancient Writings Which Relate to Pythagoras and Pythagorean Philosophy. Compiled and tr. by Kenneth Sylvan Guthrie et al. Grand Rapids: Phanes Press, 1987.

The Pythagorean Writings: Hellenistic Texts from the 1st Cent. B.C.—3rd Cent. A.D. On Life, Morality, Knowledge, and the World. Ed. by Robert Navon. Tr. by Kenneth Guthrie and Thomas Taylor. GWP 3. Kew Gardens: Selene Books, 1986.

Sapientia Jesu Filii Sirach. Ed. by Joseph Ziegler. Septuaginta 12/2. Göttingen: Vandenhoeck & Ruprecht, 1965.

Secundus the Silent Philosopher. Ed. and tr. by Ben Edwin Perry. APAPM 22. Chapel Hill: American Philological Association, 1964.

Septuaginta. Ed. by Alfred Rahlfs. 9th ed. 2 vols. Stuttgart: Deutsche Bibelstiftung, n.d.

Die Weisheit des Jesus Sirach, hebräisch und deutsch. Ed. and tr. by R. Smend. Berlin: Reimer, 1906.

II. WORKS ON THE NEW TESTAMENT

Abrahams, Israel. *Studies in Pharisaism and the Gospels.* Cambridge: University Press, 1917.

Absire, Alain. *Lazarus.* Tr. by Barbara Bray. San Diego, New York, and London: Harcourt Brace Jovanovich, 1988.

Achtemeier, Paul J. "'And He Followed Him': Miracles and Discipleship in Mark 10:46-52." *Semeia* 11 (1978) 115-45.

_____. "Gospel Miracle Tradition and the Divine Man." *Int* 26 (1972) 174-97.

_____. *Mark.* PC. Philadelphia: Fortress Press, 1975.

_____. "Mark as Interpreter of the Jesus Traditions." In *Interpreting the Gospels*, ed. by James Luther Mays (Philadelphia: Fortress Press, 1981) 115-29.

_____. "The Origin and Function of the Pre-Markan Miracle Catenae." *JBL* 91 (1972) 198-221.

_____. "Peter in the Gospel of Mark." In *Peter in the New Testament: A Collaborative Assessment by Protestant and Roman Catholic Scholars*, ed. by R. E. Brown, K. P. Donfried, and J. Reumann (Minneapolis: Augsburg Press, 1973) 57-73.

_____. "Toward the Isolation of Pre-Markan Miracle Catenae." *JBL* 89 (1970) 265-91.

Aune, David E. "Greco-Roman Biography." In *Greco-Roman Literature and the New Testament*, ed. by David E. Aune, SBLSBS 21 (Atlanta: Scholars Press, 1988) 107-26.

_____. *The New Testament in Its Literary Environment.* LEC 8. Philadelphia: Westminster Press, 1987.

_____. "The Problem of the Genre of the Gospels: A Critique of C. H. Talbert's *What is a Gospel?*" In *Gospel Perspectives: Studies of History and Tradition in the Four Gospels*, ed. by R. T. France and D. Wenham, vol. 2 (Sheffield: JSOT Press, 1981) 9-60.

Baur, Ferdinand Christian. *Apollonius von Tyana und Christus, oder das Verhältnis des Pythagoreismus zum Christentum.* Tübingen: Fues, 1832.

Beardslee, William A. "The Wisdom Tradition and the Synoptic Gospels." *JAAR* 35 (1967) 231-40.

Beavis, Mary Ann. *Mark's Audience: The Literary and Social Setting of Mark 4.11-12.* JSNTSup 33. Sheffield: JSOT Press, 1989.

_____. "The Trial Before the Sanhedrin (Mark 14:53-65): Reader Response and Greco-Roman Readers." *CBQ* 49 (1987) 581-96.

Beck, N. A. "Reclaiming a Biblical Text: The Mark 8:14-21 Discussion about Bread in the Boat." *CBQ* 43 (1981) 49-56.

Bernard, Jean-Louis. *Apollonius de Tyane et Jésus.* Paris: Robert Laffont, 1977.

Best, Ernest. *Disciples and Discipleship: Studies in the Gospel According to Mark.* Edinburgh: T. & T. Clark, 1986.

_____. *Following Jesus: Discipleship in the Gospel of Mark.* Sheffield: JSOT Press, 1981.

_____. *Mark: The Gospel as Story.* Edinburgh: T. & T. Clark, 1983.

_____. "Mark's Narrative Technique." *JSNT* 37 (1989) 43-58.

Betz, Hans Dieter. "Jesus as Divine Man." In *Jesus and the Historian: Written in Honor of Ernest Cadman Colwell*, ed. by F. Thomas Trotter (Philadelphia: Westminster Press, 1968) 114-33.

_____. *Nachfolge und Nachahmung Jesu Christi im Neuen Testament.* Tübingen: J. C. B. Mohr, 1967.

Bieler, Ludwig. ΘΕΙΟΣ ΑΝΗΡ: *Das Bild des "göttlichen Menschen" in Spätantike und Frühchristentum.* 2 vols. in 1. Darmstadt: Wissenschaftliche Buchgesellschaft, 1967.

Black, C. Clifton, II. *The Disciples according to Mark: Marcan Redaction in Current Debate.* JSNTSup 27. Sheffield: Sheffield Academic Press, 1989.

_____. "The Quest of Mark the Redactor: Why Has It Been Pursued, and What Has It Taught Us?" *JSNT* 33 (1988) 19-39.

Black, Matthew. *An Aramaic Approach to the Gospels and Acts.* 3rd ed. Oxford: Clarendon Press, 1967.

Boomershine, Thomas Eugene. "Mark, the Storyteller: A Rhetorical-Critical Investigation of Mark's Passion and Resurrection Narrative." Dissertation. Union Theological Seminary, New York, 1974.

_____. "Peter's Denial as Polemic or Confession: The Implications of Media Criticism for Biblical Hermeneutics." *Semeia* 39 (1987) 47-68.

Boucher, Madeleine. *The Mysterious Parable: A Literary Study.* CBQMS 6. Washington: The Catholic Biblical Association of America, 1977.

Breytenbach, Cilliers. "Gospel of Mark as Episodic Narrative." *Scriptura* (special issue 4, 1989) 1-26.

_____. "Das Markusevangelium als episodische Erzählung, Mit Überlegungen zum 'Aufbau' des zweiten Evangeliums." In *Der Erzähler des Evangeliums: Methodische Neuansätze in der Markusforschung*, ed. by Ferdinand Hahn, StutB 118/119 (Stuttgart: Verlag Katholisches Bibelwerk, 1985) 139-69.

_____. *Nachfolge und Zukunftserwartung nach Markus: Eine methodenkritische Studie.* Zürich: Theologischer, 1984.

Bultmann, Rudolf. *The History of the Synoptic Tradition.* Tr. by John Marsh. New York: Harper & Row, 1963.

Burkill, T. Alec. *Mysterious Revelation: An Examination of the Philosophy of St Mark's Gospel.* New York: Cornell University Press, 1963.

Calvin, John. *Commentary on a Harmony of the Evangelists, Matthew, Mark, and Luke.* Tr. by William Pringle. CalC 16. Grand Rapids: Baker Book

House, 1979.

Cangh, Jean-Marie van. *La multiplication des pains et l'Eucharistie.* LD 86. Paris: Éditions du Cerf, 1975.

Collins, Adela Yarbro. *Is Mark's Gospel a Life of Jesus? The Question of Genre.* PMLT 21. Milwaukee: Marquette University Press, 1990.

Countryman, L. William. "How Many Baskets Full? Mark 8:14-21 and the Value of Miracles in Mark." *CBQ* 47 (1985) 643-55.

Cranfield, C. E. B. *The Gospel According to St. Mark.* CGTC. Cambridge: Cambridge University Press, 1959.

Crossan, John Dominic. *The Dark Interval: Towards a Theology of Story.* Allen, TX: Argus Communications, 1975.

Culpepper, R. Allan. *Anatomy of the Fourth Gospel: A Study in Literary Design.* FFNT. Philadelphia: Fortress Press, 1983.

Dahl, Nils Alstrup. "The Purpose of Mark's Gospel." In *Jesus in the Memory of the Early Church* (Minneapolis: Augsburg Publishing House, 1976) 52-65.

Daube, David. *The New Testament and Rabbinic Judaism.* London: University of London Anthone Press, 1956.

_____. "Public Pronouncement and Private Explanation in the Gospels." *ExpTim* 57 (1945-46) 175-77.

_____. "The Responsibilities of Master and Disciples in the Gospels." *NTS* 19 (1972-73) 1-15.

Dewey, Joanna. "Mark as Interwoven Tapestry: Forecasts and Echoes for a Listening Audience." *CBQ* 53 (1991) 221-36.

_____. *Markan Public Debate: Literary Technique, Concentric Structure, and Theology in Mark 2:1-3:6.* SBLDS 48. Chico: Scholars Press, 1980.

_____. "Oral Methods of Structuring Narrative in Mark." *Int* 43 (1989) 32-44.

Dinkler, Erich. "Peter's Confession and the Satan Saying: The Problem of Jesus' Messiahship." In *The Future of Our Religious Past: Essays in Honour of Rudolf Bultmann* (New York: Harper & Row, 1971) 169-202.

Dodd, Charles Harold. *The Parables of the Kingdom.* Rev. ed. New York: Charles Scribner's Sons, 1961.

Donahue, John R. *Are You the Christ? The Trial Narrative in the Gospel of Mark.* SBLDS 10. Missoula: Scholars Press, 1973.

_____. *The Gospel in Parable: Metaphor, Narrative, and Theology in the Synoptic Gospels.* Philadelphia: Fortress Press, 1988.

_____. "Jesus as Parable of God in the Gospel of Mark." *Int* 32 (1978) 369-86.

_____. "Temple, Trial, and Royal Christology (Mark 14:53-65)." In *The Passion in Mark: Studies in Mark 14-16,* ed. by Werner Kelber (Philadelphia: Fortress Press, 1976) 61-78.

_____. *The Theology and Setting of Discipleship in the Gospel of Mark.*

298   *Follow Me!*

PMLT 14. Milwaukee: Marquette University Press, 1983.

Drury, John. "Mark." In *The Literary Guide to the Bible*, ed. by Robert Alter and Frank Kermode (Cambridge, MA: Belknap Press, 1987) 402-17.

Dupont, Jacques. "La transmission des paroles de Jésus sur la lampe et la mesure dans Marc 4,21-25 et dans la tradition Q," in *Logia: Les Paroles de Jésus—The Sayings of Jesus. Memorial Joseph Coppens*, ed. by J. Delobel, BETL 59 (Leuven University: Peeters, 1982) 201-36.

Edwards, James R. "Markan Sandwiches: The Significance of Interpolations in Markan Narratives." *NovT* 31 (1989) 193-216.

Fay, Greg. "Introduction to Incomprehension: The Literary Structure of Mark 4:1-34." *CBQ* 51 (1989) 65-81.

Fiore, Benjamin. *The Function of Personal Example in the Socratic and Pastoral Epistles*. AnBib 105. Rome: Biblical Institute, 1986.

Fiorenza, Elisabeth Schüssler. "Miracles, Mission, and Apologetics: An Introduction." In *Aspects of Religious Propaganda in Judaism and Early Christianity*, ed. by Elisabeth Schüssler Fiorenza (Notre Dame and London: University of Notre Dame Press, 1976) 1-25.

Focant, Camille. "L'Incompréhension des disciples dans le deuxième Évangile." *RB* 82 (1985) 161-85.

Fowler, Robert M. *Let the Reader Understand: Reader-Response Criticism and the Gospel of Mark*. Minneapolis: Fortress Press, 1991.

_____. *Loaves and Fishes: The Function of the Feeding Stories in the Gospel of Mark*. SBLDS 54. Chico: Scholars Press, 1981.

Freyne, Sean. "The Disciples in Mark and the *maskilim* in Daniel: A Comparison." *JSNT* 16 (1982) 7-23.

Fridrichsen, Anton. *The Problem of Miracle in Early Christianity*. Minneapolis: Augsburg Publishing House, 1972.

Friedrich, Gerhard. "κηρύσσω." *TDNT* 3.697-714.

Gallagher, Eugene V. *Divine Man or Magician? Celsus and Origen on Jesus*. SBLDS 64. Chico: Scholars Press, 1982.

Garrett, Susan R. *The Demise of the Devil: Magic and the Demonic in Luke's Writings*. Minneapolis: Fortress Press, 1989.

Georgi, Dieter. *The Opponents of Paul in Second Corinthians*. Philadelphia: Fortress Press, 1986.

Haenchen, Ernst. *The Acts of the Apostles: A Commentary*. Tr. by Bernard Noble and Gerald Shinn. Oxford: Basil Blackwell, 1971.

Hauck, Fiedrich. "παραβολή." *TDNT* 5.744-61.

Hawkin, David J. "The Incomprehension of the Disciples in the Marcan Redaction." *JBL* 91 (1972) 491-500.

Hay, Lewis S. "Mark's Use of the Messianic Secret." *JAAR* 35 (1967) 16-27.

Heil, John Paul. *Jesus Walking on the Sea*. AnBib 87. Rome: Biblical Institute Press, 1981.

Heisig, Alkuin. *Die Botschaft der Brotvermehrung.* StutB 15. Stuttgart: Katholisches Bibelwerk, 1966.

Hengel, Martin. *The Charismatic Leader and His Followers.* Tr. by James Greig. New York: Crossroad, 1981.

_____. *Crucifixion in the Ancient World and the Folly of the Message of the Cross.* Philadelphia: Fortress Press, 1977.

_____. *Studies in the Gospel of Mark.* Philadelphia: Fortress Press, 1985.

Hock, Ronald F. "The Greek Novel." In *Greco-Roman Literature and the New Testament,* ed. by David E. Aune, SBLSBS 21 (Atlanta: Scholars Press, 1988) 127-146.

Holladay, Carl R. *Theios Aner in Hellenistic Judaism: A Critique of the Use of This Category in New Testament Christology.* SBLDS 40. Missoula: Scholars Press, 1977.

Hurtado L. W. "The Gospel of Mark: Evolutionary or Revolutionary Document?" *JSNT* 40 (1990) 15-32.

Iersel, Bastiaan van. "Die wunderbare Speisung und das Abendmahl in der synoptischen Tradition." *NovT* 7 (1964) 167-94.

Jaeger, Werner. *Early Christianity and Greek Paideia.* Cambridge, MA: Belknap Press, 1961.

Jeremias, Joachim. *The Parables of Jesus.* 2nd rev. ed. Tr. by S. H. Hooke. New York: Charles Scribner's Sons, 1972.

Johnson, Luke T. "The New Testament's Anti-Jewish Slander and the Conventions of Ancient Polemic." *JBL* 108 (1989) 419-41.

Juel, Donald H. *Mark.* ACNT. Minneapolis: Augsburg, 1990.

_____. *Messiah and Temple: The Trial of Jesus in the Gospel of Mark.* SBLDS 31. Missoula: Scholars Press, 1977.

Käsemann, Ernst. "The Disciples of John the Baptist in Ephesus." In *Essays on New Testament Themes* (Philadelphia: Fortress Press, 1982) 136-48.

Kealy, Sean P. *Mark's Gospel: A History of Its Interpretation From the Beginning Until 1979.* New York and Ramsey: Paulist Press, 1982.

Keck, Leander. "The Introduction to Mark's Gospel." *NTS* 12 (1966) 352-70.

_____. "Mark 3.1-12 and Mark's Christology." *JBL* 84 (1965) 341-58.

Kee, Howard Clark. "Aretalogy and Gospel." *JBL* 92 (1973) 402-22.

_____. *Community of the New Age: Studies in Mark's Gospel.* Philadelphia: The Westminster Press, 1977.

_____. *Medicine, Miracle and Magic in New Testament Times.* SNTSMS 55. Cambridge and London: Cambridge University Press, 1986.

_____. *Miracle in the Early Christian World: A Study in Sociohistorical Method.* New Haven: Yale University Press, 1983.

Kelber, Werner H. *The Kingdom in Mark: A New Place and a New Time.* Philadelphia: Fortress Press, 1974.

_____. *Mark's Story of Jesus.* Philadelphia: Fortress Press, 1979.

_____. *The Oral and the Written Gospel: The Hermeneutics of Speaking and Writing in the Synoptic Tradition, Mark, Paul, and Q.* Philadelphia: Fortress Press, 1983.

Kennedy, George A. *New Testament Interpretation through Rhetorical Criticism.* Chapel Hill and London: University of North Carolina Press, 1984.

Kermode, Frank. *The Genesis of Secrecy: On the Interpretation of Narrative.* Cambridge, MA, and London: Harvard University Press, 1979.

Kingsbury, Jack Dean. *The Christology of Mark's Gospel.* Philadelphia: Fortress Press, 1983.

_____. *Conflict in Mark: Jesus, Authorities, Disciples.* Minneapolis: Fortress Press, 1989.

_____. "The 'Divine Man' as the Key to Mark's Christology: The End of an Era?" *Int* 35 (1981) 243-57.

Kolenkow, Anitra Bingham. "A Problem of Power: How Miracle Doers Counter Charges of Magic in the Hellenistic World." SBLSP 1976, 105-10.

Lafontaine, René, and Pierre Mourlon Beernaert. "Essai sur la structure de Marc, 8,27-9,13." *RSR* 57 (1969) 543-61.

Lane, William L. *Commentary on the Gospel of Mark.* NICNT. Grand Rapids: Eerdmans, 1974.

Lemcio, Eugene E. "External Evidence for the Structure and Function of Mark iv.1-20, vii.14-23 and viii.14-21." *JTS* 29 (1978) 323-38.

Lincoln, Andrew. "The Promise and the Failure—Mark 16:7, 8." *JBL* 108 (1989) 283-300.

Lindars, Barnabas. "Salvation Proclaimed VII. Mark 10^{45}: A Ransom for Many." *ExpTim* 93 (1982) 292-95.

Mack, Burton L. and Vernon K. Robbins. *Patterns of Persuasion in the Gospels.* FFLF. Sonoma: Polebridge Press, 1989.

Malbon, Elizabeth Struthers. "Disciples/Crowds/Whoever: Markan Characters and Readers." *NovT* 28 (1986) 104-30.

_____. "Fallible Followers: Women and Men in the Gospel of Mark. *Semeia* 28 (1983) 29-43.

_____. "The Jewish Leaders in the Gospel of Mark: A Literary Study of Marcan Characterization." *JBL* 108 (1989) 259-81.

_____. "Mark: Myth and Parable." *BTB* 16 (1986) 8-17.

_____. "The Poor Widow in Mark and Her Poor Rich Readers." *CBQ* 53 (1991) 589-604.

Malherbe, Abraham J. "Exhortation in First Thessalonians." *NovT* 25 (1983) 238-56.

_____. "'Gentle as a Nurse': The Cynic Background to 1 Thessalonians 2." *NovT* 12 (1970) 203-17.

_____. "Medical Imagery in the Pastoral Epistles." In *Texts and Testaments:*

Critical Essays on the Bible and Early Church Fathers, ed. by W. Eugene March (San Antonio: Trinity University Press, 1980) 19-35.

_____. "'Not in a Corner': Early Christian Apologetic in Acts 26:26." *SecCent* 5 (1985/86) 193-210.

_____. *Paul and the Popular Philosophers*. Minneapolis: Fortress Press, 1989.

_____. *Paul and the Thessalonians: The Philosophic Tradition of Pastoral Care*. Philadelphia: Fortress Press, 1987.

Manek, Jindrich. "Fishers of Men." *NovT* 2 (1958) 138-41.

Marcus, Joel. "Mark 4:10-12 and Marcan Epistemology." *JBL* 103 (1984) 557-74.

_____. *The Mystery of the Kingdom of God*. SBLDS 90. Atlanta: Scholars Press, 1986.

Martitz, Wülfing von. "υἱός." *TDNT* 8.336-40.

Marxsen, Willi. *Mark the Evangelist: Studies on the Redaction History of the Gospel*. Tr. by James Boyce, Donald Juel, William Poehlmann and Ray A. Harrisville. Nashville: Abingdon, 1969.

_____. "Redaktionsgeschichtliche Erklärung der sogennanten Parabeltheorie des Markus." *ZTK* 52 (1955) 255-71.

Matera, Frank J. "The Incomprehension of the Disciples and Peter's Confession (Mark 6,14-8,30)." *Bib* 70 (1989) 153-72.

_____. *The Kingship of Jesus: Composition and Theology in Mark 15*. SBLDS 66. Chico: Scholars Press, 1982.

_____. "The Prologue as the Interpretive Key to Mark's Gospel." *JSNT* 34 (1988) 3-20.

_____. *What Are They Saying about Mark?* New York and Mahwah: Paulist Press, 1987.

Maxwell, Arthur S. *The Bible Story*. 10 vols. Washington: Review and Herald Publishing Association, 1957.

Meagher, John C. *Clumsy Construction in Mark's Gospel: A Critique of Form- and Redaktionsgeschichte*. TST 3. New York and Toronto: Edwin Mellen Press, 1979.

Melbourne, Bertram L. *Slow to Understand: The Disciples in Synoptic Perspective*. Lanham, New York, and London: University Press of America, 1988.

Metzger, Bruce M. *A Textual Commentary on the Greek New Testament*. Cor. ed. London and New York: United Bible Societies, 1975.

Meye, R. P. *Jesus and the Twelve: Discipleship and Revelation in Mark's Gospel*. Grand Rapids: Wm. B. Eerdmans, 1968.

Meyer A. "Die Entstehung des Marcusevangeliums." In *Festgabe für Jülicher zum 70. Geburtstag* (Tübingen: Mohr, 1927) 35-60.

Moore, Stephen D. "Doing Gospel Criticism as/with a 'Reader'." *BTB* 19 (1989) 85-93.

Moule, Charles F. D., ed. *Miracles: Cambridge Studies in Their Philosophy and*

History. London: A. R. Mowbray, 1966.

Munro, Winsome. "Women Disciples in Mark?" *CBQ* 44 (1982) 225-41.

Neusner, Jacob. "Death-Scenes and Farewell Stories: An Aspect of the Master-Disciple Relationship in Mark and in Some Talmudic Tales." In *Christians Among Jews and Gentiles*, ed. by George W. E. Nickelsburg with George W. MacRae (Philadelphia: Fortress Press, 1986) 187-97.

Nineham, D. E. *The Gospel of St. Mark.* PGC. Baltimore: Penguin, 1963.

Ong, Walter J. "Text as Interpretation: Mark and After." *Semeia* 39 (1987) 7-26.

Osborn, B. A. E. "Peter: Stumbling-block and Satan." *NovT* 15 (1973) 187-90.

Parunak, H. Van Dyke. "Oral Typesetting: Some Uses of Biblical Structure." *Bib* 62 (1981) 153-68.

_____. "Transitional Techniques in the Bible." *JBL* 102 (1983) 525-48.

Perrin, Norman. "The Evangelist as Author: Reflections on Method in the Study and Interpretation of the Synoptic Gospels and Acts." *BR* 17 (1972) 5-18.

_____. *The New Testament: An Introduction.* New York, Chicago, San Francisco, and Atlanta: Harcourt Brace Jovanovich, 1974.

_____. *What is Redaction Criticism?* GBS. Philadelphia: Fortress Press, 1969.

Pesch, Rudolf. *Das Marcusevangelium.* 2 vols. HTKNT 2. Freiburg, Basel, and Vienna: Herder, 1976.

Petersen, Norman R. "The Composition of Mark 4:1-8:26." HTR 73 (1980) 185-217.

_____. *Literary Criticism for New Testament Critics.* GBS. Philadelphia: Fortress Press, 1978.

_____. "'Point of View' in Mark's Narrative." *Semeia* 12 (1978) 97-121.

Petzke, Gerd. *Die Traditionen über Apollonius von Tyana und das Neue Testament.* SCHNT 1. Leiden: E. J. Brill, 1970.

Powell, Mark Allan. *What is Narrative Criticism?* GBS. Minneapolis: Fortress Press, 1990.

Quesnell, Quentin. *The Mind of Mark: Interpretation and Method through the Exegesis of Mark 6,52.* AnBib 38. Rome: Pontifical Biblical Institute, 1969.

Remus, Harold. *Pagan-Christian Conflict Over Miracle in the Second Century.* PPFPM 10. Cambridge, MA: Philadelphia Patristic Foundation, 1983.

Rengstorf, Karl Heinrich. "διδάσκαλος." *TDNT* 2.148-59.

_____. "ἑπτά, ἑπτάκις, ἑπτακισχίλιοι, ἑβδομάς, ἑβδομήκοντα." *TDNT* 2.627-35.

_____. "μαθητής." *TDNT* 4.415-60.

Reploh, Karl-Georg. *Markus—Lehrer der Gemeinde: Eine redaktionsgeschichtliche Studie zu den Jüngerperikopen des Markus-Evangeliums.* SBM 9. Stuttgart: Katholisches Bibelwerk, 1969.

Rhoads, David, and Donald Michie. *Mark as Story: An Introduction to the*

Narrative of a Gospel. Philadelphia: Fortress Press, 1982.

Robbins, Vernon K. *Jesus the Teacher: A Socio-rhetorical Interpretation of Mark.* Philadelphia: Fortress Press, 1984.

_____. "Mark 1.14-20: An Interpretation at the Intersection of Jewish and Graeco-Roman Traditions." *NTS* 28 (1982) 220-36.

Sanders, E. P. *Paul and Palestinian Judaism: A Comparison of Patterns of Religion.* Philadelphia: Fortress Press, 1977.

Schmidt, Karl Ludwig. *Der Rahmen der Geschichte Jesu: Literarkritische Untersuchungen zur ältesten Jesusüberlieferung.* Berlin: Trowitzsch, 1919.

Schweizer, Eduard. *The Good News According to Mark.* Tr. by Donald H. Madvig. Richmond: John Knox, 1970.

Scott, M. Philip. "Chiastic Structure: A Key to the Interpretation of Mark's Gospel." *BTB* 15 (1985) 17-26.

Sellew, Philip. "Composition of Didactic Scenes in Mark's Gospel." *JBL* 108 (1989) 613-34.

Silberman, Lou H., ed. *Orality, Aurality and Biblical Narrative.* *Semeia* 39 (1987).

Smith, Charles W. F. "Fishers of Men: Footnotes on a Gospel Figure." *HTR* 52 (1959) 187-203.

Smith, Jonathan Z. "Good News is No News: Aretalogy and Gospel." In *Christianity, Judaism and Other Greco-Roman Cults: Studies for Morton Smith at Sixty*, ed. by Jacob Neusner, SLA 12 (Leiden: E. J. Brill, 1975) Part 1, 21-38.

Smith, Morton. "Prolegomena to a Discussion of Aretalogies, Divine Men, the Gospels and Jesus." *JBL* 90 (1971) 174-99.

Smith, Stephen H. "The Role of Jesus' Opponents in the Markan Drama." *NTS* 35 (1989) 161-82

Standaert, Benoît. *L'Évangile selon Marc: Commentaire.* LirB. Paris: Éditions du Cerf, 1983.

_____. *L'Évangile selon Marc: Composition et genre littéraire.* Brugge: Sint-Andriesabdij, 1978.

Stock, Augustine. *Call to Discipleship: A Literary Study of Mark's Gospel.* GNS 1. Wilmington: Michael Glazier, 1982.

_____. "Chiastic Awareness and Education in Antiquity." *BTB* 14 (1984) 23-27.

_____. "Hinge Transitions in Mark's Gospel." *BTB* 15 (1985) 27-31.

_____. *The Method and Message of Mark.* Wilmington: Michael Glazier, 1989.

Stowers, Stanley Kent. *The Diatribe and Paul's Letter to the Romans.* SBLDS 57. Chico: Scholars Press, 1981.

Strack, Hermann L., and Paul Billerbeck. *Kommentar zum Neuen Testament aus*

Talmud und Midrasch. 6 vols. Munich: Beck, 1922-65.

Swete, Henry Barclay. *The Gospel According to St. Mark: The Greek Text with Introduction Notes and Indices.* London and New York: Macmillan, 1905.

Talbert, Charles H. "The Concept of Immortals in Mediterranean Antiquity." *JBL* 94 (1975) 419-36.

_____. *What is a Gospel? The Genre of the Canonical Gospels.* Philadelphia: Fortress Press, 1977.

Tannehill, Robert C. "The Disciples in Mark: The Function of a Narrative Role." *JR* 57 (1977) 386-405.

_____. "The Gospel of Mark as Narrative Christology." *Semeia* 16 (1980) 57-95.

Taylor, Vincent. *The Gospel According to St. Mark: The Greek Text with Introduction, Notes, and Indexes.* 2nd ed. London: Macmillan, 1966.

Theissen, Gerd. *The Miracle Stories of the Early Christian Tradition.* Tr. by Francis McDonagh. Ed. by John Riches. Philadelphia: Fortress Press, 1983.

Tiede, David L. *The Charismatic Figure as Miracle Worker.* SBLDS 1. Missoula: Scholars Press, 1972.

Tolbert, Mary Ann. *Sowing the Gospel: Mark's World in Literary-historical Perspective.* Minneapolis: Fortress Press, 1989.

Trocmé, Etienne. *The Formation of the Gospel According to Mark.* Tr. by Pamela Gaughan. Philadelphia: Westminster Press, 1975.

Tyson, Joseph B. "The Blindness of the Disciples in Mark." *JBL* 80 (1961) 261-68.

Vorster, W. S. "Characterization of Peter in the Gospel of Mark." *Neot* 21 (1987) 57-76.

Votaw, Clyde Weber. "The Gospels and Contemporary Biographies." *AJT* 19 (1915) 45-73, 217-49. Reprinted as *The Gospels and Contemporary Biographies in the Greco-Roman World.* FBBS 27. Philadelphia: Fortress Press, 1970.

Weeden, Theodore J. Sr. "The Heresy that Necessitated Mark's Gospel." *ZNW* 59 (1968) 148-58.

_____. *Mark—Traditions in Conflict.* Philadelphia: Fortress Press, 1971.

Wilkins, Michael J. *The Concept of Disciple in Matthew's Gospel as Reflected in the Use of the Term* Μαθητής. NovTSup 59. Leiden, New York, Copenhagen: Brill, 1988.

Williams, James G. *Gospel Against Parable: Mark's Language of Mystery.* BLS 12. Bradford on Avon: Almond Press, 1985.

Wrede, William. *The Messianic Secret.* Tr. by J. C. G. Greig. Cambridge: James Clarke & Co., 1971.

Wuellner, Wilhelm. *The Meaning of "Fishers of Men".* Philadelphia: Westminster Press, 1967.

III. WORKS RELATING TO GRECO-ROMAN HISTORY AND LITERATURE, WISDOM SCHOOLS, AND LITERARY CRITICISM

Anderson, Graham. *Philostratus: Biography and Belles Lettres in the Third Century A.D.* London, Sidney, and Dover, NH: Croom Helm, 1986.

_____. "Putting Pressure on Plutarch: Philostratus *Ep.* 73." *CP* 72 (1977) 43-45.

Anderson, John Kinloch. *Xenophon.* CLL. London: Gerald Duckworth, 1974.

Armstrong, Arthur Hilary, ed. *The Cambridge History of Later Greek and Early Medieval Philosophy.* Cambridge: University Press, 1967.

Auerbach, Erich. *Mimesis: The Representation of Reality in Western Literature.* Tr. by Willard R. Trask. Princeton: Princeton University Press, 1953.

Berns, Laurence. "Socratic and Non-Socratic Philosophy: A Note on Xenophon's *Memorabilia*, 1.1.13 and 14." *The Review of Metaphysics* 28 (1974) 85-88.

Bertermann, G. "De Iamblichi vitae pythagoricae fontibus." Dissertation. Königsberg, 1913.

Beyenka, Mary Melchior. *Consolation in Saint Augustine.* CUAPS 83. Washington: Catholic University of America, 1950.

Bidez, Joseph. "Le philosophe Jamblique et son école." *REG* 32 (1919) 29-40.

Birley, Anthony. *Septimius Severus: The African Emperor.* Garden City: Doubleday, 1972.

Birt, Theodor. "Zu Antisthenes und Xenophon." *RheinMus* 51 (1896) 153-57.

_____. *De Xenophontis Commentariorum Socraticorum compositione.* Marburg: Impensis Elwerti Bibliopolae Academici, 1893.

Bonner, Stanley F. *Education in Ancient Rome: From the Elder Cato to the Younger Pliny.* Berkeley and Los Angeles: University of California Press, 1977.

Booth, Wayne C. *The Rhetoric of Fiction.* Chicago: University of Chicago Press, 1961.

Bowersock, Glen Warren. *Greek Sophists in the Roman Empire.* Oxford: Clarendon Press, 1969.

_____. "Introduction." In *Philostratus, Life of Apollonius*, tr. by C. P. Jones (Harmondsworth: Penguin, 1970).

Bowersock, Glen Warren, ed. *Approaches to the Second Sophistic: Papers Presented at the 105th Annual Meeting of the American Philological Association.* University Park, PA: American Philological Association, 1974.

Bowie, Ewan Lyall. "Apollonius of Tyana: Tradition and Reality." *ANRW* 2.16.2, 1652-99.

_____. "Greeks and Their Past in the Second Sophistic." *PP* 46 (1970) 3-41.

_____. "The Importance of Sophists." *YCS* 27 (1982) 22-59.

Boyancé, Pierre. "Sur la vie pythagoricienne." *Revue des études grecques* 52

(1939) 36-50.

Brown, Peter. "The Rise and Function of the Holy Man in Late Antiquity." *JRS* 61 (1971) 80-101.

Burgess, Theodore C. "Epideictic Literature." *UCSCP* 3 (1902) 89-261.

Burke, Kenneth. *Counter-Statement.* Berkeley, Los Angeles, and London: University of California Press, 1931.

Burkert, Walter. *Lore and Science in Ancient Pythagoreanism.* Tr. by Edwin L. Minar, Jr. Cambridge, MA: Harvard University Press, 1972.

Calderini, A. "Teoria e pratica politica nella 'Vita di Apollonio di Tiana'." *RIL* 74 (1940/41) 213-41.

Cameron, Alan. "The Date of Iamblichus' Birth." *Hermes* 96 (1968) 374-76.

Christ, Wilhelm von, Wilhelm Schmid, and Otto Stählin. *Geschichte der griechischen Litteratur,* 6th ed. HKA 7. 2 vols. Munich: Beck, 1911-13.

Chroust, Anton-Hermann. *Socrates, Man and Myth: The Two Socratic Apologies of Xenophon.* London: Routledge & Kegan Paul, 1957.

Clarke, Martin L. *Higher Education in the Ancient World.* London: Routledge & Kegan Paul, 1971.

Classen, C. Joachim. "Xenophons Darstellung der Sophistik und der Sophisten." *Hermes* 112 (1984) 154-67.

Cobet, Carel Gabriel. *Novae Lectiones Quibus Continentur Observationes Criticae in Scriptores Graecos.* Leiden: E. J. Brill, 1858.

Cox, Patricia. *Biography in Late Antiquity: A Quest for the Holy Man.* TCH 5. Berkeley, Los Angeles, and London: University of California Press, 1983.

Crenshaw, James L. *Old Testament Wisdom: An Introduction.* Atlanta: John Knox Press, 1981.

_____, ed. *Studies in Ancient Israelite Wisdom.* New York: Ktav, 1976.

Deutsch, Celia. "The Sirach 51 Acrostic: Confession and Exhortation." *ZAW* 94 (1982) 400-09.

Di Lella, Alexander A. "Conservative and Progressive Theology: Sirach and Wisdom." *CBQ* 28 (1966) 139-54.

_____. *The Hebrew Text of Sirach: A Text-Critical and Historical Study.* SCL 1. The Hague: Mouton, 1966.

_____. Review of J. A. Sanders, *The Psalm Scroll of Qumrân Cave 11 (11QPs^a). CBQ* 28 (1966) 92-95.

Dillon, John. *Iamblichi Chalcidensis In Platonis Dialogos Commentariorum Fragmenta.* PA 23. Leiden: E. J. Brill, 1973.

_____. "Iamblichus of Chalcis (c. 240-325 A.D.)." *ANRW* 2.36.2, 862-909.

_____. *The Middle Platonists: A Study of Platonism 80 B.C. to A.D. 220.* London: Gerald Duckworth, 1977.

Dodds, E. R. "The *Parmenides* of Plato and the Origin of the Neoplatonic 'One'." *ClassQ* 22 (1928) 129-42.

_____. "Theurgy and Its Relation to Neoplatonism." *JRS* 37 (1947) 55-69.

Düring, Ingemar. *Aristotle in the Ancient Biographical Tradition.* AUG 43.2. Göteborg: Elanders Boktryckeri Aktiebolag, 1957.

Erbse, Hartmut. "Die Architektonik im Aufbau von Xenophons Memorabilien." *Hermes* 89 (1961) 257-87.

Fairweather, Janet A. "Fiction in the Biographies of Ancient Writers." *AS* 5 (1974) 231-75.

Favez, Charles. *La consolation latine chrétienne.* Paris: Libraire Philosophique J. Vrin, 1937.

Fern, Mary E. *The Latin Consolatio as a Literary Type.* St. Louis: St. Louis University Press, 1941.

Forster, A. Haire. "The Date of Ecclesiasticus." *Anglican Theological Review* 41 (1959) 1-9.

Forster, E. M. *Aspects of the Novel.* San Diego, New York, and London: Harcourt Brace Jovanovich, 1985.

Fritz, Kurt von. *Pythagorean Politics in Southern Italy: An Analysis of the Sources.* New York: Octagon Books, 1977.

Gaiser, Konrad. *Protreptik und Paränese bei Platon.* TBA 40. Stuttgart: Kohlhammer, 1959.

Gigon, Olaf Alfred. *Sokrates: Sein Bild in Dichtung und Geschichte.* Bern: A. Franke, 1947.

Ginzberg, Louis. *A Commentary on the Palestinian Talmud.* TSJTSA 10-12, 21. 4 vols. New York: Jewish Theological Seminary, 1941-61.

Gordis, Robert. "The Social Background of Wisdom Literature." *HUCA* 18 (1943-44) 77-118.

Gorman, Peter. *Pythagoras: A Life.* London: Routledge & Kegan Paul, 1979.

Göttsching, Johannes. *Apollonius von Tyana.* Leipzig: Max Hoffmann, 1889.

Gray, Bennison. "Repetition in Oral Literature." *JAF* 84 (1971) 289-303.

Gregg, Robert C. *Consolation Philosophy: Greek and Christian Paideia in Basil and the Two Gregories.* PPFPM 3. Cambridge, MA: Philadelphia Patristic Foundation, 1975.

Griffin, Miriam. Review of G. W. Bowersock, *Greek Sophists in the Roman Empire. JRS* 61 (1971) 278-80.

Grosso, F. "La Vita di Apollonio di Tiana come fonte storice." *Acme* 7 (1954) 331-530.

Hadas, Moses, and Morton Smith. *Heroes and Gods: Spiritual Biographies in Late Antiquity.* New York: Harper & Row, 1965.

Hägg, Tomas. *Narrative Technique in Ancient Greek Romances: Studies of Chariton, Xenophon Ephesus, and Achilles Tatius.* AIARS Series 8, No. 8. Stockholm: Svenska Institutet i Athen, 1971.

Halliday, William Reginald. "Damis of Nineveh and Walter of Oxford." *ABSA* 18 (1911-12) 234-38.

Harrington, Daniel J. "The Wisdom of the Scribe According to Ben Sira." In *Ideal Figures in Ancient Judaism: Profiles and Paradigms*, ed. by John J. Collins and George W. E. Nickelsburg, SBLSCS 12 (Chico: Scholars Press, 1980) 181-88.

Harris, B. F. "Apollonius of Tyana: Fact and Fiction." *JRH* 5 (1969) 189-99.

Harvey, W. J. *Character and the Novel*. London: Chatto & Windus, 1965.

Hempel, Johannes. *Untersuchungen zur Überlieferung von Apollonius von Tyana*. BRel 4. Stockholm: Bonnier; and Leipzig: Voigtländer, 1920/21.

Hengel, Martin. *Judaism and Hellenism: Studies in their Encounter in Palestine during the Early Hellenistic Period*. Tr. by John Bowden. 2 vols. Philadelphia: Fortress Press, 1981.

Herzog, Gertrud. "Julia Domna." *PW* 10.926-35.

Higgins, William Edward. *Xenophon the Athenian: The Problem of the Individual and the Society of the Polis*. Albany: State University of New York Press, 1977.

Humbert, P. *Recherches sur les sources égyptiennes de la littérature sapientiale d'Israël*. MUN 7. Neuchatel: Secrétariat de Université, 1929.

Hyldahl, Niels. *Philosophie und Christentum: Eine Interpretation der Einleitung zum Dialog Justins*. ATDan 9. Copenhagen: Munksgard, 1966.

Iser, Wolfgang. *The Act of Reading: A Theory of Aesthetic Response*. Baltimore and London: John Hopkins University Press, 1978.

Jackson, Steven. "Apollonius and the Emperors." *Hermathena* 137 (1984) 25-31.

Jaeger, Werner. *Paideia*. 2nd ed. 3 vols. New York: Oxford University Press, 1945-46.

Joël, Karl. *Der echte und der xenophontische Sokrates*. 3 vols. Berlin: R. Gaertner, 1893-1901.

Jordan, Mark D. "Ancient Philosophic Protreptic and the Problem of Persuasive Genres." *Rhetorica* 4 (1986) 309-33.

Kettenhofen, Erich. *Die syrischen Augustae in der historischen Überlieferung: Ein Beitrag zum Problem der Orientalisierung*. Antiquitas, Reihe 3, Band 24. Bonn: Rudolf Habelt Verlag, 1979.

Kirk, G. S., and J. E. Raven. *The Presocratic Philosophers: A Critical History with a Selection of Texts*. Cambridge: University Press, 1966.

Knoles, Thomas Gregory. "Literary Technique and Theme in Philostratus' *Life of Apollonius of Tyana*." Dissertation. Rutgers, 1981.

Knox, B. M. W. "Silent Reading in Antiquity." *GRBS* 9 (1968) 421-35.

Lander, Mary Katherine Gloth, and Maria Francisca Kellog. *Index in Xenophontis Memorabilia*. CSCP 21. New York: Johnson Reprint Corp, 1971.

Lang, Bernhard. *Frau Weisheit: Deutung einer biblischen Gestalt*. Düsseldorf: Patmos, 1975.

_____. "Schule und Unterricht im alten Israel." In *La sagesse de l'Ancien*

Testament, ed. by M. Gilbert, BETL 51 (Gembloux: Duculot; and Louvain: University, 1979) 186-201.

Larsen, Bent Dalsgaard. *Jamblique de Chalcis: Exégète et Philosophe*. 2 vols. Aarhus: Universitetsforlaget i Aarhus, 1972.

_____. "La place de Jamblique dans la philosophie antique tardive." In *De Jamblique a Proclus*, ed. by Heinrich Dörrie (Geneva: Olivier Reverdin, 1975) 1-26.

Lee, G. M. "Had Apollonius of Tyana Read St. Mark?" SO 48 (1973) 115-16.

Leo, Friedrich. *Die griechisch-römische Biographie nach ihrer litterarischen Form*. Leipzig: Teubner, 1901.

Lévy, Isidore. *La légend de Pythagore de Grèce en Paléstine*. Paris: Champion, 1927.

_____. *Recherches sur les sources de la legénde de Pythagoras*. Paris: Leroux, 1926.

Lo Cascio, Ferdinando. *La Forma letteraria della Vita de Apollonio Tianeo*. QIFGUP 6. Palermo: Bruno Lavagnini, 1974.

Luccioni, Jean. *Xénophon et le socratisme*. Paris: Presses Universitaire de France, 1953.

McCall, Marsh H., Jr. *Ancient Rhetorical Theories of Simile and Comparison*. Cambridge, MA: Harvard University Press, 1969.

Mack, Burton. *Wisdom and the Hebrew Epic: Ben Sira's Hymn in Praise of the Fathers*. Chicago and London: University of Chicago Press, 1985.

McKane, William. *Prophets and Wise Men*. SBT 44. Naperville: Alec R. Allenson, 1965.

MacMullen, Ramsay. *Enemies of the Roman Order: Treason, Unrest, and Alienation in the Empire*. Cambridge, MA: Harvard University Press, 1966.

_____. *Paganism in the Roman Empire*. New Haven and London: Yale University Press, 1981.

Malherbe, Abraham J. *Moral Exhortation: A Greco-Roman Sourcebook*. LEC 4. Philadelphia: Westminster Press, 1986.

Marböck, Johannes. "Sir., 38,24-39,11: Der schriftgelehrte Weise. Ein Beitrag zu Gestalt und Werk Ben Siras." In *La Sagesse de l'Ancien Testament*, ed. by M. Gilbert, BETL 51 (Gembloux: J. Duculot; and Louvain: University Press, 1979) 293-316.

_____. "Sirachliteratur seit 1966. Ein Überblick." *TRev* 71 (1975) 179-84.

_____. *Weisheit im Wandel: Untersuchungen zur Weisheitstheologie bei Ben Sira*. BBB 37. Bonn: Peter Haustein Verlag, 1971.

Marchant, E. C. "Introduction." In *Xenophon IV: Memorabilia and Oeconomicus, Symposium and Apology*, tr. by E. C. Marchant and O. J. Todd, LCL (Cambridge MA: Harvard University Press; and London: William Heinemann, 1979) vii-xxvii.

Marrou, H. I. *A History of Education in Antiquity.* Tr. by George Lamb. New York: Sheed and Ward, 1956.

Mau, G. "Iamblichos." *PW* 9.645-49.

Merlan, Philip. *From Platonism to Neoplatonism.* 3rd rev. ed. The Hague: Martinus Nijhoff, 1968.

_____. "Greek Philosophy from Plato to Plotinus." In *The Cambridge History of Later Greek and Early Medieval Philosophy,* ed. by Arthur Hilary Armstrong (Cambridge: University Press, 1967) 11-132.

Mesk, J. "Die Damisquelle des Philostratos in der Biographie des Apollonios von Tyana." *WS* 41 (1919) 121-38.

Meyer, Eduard. "Apollonius von Tyana und die Biographie des Philostratos." *Hermes* 52 (1917) 371-424.

Middendorp, Theophil. *Die Stellung Jesus ben Siras zwischen Judentum und Hellenismus.* Leiden: Brill, 1973.

Minar, Edwin L. *Early Pythagorean Politics in Practice and Theory.* CCM 2. Baltimore: Waverly Press, 1942.

Momigliano, Arnaldo. *The Development of Greek Biography.* Cambridge, MA: Harvard University Press, 1971.

Moore, George Foote. *Judaism in the First Centuries of the Christian Era: The Age of the Tannaim.* 3 vols. Cambridge, MA: Harvard University Press, 1927-30.

Morrison, Donald R. *Bibliography of Editions, Translations, and Commentary on Xenophon's Socratic Writings, 1600-Present.* Pittsburgh: Mathesis Publications, 1988.

Münscher, Karl. "Die Philostrate." *Philologus,* Supplementband 10 (1907) 469-557.

Muraoka, T. "Sir. 51, 13-30: An Erotic Hymn to Wisdom?" *JSJ* 10 (1979) 166-78.

Nickelsburg, George W. E. *Jewish Literature between the Bible and the Mishna: A Historical and Literary Introduction.* Philadelphia: Fortress Press, 1981.

Nock, Arthur Darby. *Conversion: The Old and the New in Religion from Alexander the Great to Augustine of Hippo.* London and New York: Oxford University Press, 1933.

_____. "Conversion and Adolescence." In *Essays on Religion and the Ancient World* (Cambridge, MA: Harvard University Press, 1972) 1.469-80.

Notopoulos, James A. "Parataxis in Homer: A New Approach to Homeric Literary Criticism." *TAPA* 80 (1949) 1-23.

Olyan, Saul M. "Ben Sira's Relationship to the Priesthood." *HTR* 80 (1987) 261-86.

Pack, Roger. "Two Sophists and Two Emperors." *CP* 42 (1947) 17-20.

Pautrel, R. "Ben Sira et le Stoïcisme." *RSR* 51 (1963) 535-49.

Penella, Robert J. "An Overlooked Story about Apollonius of Tyana in Anastasius Sinaita." *Traditio* 34 (1978) 414-15.

_____. "Philostratus' Letter to Julia Domna." *Hermes* 107 (1979) 161-68.

_____. "Scopelianus and the Eretrians in Cissia." *Athenaeum* 52 (1974) 295-96.

Peters, Norbert. *Das Buch Jesus Sirach oder Ecclesiasticus.* EHAT 25. Münster: Aschendorff, 1913.

Pfeiffer, Robert H. *History of New Testament Times with an Introduction to the Apocrypha.* New York: Harper & Brothers, 1949.

Philip, J. A. "Aristotle's Monograph *On the Pythagoreans.*" *TAPA* 94 (1963) 185-98.

_____. "The Biographical Tradition—Pythagoras." *TAPA* 90 (1959) 185-94.

_____. *Pythagoras and Early Pythagoreanism.* PSV 7. Toronto: University of Toronto Press, 1966.

Places, Édourd des. "La religion de Jamblique." In *De Jamblique à Proclus*, ed. by Heinrich Dörrie, EFH 21 (Vandoeuvres and Geneva: Olivier Reverden, 1975) 69-102.

Purser, Louis C. "Court Religion at Rome in the Third Century." *PCAS* 10 (1911-12) 43-65.

Rad, Gerhard von. "Die Weisheit des Jesus Sirach." *EvT* 29 (1969) 113-33.

_____. *Wisdom in Israel.* Tr. by J. D. Martin. Nashville: Abingdon, 1972.

Raynor, D. H. "Moeragenes and Philostratus: Two Views of Apollonius of Tyana." *ClassQ* 34 (1984) 222-26.

Reardon, Brian P. *Courants littéraires grecs des IIe et IIIe siècles après J.-C.*, ALUN 3. Paris: Les Belles Lettres, 1971.

Rickenbacker, O. *Weisheitsperikopen bei Ben Sira.* OBO 1. Freiburg: Universitätsverlag; and Göttingen: Vandenhoeck und Ruprecht, 1973.

Rivkin, Ellis. "Ben Sira—The Bridge between the Aaronide and the Pharisaic Revolutions." *Eretz-Israel* 12 (1975) 95*-103*.

Rogers, Arthur Kenyon. *The Socratic Problem.* New Haven: Yale University Press, 1933.

Rohde, Erwin. "Die Quellen des Iamblichus in seiner Biographie des Pythagoras." *RheinMus* 26 (1871) 554-76; 27 (1872) 23-61.

Roth, Wolfgang. "On the Gnomic-Discursive Wisdom of Jesus Ben Sirach." *Semeia* 17 (1980) 59-79.

Rylaarsdam, John Coert. *Revelation in Jewish Wisdom Literature.* Chicago: University of Chicago Press, 1946.

Sanders, Jack T. *Ben Sira and Demotic Wisdom.* SBLMS 28. Chico: Scholars Press, 1983.

Sanders, James A. *The Dead Sea Psalms Scroll.* Ithaca: Cornell University Press, 1967.

_____. "The Sirach 51 Acrostic." In *Hommages à André Dupont-Sommer*, ed. by A. Caquot and M. Philonenko (Paris: Libraire d'Amérique et d'orient Adrien-Maisonneuve, 1971) 429-38.

Scholes, Robert, and Robert Kellogg. *The Nature of Narrative.* New York and London: Oxford University Press, 1966.

Schürer, Emil. *The History of the Jewish People in the Age of Jesus Christ (175 B.C.-A.D. 135).* Rev. and ed. by Geza Vermes, Fergus Millar and Martin Goodman. 3 vols. Edinburgh: T. & C. Clark, 1973-87.

Schwartz, Eduard. *Fünf Vorträge über den griechischen Roman.* Berlin: G. Reimer, 1896.

Skehan, Patrick W. "The Acrostic Poem in Sirach 51:13-30." *HTR* 64 (1971) 387-400.

_____. "Structures in Poems on Wisdom: Proverbs 8 and Sirach 24." *CBQ* 41 (1979) 365-79.

_____. "They Shall Not Be Found in Parables (Sir 38,33)," *CBQ* 23 (1961) 40.

Skehan, Patrick W., and Alexander A. Di Lella. *The Wisdom of Ben Sira.* AB 39. New York: Doubleday, 1987.

Smend, R. *Die Weisheit des Jesus Sirach erklärt.* Berlin: Reimer, 1906.

Solmsen, F. "Philostratos, 8-12." *PW* 20.1.124-77.

_____. "Some Works of Philostratus the Elder." *TAPA* 71 (1940) 556-72.

Speyer, Wolfgang. "Zum Bild des Apollonios von Tyana bei Heiden und Christen." JAC 17 (1974) 47-63.

Stanton, G. R. "Sophists and Philosophers: Problems of Classification." *AJP* 94 (1973) 350-64.

Stone, Michael E. "Ideal Figures and Social Context: Priest and Sage in the Early Second Temple Age." In *Ancient Israelite Religion: Essays in Honor of Frank Moore Cross*, ed. by Patrick D. Miller, Jr., Paul D. Hanson, and S. Dean McBride (Philadelphia: Fortress Press, 1987) 575-86.

Strack, Hermann L. *Introduction to the Talmud and Midrash.* Philadelphia: Jewish Publication Society of America, 1931.

Strauss, Leo. *Xenophon's Socrates.* Ithaca: Cornell University Press, 1972.

_____. *Xenophon's Socratic Discourse.* Ithaca: Cornell University Press, 1970.

Stuart, Duane Reed. *Epochs of Greek and Roman Biography.* New York: Biblo and Tannen, 1967.

Syme, Ronald. *Ammianus and the Historia Augusta.* Oxford: Clarendon Press, 1968.

Talbert, Charles H. "Biographies of Philosophers and Rulers as Instruments of Religious Propaganda in Mediterranean Antiquity." *ANRW* 2.16.2, 1619-51.

Tcherikover, Victor. *Hellenistic Civilization and the Jews.* Tr. by S. Applebaum. Philadelphia: Jewish Publication Society of America, 1959.

Thesleff, Holger. *An Introduction to the Pythagorean Writings of the Hellenistic*

Period. AAAH 24.3. Abo: Abo Akademi, 1961.

Todorov, Tzvetan. *The Poetics of Prose.* Tr. by R. Howard. Oxford: Basil Blackwell, 1977.

Traill, John S. "Greek Inscriptions Honoring Prytaneis." *Hesperia* 40 (1971) 308-29.

Vogel, Cornelia J. de. *Pythagoras and Early Pythagoreanism: An Interpretation of Neglected Evidence on the Philosopher Pythagoras.* Assen: Van Gorcum, 1966.

Wallis, R. T. *Neoplatonism.* London: Duckworth, 1972.

Warmington, E. H. "Introduction." In *Achilles Tatius*, LCL (Cambridge, MA: Harvard University Press; and London: William Heinemann, 1969) ix-xvi.

Welch, John W., ed. *Chiasmus in Antiquity: Structure, Analyses, Exegesis.* Hildesheim: Gerstenberg Verlag, 1981.

Wellman, Robert R. "Socratic Method in Xenophon." *JHI* 37 (1976) 307-18.

Wilken, Robert L. "Collegia, Philosophical Schools, and Theology." In *The Catacombs and the Colosseum: The Roman Empire as the Setting of Primitive Christianity*, ed. by Stephen Benko and John J. O'Rourke (Valley Forge: Judson Press, 1971) 268-91.

Williams, Mary Gilmore. "Studies in the Lives of Roman Empresses: I. Julia Domna." *AJA* NS 6 (1902) 259-305.

Witt, Rex E. "Iamblichus as a Forerunner of Julian." In *De Jamblique à Proclus*, ed. by Heinrich Dörrie, EFH 21 (Vandoeuvres and Geneva: Olivier Reverden, 1975) 35-64.

Wittaker, John. "Epekeina nou kai ousias." *VC* 23 (1969) 91-104.

_____. "Neopythagoreanism and Negative Theology." SO 44 (1969) 109-25.

_____. "Neopythagoreanism and the Transcendent Absolute." SO 48 (1973) 77-86.

Wright, Benjamin G. *No Small Difference: Sirach's Relationship to Its Hebrew Parent Text.* SBLSCS 26. Atlanta: Scholars Press, 1989.

Index of Biblical and Ancient Sources

I. Hebrew Bible and Apocrypha

II. New Testament

Subject Index

Apollonius (source for *Pythagorean Life*), 90

Apollonius of Tyana: historical, 101, 104-6; as wonder worker, 105-06; as μάγος/γόης, 113; as ideal philosopher, 116; straightforward teaching of, 122; conversations with kings, 124; wise man rather than teacher, 140; followers not described as μαθητής, 191*n*37. *See also* Miracles of Apollonius, *Theios aner*

Apomnemoneumata, 20-21, 21*n*48

Aristotle, 71, 95, 180

Aristoxenus, 90

Ben Sira: Hellenism and, 142-44. *See also* Wisdom of Ben Sira

Biographical writings: philosophical, 32-34, 37-38, 98-99; early Greek, 37-38

Call stories: absence in Iamblichus, 78-79, 117; in Xenophon's *Memorabilia*, 117; in Philostratus, 117-119

Call stories, Markan: pattern of, 172-74; synopsis, 173; lack of disciple motivation, 183-86; establishing authority of Jesus, 186-89; in characterization of disciples, 190; lack of moral criteria for followers, 194-95; lack of moral change in followers, 196-98

Call stories, narrative functions of: to provide an authoritative source, 130-31, 182-83; characterization, 182-83

Call stories, rhetorical functions of: protreptic, 176; demonstrating superiority of a teacher, 177-78; characterization of teacher or student, 180; showing dedication of student, 180; occasion for miracle, 180; showing power of teaching, 181-82; showing value of intellectual inquiry, 182.

Character: ancient view of innate character, 118

Character, literary: ancient characters different from modern literary characters, 10, 12-13; in Mark, 9-13, 15-16, 18, 292; structuring narrative through contrasting in Philostratus, 134.